English Shops and Shopping

English Shops and Shopping

An Architectural History

KATHRYN A. MORRISON

Published for

The Paul Mellon Centre for Studies in British Art

by

Yale University Press

New Haven & London

in association with

English Heritage

Second printing 2004

Designed by Gillian Malpass

Printed in Singapore

Library of Congress Cataloging-in-Publication Data

Morrison, Kathryn A.
English shops and shopping : an architectural history /
Kathryn A. Morrison. – 1st ed.
p. cm.
Includes bibliographical references and index.
ISBN 0-300-10139-2 (cl : alk. paper)
1. Stores, Retail – England – History. 2. Architecture – England.
3. Retail trade – England – History. I. Title.
NA6220.M69 2003
725′.2′0942 – dc21

2003005826

A catalogue record for this book is available from
The British Library

Frontispiece T. & W. Ide Ltd of Glasshouse Fields, Stepney, London, delivering a large sheet of plate glass to Barker's on Kensington High Street in the 1950s

Contents

Acknowledgements

This book is based on a survey of retail buildings begun by the former Royal Commission on the Historical Monuments of England in 1998, and continued by English Heritage following its merger with the Royal Commission in 1999. I am indebted to Dr Ann Robey for initiating the project, and to Dr John Bold and Dr Humphrey Welfare for lending crucial support at an early stage.

The contents of this book are based largely on observations made during sixteen months of fieldwork, spread over two years. I am grateful to my colleagues at English Heritage, Tony Calladine and Tara Draper, who accompanied me on early field trips in 1998 and 1999, but above all to Katherine d'Este Hoare, who was my constant 'shopping' companion and sounding board between October 1999 and June 2002. In the wake of our fieldwork, a survey of significant or typical sites was undertaken by English Heritage photographers: Sid Barker, Alun Bull, Steve Cole, Nigel Corrie, Caroline Craggs, James O. Davies, Mike Hesketh-Roberts, Derek Kendall, Patricia Payne, Tony Perry, Bob Skingle, Peter Williams and the aerial photographer Damian Grady. I would like to thank them all for their patience, cooperation and skill, and also to acknowledge the special contribution made by Tony Berry, who was responsible for the drawings, which are such an important feature of the book.

The text of this book owes a great deal to other people. Katherine d'Este Hoare undertook much research and writing for Chapters 1, 4 and 10; Dr Ann Robey contributed to Chapter 13; and Audrey Kirby, lecturer at the London Institute, London College of Printing, School of Retail Studies, kindly lent her expertise on supermarket and superstore design, and co-authored the case study on Tesco in Chapter 12. I am extremely grateful to all three for lightening my load.

Dr Derek Keene of the Centre for Metropolitan History in London and Dr Malcolm Airs of the Department for Continuing Education, Oxford University, both made invaluable comments on the draft text, as did several colleagues within English Heritage, especially Harriet Richardson, Alan Cox, Stephen Porter, Colum Giles and Paul Barnwell. Throughout the duration of the project innumerable other colleagues – too many to be mentioned individually – drew my attention to fascinating shops, and imparted precious nuggets of information, for which I am deeply grateful. Those who must be singled out for special thanks include Tara Draper, for providing general research assistance on London shops as well as insight into the arcane pleasures of luxury shopping; Jonathan Clarke for his advice on steel framing; and David Robinson for giving me access to English Heritage's London Historians' files. Furthermore, I greatly appreciate the constant help that was provided by the staff of the NMR search rooms in London and Swindon, and especially by Liz Smith and Suzie Pugh.

This project could not have been undertaken without the cooperation of shopkeepers, managers and owners throughout England, who gave us generous access to their premises. Nor could it have succeeded without the expertise of those individuals who allowed us to consult company archives and collections, including: Judy Burg and Alan Cooper of Boots; Isabel Hunter of Marks & Spencer; Ken Trimmer of Woolworths; Chris Williams of C&A; Tim Baker-Jones of W. H. Smith; Jeremy Burton and R. A. Whiteley of the Arcadia Group; Ursula Lidbetter and Geoff Leadbetter of the Lincoln Co-operative Society; Gillian Lonergan of the Co-operative Union Archive; Judy Faraday of John Lewis; Peter Coleman of BDP; Terry Driscoll of Ide's; Mike Seary of Dean's Blinds; Sebastian Wormell of Harrods; Steve Douglas of Tesco; and Bridget Williams of Sainsbury's. I am also grateful to Pat Sullivan, retired Project Manager of Woolworths, for supplying much historical information. Additional help was received from the staff of Cambridge University Library, the British Architectural Library, the British Library (St Pancras and Colindale), the British Museum, the History of Advertising Trust, Beamish Museum, Guildhall Library, the Museum of the Royal Pharmaceutical Society and innumerable local libraries and record offices throughout the country. Other valuable information has been supplied by local authority conservation and planning officers, including D. F. Stenning of Essex County Council, Ian Kilby of Bridgnorth District Council and Colette Hall of North Devon District Council. For facilitating access to building regulation plans, I am particularly grateful to David Drake of Lincoln City Council and David Hilton of Manchester City Council.

The publication of this book was made possible by collaboration between English Heritage, Yale University Press and the Paul Mellon Centre for Studies in British Art. I am grateful to Val Horsler, Robin Taylor and Rachel Howard of English Heritage for general support and for administrative help with the illustrations, to Gillian Malpass of Yale University Press for guiding this book from the negotiation stage through to publication, and to the copy-editor, Delia Gaze.

Finally, I would like to give very special thanks to Dr Ron Baxter, for reading and commenting on umpteen draft texts, for providing occasional research assistance and, above all, for his untiring enthusiasm and encouragement.

Introduction

THE HIGH STREET CAN BE SEEN AS A palimpsest of social change, undergoing transformations from year to year, and day to day. In this process much evidence of bygone enterprise is obliterated, yet by scratching beneath the surface of today's array of shops and stores we can uncover substantial fragments of the past (pls 1–2). Pieced together, these tell the story of how the English became a nation of shopkeepers and shoppers, and how the country's retail environment attained its present-day form.

As shoppers we embrace novelty. But we also form strong attachments, as demonstrated by the dismay that greeted the troubles of Marks & Spencer in the late 1990s. Our great retail institutions – from Swan & Edgar to Lipton's – pass with deep regret and are treasured in memory, as is the humblest local shop. Indeed, we tend to measure the social changes that have taken place in the course of our lifetime by evoking the shops of our childhood: the weighing machine in Woolworth's doorway, loose biscuits in the local corner shop, or even the blood and sawdust on the butcher's floor. To stumble across surviving examples of 'traditional' shops is a delight, but only thirty years ago we would have looked down our noses at these relics from another age.

Until the 1970s high street development was propelled by notions of progress and modernity, but in recent decades it has been dominated by the desire to recreate, albeit superficially, a lost golden age of shopping. That golden age is thought to have existed from the Georgian period until about 1950, when the death knell of 'traditional' shopping was sounded by the advent of self-service, mass car ownership and the triumph of national multiples over independent traders. Although the high street survived the initial impact of these phenomena, its character was greatly altered by pedestrianisation and the need to provide car parks. In the 1960s and 1970s its fabric suffered more deep-seated damage from the intrusive construction of precincts and malls, and more recently its economic stability, the very foundation of its being, has been seriously undermined by an explosion in edge-of-town and out-of-town shopping. But even as the Con-servative Government of the 1980s was supporting the creation of non-central shopping complexes, a sense of loss was stirring in town centres. The fear that high street shopping might vanish forever brought about fundamental changes in design phi-losophy, and instead of looking forward the high street began to look back. The most visible result is a rash of pastiche shopfronts and Victorian-style street furniture, but at a deeper level the crisis faced by the high street has compelled those involved in plan-ning processes to give greater consideration to the value placed on retail buildings by local communities, regardless of architec-tural merit.

The condition of the high street at the end of the twentieth century, standing at a crossroads of decline and regeneration, prompted English Heritage to undertake the study that has cul-minated in the production of this book. The following chapters present the history of retail buildings in England using evidence from the built environment, supplemented by documentary research when necessary. The desire to relate the subject as closely as possible to surviving fabric has been a major criterion in determining which topics are covered by individual chapters. It has proved impossible to be all-inclusive, however, and there has simply not been sufficient space within the confines of this single volume to relate the full story of village shops and corner shops, or to give serious consideration to modern architect-designed shop interiors – although these subjects have all been touched upon. Numerous other themes have been treated in greater depth, and because the history of retailing is not a simple linear story, with a beginning, a middle and an end, these are inevitably varied in nature, with many parallel and interweaving strands. Despite this, the ordering of the chapters has a general chronological thrust, carrying the reader from the twelfth century to the present day.

The fundamental human need to exchange goods in order to survive has shaped our towns and cities since the medieval period, when many county towns were not much larger than a modern village. Medieval markets affected the layout and names

1 The battered remains of a Victorian chemist's shop, exposed by the removal of later cladding, at 108–110 Icknield Street in Birmingham.

of main streets, while the houses around them were designed to incorporate small open-fronted shops or stalls (Chapter 1). Little had changed by the late sixteenth century, when the first fashionable shopping galleries were created in London's Royal Exchange (Chapter 2), and the idea dawned that elegant surroundings enabled shopping to become a leisure pursuit. It was only in the early eighteenth century, however, when glazed shopfronts became affordable (Chapter 3), that high street shops began to assume the character we now regard as 'traditional', and clear physical distinctions emerged between the shops of different classes of trader (Chapter 4).

The pace of change accelerated after the Battle of Waterloo (1815). Exchanges had passed into history and were superseded by arcades and bazaars as venues for the promenades of the *beau monde* (Chapter 5). At the same time markets were swept into purpose-built halls (Chapter 6), liberating town-centre streets for the development of high street shopping. As standards of living improved in the Victorian period, so new methods of retailing were developed to serve a more affluent working-class customer base, notably co-operative stores (Chapter 8) and multiple or chain stores (Chapter 10). Increasingly, large ironmongery, furniture and drapery emporia met the aspirations of the burgeoning middle classes, and by the 1870s the largest drapery establishments had begun their metamorphosis into department stores (Chapter 7). These sought an elegant, prosperous clientele in the first half of the twentieth century, but after the Second World War most followed the path of democratisation, opening their doors to all comers and abandoning the glamour they had

2   The fascia of Roberts, 'late buyer for Lewis's', revealed on a boarded-up shopfront on Dudley Road, Winson Green, Birmingham.

cultivated in earlier decades (Chapter 9). Once the extended period of post-war austerity was consigned to history, that homogeneous market began to fragment, and niche-market retailing came to the fore, culminating in the 'brand cathedrals' of present-day metropolitan shopping centres.

But the second half of the twentieth century heralded much greater changes than the simple democratisation, and subsequent fragmentation, of shopping. As already mentioned, many town centres were redeveloped with open-air precincts and enclosed American-style malls (Chapter 11). The first generation of super-markets was also an urban phenomenon, but by the 1970s major companies were eager to develop superstores on sites outside towns and cities (Chapter 12). Before long they were joined by a host of other retailers, who congregated in retail parks, outlet

villages and regional malls (Chapter 13). In the short space of forty years, the fickle world of shopping had been transformed with greater rapidity than at any other time in history.

As town centres fight back, reinventing themselves either as regional shopping centres on the scale of the great megamalls, or as historic havens, it is important that their heritage of retail buildings is properly assessed. This book sets out to provide a national context in which local evaluations can take place, and offers a springboard for those undertaking more theoretical or in-depth studies in the fields of retail, architectural or local history. But, above all, it is written for those who enjoy shop-ping, in the hope that a greater understanding of the built envi-ronment can enhance even the most mundane shopping trip.

I

Stalls, Shambles and Shops:
Marketing and Shopping before 1700

For centuries, urban centres have been moulded by trade, by the simple acts of buying and selling. Medieval commerce has left its clearest mark in the shape and position of our market places, and in the widths and names of our streets. Occasionally it can even be detected in those surviving structures that were built to contain shops or market stalls, or to accommodate merchants and tradesmen. The desire to preserve that legacy affects many present-day planning decisions and, in such towns as Chester, Canterbury and York, the medieval context has proved a huge advantage in maintaining a successful shopping centre that attracts visitors from near and far. The business of shopping, or marketing, however, has undergone great changes since the Middle Ages.

In medieval times the wealthy acquired many of their possessions by dealing directly with craftsmen and artisans, including carpenters, goldsmiths and tailors, either in the comfort of their homes or in the tradesmen's workshops. They could also purchase cloth, imported luxuries and small wares from retailers, who had shops in most large towns by the fourteenth century. Meanwhile, the vast majority of the population could afford little more than necessities, which were bought from pedlars, or at the market. Like the church, the market occupied a central position in the life of every man, woman and child. It ensured that food and fuel were always available, but also offered a forum for social interaction, particularly between the people of the countryside and the town. Annual fairs, where a huge variety of goods was bought and sold in large quantities, accompanied by rowdy entertainments, were especially significant events in people's lives. Today, in an age of anodyne supermarkets, malls and retail parks, it is difficult to imagine the fundamental and vital position held by the market and fair in medieval and early modern society.

★   ★   ★

The Mechanisms of Commerce

BUYING AND SELLING

Few individuals or communities enjoyed complete self-sufficiency in the Middle Ages. Most sold their surplus production and purchased what they lacked with the proceeds, all within the strictly controlled environs of the local market (pl. 4).[1] The market provided a context for the agricultural producers of the countryside to trade directly with the craftsmen and artisans of the town, with each supplying the others' wants through sale or barter. In the market one could usually procure grain, malt, meat and butter, and, since weaving, metalwork, carpentry and leatherwork were practised widely, cloth, cooking pots, tools and shoes were normally available. But not every necessity could be produced locally, and commodities such as coal, salt and fish were transported over long distances within the country. Silks, furs, spices, olive oil and wines came from even further afield.[2] These luxuries were imported by Continental merchants, traded at annual fairs and retailed in the shops of middlemen.

Markets and shops usually prospered in towns that benefited from a good harbour, a strategic river crossing or a major road junction, as well as a fertile hinterland.[3] Although numerous new towns were planted in the twelfth and thirteenth centuries, many urban centres had originated before the Conquest, and enjoyed special trading privileges, including a monopoly on buying and selling and the right to hold markets. These rights were upheld by merchant guilds and municipal authorities, although individual trades might be controlled by craft guilds, or amalgamated companies of retailers, which multiplied in the fourteenth century.[4] Boroughs charged a variety of tolls from outsiders, including 'stallage', 'pontage' and 'pesage', but as the exemptions granted in borough charters increased, so the revenue gleaned through market dues declined. Depopulation, arising from the

3   The Market House in Chipping Campden, Gloucestershire, a rich Cotswold wool town, was built by Sir Baptist Hicks in 1627. Simple secular market houses of this sort evolved from the medieval market cross.

4 Norwich market place, painted by Robert Dighton in 1799. Norwich Castle Museum and Art Gallery.

Black Death of the mid-fourteenth century and later epidemics, also reduced market income and the absolute level of trade. Many towns contracted, but at the same time others thrived and, overall, people experienced an increase in prosperity and commerce.

In the local market or shop some trade was carried out by barter, but buyers and sellers commonly resorted to an exchange of currency or credit arrangements. Simple minor transactions, throughout the medieval and early modern periods, were complicated by a shortage of small-denomination coins. Although pennies could be halved and quartered, and farthings and half-pennies were introduced in the late thirteenth century, it is difficult to imagine how small-scale business was carried out at the market, fair, shop or inn, when a farthing – the smallest coin – bought no less than a quart of ale, and when labourers earned an average daily wage of 2d.[5] Because of this, the practices of the local economy, where the buyer and seller were well acquainted, were very different from trading methods at a regional, national or international level, where merchants were strangers to one another. Local customers could accumulate debts which would be settled periodically, although it has been suggested that even the poorest household bought its necessities in bulk.[6] As for travellers, they may simply have expected to pay over the odds for their bread and ale. It was dangerous to travel with large amounts of money, so international merchants usually carried letters of credit or a bill of exchange rather than sacks of coins. At their destination, they could obtain the money they required from another merchant, or a money lender, who manipulated the rate of exchange to make the deal worthwhile.

Trading frauds and breaches of the peace at markets were tried by borough or manor market courts and punished by a stint in the pillory or stocks, or by a fine. There were also 'piepowder' ('dusty feet') courts which could settle disputes especially quickly. Misdemeanours included 'forestalling', or buying up goods before they entered the market. The disreputable practice of 'engrossing' involved buying large quantities of a particular commodity and hoarding it to stimulate demand. Equally frowned upon was 'regrating', or buying wholesale to sell retail at a profit, although that was often a practical necessity when goods had to be transported from afar. Bakers and brewers could end up in the pillory for cheating the assizes, which determined the size of loaves and the strength of ale on the basis of the price of grain, while butchers might meet the same fate for selling rotten meat. Cooks were often criticised for reheating food or using poor ingredients, and meal dealers were not above adulterating grain. All markets provided official weights and measures, as private scales or auncels were not to be trusted. To complicate matters further, weights varied greatly from place to place, and local customs proved extremely durable despite regular attempts, from the tenth century onwards, to impose national standards.[7]

★   ★   ★

With the possible exception of second-hand dealers, the first shopkeepers for whom retailing, rather than production, became a primary trade, and whose shops no longer doubled as workshops, were drapers (who dealt mainly in woollen cloth), mercers, haberdashers and grocers. Outside major commercial centres, many of these retailers operated as general merchants, selling a miscellany of goods with a slow turnover, rather than adhering to their avowed speciality. As citizens, however, they were freer from municipal interference than those engaged in fresh food trades. They could open their shops outside market hours and on non-market days, although few provincial shopkeepers considered this worthwhile, even as late as the seventeenth century.[8]

Throughout the medieval period most craftsmen, including saddlers, shoemakers, goldsmiths and tailors, sold goods of their own manufacture either from their workshop or in the market place. In addition to their own handiwork, some sold that of apprentices and outworkers who played no direct part in the retail process. As demand for their goods grew, craftsmen with premises in town centres found it profitable to concentrate on the retail side of their business, and came to rely more heavily on outworkers to manufacture their stock. In this way they became retailers rather than craftsmen, and their workshops were transformed into shops. This trend was particularly evident in Elizabethan London, where a concentration of wealthy customers was developing a taste for exotic clothing and personal accessories. Despite this, the craftsman-retailer survived, especially if he manufactured expensive customised items, such as guns or clocks.

Men and women engaged in the lowly victualling trades were compelled to sell their wares in the open market throughout the Middle Ages, so that fraud could easily be detected. While some rented open-fronted shops in the frontages of houses facing the market place, victuallers were expressly forbidden to sell from inside their own houses, behind closed doors. The marketing of foodstuffs first began to change in London under the pressure of feeding a population that is roughly estimated to have grown from 40,000 in 1377 to 120,000 in 1550 and 375,000 in 1650.[9] The authorities, possibly fearing famine, did not prevent the capital's butchers, bakers and meal-men retailing from fixed shops beyond the reach of the market. Other victuallers followed suit, especially in the new suburbs of London, which were slow to acquire their own markets. It was only in the late nineteenth century, however, with the rise of the co-operative store and the multiple provision shop, that the market ceased to be the main location for buying all kinds of food in urban societies.

Beyond the bounds of the formal market, fair and shop, some selling took place in illicit locations, such as houses or inns. In addition, hawkers and pedlars played a significant role in the distribution of goods. While some ambulatory traders cried their wares in city streets, often from trays slung around their necks, others carried their merchandise from house to house and village to village. Most travelled on foot, carrying their goods in a bundle, while wealthier hawkers had a packhorse or mule. Many traders had to combine peddling with part-time shopkeeping and market trading to make a decent living.

Markets and Fairs

MARKETS

Markets were the main users of public space in medieval towns and cities. The Domesday Survey of 1086 mentions only fifty markets, but many more must have existed at that time.[10] Most Anglo-Saxon markets probably originated spontaneously, at a convenient meeting place, and it is unclear how, or to what extent, they were regulated. From the late eleventh century onwards it was usual for the monarch to grant individuals and institutions the right to control markets and levy tolls, but some markets remained prescriptive, in other words held by custom, and not by grant. Approximately 2,000 new markets were established between 1200 and 1349,[11] some regularising existing *ad hoc* arrangements, others serving new or planted towns, but many at settlements that were no more than villages. Not all foundation charters were acted upon, and not all new markets were a resounding success – some could have an adverse impact on older markets, as the townsfolk of Wilton, Wiltshire, discovered when Salisbury was established near by in 1219.[12] The total number of markets decreased after the mid-fourteenth century, partly as a result of the Black Death. This served to strengthen, or at least sustain, remaining markets, which were mostly located in towns. It has been estimated that Tudor and Stuart England was served by about 760 markets.[13]

In the eleventh century the churchyard was the favoured venue for market trading, which usually took place on Sundays and feast days. However, a movement against Sunday trading gained ground in the early thirteenth century. Thenceforth, most markets took place on weekdays, and were moved to a designated open space in the town centre. The majority were held once a week, but large shire towns had separate markets for different commodities, held on different days, and London markets were open every day except Sunday.[14]

While some markets formed a nucleus around which the town itself developed, others were imposed on mature settlements, necessitating a certain amount of clearance. Ideally, market places occupied level ground and, although they could assume a wide variety of shapes and sizes, three basic plans emerged: linear, triangular and rectangular (pls 6a–c).[15] Some Anglo-Saxon markets were held in particularly wide streets, such as West Cheap (later Cheapside; Old English *ceap* meaning market) in London and the High Street (*Cypstret*) in Winchester, Hampshire, which followed the line of the main Roman street, connecting the east and west gates of the town. Several post-Conquest markets, like Ludlow, Shropshire (pl. 6a), also occupied a broad street, lined with narrow burgage plots. These markets frequently swelled out at one end to create a small triangular space adjoining a major route, but many medieval market places were triangular or funnel-shaped in their entirety, because they were established at the junction of three or more main roads (pl. 6b). Other markets, especially in gridlike planted towns such as Salisbury (pl. 6c), were allotted a spacious rectangular area in the town centre.[16] Even small village markets had regular triangular or rectangular shapes, and it is clear that their establishment could have a profound effect on the morphology of a settlement, sometimes shifting it away from the church to a major through route.[17] Regardless of its form, the medieval market tended to be divided loosely into different areas, each specialising in a specific commodity. As towns grew, these spilled into surrounding streets, which were often named after the trades conducted there.

MARKET BUILDINGS

By 1300 permanent structures had begun to intrude on to open market places. These islands of buildings originated as temporary stalls arranged in narrow rows devoted to particular trades, usually under licence from the civic authorities. Over time the stalls were replaced by buildings with cramped domestic accommodation or storage above a stall or shop, and many were eventually reconstructed as complete houses. In 1598 John Stow explained the origin of buildings in Old Fish Street, where London fishmongers sold their stock:

> In this Old Fish Street is one row of small houses, placed along in the midst of Knightrider Street, which row is also of Bread Street Ward: these houses, now possessed by fishmongers, were at the first but moveable boards, or stalls, set out on market-days, to show their fish there to be sold; but procuring licence to set up sheds, they grew to shops, and by little and little to tall houses, of three or four stories in height, and are now called Fish Street.[18]

Market colonisation of this nature is easily recognised in many English towns, for example in Ludlow (pl. 6a). What differentiates it from burgage plots is the absence of back yards or gardens, and it often retains its distinctive ramshackle qualities to this day.

For simple reasons of hygiene, butchers and fishmongers were among the first traders to erect substantial stalls, or shambles

5 The octagonal market cross of around 1500 in Chichester, West Sussex, provided shelter for country traders selling butter and other foodstuffs. It is elaborately decorated with panelled tracery, crockets, pinnacles and buttresses.

(usually *sceamel*), in the market place. Initially these would have been little more than humble timber shelters, with a pent roof covering a counter, like the restored fifteenth-century shambles in Shepton Mallet in Somerset, or modern market structures in towns such as Cheadle in Staffordshire (pl. 7). Most of today's Butchers' and Fleshmongers' Rows originated as shambles. The street known as The Shambles in York (pl. 8), for example, is lined by tall, jettied buildings which probably evolved from simple sheds set up under licence by the city butchers to protect their meat from the weather.

Other permanent structures were erected in the market place to shelter those selling cleaner categories of perishable foodstuffs,

6a–c (*facing page*) Three differently shaped medieval market places: a. the linear market at Ludlow, Shropshire, extending between the castle and the church; b. the triangular market in Carlisle, Cumbria, at a major road junction; and c. the rectangular market place in Salisbury, Wiltshire, laid out as part of the new town. All three were encroached upon in the medieval period.

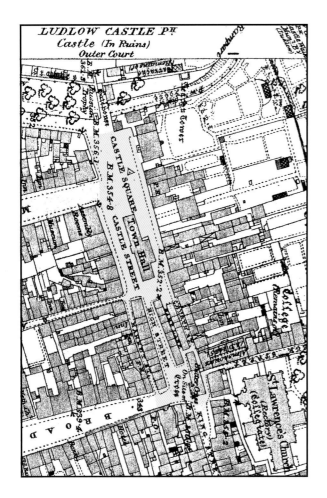

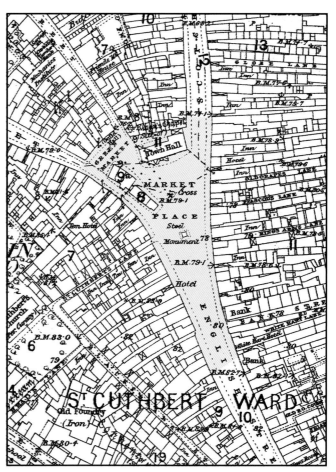

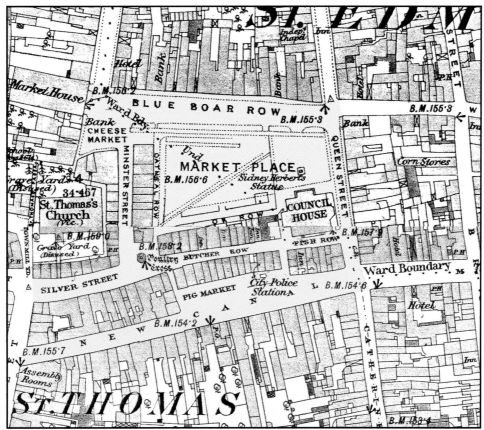

7　The modern market stalls in Cheadle, simple structures designed to shelter goods and traders, are not very different from medieval stalls. The late Georgian terrace to the rear of the market place has bow-fronted shops on its ground floor, with lodgings above.

such as butter, cheese, eggs and fruit. By the late medieval period, the simple market cross, set up to inspire honesty amongst traders, had developed into a small structure with a roof and open sides. The octagonal market cross close to the cathedral in Chichester (pl. 5), at the junction of the city's four main streets, was erected by Bishop Edward Storey around 1500 'to soocure and comfort of the poore people'.[19] The early sixteenth-century cross in Malmesbury, Wiltshire, was built so that 'personnes which resort hither in market ouvert might think upon their deare Savioure which died for them upon the Crosse, of which this faire Market Crosse is a signe ande symbole; to the ende that rogues and cozeneours may looke upon it ande cease them of theyre guile'.[20] Although simple market crosses, or market houses (pl. 3), continued to be built after the Reformation, they were usually devoid of religious imagery. One of the longest market houses ever erected must have been the Fleet Market House (pl. 9), which was designed by George Dance the Elder, Clerk of Works to the City of London, and opened in 1737. It was not until the early nineteenth century that the open-sided market house was succeeded by the enclosed market hall (see Chapter 6).

Long before that time, however, it was much more usual for an open-sided market shelter to be incorporated within the ground floor of a civic building. Such multiple-use buildings seem to have originated in the thirteenth century, although there is a possibility that the Northampton Guildhall had a market area as early as 1138.[21] An early surviving example is the Cutlers' Guildhall (pl. 10) in Thaxted, Essex, a splendid jettied structure which is generally thought to have been erected in 1393–1401, but may be later.[22] While the ground floor contained an open area for market stalls, the upper rooms hosted meetings of the Cutlers' Guild and the burgesses of the manorial borough. It has been suggested that the first floor was originally open-fronted, like that of Titchfield Guildhall, now re-erected at the Weald and Downland Open Air Museum, Singleton, West Sussex, so that officials could supervise the market place.[23] Before long, similar buildings were being erected all over the country, in a variety of styles and materials. The octagonal market building in Wymondham (1617–18), near Norwich, resembled earlier market crosses but had an upper-floor room. Those in Much Wenlock, Shropshire (main phase, 1540; extension 1577), and Ledbury, Herefordshire (c. 1617–55), were much larger timber-framed structures, while the buildings at Rothwell, Northamp-

8 (facing page)　The Shambles in York, photographed by H. Felton in 1950. The city butchers had their stalls here for centuries, but nowadays the street is full of specialist shops, catering largely for tourists.

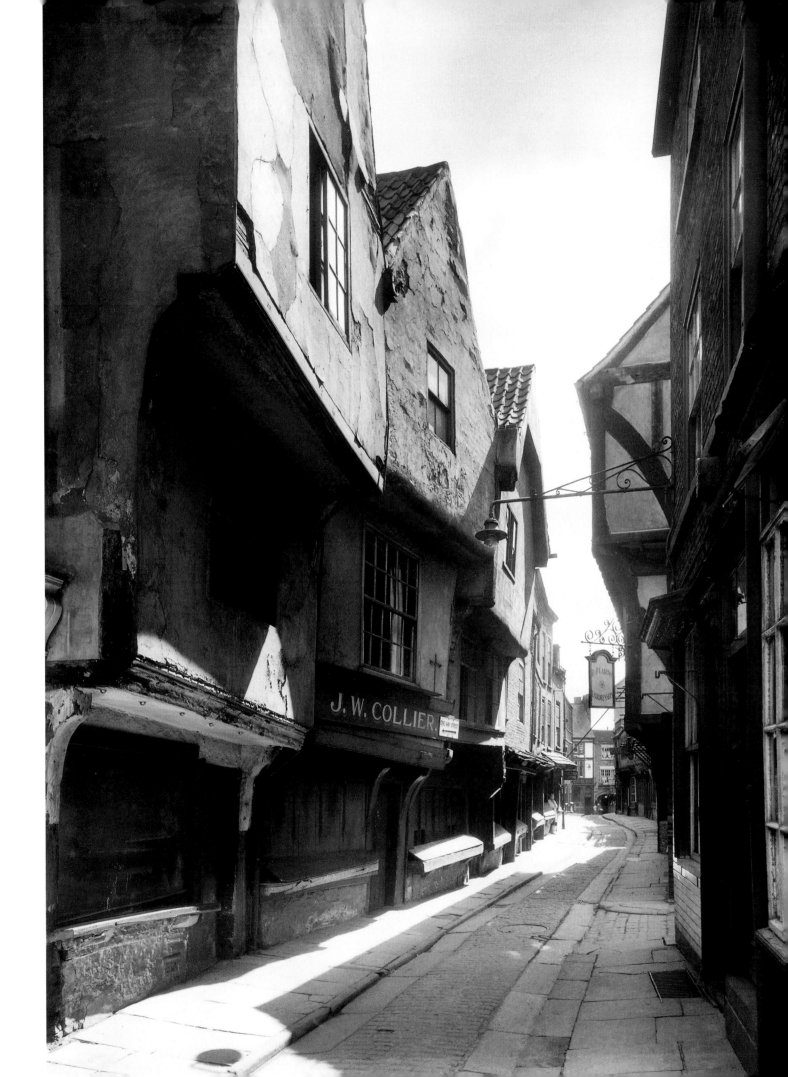

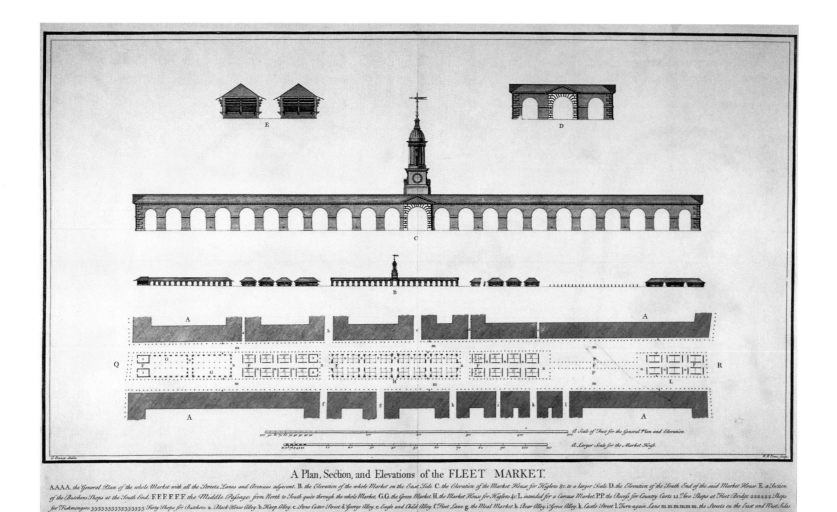

A Plan, Section, and Elevations of the FLEET MARKET.

AAAA the General Plan of the whole Market with all the Streets Lanes and Avenues adjacent. B. the Elevation of the whole Market on the East Side. C. the Elevation of the Market House for Higlers &c. to a larger Scale. D. the Elevation of the South End of the said Market House E. a Section of the Butchers Shops at the South End. FFFFFF the Middle Passage from North to South quite through the whole Market. G.G. the Green Market. H. the Market House for Higlers &c. I. intended for a Carcase Market. P.P. the Recess for Country Carts 11 Two Shops at Fleet Bridge. 22222 Shops for Fishmongers. 33333333333333 Forty Shops for Butchers. a. Black House Alley. b. Harp Alley. c. Stone Cutter Street & George Alley. e. Eagle and Child Alley. f. Fleet Lane. g. the Meal Market. h. Bear Alley i. Goose Alley. k. Castle Street l. Turn again Lane m. m.m.m.m.m. the Streets on the East and West Sides of the Market. n n n n n n n n n n. the Cross Passages between the several Shops and Market Houses o o o o o o o o o. the Cross Passages in the Market House and in the Green and Carcase Markets. 4 4 4 4 4 4 4 4 4 4 4 4 the Foot Ways between the Posts and Buildings. Q. Fleet Bridge. R. Holborn Bridge. Published April the 25, 1737 by George Dance pannx t to a late Act of Parliament.

9   London's Fleet Market of 1737 was built over the Fleet Ditch, on what is now Farringdon Street, to replace the old Stocks Market. The main building sported an impressive turret, capped by a dome and weathervane.

tonshire (1577–8), and Shrewsbury (1596), were of ashlar, revealing a new and more dignified attitude towards civic buildings. Later examples included those at Peterborough (1671) and High Wycombe (1757), and after a lull of 150 years the building type has recently been resurrected at Poundbury in Dorset (2000). The use of upper-floor rooms in these buildings varied and changed over time: although most were built as guildhalls or town halls, they could also serve as tollbooths, courts, wool halls, assembly rooms or grammar schools. A room was often reserved for market officials or weights, and some even had a gaol cell.

LONDON MARKETS

London was by far the most populous city in the land and had the busiest markets, most of which were reserved for 'foreign' traders, who came from the surrounding countryside. Only private citizens could buy in these markets, but retailers wishing to acquire stock for their shops were allowed in towards the end of the day's trading.[24] Over the centuries such regulations proved extremely difficult to enforce.

London's main medieval markets (pl. 11) straggled across the City from west to east, beginning with the livestock market just outside the City walls at Smithfield and the butchers' shambles and meal market at Newgate, continuing along Cheapside to the Stocks and Leadenhall, running down Gracechurch Street, and finally ending up on Eastcheap and Fish Street Hill (New Fish Street). In addition, much corn and fish was sold on the quays, at Queenhithe and Billingsgate, and numerous other food markets existed throughout the City. Efforts to reorganise some of these markets resulted in the construction of two substantial buildings quite unlike anything in provincial towns.

First, in preparation for a visit from Edward I in 1274, butchers' and fishmongers' stalls in Cheapside were removed to Woolchurchhaw where, around 1282, the mayor, Henry le

10   The open ground floor of Thaxted Guildhall, built around 1400, sheltered market traders, while the Cutlers' Guild met in the rooms above. From the mid-sixteenth century, the building hosted meetings of the borough council, and from the late seventeenth century it was used as a school. It was heavily restored in 1910, and this photograph was taken in 1927.

Waleys, a wine merchant with strong connections in south-west France, built a timber, covered market called the Stocks, modelled on the Halles of Paris.[25] It was rebuilt in 1406–11 (pl. 12) as a three-storey stone structure with stalls at street level and upper rooms that were rented by drapers and as domestic accommodation for single men.[26] In 1439, in response to grain shortages, the City added a granary to the Stocks and embarked upon the construction of a combined market and granary at Leadenhall.[27] Since the early fourteenth century the street in front of the mansion known as Leadenhall had been used as a market where country producers, primarily poulterers, came to sell their wares to the citizens of London. The City authorities had acquired the mansion in 1411, and now, in 1439, decided to redevelop the site to accommodate the market. The new building, completed around 1455, had a central courtyard surrounded by open arcades which sheltered stall-holders in bad weather, while the upper floors were used for the storage of grain and,

in time, a variety of other goods, including wool and lead. A simple chapel projected from the east range. As at the Stocks, the walls were topped by battlements which emphasised the status of the building and lent it a superficially defensive appearance perhaps intended to discourage raiding in time of famine.

In the course of the sixteenth century smaller market buildings, on a par with those of provincial towns, were erected at Newgate and Queenhithe, and both were depicted schematically by Hugh Alley in his *Caveat*, or plea for market reform, issued in 1588. The Newgate market house of 1547 seems to have been an open-sided market shelter without any upper-floor rooms.[28] The Queenhithe market house, on the other hand, was erected in 1564–6 with a gabled upper storey over an open, arcaded ground floor used mainly for the storage of corn.[29] Southwark market, on the south side of the Thames, came under the control of the City in 1550, and also had a small market house with an upper storey.[30] Despite the existence of such buildings, most of

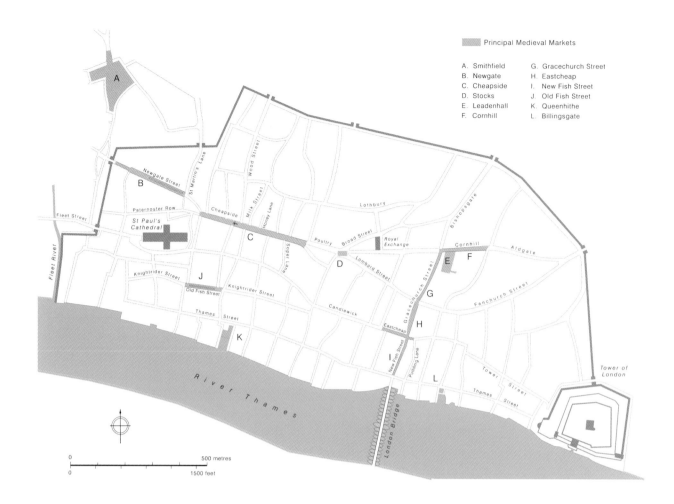

11 (*above*)   Before the Great Fire of 1666, London's streets had many markets; this map shows the location of the main ones.

London's markets continued to take place in the streets, which were lined by open-fronted shops and stalls. By 1615, under pressure from a growing population (now approximately 200,000), the markets were spilling beyond their traditional boundaries and 'Newgate Market, Cheapside, Leaden-hall, and Gracechurch Street, were unmeasurably pestered with the unimaginable encrease, and multiplicity of Market-folkes'.[31]

The Great Fire of 1666, which destroyed the Stocks but spared Leadenhall, was seen as an opportunity to remove the major retail markets from the streets.[32] The general market at Cheapside was relocated to Honey Lane and Milk Street, where it incorporated the sites of Allhallows and St Mary Magdalene, two churches that had been destroyed by the fire. Similarly, the Stocks, or Woolchurch Market, was extended south over ground

12   This schematic drawing, made in 1598 by Hugh Alley, is the only surviving depiction of the Stocks Market (1406–11) on Poultry, which burnt down in 1666. From left to right, it shows the north elevation, the west façade, and the adjoining church of St Mary Woolchurch. The column indicates a place where market offenders could be punished; it formed part of Alley's scheme for reform, and was never erected. From Hugh Alley, *A Caveat for the City of London*. V.a.318.

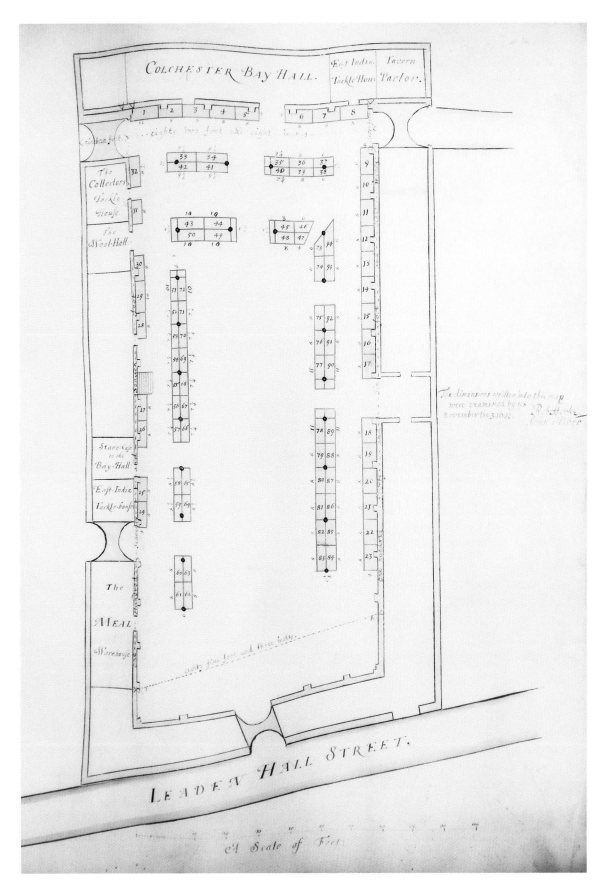

13　William Leybourn drafted this plan of Leadenhall Market in 1677, before the new wooden piazza inside the court-yard had been completed. The original stone arcades were largely blocked up, and the ground-floor rooms used as ware-houses.

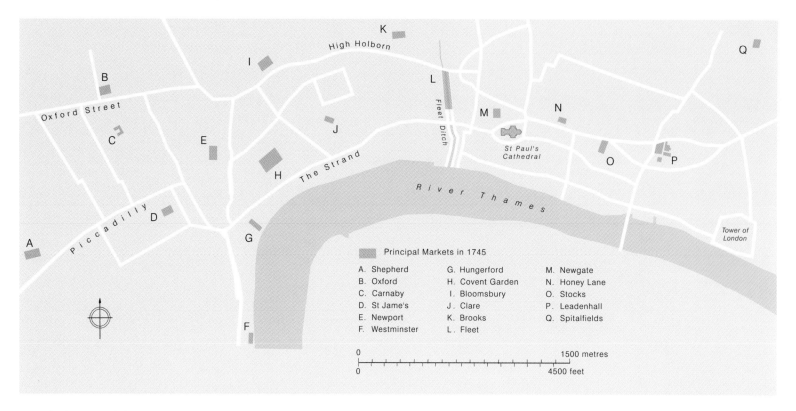

14   The location of the main London markets around 1745.

	Principal Markets in 1745		
A. Shepherd	G. Hungerford	M. Newgate
B. Oxford	H. Covent Garden	N. Honey Lane
C. Carnaby	I. Bloomsbury	O. Stocks
D. St Jame's	J. Clare	P. Leadenhall
E. Newport	K. Brooks	Q. Spitalfields
F. Westminster	L. Fleet	

formerly occupied by St Mary Woolchurch. Newgate Market moved to a new square, south of the old street market, and Leadenhall was extended by the addition of the Greenyard and Herb Market.[33] A building called the Nailgallery divided the Greenyard into a White Market – for the sale of mutton, lamb, veal, pork and poultry – and a Fish Market.

Much of the constructional work in the new markets was entrusted to Roger Jerman and, perhaps surprisingly, was carried out in wood rather than more fireproof materials. The chief feature of most of the markets was a colonnade, known as a piazza, which not only provided a covered trading area but also served to delimit the market. Piazzas were erected around the White and Herb Markets at Leadenhall, around the southern part of the Stocks, and at Honey Lane. Even the interior of the old courtyard at Leadenhall (pl. 13), now referred to as the Beef Market or Leather Market, received a new wooden piazza, constructed against the original stone arcade.[34] The northern part of the Stocks, however, was surrounded by lime trees rather than a piazza, and was dominated by an equestrian statue of Charles II.[35]

Market houses with cellars, open ground floors and upper-floor rooms were erected in the White Market, Newgate Market and at Honey Lane. The upper floors did not have civic functions, unlike their counterparts in the provinces; they were usually rented out for storage, but in 1691 that in Honey Lane

was leased to a congregation of French refugees.[36] Some of these buildings were surrounded by permanent stalls: Honey Lane Market, for example, accommodated 105 butchers' stalls fitted with boards, rails, racks and hooks. Stalls were built within the market houses of both Honey Lane and the White Market, and when the cruciform Newgate market house was rebuilt after a fire in 1685, each of its four corners housed a shop.[37] Engravings show that the ground floors of many London market houses had been enclosed by the early nineteenth century, and were used as either warehouses or shops. The market piazzas seem to have had a similar fate.

After the Fire, several new markets were created beyond the bounds of the City (pl. 14).[38] Serving the poor districts to the east was Spitalfields Market (1682), which specialised in vegetables and occupied a square with a small, cruciform market house in the centre.[39] Meanwhile, respectable society continued its inexorable shift to the west, where new residential districts required their own food supplies. At least four markets had been set up just before 1666: New or Clare Market (1657), Covent Garden Market (1661), Southampton or Bloomsbury Market (1662) and St James's Market (1664). To these were now added Hungerford Market (1680), Brook's Market (1682), Newport Market (1686), Lowndes or Carnaby Market (1720), Oxford Market (1721) (pl. 15) and Shepherd Market (1742). Several of these included market buildings with enclosed stalls or shops

15   Oxford Market House, London, was built 1726–37 to a design by James Gibbs. Around 1815–17 it was encased by two-storey units with ground-floor shops. This watercolour by J. P. Emslie was made shortly before the demolition of the building in 1880.

on their ground floors, rather than an open area for informal pitches. For example, the two-storey, H-shaped building in St James's Market, visited by Pepys when new in April 1666, had central corridors flanked by stalls or shops.[40] While some seventeenth-century market buildings admitted light through dormers in their roofs, lanterns and skylights became increasingly common in the eighteenth century. The roof of the Fleet Market House of 1737 (pl. 9), for example, incorporated skylights, and two new blocks of stalls built in Honey Lane Market in 1787–9 had covered central passages lit by clerestorys.[41] Such buildings, although humble, may have served as prototypes for early nineteenth-century arcades and market halls.

THE FAIR

The right to hold fairs coinciding with a particular religious feast was granted to powerful individuals, institutions or towns from the late eleventh century onwards. By 1500 more than 2,000 fairs had come into existence, most of which had been established before 1350.[42] Many of these were of little more than local or regional significance, but in the twelfth and thirteenth centuries England's main annual fairs served as enormous markets, where merchants from all over Europe (but especially Flanders and Italy) came to buy and sell goods in bulk, craftsmen came to buy the materials of their trade, retailers came to stock their shops, stewards of great households came to buy supplies and local people came to enjoy themselves.

Most important of all were the 'great fairs' held in Boston (St Botolph's; July), Northampton (All Saints; November), St Ives, Cambridgeshire (Easter), Stamford (Lent) and Winchester (St Giles; September). These fairs peaked between 1180 and 1220,[43] but in the late thirteenth century entered a decline from which they never recovered. Their change of fortune is ascribed to a multitude of causes, notably the rising importance of London as a permanent trading centre and the growing tendency for merchants to sell their wool and cloth direct to middlemen, who arranged for its transportation overseas through staple towns and ports.[44] The location of the staple in Calais from 1363 served further to concentrate the wool trade in London. But not all fairs had specialised in wool or cloth: sheep were traded at Weyhill in Hampshire, geese and cheese at Nottingham, herring at Great Yarmouth and horses at Horncastle. Regardless of this specialisation, a wide range of products was available at every fair. As yet, there was no distinction between wholesale and retail trading: anyone could buy anything at a fair.

At fair time the owner had the right to charge tolls and rents, and impose taxes and fines, while townsfolk suffered from restrictions upon local trading and municipal activity. Trading was prohibited within seven leagues of Winchester during St Giles's Fair, which was granted to the bishop in 1096 and initially lasted for three days. By the early fourteenth century, however, it continued for no less than twenty-four days.[45]

Some fairs were held on church property, or in town and city streets. In St Ives, for example, Ramsey Abbey owned both town and fair, and required residents to vacate their houses, or at least their front rooms, in fair time. In addition, the abbey erected temporary stalls in the streets, and permitted selling from boats moored at the quay. The area of the fair was delimited by two gates and a tollbooth. Most fairs, however, were in separate ownership from the town and took place in fields. In Winchester the fair was held some 150 yards east of the town, on St Giles's Hill, which was occupied by permanent wooden buildings and surrounded by a palisade and ditch for security.[46] Rows of stalls were rented out to different categories of trader, either to a particular trade or guild, or to merchants from a particular city or country.

One of the most important and popular fairs in early modern England was Stourbridge (or Sturbridge) Fair (pl. 16), which had been held just outside Cambridge since the thirteenth century.

16   Buildings at Stourbridge Fair, Cambridge, in 1832.

In 1724 Daniel Defoe declared it 'not only the greatest in the whole nation, but in the world',[47] and described its layout:

the shops are placed in rows like streets, whereof one is called Cheapside; and here, as in several other streets, are all sorts of trades, who sell by retail, and who come principally from London with their goods . . . In another street parallel with the road are like rows of booths, but larger, and more intermingled with wholesale dealers, and one side, passing out of this last street to the left hand, is a formal great square, formed by the largest booths, built in that form, and which they call the Duddery ... The area of this square is about 80 to 100 yards, where the dealers have room before every booth to take down, and open their packs, and to bring in waggons to load and unload.[48]

Clearly a strong distinction had been established between wholesale and retail trading. The Duddery was largely reserved for wholesale wool dealers, and Defoe remarked that Londoners now struck deals here without goods actually changing hands. By the end of the century new business and banking methods, and the provision of a permanent and settled mercantile community in London had rendered fairs all but obsolete for wholesale trading.

As their importance as trading centres waned, so the significance of fairs as places of entertainment grew: in the 1660s Samuel Pepys visited St Bartholomew's Fair in London to watch the rope walkers, and by 1700 Stourbridge Fair was renowned for its brothels. It was said that men came here from London, not to do business, but to 'Drink, Smoke, and Whore'.[49] The range of entertainments offered by fairs continued to expand until, by the mid-nineteenth century, many had become the travelling funfairs that are still with us today.

Shops

SINGLE SHOP UNITS

While commercial activity in the medieval town was focused on the market place, much additional trading took place in shops (*schoppe*, *sopa* or *shopa*), which could be kept only by freemen or citizens.[50] Shops varied in form and function: some may have been little more than stalls which would have opened on market day, while others served as craftsmen's workshops, or were used by wealthy merchants as showrooms. It is usually impossible to deduce the precise original function – or functions – of a medieval shop.

The most valuable tenements in any town were clustered around the market place, and their frontages often incorporated shops. Some stone town houses of the twelfth century may have accommodated shops or workshops within arcades on their ground floors.[51] Several such shops survive in France, and it has been argued that the so-called Jew's House in Lincoln (pl. 17), together with several other surviving English houses, were originally of that type.[52] However, no English example has survived with its ground floor intact. In England all the medieval shops that have been preserved in a recognisable state form an integral part of timber-framed buildings. The implication that medieval shop developers preferred timber to stone is supported

17 The Jew's House on Steep Hill, Lincoln, was built around 1160. It is thought to have had three arches at street level, two to the left of the entrance passage and one to the right. These may have housed shops. The present shopfront dates from the mid-nineteenth century and, like many other Lincolnshire shopfronts, is fitted with shutter boxes.

by the survival or documentation of numerous sites where a timber commercial range lay along the front of a stone house.[53] Thin wooden walls would undoubtedly have been the most economical option for shops, in both spatial and monetary terms.

Surviving shops are concentrated in rural East Anglia, often in communities that have not experienced great pressure for commercial redevelopment since the decline of the cloth trade in the late Middle Ages. Elsewhere, isolated examples have been identified in commercial centres such as Bristol, Chester, Coventry, Exeter, Oxford, Shrewsbury and Southampton. This body of material gives little impression of what once existed, as documents make it plain that town centres were thronged with shops from the thirteenth century onwards. Cheapside alone is estimated to have had something in the region of 400 shops in 1300, while Canterbury had 200 in 1234 and Chester had 270 in

18 Myddleton Place in Saffron Walden, now a youth hostel, was built in the sixteenth century. The frame of the shop which originally occupied the corner bay can still be seen.

1300.[54] Although numbers seem to have declined after the Black Death, it must be supposed that many medieval shops still stand unrecognised, camouflaged by centuries of alterations.

Then as now, location was of the utmost importance. Some medieval shopkeepers clearly favoured positions close to the church, where crowds would pass on certain days of the week. At Writtle Green in Essex, for example, a shop occupied the end bay of a house of *circa* 1500, facing the main thoroughfare to the church. At Felsted (pl. 23), also in Essex, a passage through the centre of the fourteenth-century Trinity Guildhall ('The Old School') gave access to the churchyard and was flanked by four lock-up shops. A similar arrangement existed in Hadleigh in Suffolk in the fifteenth century. Elsewhere, shops lined the approaches of river crossings, where they could attract business from foot, road and water traffic, a good example being the sixteenth-century Myddleton Place on Bridge Street in Saffron

Walden, Essex (pl. 18). Most medieval shops, however, would have faced the market place, or the streets that led off it: thriving commercial locations, in which they were more likely to be rebuilt in later centuries.

Many medieval shops, like those in Writtle Green and Saffron Walden, occupied a small proportion of a large town house. Such houses belonged to wealthy burgesses, men usually involved in wholesale trade or manufacture rather than agriculture or, indeed, retailing. Many of their houses comprised an open hall, lying parallel to the street and flanked by floored cross-wings: one for services (buttery and pantry), and the other for private domestic accommodation (parlour and solar). When a shop was included, for example at 26 Market Place, Lavenham, Suffolk (pls 19 and 20a), it usually occupied the front of the service wing. This pushed the two service rooms back, making it difficult to light the central room unless the cross-wing occupied a corner site. One solution was to combine the buttery and pantry to form a single space, lit from the rear; another was to move the shop to the high end of the hall and dispense with a parlour, as seems to have happened at 17–21 King Street, Saffron Walden, in the late fifteenth century.[55] Where there is evidence that a shop had direct access from the cross-passage or hall it is assumed that it was used by the householder. If, on the other hand, the shop did not communicate with the house, it was probably rented out as 'lock-up' premises. Such shops could have access to an upper chamber, often described as a solar or upper shop, to all intents and purposes forming a house within a house. Upper rooms were accessed by means of a stair or ladder, and could be used for either living accommodation or storage. Vertical arrangements of this sort led to the sub-division of burgage plots in many towns, but are not always detectable in surviving buildings.

Urban medieval houses did not often conform to the classic hall and cross-wings plan, a layout that required a wide plot and was better suited to the countryside. In prime commercial locations narrow burgage plots forced town-dwellers to devise ingenious variations on the standard house plan. One option was to dispense with an entire cross-wing and place the solar over the services or shop. An alternative (pl. 20b) was to set the building at right angles to the street, in which case the shop was positioned at the front, under the solar, with the open hall and a floored service wing to the rear. In such a plan, access to the domestic accommodation was from an enclosed side passage that ran through the property, once more allowing the shop to form either an integral part of the house or to function as a self-contained unit. At Leche House in Chester, a well-preserved example of the right-angle plan dating from the fifteenth century, a gallery above the passage connected the chambers at the front and rear of the building.[56] The shop itself communicated with the hall, and must have been used by the owner.

While most medieval shops would have been used as stalls, retail units or craftsmen's workshops, some could simply have been showrooms, forming part of the suite of business rooms needed by the wealthy merchants who owned imposing town houses. Such merchants concentrated on bulk trading, conducted at the quayside, fair or exchange, rather than at the market or shop, and thus required premises with substantial storage facilities, a strongroom and a counting house. They may have used their well-lit shops to display goods to prospective buyers, particularly if they were involved in the wool or cloth trade. The merchant stored his goods in a warehouse at the back of the house, or in a cellar. Vaulted cellars, or undercrofts, were used mainly for the storage of wine or other commodities that would not be affected by cold or damp, and in towns were also used

19   The area around 26 Market Place, Lavenham, was known as 'The Butchery' in the sixteenth century and so it is possible that this heavily restored shop – now a National Trust gift shop – was originally occupied by a butcher. It dates from around 1520.

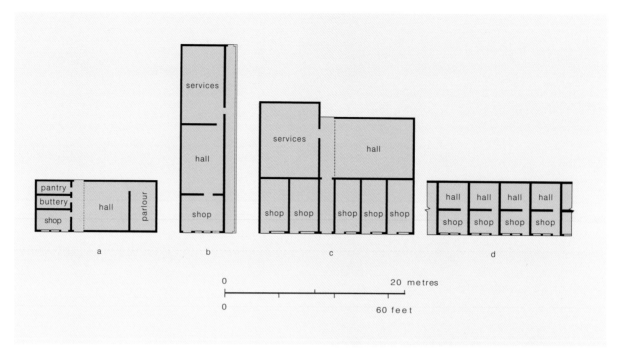

pantry		services	
buttery	hall		hall
shop	parlour	services	
		shop shop	shop shop shop
	hall		
		hall hall hall hall	
	shop	shop shop shop shop	

0   20 metres

0   60 feet

20a–d   These schematic plans show four common medieval shop arrangements: a. a shop in a parallel-hall house; b. a shop in a right-angle hall house; c. a row of shops in front of a house; and d. an independent row of shops with living accommodation for the shopkeepers.

as taverns, the wine being sold in the front compartment where customers could see it being drawn from the barrels to the rear.[57] Together with ground-floor shops, undercrofts could provide the householder with a regular income and many eventually fell into separate freeholds. At 58 French Street, Southampton, a right-angle plan house of late thirteenth-century date with a ground-floor shop, the only entrance to the undercroft was from the street, strongly suggesting that it was designed for separate letting from the outset.[58]

By 1612, when the surveyor Ralph Treswell drew plans of numerous buildings in the City of London, the 'traditional' shop-and-house plan, which would endure throughout the country for the next 350 years, was well established. In the City at that time, most shops occupied the full frontages of buildings on long, narrow plots.[59] As ever, shops could be entered directly from the street, or from a side passage that also gave admission to the house. In most cases the house was occupied by the shop-keeper and communicated directly with the shop. Some shop-keepers had enlarged their shop by removing the wall or partition that separated it from the rear room, which was often identified as a kitchen. Behind that lay a yard. It is notable that many properties with a shop also had a warehouse or cellar, and/or a counting-house. The degree of storage and office space required would, of course, have varied greatly from one type of shop to another.

★   ★   ★

ROW SHOPS

From at least the thirteenth century, and probably much earlier, blocks, terraces or rows of shops were erected on a speculative basis by religious bodies, colleges or wealthy merchants who sought a steady income. Indeed, rows were probably the most common building type to be found in medieval town centres. Some row shops included accommodation and storage facilities for the shopkeeper (pl. 20d). For example, each of the twenty-two shops at 34–51 Church Street, Tewkesbury, Gloucestershire, a row erected around 1450 by Tewkesbury Abbey, was positioned in front of its own small, heated hall, and under a first-floor chamber.[60] On the other hand, the five shops comprising the fifteenth-century row at 4–16 St James's Street in King's Lynn, Norfolk, merely had a first-floor room for storage: they had no hall and no chimney stack.[61]

In general, the absence of stairs within row shops is taken as an indication that upper rooms were rented out separately as lodgings, and that the shops were lock-ups. This seems to have been the case at the Guildhall in Carlisle, which was built in 1386–1400, and also at the so-called Abbot's House in Shrewsbury (pl. 21), erected in 1457–9 by Lilleshall Abbey. In each of these cases, access to the upper-floor accommodation must have been provided by an external staircase and gallery. Certainly, at Marshall's Inn in Oxford, now demolished, the chambers above two of the row shops were reached by stair turrets and an 'alure',

21 At the so-called Abbot's House, Shrewsbury, the shops on the ground floor seem to have been quite independent of the accommodation above. The building has been dated by dendrochronology to 1457–9.

or gallery, on the rear elevation.[62] The stairs were reached from an entry, positioned between the shops.

Several complexes have been identified where a short row of shops was combined with separate ranges of private, commercial or institutional accommodation, with the shops always occupying the commercial frontage (pl. 20c). The possibility that these arrangements originated as encroachments against house fronts is suggested by the practice of building timber shop ranges against stone houses. However, they may equally well have been planned as buffers to preserve the tranquillity of private complexes.[63] Tackley's Inn in Oxford, built about 1291–1300, and 38–42 Watergate Street, Chester, of around 1325, both had a double-range plan, with a parallel hall and adjoining service

bay, behind a row of shops.[64] In each case an entry between the shops led to a cross-passage which gave access to the hall and services. At Tackley's Inn each of the five shops formed a complete unit with a solar, probably used by the shopkeeper as a living and sleeping room. The row stood over an independently let, open-plan cellar, used as a tavern from at least 1363, while the rear range accommodated scholars at what was to become Oriel College: a happy juxtaposition for the students. At Stranger's Hall in Norwich two parallel ranges were separated by a courtyard.[65] The front range, dating from the fifteenth century, contained a row of shops with a chamber above each unit, while the rear range formed the core of a large house. Marshall's Inn, mentioned above, had a similar plan, with two

23

adjoining tenements lying behind a street range of five shops.[66] It is likely that at least one of these shops was used by the owner of the property while the remainder was let.

Occasionally, rows of lock-up shops were associated with civic buildings: these included the short rows that ran through the guildhalls of Felsted and Hadleigh, and those in the sixteenth-century moot halls of Elstow, Bedfordshire, and Aldeburgh, Suffolk. It is unclear whether the highly restored Moot Hall at Steeple Bumpstead, Essex, originally housed an open area for stalls, or a row of small shops.

SELDS

Another distinct type of commercial development, about which little is known, was the seld. While the term *seuda* or *selda* sometimes simply denoted a shop, it commonly referred to a substantial structure that accommodated numerous traders. One of the earliest documented examples, in Winchester in 1148, was a large property in which the linen trade was conducted.[67] Selds appear in documents relating to London, Chester, Winchester and other large towns until the sixteenth century. They clearly assumed a variety of physical forms: the thirteenth-century selds at St Giles's Fair outside Winchester were rows of up to fifty booths, each of which was described as a *fenestra* (window).[68] Others seem to have been long, roofed sheds, often situated behind shops on the street frontage, containing a number of chests, plots or stalls devoted to a particular trade. That in Middlewich, Cheshire, built for the use of 'foreign' (out-of-town) merchants, measured 100 feet by 22 feet (30.48 × 6.7 m) and became known as the 'great hall'.[69] Selds in Chester seem to have been equally long, but even narrower.[70] Although we know little about these buildings, how they were lit or how customers circulated inside them, they clearly represent the first attempt by retailers to exploit the interiors of urban blocks, spaces usually devoted to private rather than public activities.

The particularly well-documented St Martin's Seld was located on Soper (Shopkeeper) Lane off Cheapside, in London.[71] Around 1250 it contained approximately twenty-one small plots, or standings, and thirty or so chests. In the mid-thirteenth century this seld specialised in gloves and leather goods, but by 1300 it dealt chiefly in girdles and mercers' wares. By then there was an entry every 8 yards along Cheapside, leading behind the shops into selds that may have accommodated a total of 4,000 individual pitches for traders.[72]

After the Black Death selds became less densely occupied: in 1360 St Martin's Seld had only eleven plots, and in 1516 eleven shops stood on the site.[73] Next door, the Painted or Broad Seld on Cheapside was rebuilt in 1530 with one 'great shop' measuring 60 feet 6 inches by 21 feet (1,270 sq. ft/117.98 sq. m) and called 'The Key'. A century later it was occupied by a linen draper named Isaacson, from whose shop Pepys watched the Lord Mayor's show in 1660.[74] By then most of the Cheapside selds had become warehouses.

SHOP FRONTS

Most shops remained open-fronted and stall-like until the eighteenth century, when glazing became more affordable (see Chapter 3). As earlier surviving examples tend to belong to timber-framed buildings, their most recognisable external features are large, unglazed, arched openings. Initially these were generally round-headed or two-centred but, by the last quarter of the fifteenth century, most were four-centred, with spandrels that provided fields for carved decoration.[75] Some, however, had straight lintels on brackets, producing the shape of a shouldered arch.[76] Unlike domestic windows, openings in shops were rarely, if ever, subdivided by mullions. Their primary function was to light the internal space, especially when it was used as a craftsman's workshop or a rich trader's showroom, but some had other uses.

While apothecaries, metalworkers and drapers sold valuable commodities and probably invited customers inside their shops for reasons of comfort and security, those selling small items of little value, or fresh foodstuffs, would have used window openings as counters to capture passing trade on market day. For this to work, the sill had to be at a low level. High sills, for example on High Street, Ashwell, Hertfordshire, or inaccessible windows, such as that on French Street, Southampton, therefore suggest that trading took place indoors. Trading must also have been carried out indoors when the area beneath the shop window was rented as a stall – a common practice in major commercial centres from at least the twelfth century.[77]

Those trading through their shop window ran a great risk of theft, and were exposed to the effects of bad weather. Those trading indoors, on the other hand, could protect openings with lattices of willow branches, or laths. Every shop had solid wooden shutters for night-time security, but few examples of these survive. Contemporary illustrations and repair accounts suggest that most shop shutters were external, and hinged top and bottom rather than at the side.[78] The bottom shutter could be lowered and supported on brackets or legs to create a stall-board for the display of goods, while the top shutter could be raised to form a canopy, as at the National Trust's heavily restored shop in Lavenham (pl. 19). But that arrangement was by no means universal. The surviving shop windows in Trinity Guildhall, Felsted (pl. 23), are fitted with internal oak shutters, attached to the jambs by iron hinges, and another variation has been detected at 2 St Ann's Street in King's Lynn, where the upper shutter was attached to the lintel and swung inwards by means of a pulley system.[79] It is possible that different types of shop

22 The Pentice on Winchester High Street occupied the site of a former royal palace and provided a covered walkway along the front of a row of drapers' shops. The mock timber-frame building with the twin gables on the right was built by Boots in 1905.

23 The two openings in the side of this passage through the fourteenth-century Trinity Guildhall (The Old School) in Felsted are typical of medieval shop windows, but the surviving shutters are a rarity.

required different shutter systems, or even that some combined external and internal shutters.

Shop doorways were generally narrower than house doorways, probably to maximise the frontage available for windows. In food shops the doors were often split, with a lower gate that prevented animals entering. Some doorways, such as that at 10–11 Lady Street, Lavenham, may have been fitted with internal shutters, presumably for extra security.[80]

Many shops occupied jettied buildings. Jetties provided additional space on the upper floors of buildings, but above shops they had several other advantages: they diverted rainwater from the stall-board and offered some shelter for customers, while their projecting bressumers made it easy to secure canopy-shutters to

buildings. Where a jetty was lacking, or of insufficient projection, the shop could be protected by a small lean-to roof which was slated, leaded or tiled, and known as a pentice. These were common from the thirteenth to the seventeenth centuries,[81] after which rainwater pipes superseded one of their main functions. Mortices that may relate to a lost pentice can be seen on the frame of a shop at 30 King Street, King's Lynn.[82] Although several late examples of pentices survive, for example at 6 Salisbury Street in Blandford Forum, their components have probably been replaced over the years.

Occasionally, upper floors projected over the pavement and were supported on posts, creating a colonnade, arcade or gallery. Like the *cornières* found in the market places of thirteenth-century

24   The remnants of earlier buildings lurk behind Victorian façades (including Boots, now Evans) on the south side of Eastgate Street in Chester. Much of the medieval row system has also survived. As well as giving access to shops and houses, row walkways accommodated raised stall-boards which created headroom over the entrances to undercrofts.

bastides in Gascony,[83] this idea probably harked back to the arcades that surrounded Roman markets. A good surviving example is the fourteenth-century Pentice (pl. 22) on Winchester High Street, which ran along the front of a row of drapers' shops.[84] The Rows in Chester (pl. 24), which seem to have developed gradually from the late thirteenth century, are quite different in form for most of their length.[85] There, the covered walkways were raised above semi-subterranean undercrofts and reached periodically by short flights of steps. This appears to have been a response to Chester's distinctive topography and was not repeated systematically in any other English town. The idea of the colonnade or piazza was revived in the late seventeenth

century, both in post-Fire London markets (see above), and in fashionable shopping streets such as the Pantiles in Tunbridge Wells, Kent.

Although increasing amounts of documentary and illustrative material are available for seventeenth-century shops, little survives in a recognisable state.[86] In 1907 it was reported that the last surviving shop front of that date, in Exeter, had been demolished two years previously.[87] Despite this, it is clear that one of the commonest forms of shop in the seventeenth century was the 'bulk' shop. Instead of a simple pentice, these shops were protected by canopies so large and heavy that they threatened to pull walls down, and instead of simple stalls, great solid bulks of

brick or wood projected beneath shop windows. The stall-board provided a permanent top to the bulk, which usually had a hatch in the front, and could be used as secure storage, or even as shelter for the homeless. Bulk shops were often treated as encroachments, liable to rents or removal by city authorities, which is why so few survived, even into the nineteenth century. One of the last examples, a poulterer's shop in Clare Market, London (pl. 25), is said to have been destroyed in 1878.[88]

While faithful representations of British shops are thin on the ground before the eighteenth century, several Dutch paintings of the mid- to late seventeenth century illustrate shops that may not have been very different from their English counterparts. These paintings show how common pentices and bulks had become, and how they could be supported in a variety of ways, including posts or brackets. Underneath pentices, open windows were used to display goods. Dutch bakers, for example, arranged their bread on a white cloth, pinned across the opening (pl. 26). Some pentices seem to have had narrow fascias that displayed the name of the shop or its proprietor, but hanging signs bearing trade symbols were more common. As an alternative, the trade symbol could be applied to the façade, and it is possible that a leg depicted in the pargetting of a house on Church Street in Saffron Walden flagged the presence of a hosier's shop.

★   ★   ★

27 Interior of a perfumer's shop, illustrating John Lydgate's *Pilgrimage of the Life of Man*, in the British Library manuscript Cotton Tiberius A. VII f. 93. This dates from the mid-fifteenth century, and is a particularly early depiction of a shop counter.

SHOP INTERIORS

The only information we have about the interiors of medieval shops comes from contemporary documents, which are not always easy to interpret, and from occasional manuscript illustrations (pl. 27). It is clear that medieval shops were extremely small by modern standards, becoming larger after the Black Death when many premises amalgamated.[89] In 1220 a row of ironmongers' shops fronting Poultry in London had a mean width of 7 feet 4 inches (2.24m), with individual units ranging from 6 feet 10 inches (2.08m) to 9 feet 2 inches (2.79m) in breadth and from 12 feet 10 inches (3.91m) to 18 feet 9 inches (2.25m) in depth.[90] These small shops can have offered few comforts. With their open fronts, they must have been very cold, except at the height of summer. Although few had a chimney stack or hearth, there is always the possibility that they were heated by braziers. Lighting would have been provided by candles or torches, when necessary.

Although illustrations show shelves, and wills and inventories mention cupboards and benches, the main requirement for the medieval shopkeeper was a chest or coffer, which was used to store goods and to serve as a counter. At times a number of chests existed within a single shop, suggesting that it was occupied by several retailers. Multiple occupancy certainly occurred:

in 1293, for example, the ironmonger Hugh de Chelmeresford and his wife Alice sold their small shop on Soper Lane off Cheapside but reserved a space within it, plus a stall in front of the window, for Alice's use during her lifetime.[91] Trading conditions must have been very cramped.

Some London shops had reached a considerable size by the fifteenth century. A 'great shop' measuring 22 feet 4 inches by 18 feet (approximately 400 sq. ft/37 sq. m) formed part of a house built, almost certainly for occupation by grocers, on Bucklersbury by the Dean and Chapter of St Paul's in 1405.[92] Next to it was a 'sotelhous', which has been interpreted as a showroom, and a warehouse. Some years later, in 1475, a Cornhill draper's shop was furnished with a 'piece of black bukram stained above round about the shop' and a 'cowcheborde [probably a counter for laying out cloth] boarded behind and covered above with boards and canvased from the backside to the ground', another 'cowcheborde' with a canvas rear, and a 'shewyng borde'.[93] The warehouse behind the shop held more cowchebords and a 'shewyng table'. Different types of trader undoubtedly required different types of fittings, about which we know little: while mercers would have needed chests and cupboards, for example, tanners selling leather would have had tables.[94]

Treswell's surveys show that most shops remained small in the early seventeenth century, although quite a number now had

28

the comfort of a fireplace. Once again, Dutch paintings offer our only glimpses of seventeenth-century shop interiors, providing evidence for the existence of neat shops with glazed fronts and counters arranged parallel to side walls. One of the earliest is a painting of 1665, attributed to Emanuel de Witte, amongst others, which depicts the inside of a very smart apothecary's shop with a tiled floor, a panelled counter and a glazed window.[95] Around 1680 Job Berckheyde (1630–93), a butcher's son from Haarlem, painted the interiors of at least two bakers' shops, each equipped with wall-shelves and a counter.[96] Inventories make it clear that English shops of the same period had chests of drawers, although we do not know how they were arranged in relation to counters. In 1668, for example, a shop in Horsham, Sussex, belonging to Robert Hurst, a tallow chandler, contained 'one Counter', and 'twoe nests of boxes with other small boxes'.[97]

The environment of marketing and shopping had changed little between the twelfth and the seventeenth centuries, although more shelters had been erected to protect market traders, and shops had grown in size, and become less like stalls. Towards the end of this period two separate phenomena helped to usher in a new approach to shopping. The first of these was the building of the Royal Exchange in London, which introduced the idea of the fashionable and leisurely shopping promenade. The second was the glazed shopfront, which did much to encourage outward display and the habit of browsing. The impact of these developments will be examined in the following two chapters.

EXETER CHANGE
will close
on
Saturday
18 April
1829

EXETER CHANGE
will close
on
Saturday
/April
1829

'Of Fine Shops and Fine Shews':
The Birth of Fashionable Shopping in London

Bᴄ ᴛʜᴇ ʟᴀᴛᴇ sɪxᴛᴇᴇɴᴛʜ ᴄᴇɴᴛᴜʀʏ Lᴏɴᴅᴏɴ ᴡᴀs ᴛʜᴇ ᴜɴᴅɪs-ᴘᴜᴛᴇᴅ social and business centre of the country, with a permanent population more than ten times that of the largest provincial city. Furthermore, many of its more fortunate citizens had a surplus of cash in their pockets and sufficient free time in which to spend it. In this environment, shopping as a pastime – as something different from straightforward buying – was nurtured in the galleries of the Royal Exchange. Although dark and cramped, these long rooms, lined with fashionable stalls, provided a safer and more congenial location for shopping than the rowdy streets, which were still choked by markets. Opportunities for pleasurable shopping were, however, greatly extended in the late seventeenth and eighteenth centuries, with the construction of fine new streets, free from rough market traders. Elite shopping avenues appeared much more slowly outside the capital, where one of the first developments, mixing shops with other high-class amusements, was the colonnaded Pantiles in Tunbridge Wells (begun *c.*1698).

It has been suggested that a 'consumer revolution' took place in the mid- to late eighteenth century, that the pace of change noticeably accelerated and that the seeds of modern retail practice were sown.[1] This perception may owe a great deal to the fact that it is really only after 1750 that we begin to get detailed descriptions, or even pictorial representations, of large retail establishments in London. Even less is known about their equivalents in the provinces, although large shops called 'warehouse' or 'emporium' certainly existed in towns such as Bath and York before 1800. These were, in many respects, precursors of the great retail businesses of the nineteenth century.

★   ★   ★

Shopping before 1666

London may have been of great national importance, but in the early to mid-sixteenth century Antwerp was the chief trading centre in Northern Europe. The Oude Beurs, established in 1512 as a meeting place for merchants, had an arcaded courtyard and a bell tower, in Italian fashion. The Nieuwe Beurs, which followed in 1531, included a *pandt*, or shopping gallery. Sir Thomas Gresham, a financier who had lived and worked in Antwerp for many years, was extremely impressed with these developments and took the Nieuwe Beurs as the model for the Royal Exchange, which he built on Cornhill, London, in 1566–8. Gresham even employed an architect from Antwerp, Hendryck van Paesschen, and imported ornamental stonework from that city.[2] Although it housed London's first fashionable shopping promenade, the Royal Exchange was intended primarily as a free public meeting place for merchants who had previously conducted their business in the open air on Lombard Street. The imposing new building (pl. 29) had a paved central courtyard surrounded by arcades with benches against the walls. The courtyard could accommodate up to 4,000 merchants, who were summoned twice a day by the ringing of a bell.

The four ranges of the Royal Exchange contained a total of 120 shops or booths, located in the basement and on the upper floors. The basement, known as 'New Venice', was deemed 'a dark and solitary place',[3] and was soon transformed into a storage area. The more attractive shops of the Pawn and Upper Pawn, above the arcades, received some natural light from windows on the exterior of the building, but were also fairly dark. They were extremely small, measuring just 7 feet 6 inches by 5 feet (2.29 × 1.52m),[4] and in 1599 a tenant complained that the space was 'so little that a man of reasonable bignesse cannot turne him-selfe'.[5] The shops had open fronts with stall-boards on which a miscellany of goods was displayed, including 'mousetrappes, bird-

29 Wenceslaus Hollar made this etching of the Royal Exchange, London (1566–8), in 1644. Statues in niches around the courtyard represented English monarchs.

cages, shooing-horns, lanthorns and Jewes-trumpes'.[6] Shoppers identified the shops by their hanging signs, which depicted animals and birds. Shop rents were supposed to meet the running costs of the establishment, but many shops remained untenanted until 1571, when an impending visit from Elizabeth I prompted Gresham to offer preferential rents. From then until the end of the seventeenth century the Royal Exchange shops were a great success, although the establishment had its vicissitudes, being renamed the Great or Old Exchange during the Commonwealth, and having to be rebuilt after the Great Fire.[7]

To the fury of the Royal Exchange shopkeepers, and indeed the Lord Mayor himself, in 1609 Robert Cecil, 1st Earl of Salisbury, erected a rival exchange on the south side of the Strand. The initial designs, prepared by Inigo Jones,[8] were not accepted by the earl, and the eventual architect was probably Simon Basil, Surveyor of the King's Works. Upon completion the building was christened 'Britain's Burse' by James I, but its more common name was the New Exchange.[9] In form, it resembled a single range of the Royal Exchange. It was anticipated that merchants would gather within an arcaded walk, 201 feet (61.3 m) in length, which ran along the street frontage. The interior was arranged as a shopping complex comprising a cellar, a single row of ground-floor shops, two rows of first-floor shops and an attic. On the ground floor the passageway was only 10 feet (3.05 m) wide, and the shops, or booths, 5 feet 6 inches (1.68 m) deep. These shops were leased to traders selling modern luxuries such as books, lace, hats and perfumes, and rules were drafted to control their conduct, ensuring, for example, that they would not 'throw or pour out into the walk or range or out at any of the windows any piss or other noisesome thing'.[10] After slow trading, the upper shops were replaced by sixteen small apartments in 1627, but an upsurge in the Exchange's fortunes led to the installation of booths within the arcade and, in 1638–9, the reinstatement of the upper-floor shops. In the 1660s the establishment was much patronised by the Navy administrator Samuel Pepys and his associates, chiefly, it would seem, to buy large quantities of gloves.

Particularly large or expensive purchases, of course, continued to be made from shops rather than booths in exchanges. While it is unlikely that the most genteel shops in seventeenth-century London ever took the form of bulk shops (see pl. 25), evidence for their appearance is thin on the ground. Some must have been quite impressive by 1664, if we are to believe the opinion of Samuel Sorbière, a French visitor, who commented:

> Perhaps there is no town in the world where there are so many and such fine shops. Their displays are not the richest, but their appearance is pleasing: for they are large, and have niches and decorations rivalling those of a theatre. The layout of each one is quite different, delighting the gaze and attracting the eyes of passers-by.[11]

Much of our information about mid-seventeenth-century London shops comes from the colourful diary kept by Samuel Pepys between 1660 and 1669.[12] The emerging professional classes, to which Pepys belonged, were now amongst the country's most avid consumers, partly because they had less space and fewer servants to make things at home, and partly because of their unbounded social aspirations. The aristocracy and landed gentry could still live off their estates, if they had the inclination to do so, especially during the summer months, when they retired to the shires.[13] For the rest of the year, many entered the social whirl of London, where they set fashions, such as scallops (lace bands) and vizards (masks), for the likes of Pepys and his wife to emulate.

Although little is known about the appearance of London's shops on the eve of the Great Fire, from Pepys's diary and other contemporary sources it is at least possible to work out where they were located. The best shops, with the highest rents, were still on Cheapside, which was a mixed shopping thoroughfare with the premises of manufacturing trades located behind the shops, on side streets.[14] The chests and plots that had accommodated a great number of businesses in the thirteenth and fourteenth centuries had gradually given way to a smaller number of larger shops. Famously, the wives of Cheapside tradesmen sat outside their husbands' doors to sweet-talk would-be customers.[15] Indeed, flirting, victuals and wine all seem to have played a vital role in seventeenth-century shopping.

Many of London's finest drapers were located just off Cheapside, on Paternoster Row, but Pepys also mentioned a corner draper's shop in Aldgate, which may later have become E. Moses & Son, and the shop of Mr Neville, a draper in St Paul's Churchyard.[16] The shops that lined London Bridge were less fashionable, but extremely popular. They included haberdashers, hosiers, glovers, mercers and drapers.[17] Second-hand clothes could be bought from brokers on Houndsditch and Long Lane, while ready-made footwear was sold mainly in Blackfriars and St Martin's. When he decided to wear a periwig, Pepys visited shops around the Temple.[18]

In 1664 Sorbière was impressed by the numbers of booksellers' shops in London, especially in St Paul's Churchyard and Little Britain.[19] Pepys bought most of his books from Joseph Kirton at the sign of the King's Arms in St Paul's Churchyard, but he also patronised the book and stationery stalls in Westminster Hall, which resembled selds and exchanges.[20] In 1662 he bought a sword in Fleet Street, where armourers and cutlers congregated, but he also made small purchases from the cutlers in Pope's Head Alley, opposite the Royal Exchange.[21] Occasionally, Pepys mentions the purchase of a piece of furniture, such as a chest of drawers or a dining table.[22] These items may have been second-hand, since it is generally thought that most seventeenth-century furniture was custom-made. A huge variety of other retailers was now scattered throughout London, including grocers, coffee sellers, hatters, tobacconists, china and glass dealers, apothecaries and saddlers. Other trades were still dominated by craftsmen, who sold guns, watches, clocks, spectacles, musical instruments and other items of their own manufacture direct to the public.

Shopping after 1666

Since most City shops were destroyed by the Great Fire, many traders moved west after 1666, settling in Covent Garden, the Strand or Holborn. Amongst them was Pepys's mercer, Bennet.[23] By the early eighteenth century, however, the most fashionable shops had gravitated even further west, to the area around St James's, where some of the most exclusive London shops can be found to this day. They include the wine merchants Berry Bros & Rudd (pl. 30), founded in 1698, and the grocers Fortnum & Mason, founded in 1707.

The City itself was rebuilt along its original lines, but with wider streets. Regulations were introduced to govern the extent of shop projections, something that seems to have been a matter of concern even before the fire, since in 1663 Pepys wrote: 'to Westminster, where all along I find the shops evening with the sides of the houses, even in the broadest streets; which will make

30 The famous London wine merchants Berry Bros & Rudd trace their origins to an Italian warehouse opened by a Mrs Bourne at 3 St James's Street in 1698. The business had become a coffee house by the time it was rebuilt in the 1730s. The gigantic coffee scales, which date from that period, have been used to weigh customers since 1765.

the City very much better than it was'.[24] In 1666 projections from shops in narrow streets were prohibited, but it was lawful on main roads for 'the Inhabitants, to suffer their Stall Boards (when their Shop Windows are set open) to turn over and extend Eleven Inches, and no more from the Foundation of their Houses into the Streets, for the better conveniency of their Shop Windows'.[25] The results of this can be seen in a late seventeenth-century view of Cheapside (pl. 31) – still a very important shopping street – which shows that the shops were rebuilt with open fronts, pentices and stall-boards. It would seem that the New Exchange acquired glazed shopfronts as early as 1667, when Pepys remarked: 'I walked in the Exchange, which is now made pretty, by having windows and doors before all their shops to keep out the cold.'[26]

The New Exchange remained popular for the rest of the century, despite the opening of two more exchanges – really no more than shopping galleries – on the Strand. One of these, the Middle Exchange or Salisbury Exchange, opened in an upper room of Great Salisbury House in 1672, and although it was later extended to the rear it lasted only until 1694, when it was demolished to make way for Cecil Street. The other, the Exeter Exchange (or Change), was purpose-built in 1676 for the Earl

of Exeter, and endured until 1829 by the simple expedient of adapting to the times. Over the years its upper floor served as an auction room, then, from about 1773, as a celebrated menagerie, while the ground floor continued to accommodate small shops in the form of stalls (pl. 28). Meanwhile, the shops in the Royal Exchange had entered a sharp decline and given way to office accommodation.[27] Its erstwhile rival, the New Exchange, was demolished in 1737.

In all of London's exchanges, most of the shopkeepers were female. This made these establishments particularly attractive to men like Pepys, who relished flirting in the New Exchange, but it also laid them open to accusations of immorality.[28] The fate of the Middle Exchange appears to have been sealed when it acquired the nickname of 'Whores' Nest',[29] and in 1699 the writer Ned Ward referred salaciously to the 'seraglio of fair ladies' in the New Exchange, 'who I suppose had drest themselves up for sale to the best advantage, as well as the fripperies and toys they deal in'.[30] Ostensibly, the exchanges declined because fashionable society had drifted further west, where the *ton* now liked to promenade along Bond Street. It is worth remarking, however, that existing establishments made no attempt to follow their customers, and no one set up new exchanges in more central locations until the early nineteenth century, when this form of retailing was revived (significantly, under a different nomenclature) by the Soho Bazaar (see Chapter 5). Furthermore, most of the exchanges that were built in provincial cities were designed primarily for the business community, and not as shopping centres.[31] The reputation of exchange shopping galleries, it would seem, had been irredeemably sullied by innuendo.

Eighteenth-Century Shops and Showrooms

Inventories suggest that shop interiors remained small and sparsely furnished until the second half of the eighteenth century, but there were clearly some exceptions in London.[32] In 1726 Daniel Defoe complained: 'never was such painting and gilding, such sashings and looking-glasses among the shopkeepers, as there is now.'[33] He particularly deplored the sum of £300 expended on a pastrycook's shop in London some years before, in 1710. That had comprised:

1. SASH windows, all of looking-glass plates, 12 inches by 16 inches measure.
2. ALL the walls of the shop lin'd up with galley-tiles, and the Back-shop with galley-tiles in panels, finely painted in forest-work and figures.
3. Two large Peir looking-glasses and one chimney glass in the shop, and one very large Peir-glass seven foot high, in the Back-shop.

31   This view of St Mary-le-Bow on Cheapside was made by Robert Thacker around 1680. It shows the appearance of the shops and houses erected on this major shopping thoroughfare after the Great Fire of 1666. By 1750 they had all acquired glazed shopfronts.

4.   Two large branches of Candlesticks, one in the shop and one in the back-room.

5.   THREE great glass lanthorns in the shop, and eight small ones.

6.   TWENTY five sconces against the wall, with a large pair of silver standing candlesticks in the back room, value 25l.

7.   Six fine large silver salvers to serve sweet-meats.

8.   TWELVE large high stands of rings, whereof three silver, to place small dishes for tarts, jelleys, &c., at a Feast.

9.   PAINTING the ceiling, and gilding the lanthorns, the sashes, and the carv'd work, 55l.[34]

According to Defoe, all this pastrycook actually needed was a pair of ovens and some stock, amounting to £45. But Defoe's pastrycook was not alone amongst his profession in coveting rich decorations. One of the earliest surviving glazed shopfronts in

London (pl. 32), and one of the most ornate at that, is known to have been erected for a pastrycook, Samuel Horton, at 15 Cornhill.[35] Some years later, in 1786, a German visitor, Sophie von la Roche, was particularly attracted by a pastrycook's shop 'surrounded, like a large spacious room, by glass cases, in which all kinds of preserved fruits and jellies are exhibited in handsome glass jars'.[36]

Defoe supposed excess in shop design to be 'a French humour', proclaiming that: 'a gay shop and a mean stock is something like the *Frenchman* with his laced ruffles, without a shirt'.[37] Despite his pleas for frugality, the notion of the shop as an elaborately crafted backdrop for sumptuous displays was perfectly suited to a world in which ladies could now take their carriages to Ludgate Street and divert themselves by visiting one mercer's shop after another, without intending to make a purchase.[38] By the second half of the century shopping had become a popular

32 In the late eighteenth century this shop on Cornhill, London, belonged to the pastrycook, or confectioner, Samuel Horton, who reportedly made his fortune selling small pies and highly spiced turtle soup in a breakfast room behind his shop. The shopfront is usually dated to around 1770.

pastime. Disposable income for non-essentials was no longer restricted to the moneyed elite that had sustained the exchange gallery shops and the specialist retailers of the seventeenth century.[39] Stimulated by social competition, the tastes of the nobility were being emulated by the swelling ranks of the middle classes, and rapid changes in the fashion of clothes were affecting more people than ever before, much to the delight of the country's mercers, drapers and haberdashers. Consumer demand was catered for by home manufacture, as yet largely unmechanised, and by copious imports of luxury and novelty goods from far-flung corners of the globe. The range and quantity of goods available for buying and selling increased hugely, commensurate with the growing spending power of the nation.

This was most manifest in London, which continued to dictate the fashions of the entire country.

After 1750 there was a notable increase in the size of stylish shops, the largest of which were now referred to as 'warehouses', 'magazines' or 'repositories'.[40] The skylight was an important feature of this development. As early as 1726 Defoe had complained that 'every false light, every artificial side-window, skie-light, and trunk-light' was exploited to make goods, and especially fabrics, look finer than they really were.[41] In 1755 André Rouquet, a Frenchman who had lived in England, remarked that London shops were made as deep as possible and that their rear portions were lighted from above: 'a kind of illumination which joined to the glasses, the sconces, and the rest of the furniture, is in regard to those who are passing by, frequently productive of a theatrical effect, of a most agreeable vista'.[42] Descriptions such as this, together with images on trade cards, reveal that retailers cultivated an opulent, domestic atmosphere. Some boasted magnificent showrooms (or 'ware rooms'), which were quite separate from the area to the front of the ground floor where sales were processed. Amongst the best-known showrooms were those of Josiah Wedgwood. In 1767 he outlined his idea for an 'elegant, extensive & convenient shew-room', with displays of table services and vases that would be changed every few days.[43] In the following year Joseph Pickford, the architect of Wedgwood's Staffordshire factory, 'Etruria', was sent to London to design and fit up first-floor showrooms at the firm's new warehouse at 1 Great Newport Street in Covent Garden. Before long these premises became too small, and in 1774 Wedgwood moved to Portland House, a seventeenth-century building on Greek Street in Soho. A previous occupant, who had belonged to the medical profession, had added a dissecting room to the rear, and to this Wedgwood added a gallery, one of the first documented examples of this architectural form

in a shop.[44] The main shop and counting-house were on the ground floor, but the grand first-floor rooms were used as showrooms, and there were extensive workshops to the rear. After Wedgwood's death in 1795, the warehouse moved to York Street, off Piccadilly. A view of the showroom there (pl. 33), published by Rudolph Ackermann in 1809, reveals it to have been a large salon, lit on one side by tall sash windows, with goods displayed in glass-fronted cabinets along the walls and on tables in the centre of the room.[45] Ackermann's views of other high-class London showrooms demonstrate that Wedgwood's premises were not unique. Morgan & Sander's furniture shop on Catherine Street near Covent Garden, for example, was newly refurbished with a staircase of inlaid wood leading up to a palatial first-floor showroom, with a rear section lit by sloping roof lights.[46] Much of the furniture was made on the premises, but the firm also employed around 1,000 outworkers.[47]

At Ackermann's own premises on the Strand the main showroom was lit by two roof lights, one rectangular and the other circular.[48] In 1810 this became one of the first shops in London to be lit by gas.[49] Another top-lit showroom belonged to the

33   The interior of Wedgwood's first-floor showroom on York Street near St James's Square, London, showing customers browsing amongst open displays. Ackermann 1809, plate 7.

34   The main sales-room in James Lackington's bookshop in Finsbury Square, London. The 'literary lounge' and rotunda galleries may be seen in the background, while the inside of the shopfront is on the left. The drawing being perused in the foreground seems to be a section of the rotunda. Ackermann 1809, plate 17.

glass-makers Pellatt & Green in St Paul's Churchyard, who had recently patented their 'Glass Illuminators', which admitted daylight to the internal parts of ships and buildings.[50] Depictions of such showrooms indicate that retailers were keen to display their merchandise in ideal light conditions, and that customers were encouraged to browse and handle objects on open display. Even more precociously, shoppers perusing the 'worser seconds' in Wedgwood's shop in the 1760s could 'serve themselves'.[51] Presumably these were not amongst Wedgwood's better customers, who would have expected full attention from the sales staff.

One of the largest and architecturally most innovative London shops at the turn of the nineteenth century belonged to James Lackington, 'the father of cheap bookselling and cheap reprinting'.[52] His bookshop, 'The Temple of the Muses', was built

35   The cupola over Lackington's rotunda gallery may be seen in this engraving. The building, which had been taken over by Jones & Co., was destroyed by fire around 1842. From Shepherd & Elmes 1827–31, opposite 124.

36　The first-floor furnishing fabric showroom of Harding, Howell & Co., London, a shop sometimes regarded as a proto-department store, as it was in 1809. Ackermann 1809, plate 12.

on the south-west corner of Finsbury Square around 1789–91, probably to a bespoke design by the office of George Dance the Younger.[53] The centre of the building was dominated by a vast 'ware room' (pls 34–5), with cast-iron columns supporting four book-lined circular galleries, fitted into the base of a dome and lit by a cupola.[54] Well-stocked bookshops could also be found outside London, although not quite on Lackington's scale. In the North, bibliophiles would have flocked to 'The Sign of the Bible' on Stonegate in York, which was run by the Todd family from 1762 until 1837, and had a spacious, top-lit warehouse, its walls lined from top to bottom by books.[55]

As well as possessing impressive premises, many large Georgian shops are known to have refused credit, marked goods with fixed prices, advertised and even introduced a limited range of customer services: all features associated with 'modern' retailing. As early as 1726 Defoe reported that some shops had tried in vain to ban credit.[56] Ferry's shop in Bath applied fixed prices and a cash-only policy in the 1740s; Todd's predecessor in York, John Hildyard, had adopted the same strategy by 1751, as had

Wedgwood and Lackington by the 1780s.[57] By the end of the century it was common practice, in London and Bath at least, to refuse credit to all but the most exalted or trusted customers.[58] New 'cash' customers were attracted by advertising which, although considered the height of vulgarity, was practised covertly in the guise of seemingly unsolicited magazine articles or trade cards. On one handbill, Lackington bragged that the Temple of the Muses was 'the Finest Shop in the World'.[59] Another way to woo custom was to provide extra comforts and services. To one side of his main showroom, actually on the ground floor of his own residence, Lackington opened two rooms 'for such Ladies and Gentlemen as wish to enjoy a literary Lounge', equipped with books in glass cases.[60] Although little evidence survives, other large shops of the period may have had rooms where customers could relax.

One establishment known to have offered refreshments was Schomberg House at 89 Pall Mall, where wines, tea, coffee and sweetmeats were served in the breakfast room. Schomberg House had been built as a private residence, but was converted into a shop by Dyde & Scribe in 1784, then taken over by the chintz dealers Harding, Howell & Co. in 1796. Their 'Grand Fashionable Magazine' was one of the most extensive retail establishments in London.[61] The ground floor was converted into four departments, or shops, separated only by glazed mahogany partitions. A wide range of goods was sold, including furs, fans, haberdashery, silks, muslins, lace, gloves, jewellery, fancy goods, perfumes, millinery, dresses and even small furniture. Furnishing fabrics, the mainstay of the business, were displayed on the first floor (pl. 36), and above that were workshops. This shop held virtually the full range of any large draper's stock before real diversification set in in the 1870s and 1880s.

With the exception of the Exeter Change, enclosed shopping centres had vanished by 1800. Certainly, covered pavements were now in vogue, but it was another twenty years before the idea of the interior shopping promenade was reinvented in the form of the bazaar and the arcade (see Chapter 5). It is clear, however, that many streets, including Bond Street and Oxford Street, had been paved and lit, were lined by shops with glazed fronts and were now quite suitable for genteel recreation. Large, fashionable retail premises could be found on the most handsome streets. The grandest showrooms imitated the style of private salons, from which they were sometimes adapted, but Lackington's bookshop reveals that cast-iron construction was already encouraging some ambitious retailers to explore more novel means of arranging their shops, in Lackington's case by giving it a vertical rather than a horizontal emphasis. Such experiments laid the foundations for the great emporia of the nineteenth century (see Chapter 7), which were constructed not just in London, but in large towns and cities throughout Britain.

3

Beguiling the Gaze:
Shopfront Design 1750–2000

SINCE THE EIGHTEENTH CENTURY one of the most important aspects of shop design has been the shopfront (pl. 37). It must be eye-catching and seductive; it must lure the passer-by off the street and into the shop. Over the last 200 years shopfront design has caused great conflict between retailers, on the one hand, and architectural purists and the conservation lobby on the other. If shopfronts are offensive to the eye, however, critics can take comfort in knowing that they are amongst the most ephemeral objects within the built environment, constantly subject to the whims of fashion and the pressures of commercial redevelopment. We might, therefore, think that those surviving from the eighteenth and nineteenth centuries would be rarer than those of any other period, but in fact it is the art deco and modern shopfronts of the 1920s and 1930s, and the best 'contemporary' designs of the 1950s and early 1960s, that seem to have disappeared, almost without trace.

This chapter concentrates on technological and stylistic factors that affected shopfront design throughout the country,[1] and does not attempt to identify regional traits, which are usually based on local carpentry and sign-painting traditions. The preferences of certain classes of trader are dealt with in Chapter 4, while the approaches of co-operatives, multiples and department stores are discussed in later chapters.

Georgian Shopfronts

Medieval and early modern shopfronts formed an integral part of the buildings to which they belonged. They bore little resemblance to the light screens with which we are familiar today, which are quite separate from the structure of the building, and can be changed at will. The key element in this transition was glass, which offered protection from the elements and security from thieves. Window glass had, of course, been around for cen-

turies, but its high cost restricted its use to prestigious buildings. It would have been considered a preposterous extravagance for a shop, although it is hard to believe that London's top retailers did not have shops with fixed glazing by the middle of the seventeenth century, especially given Pepys's revelation that the shops in the New Exchange acquired windows in 1667 (see p. 34). Although some early shopfronts were erected with canted bay windows in brick surrounds, the majority involved the complete removal of the load-bearing wall at ground-floor level, and its substitution by a massive timber bressumer borne on strong supports. The screen applied to the front of this post-and-lintel structure was usually of softwood, and comprised a cornice, doors and glazed windows.

The glazed front did not oust the open front at a stroke: a view of Bishopsgate in London (pl. 38), dating from 1737, shows the two types coexisting. As late as 1807 Robert Southey asserted

37 A guide to shopfront terminology.

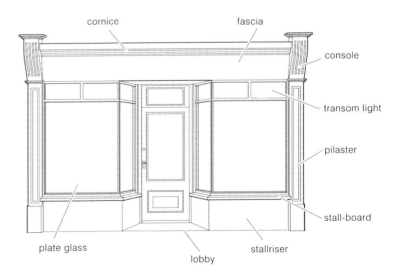

THE WEST PROSPECT OF THE CHURCH OF St ETHELBURGH.

To Sir Robert Godschall Kn.^t
Alderman of the Ward of Bishopsgate.
London.

This Plate is Humbly Inscribed by the Proprietors Robert West and William Henry Toms.

38   Shops and stalls were commonly erected against the fronts of churches during the medieval period. Here we see shops in front of St Ethelburga, Bishopsgate, London, in 1737. The church was gutted by an IRA bomb in 1993. It was reopened in 2002 as a Centre for Reconciliation and Peace.

that 'glass windows were seldom used in shops before the present reign, and they who deal in woollen cloth have not yet universally come into the fashion'.[2] By the middle of the nineteenth century, however, it was only fresh food shops that retained open fronts, while retailers of all kinds of dry goods had adopted glazing. In later years open fronts were occasionally revived, for example by the Victorian penny bazaars, and the mall shops of today.

By 1750 Cheapside was lined by shops with glass windows.[3] These businesses announced their presence by hanging signs, displaying age-old symbols such as three balls for a pawnbroker or a striped pole for a barber. Signs could be handed down from one occupant to the next, regardless of their trade. One observer claimed: 'I have seen a *Goat* set up before a perfumer and the

King's Head before a sword-cutler's.'[4] The shop windows had modest classical frames with pilasters supporting a thin entablature, not yet used as a name-frieze or fascia. The fascia (pl. 39) came into its own after 1762, when a law was enacted in London prohibiting the hanging of signs, although innkeepers, pawnbrokers and barbers persisted in using them. The legislation was not implemented immediately, but the switch from hanging signs to fascias proved pivotal in the development of what is now regarded as the 'traditional' shopfront. By 1807 Southey could remark of London: 'every shop has an inscription above it expressing the name of its owner, and that of his predecessor . . . and if the tradesman has the honour to serve any of the royal family, this is also mentioned, and the royal arms in a style of expensive carving are affixed over the door'.[5]

39 The fascia of Jacob & Johnson at 57 High Street, Winchester, retains its original 'English' lettering. Jacob & Johnson, booksellers and printers, were proprietors of the *Hampshire Chronicle*, which still occupies the building.

Shopfronts of the eighteenth century are difficult to date precisely, because designs spread slowly from London to provincial towns, and from exclusive shops to those with a broader customer base. Several London shopfronts, surviving either *in situ* or in museums, are thought to date from the middle of the century. One of these, which belonged to the confectioner Samuel Horton (pl. 32), later Birch, Birch & Co., at 15 Cornhill, had three round-headed sash windows and a part-glazed double door under a semicircular fanlight, all within a delicately ornamented Adam-style surround, topped by a simple fascia with hollowed ends. One of the earliest surviving bow fronts is that of the former tobacconists Fribourg & Treyer on Haymarket (pl. 41), which is usually dated to 1754. The house above the shop was served by a separate entrance to the right of the shopfront.

Bow fronts may have become so popular because they enabled shopkeepers to uphold ancient rights of encroachment, but their projection was restricted in some cities, including London and Bath. The London Building Act of 1774 limited projections to 10 inches (cornice 18 in.; 0.25/0.46 m) in streets 30 feet (9.14 m) wide, and 5 inches (cornice 13 in.; 0.13/0.30 m) in narrower streets, encouraging the development of shallow segmental bows. Projecting windows of all kinds made displays more conspicuous and admitted more light to interiors than flush windows. It was only in the era of gas lighting that window displays were given solid backs that blocked out daylight. Stall-boards were supported by brackets, leaving space for a cellar light or basement area, which was protected by grilles. If it was not necessary to light a cellar, stallrisers could be panelled, or faced to match the rest of the building.

The West End took over from the City as London's primary shopping district in the course of the eighteenth century. Sophie von la Roche described the shops of Oxford Street in 1786: 'behind the great glass windows absolutely everything one can think of is neatly, attractively displayed, and in such abundance of choice as almost to make one greedy'.[6] Undoubtedly, she was referring to the size of the windows rather than the size of their individual panes. The glass was most likely to be crown glass, spun in discs or crown-tables of up to 5 feet (1.52 m) in diameter and then cut into small squares, which were held in place by glazing bars of fat ovolo section. The bull's eye, or pontil, from the centre of the crown-table was seldom used. In the 1780s cast-plate glass had to be imported from France, but by the following decade it was being made in Britain by the British Plate Glass Manufacturer, which offered plates measuring up to 6 feet 3 inches by 9 feet 9 inches (1.91 × 2.97 m). These were extremely expensive, and so deep astragal-and-hollow mouldings were substituted for ovolos to make small panes of glass look larger in shop windows. The precious glass was protected out of business hours by wooden lifting shutters secured by iron straps. Some jewellery shops (for example, Tessier's, New Bond Street, London) still use these today, and telltale shutter grooves can often be seen under architraves or fascias, while iron shutter-bar keeps remain affixed to pilasters. In some cases, shutters were pinned to the cill, above the stall-board.

Sophie von la Roche also reported that Oxford Street shops were 'splendidly lit' in the evenings.[7] At that time shopkeepers depended on candles and oil lamps. The most effective were Argand lamps and sconces, which had been introduced as

40 The original small-paned glazing in the main windows of this bow shopfront, erected around 1793 at 16 Argyle Street, Bath, has been replaced with plate glass.

recently as 1784. Indeed, of all the shops on Oxford Street, Sophie most admired one selling Argand and other lamps.[8] The Argand lamps worked on the hollow wick principle, emitted as much light as seven candles and remained popular into the 1830s.

In 1792 I. and J. Taylor published around twenty original designs for shopfronts. Although these all adopted similar rococo ornamentation, they showed great inventiveness, demonstrating variations on the standard bow front that can often be paralleled by surviving examples. In some, the door, as well as the windows, was placed within the bow (pl. 40). Others involved salient or inset bows flanked by doors, or doors flanked by bows under a serpentine entablature (pl. 43). Several designs presented flush frontages, with part-glazed shop doors, transom lights or fan-lights, stepped entablatures and arched windows. The shopfront of the Temple of the Muses, on Finsbury Square in London

(pl. 35), was of that type. It was designed around 1789–91 by George Dance's office, which had preferred richly ornamented bow fronts twenty years earlier.[9]

Flat-fronted bows with quadrant-shaped sides were particularly fashionable after the Napoleonic wars, although an example from Artillery Lane in London, erected for the silk mercer Samuel Rybot, is commonly dated to 1756. Flattened bows were built in the Royal Opera Arcade (1817), in the Burlington Arcade (1818; see pl. 100) and on Woburn Walk (1822; pl. 42), but flush fronts were preferred on Regent Street (pl. 44), which was created between 1819 and 1823 and was probably the first major London street to be deliberately laid out for shops since the post-Fire rebuilding of Cheapside. One of the most innovative aspects of Regent Street was the way that the façades were supported on iron columns, meaning that 'the architecture of the

41 Fribourg & Treyer's former shop at 34 Haymarket, London, now a gift shop, is thought to date from the mid-eighteenth century. The interior still houses the glazed screen that originally separated the small shop from the back room.

42 Woburn Buildings (now Woburn Walk) in London was developed by Thomas Cubitt in 1822 as two rows of houses with ground-floor shops. Each shopfront comprised a central bow window with a part-glazed shop door on one side and a fully panelled house door on the other. The shopfronts were separated by twinned pilasters.

shops . . . can be changed as the fashions of the day, or the character of the goods to be displayed within them required'.[10] Although these Regent Street shops are long gone, rows of similar, if humbler, shopfronts can still be seen in small market towns such as Woodbridge in Suffolk. In London and the provinces alike, there was little concern about the relationship between the apertures on the ground and upper floors, but by respecting floor heights and property widths, shopfronts maintained pleasing proportions along the Georgian shopping street.

★   ★   ★

Victorian Shopfronts

Bow shopfronts remained common in provincial towns into the 1850s and 1860s.[11] By then, however, the availability of relatively inexpensive sheet and plate glass had revolutionised shopfront design in the metropolis. In 1832 the Chance Brothers of Birmingham introduced the mass production of German sheet glass to England, using the cylinder process to produce panes measuring 4 feet by 3 feet (1.22×0.91 m). The decline of the crown-glass industry was hastened by the removal of excise duty in 1845, which caused prices to tumble, and by the repeal of the Window Tax in 1851. These steps boosted the production of both sheet glass and cast-plate which, although the more expensive of the two, had a better surface. John Tallis's street views of London, published in 1838–40 and 1847, show the extent to which large panes of glass were adopted for shopfronts between those dates.[12] (They also demonstrate that there was little architectural differentiation as yet between shops selling different categories of dry goods.)

When the author and lithographer Nathaniel Whittock wrote his book on shopfront design in 1840, he complained about the lack of invention amongst London shopfronts, and the tendency for shopkeepers to imitate one another's designs rather than express their individual character.[13] He reported that in 1835 the fashion was to paint shopfronts in imitation of white veined

43 (*right*) This early nineteenth-century bow window at 5 Corn Market, Worcester, has an unusual serpentine shape, and retains its original glazing bars.

44 (*below*) This view of Regent Street by Thomas H. Shepherd shows that retractable blinds were being used to carry advertisements by around 1830. The Quadrant colonnade, just visible on the right, was removed in 1848 at the request of the shopkeepers. From Shepherd & Elmes 1827–31.

tea dealers James Gilbertson & Son.[14] Another singular shopfront belonged to Saunders & Woodley, the Regent Street upholsterers. It had supports in the form of palm trees, rather similar to those inside the Royal Norfolk and Norwich Bazaar (pl. 94). Further down Regent Street, Sangster's umbrella shop adopted an ornate Louis Quatorze style, while the shopfront of a seal engraver on Gerrard Street was Gothick. Whittock's advocacy of picturesque styles seems to have gone largely unheeded, although a neo-Elizabethan shop was built on the corner of Oxford Street and Berners Street in 1841, and a Moorish shopfront was erected for the architectural metalworkers Cottam & Hallen at 76 Oxford Street in 1843.[15] Very few examples of such shopfronts survive. Typically, later developers took less exception to the simpler shopfronts of the period, which survive in great numbers in some towns.

In the 1830s and 1840s most shopfitters opted for classical designs. Delicate Georgian ornamentation and Regency simplicity gave way to sturdy neo-classical forms, involving the bold

45   The Egyptian style was in vogue in the mid-1820s when this building was erected by a tea dealer at 42 Fore Street in Hertford. Originally each shop window was divided by two vertical and three horizontal glazing bars.

46   The spectacular shopfront erected by the drapers Harvey & Son on Ludgate Hill, London, around 1841 was described by Henry Mayhew as 'the wonder of all London when it was first put up' (Mayhew 1865, 208). In this view, the mezzanine gallery and barrel vault of the interior can be seen through the plate-glass windows.

marble, but he recommended the more gaudy recent trend for replicating the effects of coloured marble, stone or wood, and gilding capitals. From Whittock's book and the streetscapes published by Tallis we can see that a few London firms had already adopted exotic and eye-catching designs by 1840. One of the oldest of these was the Chinese-style façade designed by J. Papworth for Sparrow's Tea Warehouse on Ludgate Hill in 1822–3, although the shopfront itself was relatively conservative. An Egyptian-style façade in Hertford (pl. 45), which survives complete with its shopfront, was probably built around 1825 for the

47 Queen Charlotte's coat of arms adorns this chemist's shop at 8 Argyle Street, Bath, which was erected around 1828.

application of half or three-quarter columns carrying heavy entablatures. Numerous shopfronts of that type – whether Doric, Ionic, Corinthian or Composite – have survived throughout the country. The chemist's shop at 8 Argyle Street in Bath (pl. 47), dated *circa* 1828, is a particularly early example. The shopfront at 43 Eastcheap in London probably dates from about 1840, while several provincial examples were erected in the 1850s. These shopfronts may originally have been elaborately painted, with the coloured marbling so vividly described by Whittock. The designs, however, were heavily criticised by architects, especially for their irregular intercolumniation, which was often caused by the need to have two doors, one for the shop and another for the house.[16] Shop and house doors were usually distinguishable from one another by their positions, but for extra clarity the house door could have solid panels while the shop door was part glazed.

Modernity in early Victorian shopfront design was represented by 9 Ludgate Hill, erected in 1841 for the linen draper John Harvey (pl. 46). Designed by John Henry Taylor, this shopfront rose through two storeys and had an entrance lobby flanked by sheets of curved plate glass.[17] The name on the cill may have

been executed in repoussé sheet brass or copper, a technique that had recently been introduced from France. The unprecedented height, the entrance lobby and the curved plate glass were all novelties and had a sensational impact. A prime example of this kind of shopfront outside London was Leach's (later Pendlebury's) emporium in Wigan, which was built in 1848 with a high plate-glass shopfront, divided into three bays by fluted Ionic columns.[18] Such tall shopfronts were made structurally possible by using cast-iron rather than timber bressumers and posts, but they caused an outcry because they gave the impression that upper floors were unsupported. Sometimes these observations were valid, especially on corner sites with returned shopfronts, as proved by the sudden collapse of a shop in Pond Street, Fulham, in 1848.[19]

It was also in the 1840s that the Palladian or Italianate style started to be used for shopfronts. It was characterised by tall, elegant arcading, which Whittock thought particularly apt for drapers. The first stirrings of this fashion can be glimpsed in late Georgian shopfronts, such as 8 Argyle Street in Bath (pl. 47),[20] and a few arcaded shopfronts with only one or two horizontal glazing bars had been built by 1840, such as Shoolbred's

48 Benson's shopfront at 25 Bond Street, London (now Tiffany's), was installed in 1866 by John Drew & Co., and was mistakenly attributed to F. P. Cockerell in *The Builder*, much to the architect's chagrin. *The Builder*, 3 March 1866, 153.

neo-classical shopfront on Tottenham Court Road in London (pl. 124). Sandeman and Leighton's *Grand Architectural Panorama* shows that numerous arcaded shopfronts existed on Regent Street by 1849.[21]

Before long, prominent classical columns were ousted by simpler pilasters, and full entablatures gave way to fascias that terminated in consoles. The use of consoles (or blocks supported by brackets) to terminate fascias first occurred in the early 1830s, although elongated brackets had been used decoratively on shopfronts of the eighteenth and early nineteenth centuries, particularly to frame fanlights. Several examples of these can still be seen on Stonegate in York. Consoles featured in some of Papworth's designs from around 1830,[22] and were recommended in 1834, in a letter to Loudon's *Architectural Magazine* deploring the common trick of scooping out the ends of friezes, giving a profile like a scotia (pl. 32).[23] The correspondent remarked that one or two shopfronts in London already had consoles. These were either moulded in Roman (hydraulic) cement or carved in wood, and their decoration was usually classical in derivation, acanthus and palmettes being favourite motifs.

Individual window panes became taller and narrower in the 1850s and 1860s, commonly measuring 7 to 8 feet (2.13–2.44 m) high by 3 to 4 feet (0.91–1.22 m) wide.[24] They could descend to the pavement, and were topped by either elliptical or semi-circular arches (pl. 48). Vertical glazing bars now assumed the form of colonnettes, sometimes with vestigial capitals and bases, and carved spandrels. The thinnest bars of all were made from hardwood or metal rather than pine.[25] Horizontal glazing bars could be reduced to mere beadings, and on occasion two panes

of glass were butted together without a glazing bar, for example at 13 St Mary's Street in Stamford, a neo-classical shopfront erected about 1850.[26]

Shops still opened late, usually until 8 or 9 o'clock at night, depending on the season, although the early closing movement, which originated in 1842, was gaining ground. Gas street lighting was now in general use, but shopkeepers took additional steps to illuminate their displays by external gas lamps, with impressive results. As early as 1843 Knight's *London* described the lighting of George Hitchcock & Sons, a drapery shop in St Paul's Churchyard:

> Here we find a shop whose front presents an uninterrupted mass of glass from the ceiling to the ground; no horizontal sash bars being seen, and the vertical ones made of brass. Here, too, we see on a winter's evening a mode of lighting recently introduced, by which the products of combustion are given off in the street, instead of being left to soil the goods in the window: the lamps are fixed outside the shop, with a reflector so placed as to throw down a strong light upon the commodities in the window.[27]

Occasionally, Victorian shopfronts incorporated technological innovations that were attractions in their own right. One of the most sensational must have been the revolving window constructed by a Mr Coombs for an outfitter's shop – probably a branch of E. Moses & Son – on New Oxford Street in 1861.[28] It was 11 feet 9 inches (3.58 m) in diameter and 12 feet (3.66 m) high, weighed two and half tons and was activated by a heavy weight below, connected with moving wheels. According to *The*

49 Mr Gill, the general manager of Thomas Goode's china shop on South Audley Street, London, demonstrates the opening mechanism of its main doorway, installed in the 1880s. The opulent showrooms, which retain much of their Victorian decoration, can be glimpsed inside the shop.

Builder, it created draughts. Rather more successfully, in the 1880s Thomas Goode of South Audley Street installed an automatic door (pl. 49), which is still in working order today.

More mundanely, shopfronts required protection in the form of blinds and shutters. Roller blinds, or awnings, had been introduced in the early nineteenth century, both to keep goods cool and to shelter window-shoppers from the elements. They were generally housed behind the cornice and opened using a pole with a hooked end. They remained common – indeed, virtually universal – until the middle of the twentieth century, and can still be seen in use on occasion. Often the blind survives, even if it is never unfurled, and although Haskin's did a great trade

in the nineteenth century, the commonest manufacturer's name, to be seen on blind boxes on high streets throughout the country, is 'J. Dean of Putney'. The company was founded in 1894 and still trades today as Deans Blinds & Awnings. Having made his fortune, John Dean became chairman of Fulham Football Club; out of season, the players are said to have worked in Dean's factory.[29]

Outside business hours, shop windows continued to be protected by wooden lifting shutters, often with painted advertisements on their backs. In some regions, such as Lincolnshire (pl. 17), the local fashion was for shutters that folded into boxes positioned to either side of the window, but this reduced the area that could be taken up by glass.[30] Revolving iron shutters, usually housed behind the fascia, were patented in 1837 by Bunnett & Co., and first used by Swan & Edgar in London.[31] Early examples were operated by a winch handle connected with a ratchet wheel and pulley, but by 1850 these had been ousted by Clarke & Co.'s patent self-coiling shutters. Many other patents existed. Benson's arcaded shopfront on Old Bond Street (pl. 48), dating from 1866, was secured by Francis's revolving iron shutters, which allowed the marble columns to remain visible when the shop was closed.[32] The end of shuttering was heralded in the late 1860s, when it was reported that American shopkeepers were leaving the lights on inside shops, and simply raising security screens between window displays and interiors.[33] Nevertheless, early twentieth-century photographs of streets in English towns, taken in the early morning or on Sundays, show most shops tightly shuttered. It was the arrival of Gordon Selfridge, with his new-fangled American methods (see Chapter 9), that eventually brought about the change.

In the late Victorian period two-tier shopfronts became very popular. They had first appeared in the 1830s: Whittock published an example because he found this feature remarkable, and a few others can be seen in Tallis's street views.[34] Some, such as Fortnum & Mason's of 1834–5, incorporated an entresol lunette, a feature favoured by architects because it provided an intermediate level between the unbroken glass of the ground-floor shopfront and the solid masonry of the upper floors. By the 1880s and 1890s the primary function of two-tier shopfronts was to light first-floor showrooms, but they also permitted travellers on the open upper levels of horse-drawn omnibuses to window-shop from an elevated position, and could catch the eye of pedestrians on the opposite side of the street.[35]

Multi-storey shopfronts were often manufactured from cast iron. Like full iron and glass façades (see Chapter 9), cast-iron shopfronts became particularly popular with certain categories of trader, especially ironmongers and furniture dealers, in the aftermath of the Great Exhibition of 1851. Indeed the fashion started much earlier: Papworth, the architect of Sparrow's Tea Warehouse, experimented with cast-iron shopfronts around 1830,

50 This cast-iron shopfront at 35 High Street, Witney, Oxfordshire, was installed by the ironmongers Thomas Clark & Son around 1870.

and Cottam & Hallen's Moorish shopfront of 1843 was largely of cast iron.[36] Sometimes only a few components of a shopfront were of iron, such as columns or spandrels, but many complete iron fronts were manufactured. Some of the most ornate surviving examples can be seen in the small market town of Witney in Oxfordshire (pl. 50) and on South King Street in Manchester: these are all undated, but were probably installed in the 1870s. Later examples include Jesse Boot's cast-iron, two-tier shopfront of 1882 (see pl. 212), which was made by the Nottingham firm of Goddard & Massey. Nationally, one of the foremost manufacturers was Walter Macfarlane of Glasgow. Macfarlane's was also one of the main producers of glass-roofed, cast-iron verandas, which offered a popular and permanent alternative to canvas blinds in spa towns and seaside resorts. These verandas still lend a distinctive character to towns such as Southport and Harrogate.

Criticism of flimsy plate-glass constructions may have inspired the erection of a number of solid masonry shopfronts in the 1870s and 1880s. To begin with, these adopted a Gothic Revival style, characterised by angular, geometric forms, with much use of chamfering, incised detailing and shouldered arches. The display windows were sometimes recessed behind a row of free-standing cast-iron columns, as at 6–8 Bow Lane in London. Versions of this style executed in wood can be found occasionally, for example at 6 Market Place, Leicester, which has similar details to the model shopfronts published by Joseph Barlow Robinson in 1869.[37] In the late 1870s and 1880s, pink granite was often used with ashlar. Hayman's Pianoforte Warehouse in Launceston,

51 Henry Hayman of Launceston, Cornwall, was a photographer and cabinetmaker, renowned for his musical instruments. His Pianoforte Warehouse at 22 Church Street, part of a much larger commercial complex, was probably built around 1880.

Cornwall (pl. 51), combined semicircular arches with Gothic touches, while Jolly's on Milsom Street in Bath, erected in 1879, is in the French classical style that was coming into vogue with drapers. By the late 1880s terracotta had taken over as the favourite material for substantial shopfronts with grand, or grandiose, aspirations.

Most shopfronts were less restrained. Lettering gradually spread all over the Victorian shopfront (pl. 53),[38] and indeed over the entire façade, something that can still be seen at James Smith's umbrella shop on New Oxford Street in London, which dates from about 1870 (pl. 52). Smith's illustrates the method by which lettering was painted directly on to the back of glass. Another popular technique was to carve wooden fascias and stall-boards with v-section letters, which were then gilded and covered by glass. The same effect could be obtained by impressing letters of v-section into copper sheets with steel dyes and covering them with glass (Brilliant signs). Elsewhere, stock letters in wood, metal or porcelain could be purchased for use on fascias. The most common were half-round wooden letters, usually gilded rather than painted. Most simply, fascias could just be hand-painted, often with shadow letters. Fragmentary examples of all these techniques can still be discovered throughout the country, often lying under later signboards. The crowded window displays that were typical of late Victorian shops, and which offered still more opportunities for signage, are occasionally replicated to good effect by traditional shopkeepers, for example the outfitters F. Hazell Smith in Leamington Spa, Warwickshire, and R. J. Hambling in Newark, Lincolnshire.

STICKS

JAS. SMITH & SONS

UMBRELLAS

HAZELWOOD HOUSE

53 · 53

New Oxford Street

James Smith & Sons · ESTABLISHED 1830 · James Smith & Sons

LADIES UMBRELLAS. GENTLEMENS UMBRELLAS. JAMES SMITH & SONS UMBRELLAS RECOVERED. RIDING CROPS & WHIPS. LIFE PRESERVERS.
TROPICAL SUNSHADES. BOX FRAMES. ENGLISH AMERICAN RENOVATED & REPAIRED. IRISH BLACKTHORNS. DAGGER CANES.
GARDEN & GOLF UMBRELLAS. GOLD & SILVER MOUNTS. UMBRELLA & STICK STORES STICKS REPOLISHED. MALACCA CANES. SWORDSTICKS.

53 53

James Smith & Sons 53   53 James Smith & Sons

53 Surviving examples of late Victorian and Edwardian lettering.

a. Pellow Bros., tobacconists, 17 Fore Street, Bodmin, Cornwall, *c.*1905.

b. W. Pattinson, chemist, 1 Cattle Market, Hexham, Northumberland *c.*1900.

c. Frank H. Sayers, photographer, 28 King Street, Great Yarmouth, Norfolk, *c.*1900.

d. T. H. Cooper, draper and silk mercer, 6 Market Place, Kirkby Moorside, Yorkshire, *c.*1905.

e. T. L. Hamlyn & Son, signwriters and decorators, 15 Buttgarden Street, Bideford, Devon, *c.*1900.

f. W. Kelsey, dairyman, 55 The Street, Ashtead, Surrey, late nineteenth century.

g. G. N. Naish & Son, bootmakers, 4 The Mall, Clifton, Bristol, *c.*1890.

h. John Freeman, chemist, 108–110 Icknield Street, Birmingham, *c.*1880.

i. R. P. Wheadon, draper, 19–21 Silver Street, Ilminster, Somerset, *c.*1910.

52 (*facing page*) James Smith & Sons' umbrella shop on New Oxford Street in London is one of the most famous Victorian shops still in existence. It dates from around 1870.

Transom lights were widely adopted in the 1870s to hide the internal gas lamps installed to illuminate window displays after dark. They were usually fitted with decorative glass, concealing the light fittings from view yet allowing daylight to filter into the shop above the display. The heat generated by window lamps made it all the more important to insert metal grilles (often of the sliding 'hit-and-miss' type) above transom lights, to improve ventilation and reduce condensation inside the glass.[39] Large ventilation grilles on food shops could be highly decorative.

The open shopfronts of butchers, fishmongers, dairymen and greengrocers had always been different from those selling non-perishable commodities. These traders adopted large double-hung sash windows in the late Georgian period, and adhered to that format until new standards of hygiene were imposed in the 1950s. The lower sash was usually hung on weights and fitted on the outside with large brass handles so that it could be thrown up with ease. An alternative arrangement was to install windows that folded back or could be lifted out, in the same manner as lifting shutters. Traders then displayed their produce in the open window, and occasionally stood outside to serve people on the pavement. White marble cills kept meat and fish cool, and marble or polished granite was used as a veneer beneath the windows, or for lobby floors. The impression of hygiene in these shops was enhanced in the late Victorian period, when it became usual to clad pilasters and stallrisers with glazed bricks or tiles, often decorated with swags or cornucopia, and with the name of the proprietor.

Shopfronts, 1900–1939

Edwardian shopkeepers faced a greater choice of styles than ever before. The majority selected a tame Queen Anne style, while more upmarket traders, like Hatchard's of Piccadilly, reacted to the perceived vulgarity of plate glass by adopting neo-Georgian designs. Others opted for art nouveau, which is said to have originated at a shop erected in Paris in 1895.[40] All of these styles continued to be produced into the early 1920s. While none of the more avant-garde art nouveau shopfronts of the early 1900s – such as those designed by George Walton for Kodak – survives, two high quality examples of about 1920 still exist in Cambridge: the former Stetchworth Dairy on Market Street (pl. 55) and Fitzbillies on Trumpington Street.

Even the most modest Edwardian shopfront was usually extremely well made, and large numbers have survived to the present day. Despite the influence of the Arts and Crafts movement, they generally made use of broader sheets of glass than their Victorian predecessors, and their mahogany frames often had slender colonnettes and carved spandrels topped by leaded transom lights incorporating pontils (or bull's eyes) and stained

glass. From around 1910 until the 1930s it was fashionable to hang a pelmet across the top of the main display windows, beneath the transom lights. Shop doorways usually occupied recessed lobbies with chequered tile, marble or mosaic floors, which might incorporate the name of the retailer (see pls 81–2), and soffits which could be panelled and decorated with plaster work or mirror glass (pl. 216).

Entrance lobbies were favoured because they increased the display area, an idea that was taken to extremes in the so-called arcade shopfronts which were highly popular between 1900 and 1939.[41] In these, the shop entrances were set back and the area between them and the building line was occupied by a collection of windows and showcases, some isolated, so that a far greater amount of merchandise could be exhibited to potential customers under cover. Many large drapery stores installed extensive arcades (pl. 245), while single island display cases were particularly popular with shoe shops (pl. 54). By the late 1930s, however, the trade press was expressing its disapproval of arcade shopfronts, claiming that they were being frequented at night by courting couples. After the Second World War, arcade fronts were thought to waste valuable retail space and to conceal entrances. They were also difficult to tend and to light, especially the island showcase elements, which were not accessible from within the shop. They were gradually replaced, and only modest examples have survived, mainly in seaside towns. The only known survivor in London is Blustons gown shop at 213 Kentish Town Road.

Under French influence, rather than sacrificing space for island display cases, some small shops installed projecting 'show-case' windows, with dome-like metal or glass roofs. The shops on Sicilian Avenue in Holborn, London, dating from 1906–10, are of that type, and examples survive throughout the country (pl. 56), dating from around 1900–30. Some shops, including several on Regent Street, suggested the existence of a showcase even more tentatively, merely by curving the front of a window.

Before 1914 animated controversy was provoked by the rebuilding of Regent Street, when it was proposed that Norman Shaw's heavy-handed design for the shops on the ground floor of the Piccadilly Hotel – described as 'a series of railway arches' – be adopted throughout the street.[42] Even the most serious shopfront critics considered trabeated designs to be more appropriate than arcuated ones, and believed that only the most exclusive shops, which carried out business by repute rather than display, would be happy with such heavy piers and such a limited display area. The argument was eventually resolved when Sir Reginald Blomfield revised the designs for the remainder of the Regent Street Quadrant.

By now the Victorian fashion for cast-iron shopfronts had faded, but interest in the use of architectural metalwork was rekindled when several large stores, notably Selfridges, were built

54 Island display cases were particularly popular with boot and shoe dealers. This rare surviving example belonged to Briggs & Co.'s shoe shop, which opened on Barnstaple High Street, Devon, around 1928.

55   Stetchworth Dairies erected this shopfront on Market Street, Cambridge, about 1923.

with infill panels of iron and glass on their upper storeys (see Chapter 9). Shopfronts in France had commonly been manufactured from gunmetal (akin to bronze) and other metals in the nineteenth century,[43] but it was only in the 1920s that bronze, often combined with polished granite or marble, became a popular material in Britain. Many of the new shopfronts erected on Regent Street were of bronze,[44] and many were designed by Frederick Sage & Co., the foremost shopfitting firm of the day. Sage's had been founded in London in 1860 by a carpenter's son from Ipswich, and secured its reputation by fitting out Harrods'

The fashion for such shopfronts, which were really little more than neutral frames for sophisticated window displays, was promoted by the publication of recent shops in New York, Paris and Berlin in the British architectural press.[45] Before long, émigré architects were creating this style of shopfront on English soil: Erno Goldfinger designed the Helena Rubenstein salon in Grafton Street, Mayfair (1928), while Walter Gropius & Maxwell Fry were responsible for an electrical goods shop at 115 Cannon Street in the City (1936; restored 1980s). Equally influential were the striking and much-publicised designs created for Cresta Silks

56 Projecting show windows with domed roofs were very popular between 1900 and 1930. This example, now Oxfam, is located at 39 West Street in Oundle, Northamptonshire. The name of the original proprietor – International Stores – has been obliterated from the mosaic paving of the entrance lobbies.

57 This advertisement of 1930, for the shopfitters A. Edmunds & Co. of Birmingham, illustrates the front of a gown shop in an art deco style, and expresses the importance attached to shopfront design. Hammond 1930, n.p.

MOST VITAL SALES FACTOR—
THE SHOPFRONT

MORRISONS

One of many Contracts for a satisfied customer

First contact with the Buying Public is most frequently made through the Shopfront. It is surely of paramount importance that its design and execution should be in the hands of a reputable firm, who are actual manufacturers, with a wide experience and a fund of modern ideas. Send us your inquiries for Shopfront work of all descriptions, Interior Fittings, and complete installations for any class of business.

A. EDMONDS & CO. LTD.

Head Office—
89-99 CONSTITUTION HILL, BIRMINGHAM
29-30 HIGH HOLBORN, LONDON
234 SAUCHIEHALL ST., GLASGOW
Agencies Abroad: CALCUTTA. NEW ZEALAND. JOHANNESBURG.
BUENOS AIRES, ETC.

new store between 1900 and 1905. Its main competitors included Harris & Sheldon, Haskin's, Parnall's and Pollard's.

In the early 1920s a neo-classical style was adopted for middle-market shops throughout the country, and was usually executed in a mixture of metal and granite (pls 251 and 252). Bent glass, decorative spandrels and arc lights were already out of date when the angular Jazz Modern style was introduced to England by Joseph Emberton, who had been inspired by the Paris *Exposition Internationale des Arts Décoratifs et Industriels Modernes* in 1925. His highly decorative version of this style could be seen in the shops he designed for Madelon Chaumet, Lotus & Delta shoes and Austin Reed, and by the 1930s ordinary high street shops were freely incorporating such art deco elements as geometric glazing, sunburst grilles and stepped fascias (pl. 57).

Meanwhile, there was a movement towards cleaner lines and purer geometric shapes accompanied by minimal decoration.

58   The shopfront of Fox's umbrella shop at 118 London Wall is a classic Modern design of Vitrolite and chrome, featuring non-reflective windows and neon letters.

by Wells Coates. One of the best surviving Modern shopfronts of the 1930s is Fox's umbrella shop on London Wall (pl. 58).

Avant-garde British shopfronts of the late 1920s and early 1930s were characterised by the use of smooth, shiny materials such as chrome and Vitrolite (a self-coloured glass made by Pilkington's, usually in black, primrose, pale green or orange, see pl. 142). In terms of design they rejected the classically derived frame of fascia and pilasters in favour of a flush surround without brackets or mouldings. On major shopping streets, Vitrolite or polished granite facings could extend over entire façades, as could signage. Lettering (pl. 59) was usually three-dimensional, of either wood or stainless steel, and could be illuminated. It often adopted a sans-serif face, and incorporated fat down-strokes and hairline crossbars.

By the mid-1930s Emberton had abandoned art deco for International Modernism, and in 1935 he designed Simpson, Piccadilly, which was fitted with non-reflective display windows. The problem of reflections on glass had exercised shopfitters for some time, and in the 1920s it was discovered that horizontal glass curves had non-reflective properties. The first such designs seem to have comprised a single concave curve, but by the mid-1920s this was topped by a smaller curve, bringing the display forward. Matt black baffle boards at the top and in a pocket at the bottom of the window absorbed every ray of light reflected, giving shoppers a clear view of the goods on display. Early examples also had black ends, but by the mid-1930s these were commonly replaced by mirror glass, an idea sometimes said to be of French origin.[46] The invention of non-reflective glazing was attributed to Gerald Brown in 1932, when it was reported that it had been patented by 'a well-known firm of shopfitters', probably a reference to E. Pollard & Co. Ltd, although Haskin's, which merged with Pollard's in the mid-1930s, also sold this type of window. One of the earliest documented examples was the Ford car showroom on Regent Street (1930; G&A Brown),[47] and the best surviving examples in London are Simpson's (1936), Fox's (c.1935) (pl. 58) and Heal's (the 1962 extension, now Habitat).[48] It is interesting to note that the cills of Heal's are much lower than those of Simpson's, something that was determined by the nature of the goods on display. The few curved non-reflective windows known to survive outside London include those of Lee Longland's furniture store (c.1935) at 224 Broad Street in Birmingham.

Other advances in the lighting of window displays took place in the 1930s. A sophisticated innovation was the introduction of a laylight or toplight behind a solid canopy. At Peter Jones on Sloane Square (1936) this was at a different angle to the plate-glass display windows; light was directed on to a curved soffit (cyclorama) and redirected on to the display. Two spotlights, one just in front of the toplight and the other in a channel at the base of the display, lit the goods by night. In 1938 C&A's new

shopfront on Bird Street, London, was advertised as having 'the only daylight windows in the world'. Its '650 daylight lamps, totalling 120,000 candle power, literally put all the other shops in the shade, making them look quite yellow by comparison'.[49] The store was bombed in 1940.

Shopfronts, 1945–2000

The development of shop design, together with so many other aspects of Western European culture, was frozen for the duration of the Second World War. Throughout the late 1940s new shops and shopfronts tended to be temporary and utilitarian, their design severely inhibited by austerity lighting, cost controls and restrictions on building materials. One of the few new shopfronts to attract attention in these years belonged to a London shoe shop, Jack Jacobus on Shaftsbury Avenue (pl. 60). The arcaded construction, produced by applying cement render to expanded metal, masked a temporary timber shopfront that had been erected following bomb damage.[50] The boldness of this design – now superseded by a conventional pub frontage – was rare at a time when it was generally only major exhibitions, such as the

a

b

c

d

59 Examples of lettering dating from the late 1920s and 1930s.
a. McClures, blouse specialists, High Street, Shrewsbury, 1927.
b. Wakefield Jewellers, West Street, Horsham, West Sussex, c.1935.
c. H. Wilmott, butcher, 1602 Coventry Road, South Yardley, Birmingham, c.1930.
d. The Anatomical Boot Co., Colmore Row, Birmingham, c.1930.
e. Tom Purves & Sons, tailors, Botchergate, Carlisle, c.1935.

e

Building Exhibition at Olympia, that offered designers an opportunity to display goods in an innovative or striking manner.

The standard 1950s shopfront was often splayed asymmetrically in plan (pl. 209), so that window-shoppers were unwittingly drawn towards the entrance. For larger shops and stores, arcade shopfronts were now obsolete; instead, deep square lobbies were the height of fashion. These could be lined by boxy display cases (pl. 61), and were separated from the shop itself by a glass wall set with frameless armour-plated doors with push handles, a ruse that eroded the distinction between the exterior and the interior of the shop. The transparency of the shopfront was often further emphasised by the substitution of clear cement for solid glazing bars. Some glass lobbies, like that of New Deansgate House, a new co-operative store in Manchester (1958), rose two storeys in height.

Many shop windows of the 1950s developed the theme of the picture frame, by having a salient concrete or stone surround, or by installing shadow boxes (pl. 72). These involved shallow, glass-fronted boxes treated like illuminated pictures, a trick picked up from high-class couture and jewellery shops of the 1930s. Shop-fitters had all but stopped producing curved non-reflective windows. As well as the expense, difficulties in replacing breakages and problems of maintenance, these placed goods further away from the building line, so that the shopper had to stand

directly in front of the window to view them. In 1955 the shop architects Brian and Norman Westwood reported that:

> In Manchester, such a window had to be taken out because mothers used to stand their children inside the base of the window so that they could feel the glass themselves and see that it really existed. For this reason crowds collected outside the shop, but very little was sold.[51]

Despite such experiences, a curved non-reflective window was installed at the Newbury branch of White of Cheltenham in 1962. It was designed by F. Sage & Co. and had aquaria set into the stallrisers.[52] By then other stores were installing non-reflective windows with cheaper tilted glass. At Kingstone's in Leicester in the late 1930s the glass had sloped inwards towards the top, and the underside of the canopy had a black anodised aluminium finish to reduce reflections from the street. Later examples sloped inwards towards the bottom. A more expensive option was to light windows so strongly from the interior that reflections were all but eliminated. Glass – manufactured by the float process from 1959 – was now protected out of business hours by collapsible grilles rather than solid shutters.

Common post-war facing materials included timber, glass bricks and Vitrolite. Small mosaic tiles, often in hues of grey and blue, became ubiquitous in British towns in the late 1950s and

early 1960s, as did monochrome or coloured 'crazy paving'. As ever, signage was treated in a variety of ways. One particularly long-lived design comprised a high fascia of narrow vertical mahogany slats to which blocky Egyptian lettering, with slab-like serifs, was affixed (pl. 61). That fashion had appeared by 1950, and lingered into the early 1970s. A common variant was red lettering edged with white, once favoured by Tesco (pl. 291); examples can still be seen in seaside towns, which hold a strong preference for garish signs.

By the end of the 1960s the internally lit plastic box sign and the flush aluminium surround had become ubiquitous. A number of 'swinging sixties' shopfronts with pop graphics offered some relief from this drabness. The majority, such as Gandalf's Garden on King's Road, Chelsea, and a cluster of boutiques on Carnaby Street, simply adapted existing shopfronts and façades by using liberal quantities of paint, creating psychedelic effects, but the zany 'Granny Takes a Trip' on King's Road had half a car bursting through its front.[53] Other boutiques of the late 1960s adopted space-age styling. Just Looking (1968), once again on King's Road, was faced in aluminium and had circular display windows and computer-style graphics.[54] Such shops were rare outside London, and few survive.

In the 1970s the affordability of air curtains – developed after the war on the Continent – transformed shopfronts.[55] In most designs, warm air passing through louvres in the lobby ceiling was extracted through a grille in the floor, where it was purified, filtered and recirculated through vertical ducts. This enabled doors to remain open without loss of heat from the interior, and further eroded the barrier between the exterior and interior of the shop. Air curtains were first used mainly for mall shops, or for mall entrances themselves, but the pioneering Elephant & Castle (1965) in south London and the Bull Ring (1964) in Birmingham had conventional shopfronts despite their controlled environments. One retailer in the Bull Ring is even said to have put up a weather drip, as if it was still necessary to protect his shopfront from the elements.[56]

The revival of the 'traditional' shopfront in the mid- to late 1970s, beginning with major projects such as the refurbishment of Covent Garden, can be attributed to the growing influence of the conservation lobby, a sense of nostalgia for pre-war shopping and the aesthetic rejection of Modernism. This turnaround was encouraged by guidelines for shopfront design which stressed the importance of good proportions and the need to respect property divisions and neighbouring façades. Aluminium and plastic fell out of favour, and designers returned to timber. Unfortunately, many so-called traditional shopfronts of the 1980s were made of softwood stained to resemble oak or mahogany rather than painted. They took generic classical forms, usually executed in a highly simplified manner, with chunky machine-made mouldings stuck to frames. Their 'olde worlde' windows featured small panes of unconvincing bottle glass, while the glazing bars themselves were often too thick and of square sections. From close up these pastiche shopfronts could never be confused with the real thing, but from a distance they managed to detract from the visual impact of genuine Georgian, Victorian and Edwardian shopfronts, with which they were often interspersed. With the benefit of hindsight, it is clear that the approach to urban shopfront design in the 1980s mirrored ideas developed in the themed malls of out-of-town shopping centres.

The desire to create a modern version of the past placed constraints on innovation but, since the revival of Modernism in the early 1990s, numerous carefully considered designs of the utmost simplicity have been produced (pl. 191). Many have completely abandoned the traditional shopfront and dispensed with window displays in favour of a fully glazed frontage which gives a direct view into the shop, an idea that can be traced back to haute couture shops of the 1930s. Simple modern styles that respect their architectural setting are suitable for erection anywhere. More adventurous, eye-catching designs (pl. 62) are more at home in metropolitan shopping centres or in malls than in historic centres and traditional market towns.

62   This Jigsaw shop on Brompton Road, London, was designed by Branson Coates Architects in 1990. A simple glass screen – typical of modern frontages – is enlivened by a copper-clad column which sprouts winglike volutes.

4

Tradition on the High Street: Specialist Traders and their Shops

FOR CENTURIES, MOST HIGH STREET SHOPS were occupied by small, specialised enterprises that required skilled shopkeeping and, sometimes, a high level of craftsmanship. Over time, each trade developed a form and style of shop that best suited its individual requirements, particularly in terms of display and sales methods, but also to accommodate manufacturing processes. What was common to all trades, until the middle of the twentieth century, was the practice of living over the shop. Very often, when shopkeepers moved their families away from the business, they continued to use upper floors for storage.

While jewellers and chemists survived the social and economic upheavals of the twentieth century, and still have a conspicuous presence in every shopping centre, other traders have fared less well. Mercers, drapers, haberdashers, upholsterers and even, to some extent, house furnishers, have been superseded by department stores, while grocers, bakers, fishmongers and butchers have been ousted by supermarkets, and the ranks of tailors, furriers, milliners and hatters have been depleted by changing fashions. But the greatest threat to the specialist independent trader in the course of the twentieth century was the multiple; these eventually monopolised every retail sector, and came to dominate English high streets from Carlisle to Truro. With their centralised warehousing, multiples had less use for upper floors than independent traders, and frequently eliminated halls and stairs to maximise ground-floor sales space. As a result, disused and poorly maintained upper floors contribute to the aura of decay that plagues so many commercial centres.

The six traditional shop types covered here – jewellers, chemists, drapers, shoe dealers, grocers and butchers – have historically been amongst the most distinctive and enduring of all, but representatives of a great many other specialist trades still maintain premises that have served their purpose for generations, from the sumptuously fitted glover's and hosier's shop that forms part of Arnison's store in Penrith to G. Smith & Sons' tobacconist's shop on Charing Cross Road in London.

Jewellers' Shops

Jewellers' shops have always been amongst the most exclusive retail establishments. In the eighteenth century London's goldsmiths occupied some of the capital's most expensively fitted shops: behind the counters the walls were lined with high glass-fronted presses for the display of plate, while smaller articles were shown in glass cases or kept in drawers.[1] Such businesses produced most of their own stock, but cheaper jewellers were already enjoying a brisk trade in trinkets and watches that had been manufactured by an army of outworkers.[2] These had a lot in common with the fancy goods shops that sold toys and baubles in spa towns like Bath and Tunbridge Wells, although they occasionally retained a small workshop to carry out repairs. Beneath them, at the bottom of the jeweller's hierarchy, were pawnshops.

Throughout the early nineteenth century there was little to distinguish the shopfronts of jewellers from those of other traders. In the 1850s and 1860s, however, a number of upmarket jewellers on London's Bond Street installed arcaded shopfronts with plate-glass windows. These included Tessier's (1857), Asprey's (c.1865) and Benson's (1866; pl. 48), all of which survive today. The interiors of the capital's finest jewellers' shops were highly opulent: in 1865 Hunt & Roskell's Bond Street establishment was described as 'a hollow square of glittering plate', lined with glass showcases.[3] Provincial jewellers had simpler shops. Henry Ellis's first shop, established in Exeter in 1814, was a humble affair with a workbench, a counter and clocks hanging on the walls.[4] Much of the stock was purchased in London.

---

63   The figures in the carillon above Baker's jewellery shop (1904) in Gloucester represent Time, accompanied by Ireland, England, Scotland and Wales. The clock projects into the street so that it can be seen from a distance.

64   The line in the pavement along the front of Reid's jewellery shop (*c.*1900) in Newcastle upon Tyne houses a solid metal shutter. In the background are the mirror-glass walls of the Eldon Square Shopping Centre.

Security was of the utmost importance to jewellers, and simple lifting or rolling shutters were inadequate for some. Ellis made his shop 'rogue proof' by lining his shutters with iron and fitting a bell to alert him when a customer entered the shop.[5] In Hunt & Roskell's shop and workshops items of value were collected in a basket each night and lowered by means of a rope and windlass through trapdoors in the floors of the building into a 'well'.[6] In 1871 John Dyson of Briggate, Leeds, installed a hydraulic mechanism that lowered the window display into the

basement, and thirty years later Reid & Sons of Blackett Street, Newcastle upon Tyne, put in a thick iron shutter (pl. 64) that was lowered into the basement during the day and cranked up by hand at night, effectively turning the shop into a safe.

By the late nineteenth century even provincial jewellers had ornate hardwood shopfronts that made ample use of etched and bevelled glass and provided a rich, glittering setting for items on display. The well-lit windows usually had high stall-boards, which brought objects as close to eye level as possible, while deep

65   Dyson's shop on Briggate in Leeds has been restored as part of the Marriott Hotel. The interior fittings date from around 1900.

lobbies served to extend the overall length of the display and drew the window-shopper towards the entrance. Window display was of supreme importance, as many people felt intimidated by the grand interiors of jewellers' shops, and preferred to examine the stock, and the prices, before entering to make a purchase.

To signal their presence, jewellers attached a clock of their own manufacture to the façades of their buildings. The figural carillon and clock above Baker's shop in Gloucester (pl. 63), made in 1904, takes up the entire first-floor elevation. The exte-

rior of Dyson's shop in Leeds sports not one, but two large brightly coloured clocks, one of which has a gilded time-ball attached. The time-ball was linked to Greenwich and dropped at exactly 1 p.m. each day, enabling those in central Leeds to adjust their timepieces.

The lavish interiors of numerous late Victorian and Edwardian jewellers' shops have survived, partly because of their sheer quality, and partly because jewellers have retained counter service, giving us a flavour of what shopping was like in the days

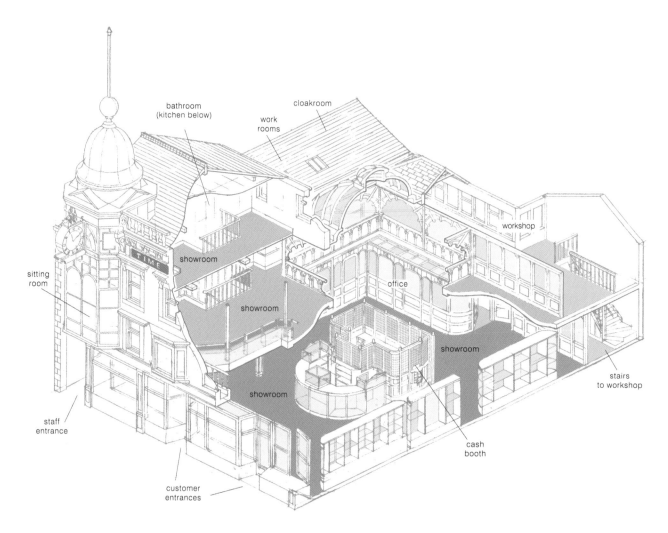

bathroom
(kitchen below)

cloakroom

work
rooms

workshop

sitting
room

showroom

showroom

office

showroom

staff
entrance

showroom

stairs
to workshop

customer
entrances

cash
booth

66   This cutaway view shows the layout of Dyson's premises.

before self-service. John Dyson's shop (pls 65–6) was recently restored by a hotel chain that wanted to use it as a themed restaurant: the shopfront was retained, as was much of the ornate interior, with its two galleries, central counter, glass-fronted display cases, mirrors, gilded lettering, decorative plasterwork and huge chandeliers.[7] Even the workshop, lit by a sloping roof light to the rear of the gallery, was kept. Dyson's evidently merited preservation, and although its pristine, highly restored interior has lost a certain air of authenticity, the end result is preferable to reassemblage in a museum, something that is seldom achieved with integrity. As a public restaurant, however, it was not successful, because people mistook it for a jeweller's shop.

Many jewellers favoured a Modern style in the 1930s. One notable feature of their shopfronts was the shadow box, which enhanced items by displaying them in isolation, like artworks. Such tactics were too wasteful of space to be taken up by the cheap jewellery chains that had begun to expand in the early twentieth century. The most prominent of these was, and still is,

H. Samuel's, which was established in Manchester in 1863 as a small watchmaking and jewellery business. Branches were eventually established throughout Lancashire before spreading countrywide, and three factories opened in Birmingham between 1912 and 1945. Samuel's was responsible for building numerous town-centre premises in a harsh modern style in the 1960s and 1970s. Even at that date, the ground-floor shops themselves remained relatively small and intimate, and were entered through deep, funnel-like lobbies lined by boxy display cases. Since the 1970s, Half-Price Jewellers have taken this approach to extremes. Their open shopfronts continue around the walls of the 'shop' space, which resembles a foyer. Goods are paid for and collected at a cash desk, protected by a glass screen, at the far end of the 'shop'. Half-Price Jewellers, found mainly in the North, are far removed from the glamorous world of the Bond Street jeweller.

★   ★   ★

Chemists' Shops

Modern-day chemists are descended from the apothecaries of the seventeenth century, who treated those unable to afford a physician and prescribed drugs to patients. Retail chemists and druggists became a distinct group within the medical profession in the eighteenth century, but were not served by an organisation of their own until the Pharmaceutical Society of Great Britain was formed in 1841. Chemists could manufacture and dispense drugs and medicinal compounds, but not prescribe them. A statutory register of chemists and druggists was set up

67   Carboys and specie jars were displayed in the individual window panes of A. Deck's chemist's shop in Cambridge in 1810. This both extended the shelving available to the chemist inside the shop and signalled the nature of the business to passers-by. Deck had installed a more modern plate-glass shopfront, like that in plate 68, by 1872.

in 1852, and the Pharmacy Act of 1868 made it mandatory for chemists to pass an examination and register with the Society. A ruling in the House of Lords made it possible, from 1880, for limited companies to run pharmacies, opening up the trade to unqualified businessmen like Jesse Boot, who had started out as a herbalist (see p. 209). Now Boot could call his establishment a chemist's shop and open a dispensary counter, so long as he employed a qualified pharmacist.

In the Georgian period, chemists tended to use each small pane of window glass to frame a single jar or bottle, which sat on a shallow shelf hidden behind a horizontal glazing bar (pl. 67). As window panes became larger, the series of superimposed shelves was replaced by a single, broader shelf, which supported carboys filled with coloured liquids.[8] After dark, these were lit from behind by oil lamps or gas jets. Externally, the shelf could be masked by a lettered strip, often with black letters on a gilt ground (pl. 68). Together with the specie jar, the carboy was widely adopted as a symbol of the chemist's business, and figured on fascias and hanging signs. Other common chemists' symbols were the pestle and mortar, and the attribute of the Greek physician Aesculapius, a snake entwined around a staff (caduceus) or a cup. Snakes are coiled around the columns flanking the doorway of a Georgian shop in Beverley, Yorkshire, and wrapped around chalices on the consoles of a mid-Victorian shop on King's Parade in Cambridge. A bust of Aesculapius crowns the façade of an apothecary's shop in Bilston, Wolverhampton.

From the seventeenth century the walls of apothecaries' and chemists' shops were lined with sets of small drawers (the drug run) and shelves carrying jars and bottles.[9] These carefully labelled drawers and containers were used to store small quantities of drugs and chemicals in natural, liquid or powered states. As with jewellery shops, many chemists' retain fixtures and fittings from the late nineteenth and early twentieth centuries: Pugh's shop, now Clowes', in Buxton was fitted out by S. Maw, Son & Thompson of Aldersgate Street, London, in 1899.[10] Glass-fronted wooden counters surround the room, their position fixed by the hot-water heating pipes that curve around their plinths. Originally, one side of the shop seems to have been devoted to toiletries and the other to patent medicines, while the dispensary counter was located to the rear, where it was protected by a screen (now removed), for the sake of customer privacy. Behind the counters (pl. 69), the walls are still lined with shelves of jars and glass-knobbed drawers, although some have been removed to make way for modern products. Many of the jars retain their original contents, and it is claimed that the vividly coloured water in the back-lit carboys in the windows has never been changed, or even topped up. Several shops similar to Pugh's have been reassembled in museums.

To produce their own drugs and medicines, chemists needed a laboratory or a manufacturing plant. The laboratory of the

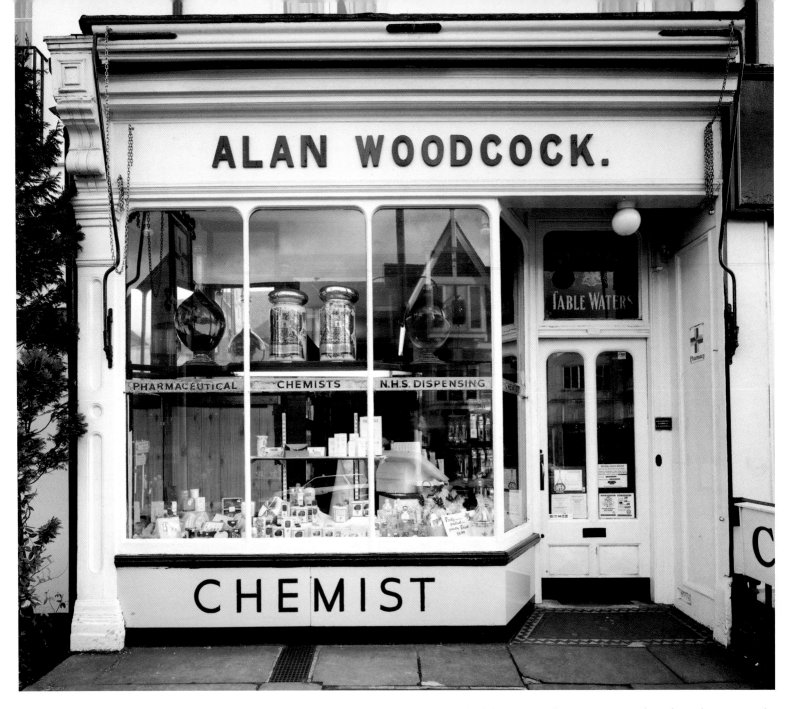

68   The carboy shelf in the window of this shop at 136 High Street, Dorking, Surrey, is typical of chemists' window arrangements throughout the country. The lettering on the stallriser and fascia probably dates from the late 1930s, but the National Health Service notice must have been put up after 1948.

London chemist John Bell was located behind his Oxford Street shop, established in 1798 and rebuilt in 1806.[11] A view dating from the 1840s (pl. 71) shows the laboratory man, John Simmonds, assisted by a young apprentice, but at that date some pharmacists still used a dog to turn the pestle in the mortar using a turnspit cage.[12] Some years later the chemist Charles F. Loggin of Stratford-upon-Avon is known to have built manufacturing premises that included an engine for making sheep dip, cattle dressings and drugs.[13] In 1903, when T. E. Butler built his new premises on Leicester High Street, he incorporated a permanent advertisement for Sea Breeze Saline (pl. 70); a headache con-

coction produced at his factory on Town Hall Lane. Chemists commonly manufactured insecticides, products for the farming community, carbonated water, perfumes and even chocolate and curry powders, as well as medicinal remedies. They were also pioneers in photography, and some practised as dentists and opticians.

To a greater degree than jewellers, chemists succumbed to the Modern movement of the 1930s, embracing new materials that gave an impression of cleanliness and efficiency. Shop layout gradually changed, first of all by exposing the dispensary counter to general view and then, in the 1950s and 1960s, by adopting

69 The interior of Pugh's, now Clowes', in Buxton, Derbyshire, was fitted out in 1899.

partial self-service. This involved the replacement of some counters by free-standing display units. The typical post-war chemist's shopfront had a metal-framed plate-glass window within a marble surround. Although the carboy shelf had disappeared, individual bottles or jars could still be exhibited in shadow boxes, as at Handford & Dawson's shop in Harrogate (pl. 72). There is little to distinguish more recent chemists' shops and shopfronts from neighbouring businesses.

* * *

Drapers' Shops

Many nineteenth-century drapers were specialists: London was thronged with shawl warehouses, crinoline warehouses, mourning warehouses, tartan warehouses, silk mercers, linen drapers and woollen drapers. These were larger than most other specialist shops, and many expanded their stock to become general drapers, usually arranging each class of goods in a separate shop or department. Large drapery shops, or stores, are discussed in Chapter 7.

With the spread of the department store in the early twentieth century, many small drapers' shops closed down. A few

CHEMISTS
BY
EXAMINATION

FOR HEADACHE DRINK
SEA BREEZE

SEA
BREEZE
SALINE

SAVES
LIFE

71 The 'elaboratory' behind John Bell's shop at 338 Oxford Street, London, was probably built in 1806 and survived until the 1850s. This mezzotint is based on a painting by W. H. Hunt.

survive in small towns, occupying premises that grew by spreading upwards into living rooms, and backwards over former gardens and yards. Like Potter's in Buxton or Dyer's in Ilminster, Somerset, they are generally departmentalised to a degree, and retain a selection of fixtures and fittings dating from various eras. Dyer's (pls 73–4) is one of the best preserved traditional drapers' shops in the country, a living museum of shopfitting.

The house and shop occupied by Dyer's dates from the eighteenth century. When the business was founded by R. P. Wheadon in 1870, the shop occupied only 180 square feet (16.7 sq. m), but by the time of the firm's Diamond Jubilee in 1930 it had grown to 5,400 square feet (501.7 sq. m).[14] It spread throughout half the building, into a two-storeyed rear extension and, eventually, into a neighbouring property that was once used as a cinema. Although the business was purchased by R. A. Dyer in 1937, much of the present layout was determined around 1910. It was probably then that Wheadon installed the twin-lobby shopfront, with swags of drapery on the fascia and his name repeated in the mosaic tiles of the lobby floors (pl. 53i) and in the etched glass of the entrance doors. A narrow bay at the extreme right of the shopfront may originally have contained an entrance for the dressmakers who worked on the first floor.

Inside Dyer's, the layout is highly typical of the proto-department stores of the late nineteenth and early twentieth centuries, before the major rebuilding programmes of the inter-war period took effect. In the haberdashery department (pl. 73), three pairs of bentwood chairs are arranged for customers in front of a continuous line of counters: the older ones with solid fronts and solid tops; the later ones of lighter wood, with glass fronts

72 The 1960s shopfront of Handford & Dawson's chemist's shop in Harrogate, North Yorkshire.

and tops. In the curtain department, the counters have measuring rules set into their surfaces. The wall behind the haberdashery counters is lined with a variety of shelves and drawers, not dissimilar to the arrangement in a traditional grocer's or chemist's shop. The shelves in the curtain department are divided into sections, just the right size to hold bolts of cloth. Beside the stair-

70 These pictorial tiles formed a permanent advertisement on the façade of Butler's chemist's shop (1903) on Leicester High Street.

73 The haberdashery department of Dyer's in Ilminster, Somerset, has changed little since the 1930s.

cases, to the rear of the main sales area, is an enclosed cash desk with a clock, wooden change drawer and safe. Upstairs, the millinery department is lit by four windows. Between these are large mirrors and underneath them are large, numbered, hat drawers.[15] Amongst ephemera here are a hat stretcher and a number of manufacturers' hat stands. In the children's department is a 1920s child mannequin, while downstairs are 'Le Roy' pattern drawers, a 'Pretty Polly' parrot (pl. 74) and a 'counterslip' gadget for storing and cutting rolls of brown paper. All of these add to Dyer's charm. Until its closure in 2002, Grout's in Palmers

Green, north London, exhibited similar paraphernalia, including what was probably the last overhead cash railway in the country to survive *in situ* (pl. 75). The snaking pipes of Lamson pneumatic tube systems (see Chapter 10, note 76) can still be glimpsed on the walls and ceilings of some drapery stores, such as Fairhead's in Ilford, in east London, although they have inevitably given way to stand-alone cash registers.

★ ★ ★

74 An advertisement for Pretty Polly stockings in Dyer's shop in Ilminster.

75 (*below*) The interior of Grout's shop in Palmers Green, north London, photographed just after it closed in April 2002. The business was founded as a general and fancy draper's shop by Alfred Grout in 1914 and was extended in 1922. Over the counters can be seen the cash railway ('The Gipe' patent), which was last used in 1989.

Shoe Shops

As with jewellery, the boot and shoe trade originated with crafts-men making and selling goods from their workshops, and only slowly moving into either pure manufacturing or pure retailing. That process was propelled by developments in the mass production of ready-made footwear. Shoes could be bought 'off the peg' in the late medieval period, but it was in the eighteenth century that the manufacture and sale of ready-made boots and shoes intensified. In 1738 a London shoemaker is known to have employed 162 people working on an assembly-line basis.[16] The quality of ready-made footwear at that date was so poor that it had to be replaced regularly, stimulating demand, and by the 1750s 'Yorkshire shoe warehouses' selling cheap shoes had become a common sight on London streets.[17] Outside the capital, shoe selling remained inextricably bound up with small-scale manufacture into the nineteenth century.

76 Boning a boot in the workshops of James Lobb, shoemakers. The firm continues to make boots and shoes in a traditional way, although it occupies modern premises in a 1920s building on St James's Street, London.

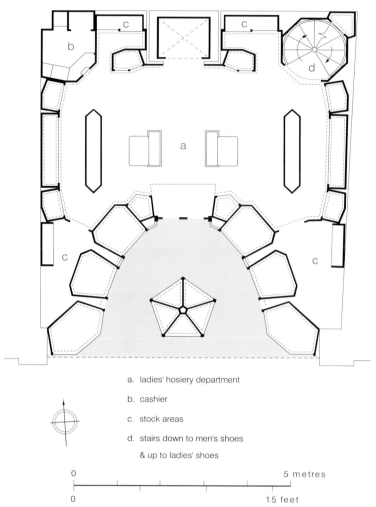

a. ladies' hosiery department

b. cashier

c. stock areas

d. stairs down to men's shoes
    & up to ladies' shoes

0   5 metres

0   15 feet

77 The Earl & Earl Ltd (Lotus & Delta) shoe shop on New Street in Birmingham, designed by Joseph Emberton in 1928, had extensive display windows and showcases. Based on Birmingham Building Regulation Plan 46769, Birmingham Record Office.

From the 1870s the mechanisation of certain manufacturing processes encouraged the formation of multiple companies that sold mass-produced boots and shoes to the working classes. Some of these multiples originated as manufacturers, while others started out as retailers. The co-operative movement soon jumped on the bandwagon: the Co-operative Wholesale Society opened its first footwear factory in 1873, and before long co-operative societies all over the country had opened boot and shoe shops. For some years, these shoe shops tended to be small and dark: the most important element was an extensive window display with prominent price tickets. By the end of the century, more refined manufacturing techniques were producing better quality footwear, encouraging multiple shoe shops to improve their premises and attract middle-class custom. Inevitably, small bespoke shoemakers gradually lost their trade to the multiples, which owned between 18 and 22 per cent of British shoe shops

78 Amos Atkinson's shoe shop, 12 Northumberland Street, Newcastle upon Tyne (1950). A typical shoe shop interior, with walls lined by shoe boxes.

by 1900.[18] Soon only shoemakers with an upper-class clientele still made bespoke shoes on the premises. The best-known shop of that type to survive to the present day is John Lobb's on St James's Street, London. Shoes are made by hand in the basement and ground-floor workshops (pl. 76), using the same techniques as when the business was first established in 1849, but the company also has a factory in Northampton. Cobbling, or shoe repairing, had developed as a separate trade, or an adjunct to retailing, by the late nineteenth century.

Shoe shops depended as heavily as jewellers on window display. A particularly fine surviving shopfront was erected for F. Pinet on New Bond Street in 1906. It is in a French rococo style with an ornate bronze frame set into the glass of each separate window. More typical of the first half of the century were arcade fronts with island showcases (pl. 54). These were favoured because they provided a long display space that enabled customers to browse under cover. The jazzy art deco designs produced by Joseph Emberton for Lotus & Delta in the late 1920s

generally incorporated a single isolated showcase (pl. 77).[19] In 1932 Gordon Jeeves designed a streamlined modern shopfront, reminiscent of an American diner, for Lilley & Skinner on Oxford Street, featuring eight showcases, five of them island cases, in addition to three large shop windows.[20] This was rivalled by Dolcis, whose architect Harry Simcock produced a design with eight island display cases, also for a site on Oxford Street, in 1936.

Display was less crucial inside the shop. A view of the inside of Pattison's shoe shop on Oxford Street in the 1820s shows that shoes were stored on open shelves in alcoves.[21] By the end of the century, although it was customary to display examples in the window, most of the stock was stowed in boxes that lined the walls of the shop from floor to ceiling. That remained typical into the 1950s (pl. 78) and can still be seen in traditional shoe shops today. By 1900, however, large metropolitan shoe shops and shoe departments in large stores (pl. 165) had begun to display specimen footwear on cast-iron stands in free-standing glass cases. Some shops introduced unusual gimmicks: in 1901, for example, Willoughby Jones of Portsmouth displayed his waterproof footwear in a tank of water, together with goldfish and freshwater lobsters imported from South Africa.[22] In the 1930s some Russell & Bromley shops also included aquaria for the amusement of their customers: one was sunk into the floor of the Ealing branch, while another was built into a showroom partition in Ilford.[23] By then children's departments tended to be brightly painted and furnished with toys to create a nursery atmosphere. Standard equipment included mirrors, foot measures and x-ray cabinets.

In the 1950s shoe shops greatly changed. Arcade fronts gave way to deep lobbies, which could take up a larger ground area than the shop itself, and occasionally rose through two storeys. The plate-glass show windows now gave inviting views into the shop rather than having solid backs. Inside, many switched to a salon system, with concealed stock fixtures. Single shoes, one from each style, were arranged on racks around the walls where they could be freely examined by customers, and pouffe-type seating or chairs were provided, under tungsten spotlights. Dolcis became a design leader in the hands of its new house architect, Ellis Somake, who used gay colours and geometric patterns to maximum effect.[24] Few of Dolcis's dark marble shopfronts of this period have survived, and their Festival of Britain style interiors have all been remodelled.

Somake subsequently became Chief Architect to the part of the British Shoe Corporation that comprised Saxone, Dolcis and Lilley & Skinner, a position he retained until 1970. The British Shoe Corporation, which was developed by Charles Clore in the 1950s, also included Curtess, Truform, Manfield and Freeman Hardy Willis. For many years it presented formidable opposition to independents and smaller chains, but it spelled the beginning of the end for British shoe manufacture by gradually moving production to the Far East.

In the last quarter of the twentieth century shoe retailers faced stiff competition from fashion retailers and chain stores such as Next and Marks & Spencer; they also had to contend with cheap imports and the fashion for trainers, which were generally sold through sports shops. As a result, many high street shoe shops closed, and in 1997 the British Shoe Corporation was disbanded, leaving Clark's (including K Shoes and Ravel) as the main U.K.-based shoe manufacturer and retailer. Manufacturers' brands are now of greater significance than retailers' brands, with many selling through concessions in department stores. New chains target niche markets, notably the 15–35 age group. They include Schuh, Sole Trader and Dr Marten's. Dr Marten's Dept Store in Covent Garden is housed in a *palazzo*-style building. Internally, its five above-ground storeys have been stripped out, the walls left bare or cemented, and an internal structure of floors and

staircases in galvanised steel mesh inserted to provide the required industrial ambience. Display units are of roughly sawn wood and galvanised steel, and the 'Doc' Marten's image is further reinforced by the use of assertive rock music. This 'brand cathedral' is far removed from the straightforward shoe shops of the past.

Grocers' Shops

The grocery trade, which originated with the spicers and pepperers who formed their own guilds in the fourteenth century, was not an easy one to enter. In London it required the completion of a seven-year apprenticeship, after which an individual had to be recommended by six well-established grocers before he could join the Grocers' Company.[25] Some idea of the contents of a sixteenth-century grocer's shop is supplied by the following list of items in the shop of the London grocer William Mase in 1573: a counterbeam with scales; five pairs of small scales; a brass mortar with its stock and two iron pestles; twenty-nine old 'standers' (casks); seventeen sugar and five candy chests; three currant butts; two old shop counters; two 'sessers' (scissors?); a hanging candlestick; brass and lead weights; shelves; shelf-cloths and twelve old trays with old boxes.[26] Such shops could be recognised by hanging signs depicting sugarloaves.

Although all kinds of groceries were sold by general shopkeepers throughout England in the seventeenth and eighteenth centuries,[27] the dedicated grocer stocked luxury articles for a wealthy clientele, including dried fruit, spices, coffee, cocoa and sugar. By the early eighteenth century the most important item of all was tea, which was imported by the East India Company from 1658 and became hugely popular in a relatively short space of time. From that date many grocers dubbed themselves tea-dealers.

Critics grumbled that grocers 'reap large Profits from their Business; but require no great Genius to fit them for their Trade'.[28] Although they were not generally manufacturers, there was much art to their shopkeeping: they blended their own tea, ground and roasted coffee, cleaned fruit, and weighed and packaged many other goods. One of the most prestigious businesses was Fortnum & Mason's, which was established in 1707 on Duke Street, London, and attracted the custom of the court. Like other grocers, its wares would have been arranged in rows of canisters and fitted drawers behind the main counter, an arrangement paralleled in contemporary chemists' shops. There was still a great difference between grocers and provision merchants, such as butter factors or cheesemongers. The most superior provision dealers were Italian warehousemen, who sold a wide variety of imported delicacies. Typically, 'smoked salmon and Dutch her-

79   The interior of Morel Brothers, Cobbett & Son Ltd, a high-class grocery shop at 210 Piccadilly, which was designed by John Robinson and built around 1890. While the upper floors were let, the two basements, ground and mezzanine floors were occupied by the firm. The shop – photographed by Bedford Lemere in 1894 – was 25 feet (7.62 m) high from floor to ceiling.

80 A former Home & Colonial shopfront at 12 Derby Street, Leek, Staffordshire, with characteristic coloured bottle-glass transom lights. The fascia would originally have been covered by glass.

rings, fine new French olives, and new rein deer tongues' were advertised by John Burgess's Italian Warehouse on the Strand in 1788.[29] Burgess's was particularly famous for its sauces and ketchups, which are still manufactured under the same name although the shop is long gone.

From the mid-nineteenth century grocers began to stock a wider range of processed foods (including cornflour and tinned goods) and fresh foodstuffs (such as cheese and bacon), which were previously considered outside their province.[30] By the end of the century grand London grocers included Harrods, which imitated the methods of the middle-class co-operatives (see p. 138), and Morel Brothers, Cobbett & Son Ltd, which erected new premises at 210 Piccadilly (pls 79 and 181) around 1890.[31]

Both of these firms sold a huge range of foodstuffs, including groceries, tea and coffee. Throughout the nineteenth century, those who specialised in tea often adopted exotic styles (pl. 45). The shopfront of Stewart's on Grainger Street, Newcastle, was topped by a series of oriental figures, pagodas and palm trees, rather similar to the decoration above the doorway of the London tea importers Twining's, whose products were sold by shopkeepers countrywide. As an expanding railway network improved distribution, large-scale wholesale grocers became established in provincial towns. When Roberts & Roberts rebuilt its wholesale and retail business on Leicester High Street in 1898, it included two floors of open-plan offices above two separate shops. To the rear was a vast warehouse, sixteen bays long and three storeys high, with a partially covered yard and ample stabling. Roberts & Roberts clearly undertook an extensive delivery service supplying smaller grocers who, in turn, delivered goods to their customers' homes. When customers visited a grocer's shop, perhaps just to settle their account, they were provided with chairs at the counter and treated with deference, much as they would have been in a draper's shop.

As food became cheaper, the requirements of the urban working and lower-middle classes were met, not just by markets but by co-operative stores (see Chapter 8) and provision chains, which initially stocked a very restricted range of dairy and grocery products, purchased in bulk and sold cheaply at a narrow profit. Amongst the most successful provision chains were Home & Colonial Stores, which first opened on Edgware Road, London, in 1883, and the Maypole Dairy Company, which had originated in Birmingham in the first half of the century. Both were phenomenally profitable, and by 1889 the founder of Home & Colonial, Julian Drewe, could retire to spend his accumulated wealth on the construction of Castle Drogo in Devon.[32] Another significant chain that eventually spread countrywide was Lipton, which started in Glasgow in 1876 and expanded substantially after becoming a limited company in 1898. Rather more up-market was J. Sainsbury's: in contrast to the original dairy on Drury Lane near Covent Garden, the Croydon branch of 1882 had expensive fixtures and fittings and attracted a middle-class clientele.[33]

In the late nineteenth century the typical provision shop had a small lobby, plate-glass windows, and pilasters and stallrisers clad in oxblood or dark green glazed bricks. Home & Colonial shops (pl. 80) were distinguished by their coloured 'bottle glass' transom lights. Maypole Dairy's shopfronts (pl. 81), made by Harris & Sheldon of Birmingham, were of particularly high quality: they had mirrored soffits and pilasters, and the Maypole name or monogram was worked into the mosaic floors and bronze door handles. The interiors of important branches of both Home & Colonial and Maypole were decorated with pictorial tiles, which occasionally survive while all other fixtures have been swept away. Lipton's early twentieth-century shopfronts were simpler and less uniform than Maypole's, but the interiors were equally lavish, with black and white chequered tile floors, and cream-coloured glazed wall tiles incorporating colourful swags and mouldings. A remarkably intact Lipton's interior in Chesterfield (pls 82–3) clearly sold provisions on one side, and groceries on the other,[34] with the former having a sash window and tiled counter, and the latter a fixed display window, a mahogany counter and wooden shelving. Marble slabs would have kept the butter, cheese, bacon and ham as cool as possible, and there was a cash desk at the back. This is an extremely rare survival of an early twentieth-century multiple shop. Sainsbury's shops were similar but deeper, as the original shop was often augmented

81 The entrance of a former Maypole Dairy shop, now a clothes shop, at 15 King Street, Ludlow, Shropshire. A tile panel manufactured by Pilkington's, depicting figures in Elizabethan costume dancing around a maypole, can just be glimpsed on the wall through the open door.

by a single-storey rear extension with a roof light. Sainsbury's assistants were usually accommodated on the upper floors.[35]

It was hard for the independent middle-market grocer to compete with multiple provision shops, which continued to dominate the high street until the 1950s, when a new phenomenon arrived – the self-service supermarket (see Chapter 12). Ultimately, that forced the traditional grocer to expand and convert, as did Jackson's in Hull (pl. 84),[36] or shut up shop forever. One of the most architecturally striking post-war grocery stores was David Greig's branch in Canterbury, designed

83   The interior of Lipton's in Chesterfield, with characteristic glazed tiles on the walls and black and white chequered floor. The motto above the grocery counter reads 'The Business on Which the Sun Never Sets'.

82 (*facing page*)   The exterior of a former Lipton's shop (now Jackson's the Bakers) on Low Pavement, Chesterfield, Derbyshire, with a sash window lighting the side dedicated to fresh foods, and fixed glazing in front of the grocery counter.

84   William Jackson of Hull started out as a grocer and tea dealer in 1851. By 1913, when this shop was erected at 118–120 Newland Avenue, the firm had numerous branches and sold a great variety of foodstuffs. Many of Jackson's shops were designed by the local architects Gelder & Kitchen and featured blue and gold mosaic panels. This branch was converted into a 'superette' around 1960.

by Robert Paine & Partners and built in 1954.[37] With its high food hall and distinctive zigzag roofline (pl. 85), it attained a much higher standard of design than any contemporary supermarket.

Butchers' Shops

Butchers' shops have been governed by health and hygiene regulations for hundreds of years. In the medieval period they were gathered together in shambles and had to abide by local regulations concerning the slaughter of animals and disposal of offal. It was only in the nineteenth century that butchers began to set up fixed shops that were not part of a market. Like stalls in shambles, however, these had open fronts or windows that could be opened wide to expose displays to passers-by (pl. 86).

In 1843 it was considered that 'a sash-window to a butcher's shop would be quite a solecism',[38] but by the last quarter of the century sash windows were widely adopted. The butcher could raise or remove the lower sash to expose a display of meat, while the fixed upper sash provided some shelter. The butcher's sash may have been preceded by windows that operated in the same manner as lifting shutters (pl. 90), while others folded like concertinas. Often there was a grille along the top, to ventilate the shop. Protection from the sun and rain was provided by blinds, but some butchers' shops had fixed canopies, and most were located on the shady side of the street. It was found that timber stall-boards absorbed water and blood,[39] and so by the Edwardian period it was common for these to take the form of white marble slabs, which usually had a forward tilt and incorporated gutters and drains. In the mid-twentieth century granite became a popular material for stallrisers, which could be incised with

85   David Greig's Canterbury branch of 1954, now adapted for Superdrug.

the shopkeeper's name. Like cheaper marble or glazed tiles, granite enhanced the impression of cleanliness. On the other hand, the long-lived practice of covering frontages with hanging carcasses (pl. 87), especially at Christmas and on other festive occasions, was anything but hygienic. Sometimes the hooks and rails used for these displays still survive.

The butcher's shop was often entered through a split 'Dutch' door, to prevent dogs entering. Inside, carcasses hung from hooks on rails attached to the ceiling. In the nineteenth century rails were usually of rough iron, fashioned by the local blacksmith, but by the early 1900s stainless steel was preferred. Some rails were fitted with a trackway to help manoeuvre heavy carcasses around the shop. The floor was covered in sawdust to absorb blood,[40] and fittings always included a large wooden chopping block (pl. 88). So that the butcher did not have to handle money or enter accounts with his bloodied hands, separate cash booths

were installed at the rear of the shop. Some of these are still used for their original purpose, for example at Allingham Bros. in Hitchin, Hertfordshire. Booths could be quite decorative, of high-quality hardwood, and sometimes incorporated a clock. Although matchboarding remained common, for reasons of cleanliness internal walls and shopfronts were often clad with tiles (pl. 89). These frequently included depictions of animals that were far removed from the reality of butchery.

Many city butchers bought 'dead meat' from wholesalers and carcass butchers. The majority, however, either raised their own animals or, more likely, bought them at local livestock markets. If no local authority abattoir existed, animals were brought 'on the hoof' to a small slaughterhouse at the rear of the shop, where they were killed. Externally, there was little to distinguish slaughterhouses from other outbuildings. Inside they contained equipment such as dehairers, scalding tanks and scraping tanks.[41] Other

86 (*above*) A row of open-fronted butchers' shops on Aldgate High Street, London, drawn by Robert Schnebbelie in 1817. The meat market at Aldgate was established in the early eighteenth century and survived until the late nineteenth.

87 Baker's butcher's shop on Hendon Road in Sunderland, photographed at Christmas 1921.

88 (*facing page*) The interior of A. Scarratt (formerly Mogridge & Sons), 47 High Street, Ilfracombe, Devon. Wooden chopping blocks like this once formed an integral part of butchers' counters.

facilities included processing rooms, where by-products such as sausages, haslets and lard could be made, and rooms where meat was cleaned and dressed. Before refrigerated cold rooms became commonplace in the early 1900s, fresh meat was stored on natural ice in a back room or cellar, and joints were salted in brine tanks.[42]

Multiple butchers largely developed as a result of the importation of cheap frozen meat from the colonies and South America from the 1870s. Their shops did not have slaughterhouses; they were very basic, and sold meat cheaply for cash.[43] The most successful included James Nelson & Son's, the River Plate Meat Co. and Eastman's, which was eventually taken over by Dewhurst's. Like all butchers, these companies made increasing use of fixed glazing from the 1920s onwards. This can be contrasted with the approach of fishmongers, including the Mac Fisheries chain, which retained completely open fronts for many more years. In the late 1940s Dewhurst's adopted chrome and plate-glass shopfronts, and established a uniform interior decor of white tiles with a black border. Some years later it introduced brightly coloured square panels depicting farmyard animals, a programme that is only now being phased out of Dewhurst's shops.[44]

a

b

כשר

c

d

89a–e   Butchers' tiles: (a) Mr E's (formerly
Harry Anderson's), 12 The Waits, St Ives,
Cambridgeshire; (b) Mr E's (formerly Harry
Anderson's), 12 The Waits, St Ives;
(c) P. Galkoff's sign for kosher meat,
Pembroke Place, Liverpool; (d) Johnson's
(formerly William North & Son), West Street,
Oundle, Northamptonshire; (e) former
Dewhurst's, Avenue Road, Freshwater, Isle of
Wight.

e

Like many other traders, butchers introduced an element of self-selection in the 1960s, displaying wrapped meat in refrigerated cabinets. By then few butchers retained their own slaughterhouse. That was largely the result of government control and rationing during the war, along with the effects of the Slaughterhouses Acts of 1954 and 1958, which placed the administration of slaughterhouses in the hands of local authorities.[45] Numbers of butchers' slaughterhouses declined still further with the adoption of EU standards in the 1990s and today only a handful survives. Despite this, several high-class butchers are still involved in rearing their own animals, smoking bacon and making sausages and puddings; they are still producer-retailers. At the other end of the scale are the discount butchers with open shopfronts who have brought the atmosphere of the market stall to the high street.

Butchers' shops *seem* to survive in greater numbers than those of other tradesmen. This may be because, of all traditional shop types, they are the most instantly recognisable. Some of the oldest surviving shops in the country were built for butchers, while the shops of many other traders discussed here evolved their 'traditional' form only after the adoption of the glazed shopfront. Coexisting with these shops on the high street are modern specialists such as mobile phone shops, most of which achieve distinctiveness through the most superficial means and are unlikely to leave any physical trace once they are superseded by the next generation of shops.

90 This former butcher's shop at 1 Nelson Place East in Bath has a fixed canopy and glazed lifting shutters. Glazed shutters were usually used on windy corner sites, where they could be put up to protect produce during business hours but still gave a view of the goods on sale.

5

Shopping in Style: Bazaars and Arcades

AT THE END OF THE NAPOLEONIC WARS, a number of English entrepreneurs introduced the interrelated concepts of the bazaar and the arcade to fashionable metropolitan consumers.[1] Like the exchanges of the seventeenth century, bazaars and arcades collected a variety of traders under one roof, and were controlled by a single proprietor who imposed stringent regulations to uphold the respectability of the establishment. While traders in bazaars lived out and were assigned counters in vast open-plan spaces, those in arcades rented small shops with cramped living accommodation, arranged along the sides of well-lit corridors. As it transpired, the arcade had a much longer life than the bazaar, continuing to be popular with the bourgeoisie in industrial cities and seaside towns throughout the Victorian and Edwardian eras and, with some adaptation, experiencing a renaissance in the glazed malls of the 1980s and 1990s.

Bazaars

Bazaars were the most architecturally adventurous retail establishments of the early to mid-nineteenth century. In fact, it is no exaggeration to claim that the proprietors of bazaars were the first to create places of theatre and spectacle as settings for retail activity. Many years before the famous Paris Bon Marché was built, English and French bazaars exploited the technological potential of iron and glass to create vast centralised spaces surrounded by galleries and lit naturally from above. Furthermore, they combined shopping with entertainments and services to an unprecedented degree. When English drapers began to transform their premises into department stores, they had much to learn from the earlier bazaar tradition.

Although the Exeter Change was described as a bazaar in 1807,[2] the building that housed the first true bazaar still stands at 4–6 Soho Square in London, albeit much altered.[3] It was built as a warehouse in 1801–4 by John Trotter, who controlled government stores during the French Wars.[4] Soon after Waterloo, Trotter transformed it into the Soho Bazaar, which opened in February 1816. Several rooms on two floors were laid out with mahogany-topped counters that were rented out on a daily basis to 200 female traders. A contemporary children's book, *A Visit to the Bazaar* (1818), listed no less than thirty-one distinct classes of goods for sale, all of British manufacture. As with exchange shopping galleries, the fact that the traders were women invited suggestions that their virtue, as well as their merchandise, was up for sale. This was insinuated in several literary works, such as Humphrey Hedgehogg's poem *The London Bazaar, or where to get cheap things* (1816), and the Soho Bazaar was famously caricatured by George Cruikshank as a place populated by flirts and dandies. Trotter combated attacks upon the reputation of his establishment by imposing rigorous rules on the traders, who had to dress plainly, 'without feathers or flowers'.[5] They were compelled to apply fixed, marked prices, which reduced their dialogues with customers to a minimum, and they seem to have been obliged to take their meals on the premises. Trotter also employed porters to turn away persons 'calculated to lessen the respectability of the place'.[6]

Before long other traders were adopting Trotter's organisational structure and, like him, installing conservatories, exhibitions and picture galleries as additional attractions.[7] As no informative illustrations showing the interior of the Soho Bazaar have survived, it is difficult to know whether the building was as influential as the retail concept. We know only that the walls of the main room were draped with red cloth, that the beams

91   The decoration of the Pantheon Bazaar, which opened on Oxford Street in 1834, was executed in papier mâché rather than plaster, and the arabesques were painted on canvas. In 1859 George Augustus Sala described looking down upon 'a perfect little ant-hill of lively industry' from the gallery (Sala 1859, 175), but the spatial effect was destroyed after 1867, when Gilbey's acquired the building and floored the well.

WINTER FASHIONS from NOVᴿ 1833 to APRIL 1834, by B. READ, Pall Mall, Sᵗ James's & 12, Hart Sᵗ Bloomsbury Square, LONDON.

92   The Queen's Bazaar on Oxford Street was chosen as the backdrop for this fashion plate of 1833. The gallery was said to be 200 feet (60.96 m) long. Guildhall Library, Corporation of London.

were painted with inscriptions, and the end walls hung with mirrors.[8] Rather more is known about the Royal Bazaar (later known as the Queen's Bazaar), which opened at 73 Oxford Street in 1828 and featured a galleried well lit by glazed domes.[9] The building had a very short life, as it was destroyed in 1829 by a fire that started at a dioramic exhibition showing, somewhat ironically, 'the Destruction of York Minster by fire'.[10] Its replacement had the narrowest of frontages, graced by caryatids, but then swelled out behind its neighbours to occupy a considerable footprint.[11] Once again, the interior (pl. 92) was arranged around a top-lit galleried well, as was part of the Tudor-style Western Exchange, a bazaar established at 10 Old Bond Street around 1819–20.[12] Significantly, the Queen's Bazaar and the

Western Exchange both occupied sites that had previously accommodated stables. Another example of that was the Horse Bazaar which opened in the former Life Guards' stables on King Street in 1822, forming the nucleus of what would become the Baker Street Bazaar (see below, p. 96).

London bazaars may have exercised some influence on the Bazar de l'Industrie, which was erected in Paris in 1827–9 to a design by Paul Lelong.[13] Its apsidal plan was derived from ecclesiastical architecture, and its central nave was in the form of a two-storey galleried well, lit from above by a glass vault on a deeply coved base.[14] This has been hailed as the first example of a multi-level commercial space lit from above, but the story is not quite that simple: not only did two London bazaars have top-lit galleries by 1828, but Lackington's bookshop (see p. 38) had galleries lit by a cupola as early as 1791. In its scale and execution, however, the Bazar de l'Industrie can be seen as a major step on the route leading to the *grands magasins* of the later nineteenth century. In the shorter term, it helped to establish the accepted architectural form for most, but not quite all, future *bazars*, including the Bazar de Boufflers or Galerie de Fer, which was rebuilt in iron after a fire in 1829.

In England, the bazaar phenomenon was not exclusive to London; indeed, by the early 1830s every major city appears to have had at least one bazaar. In Manchester, for example, a draper named John Watts had founded a bazaar in 1821. Ten years later he moved it into new premises on Deansgate which included counters for male traders on the first floor and for females on the second, together with an 'exhibition of works of art, including diorama, physiorama, etc'.[15] In a similar vein, Jolly & Son's 'Bath Emporium', which opened in a row of houses on Milsom Street in 1831, combined a draper's shop with a bazaar that sold 'multifarious articles'.[16] Jolly had previously owned a wholesale woollen warehouse in London under the amusing name of Nice & Jolly, and also ran a bazaar in Margate, Kent.[17] In Bath, he would have competed with the Auction Mart and Bazaar on Quiet Street, a narrow building of 1824, attributed to Henry Goodridge,[18] which survives today as a bank and restaurant.[19] Kettlewell's Bazaar, which opened in 1826 on the first floor of the Shambles on Briggate in Leeds, had similar long, narrow proportions but was almost certainly a less refined establishment, as were the bazaar galleries of contemporary market halls (see p. 113).[20]

From 1830 increasing expertise in the use of cast iron encouraged the erection of bazaars with galleries. One of the best-documented examples is the Norfolk & Norwich Royal Bazaar (pls 93–4), which was built on St Andrew's Street in Norwich in 1831.[21] Beyond the hat shops that flanked the entrance lay the main hall. Two staircases led to a gallery where toys and fancy goods were sold, and which was partly fitted up to exhibit pictures. The gallery itself was upheld by ornamental iron columns shaped to imitate palm trees, a fashionable conceit at this time. Other rooms, probably in the street block, included offices, a reading room and accommodation for the secretary. The regulations were almost identical to those of Trotter's and Watts's bazaars.[22] Peter Thompson, the co-originator, architect and later owner-occupier of the Norwich Bazaar, eventually abandoned his chosen career to become an antiquarian forger, specialising in the work of Wenceslaus Hollar.[23]

Meanwhile, in 1834, the most distinguished of all bazaars, the Pantheon, opened opposite the Queen's Bazaar on Oxford Street. The interior of James Wyatt's building, which had been erected in 1772 to host 'the nocturnal adventures of the British aristocracy', was rebuilt by Sydney Smirke in 1834 with a vast

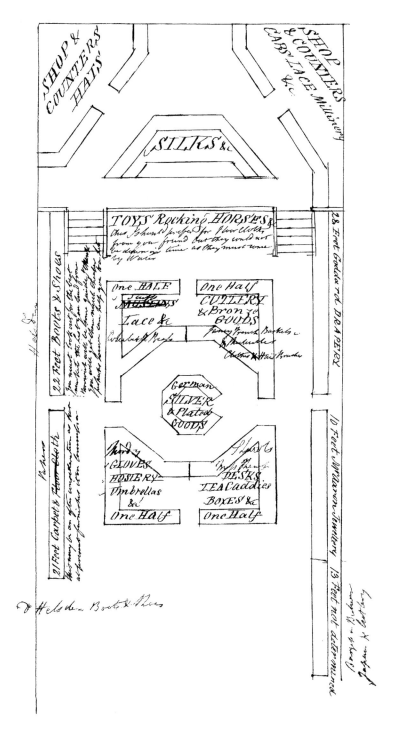

93 The Norfolk & Norwich Royal Bazaar of 1831, shown here with the entrance at the top, was laid out with 680 feet (207.3 m) of counters. In the centre of the open-plan ground floor, island counters were loaded with silks, 'German silver and Plated goods', lace, cutlery, hosiery and 'desks, tea caddies, boxes &c'. Norfolk Record Office so 18/87.

rectangular hall (116 × 88 ft/35.4 × 26.8 m) covered by a part-glazed barrel vault (pl. 91).[24] Towards the rear was a circular refreshment room, an elegant conservatory for the sale of flowers and plants (pl. 95) and a room where ladies could await their

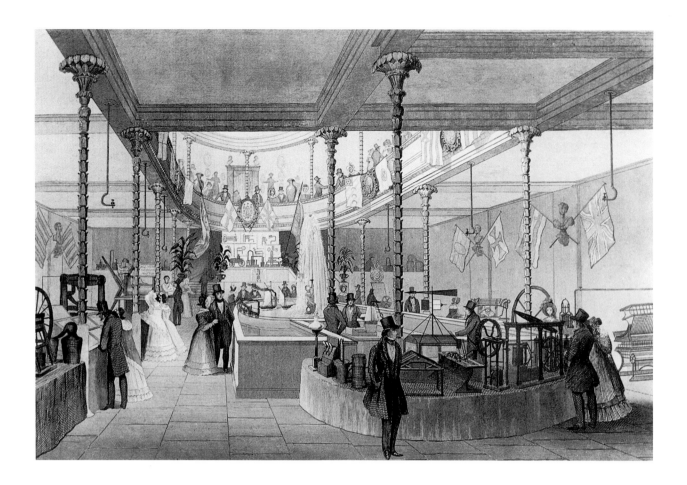

94 (*above*)   This engraving shows the Polytechnic Exhibition, which was held in the Norfolk & Norwich Royal Bazaar in 1840. The building seems to have been let for various purposes from the early 1840s onwards. It became a cinema in 1910, and was demolished in 1964.

95   An alcove at one end of the conservatory in the Pantheon Bazaar, erected by the firm D. & E. Bailey, was reserved for the sale and exhibition of ornamental birds. As Sala described it: 'the place is but a niche, a narrow passage, with a glass roof and a circle at the end, where the fountain is, like the bulb of a thermometer; but to me it is very delightful' (Sala 1859, 182).

carriages. Pictures were sold in a range of rooms on the first floor of the entrance block.

Early Victorian London was served by numerous bazaars, including the Pantechnicon on Motcomb Street in Belgravia, the Lowther Bazaar opposite the Lowther Arcade (see p. 100), and the St James's Bazaar. The largest of all, secreted behind respectable terraced houses, was the Baker Street Bazaar.[25] The former Life Guards' stables were rebuilt and extended in piecemeal fashion over many decades, creating a rambling complex. By the mid-1830s the upper rooms included a furniture department and a 'miscellaneous' department,[26] as well as Mme Tussaud's waxworks, and in 1843 a furnishing ironmongery warehouse known as the Panklibanon (pl. 96) was 'fitted to meet

96   The Panklibanon, an ironmongery store, was erected in 1843 within the Baker Street Bazaar. Marks & Spencer's head office was later built on the site. *The Builder*, 24 June 1843, 254.

97   The London Crystal Palace Bazaar, built in 1858 to a colourful design by Owen Jones, was bought by Peter Robinson in 1876 and was absorbed by his huge drapery emporium at Oxford Circus in 1889. The building was demolished to make way for a new store after the First World War. *Illustrated London News*, 6 November 1858, 440.

the requirements of the higher ranks of society' within the north range.[27] The Panklibanon stocked a wide range of merchandise, from showers to coffee machines. Its spacious showroom was divided into a broad nave and aisles, with supports carrying a delicate, arcaded gallery which, in turn, carried the decorative trusses of the part-glazed double-pitched roof. As well as an ornate staircase, which split into two flights at mid-height, there were two gallery projections which can only have been viewing platforms, designed to encourage customers to admire their surroundings, or to see and be seen. The remainder of the Baker Street Bazaar probably resembled Aldridge's horse and carriage depot on St Martin's Lane, which was rebuilt with a cast-iron roof and gallery in 1844.[28]

London's most architecturally innovative bazaar was the London Crystal Palace, an L-shaped structure with entrances on Oxford Street and Great Portland Street, which opened in December 1858.[29] The architect, Owen Jones, who had been Superintendent of the Works for the Great Exhibition of 1851, introduced bright colours and sophisticated lighting to the spacious interior, which was built of iron and glass (pl. 97). The 36-foot (10.9 m) high barrel vault was made of stained glass, set within fibrous plaster frames suggestive of ribbed construction, and was protected by an outer skin of opaque glass, set in an iron frame. By day, the interior basked in luminous coloured light, and after dark star-shaped gas lamps highlighted the gilded ribs and painted surfaces of the building. Rather than expecting this gemlike light to damage the appearance of the goods, Jones believed that the light streaming through the glass would combine optically to produce a scientifically white light, ideal for the display of goods.[30] Significantly, this bazaar had more than one refreshment room, 'one of them private, for ladies, with lavatories and other conveniences'.[31] The Soho Bazaar had a ladies' dressing room, and the Pantheon had a refreshment room, but this was one of the first West End retail establishments openly to provide water closets for customers, something that would have greatly encouraged women, in particular, to prolong their visits. Those who did not frequent this establishment had to wait another twenty-six years before the Ladies' Lavatory Company opened its first facilities at Oxford Circus, greatly easing the trials of a day-long shopping trip.[32]

The last bazaar to be built in London was the Corinthian Bazaar (1867–8; Owen Lewis) on Argyll Street off Oxford Circus, which hoped to profit from the impending closure of the Pantheon. Amongst its attractions were a ladies' cloakroom, a refreshment room and an aviary. Unfortunately, it failed to prosper: in 1871 it was converted into a circus, and in 1910 was rebuilt, behind the old façade, as the Palladium Theatre.[33] All fashionable retail formats eventually lose their sparkle, and by the end of the nineteenth century the word 'bazaar' was more likely to refer to a cheap penny bazaar, like Marks & Spencer's (see

pl. 236), to a temporary charity bazaar or to one of the Christmas bazaars that were set up for the sale of seasonal novelties in drapery stores. But while few true bazaars still traded, the arcade was enjoying its heyday.

The First Arcades

While the bazaar was probably an English invention, based on the older tradition of the exchange,[34] it is commonly understood that the direct precursor of the arcade was the Galeries de Bois of 1786, which completed the quadrangle of buildings surrounding the gardens of the Palais Royal in Paris. The three earlier ranges, begun in 1781, had been built of stone, with colonnades sheltering shops on the ground floors. These resembled covered pavements in English towns, such as The Pantiles in Tunbridge Wells (begun c.1698) and Bath Street in Bath (1791). The Galeries de Bois, however, comprised rows of wooden shops separated by covered passageways lit by skylights. The formula was a great success, and more permanent arcades were soon erected nearby, beginning with the Passage Feydeau in 1791 and the Passage du Caire and Passage des Panoramas in 1799. Many of these Parisian arcades were associated with theatres or other places of entertainment.

The first English arcade, the Royal Opera Arcade, was designed by John Nash and George Repton as the entrance to the London Opera House, and opened in 1817. Small shops lined one side of the covered corridor, which was vaulted in eighteen square bays with circular skylights, an unusual design that was repeated only in the Lowther Arcade (1830; Witherden Young) on the Strand and the Royal Arcade (1832; John Dobson) (pl. 98) in Newcastle upon Tyne, both of which have been demolished. The living accommodation over the shops, which had to be lit by lunettes and skylights, was accessible by rear staircases.[35] Hot on the heels of this development came the most famous and, at 585 feet (178 m), the longest of all British arcades, the Burlington Arcade, which was built in a much more commercial location, lying parallel to Old Bond Street. It was designed by Samuel Ware for Lord George Cavendish, and opened in 1818. In contrast to the Royal Opera Arcade, the shops lined both sides of the corridor (pl. 100), and the upper storeys, corresponding to the shopkeepers' living quarters, were allowed to rise full height under the double-pitched roof, which was divided into sections by transverse arches, and held large skylights. As at the Royal Opera Arcade, the shopfronts assumed the currently fashionable form of flattened bows with quadrant-shaped corners. Just inside the main entrance on Piccadilly, the line of the shopfronts was set back to accommodate the sober classical façade, which comprised three round-headed arches of equal height.

98   The Royal Arcade in Newcastle upon Tyne (1832; John Dobson) was demolished in 1960, a year after this photograph was taken. A 'copy' was erected on the ground floor of an office block named Swan House in 1970.

The *bon ton* of Regency London flocked to the Burlington Arcade to indulge their appetite for expensive trinkets, and to exhibit their finery away from the dirt and din of the streets. To preserve an air of exclusivity and tranquillity the arcade was policed by beadles, who strictly enforced rules preventing visitors from whistling, singing, playing musical instruments, carrying parcels or pushing prams.[36] Only select trades were allowed to rent arcade shops, to the automatic exclusion of any that could be classified noisy, noxious or offensive. As in bazaars, the rules adopted by arcades guarded against the possibility that they might degenerate, like their predecessors the exchanges. Despite this, the upper rooms of a particular 'friendly bonnet shop' in the Burlington Arcade were used, at one time, for prostitution.[37]

None of the other arcades that opened in late Georgian or early Victorian London was as successful as the Burlington

Arcade, largely because none benefited from such a plum location. The Lowther Arcade on the Strand had three-storey internal elevations and flush-fronted shopfronts. The building was much admired, but it quickly became renowned as a centre for cheap toy shops rather than fashionable knick-knacks. In 1865 Henry Mayhew made the peculiar observation that all the shop girls in the Lowther Arcade appeared to be web-footed, also noting that the unpopular Royal Opera Arcade was known as 'the Arcade of the Melancholy-Mad Bootmakers'.[38] Further east along the Strand, an arcade called the New Exeter Change was built in 1844 to a design by Sydney Smirke, the architect of the Pantheon Bazaar. Its short corridor was cleverly set on a diagonal to increase its length, but still it contained only eleven shops.[39] According to Mayhew, it was notorious for its 'double line of tenantless shops, and the lugubrious aspect as well as stern

99   The Lower Arcade in Bristol, erected in 1824, adopted a fashionable Greek Revival style.

100 The most successful arcade in England is undoubtedly the Burlington Arcade in London. By 1905, when this photograph was taken, some glazing bars had been removed from the shop windows and gas lighting had been installed; otherwise it had changed little since it first opened in 1818.

manners of its hermit-like beadle'.[40] It was demolished in the early 1860s.

The outstanding success of the Burlington Arcade encouraged the construction of refined arcades in flourishing ports, and in seaside and spa resorts. One of the first, still demonstrating a certain hesitancy about this new building type, was the Pelham Arcade in Hastings. It was designed by Joseph Kay for a terraced site under the cliff, and opened in August 1825. The twenty-eight shops had simple counters set within arched openings rather than glazed shopfronts, but they nevertheless sold fashionable goods, and high society came here to promenade and listen to music on summer evenings.[41] The corridor had a pitched roof which was ceiled at collar level and set with skylights.

More mature arcades were constructed in Bristol and Bath,

although the latter was unfortunately bisected by a lane. The form of the Grecian-style Upper and Lower Arcades in Bristol (1824–5; James Foster; pl. 99) closely resembled the Burlington Arcade, but the roofs held larger skylights. Only the Lower Arcade survived the Second World War. The Corridor in Bath (1825; H. E. Goodridge) incorporated Assembly Rooms on the first floor. While bazaars always included amusements in the form of conservatories, exhibitions or waxworks, English arcades were only sporadically associated with places of entertainment, and all too often with theatres or assembly rooms that did not open at the same time as the shops. The first roof of The Corridor, long since replaced, contained skylights with coloured glass, which had a darkening effect. A few years later, the Argyle Arcade in Glasgow (1827; attributed to John Baird) was the first of its kind to have a continuous iron and glass roof.

The relatively slow acceptance of arcades throughout the rest of England was sometimes ascribed to the uniformity, or even monotony, of their long straight corridors. In Paris, the Galerie Colbert of 1826 had included a central rotunda. The well-preserved Royal Victoria Arcade in Ryde on the Isle of Wight (1835; William Westmacott) adopted this idea, placing a rotunda at the crossing of its three arms. A decade later, the New Exeter Change incorporated a ceiled polygonal space at either end of the corridor, just inside each entrance. The corridor had a glazed roof which was described at the time as 'pseudo-hypœthral', having a continuous ridge light in the form of a pointed barrel on deep covings.[42] It was some time, however, before English arcades were built with full barrel vaults, in the manner of the Galerie d'Orléans, which replaced the Galeries de Bois in 1828.

Victorian Arcades

On several occasions over the course of the nineteenth century the arcade was presented by those involved in utopian urban planning as the ideal architectural form for shopping centres. Its appeal lay in the fact that it served as a pedestrian thoroughfare, and was not just a simple shopping development. While it was difficult to fit arcades effectively into existing fabric, they were thought highly appropriate for the remodelling of large urban areas, or for new towns and cities. Thus, in 1842 Frederick Gye, son of the proprietor of Vauxhall Gardens, proposed to connect Bank to Trafalgar Square by a gigantic arcade, 70 feet (21.3 m) high.[43] In 1855 arcades formed the basis of two schemes, William Moseley's design for a 'Crystal Way' and Joseph Paxton's 'Great Victorian Way', which were produced for the Select Committee of Metropolitan Communications. The 'Crystal Way' was conceived as a long building with a railway on the lower level, lying 12 feet (3.66 m) below the street, and with a walkway lined by shops and covered by a glass roof on the upper level. Paxton's much more expensive proposal involved a 10-mile (16 km) boulevard, or glazed arcade, that would encircle central London.[44] Many years later, in 1898, Ebenezer Howard published his plan for a garden city, based on concentric rings.[45] A central park was encircled by a glass shopping arcade called the 'Crystal Palace', part of which was to be used as a winter garden. Despite this, the first garden city to be created, at Letchworth, Hertfordshire, in 1903, was built with conventional shopping streets.

In the 1870s arcade building resumed with a vengeance, mainly in the industrial cities of the North and Midlands, indulging the desires of the prospering middle classes. Interest in arcades may have been reawakened by the building of the Galleria Vittorio Emanuele II in Milan in 1865–7, although nothing on this scale was even attempted in England.[46] Some cities displayed more of a penchant for arcades than others, and

top of the list were Manchester, Leeds and Birmingham. The first and most splendid arcade to be built in Manchester was the Barton Arcade (pl. 101) of 1871–3, by Corbet, Raby & Sawyer, which formed part of the Deansgate widening scheme.[47] Leeds, more than any other city, used arcades to extend its communications network. Thornton's Arcade of 1877 and the Queen's Arcade of 1889 were both erected on former inn sites on Briggate, which had been the main shopping street in the city since the thirteenth century. A number of arcades were also built in Birmingham, beginning with the Great Western Arcade of 1875, which straddled a railway tunnel. For some reason, Liverpudlians had little interest in arcades, erecting their first (now Allsports) on Lord Street as late as 1901.

The fashion for arcades endured until about 1910. Despite accusations of monotony, the most successful plan remained the straight corridor, which was usually about 15 feet wide, with an entrance at either end. Such a straightforward layout was not always possible, however, and arcades had to conform to the vagaries of their chosen site. Corridors were often curved, angled or linked ('Y', 'H', 'L' or 'T' shaped), and some developers even risked constructing corridors that formed a dead end, or had secondary entrances on minor service streets with little pedestrian traffic.[48] As in Leeds, long narrow sites that had been laid out as burgage plots in the medieval period and later become inns or alleys were ideal for arcades. Occasionally, as at the Wayfarer's Arcade in Southport (pl. 102), built as the Leyland Arcade in 1896, the site widened out to provide a central space that could be covered by a spectacular glass roof.

Many city arcades formed part of buildings with multiple functions, such as offices, hotels, apartments, billiard rooms or even Turkish baths. Inevitably, this affected their character and appearance. Glass roofs generally abutted the rear walls of entrance buildings, creating low, tunnel-like foyers, which were closed by wrought-iron gates at night. As at the Barton Arcade, the main entrance often occupied a single bay on the ground floor of a building with a conventional elevation, and was treated with little more prominence than a carriage arch. Ironically, it was only on back lanes that façades could be treated as eye-catching glass walls, for example at the Barton Arcade and the Wayfarer's Arcade.

The arcade as a stand-alone building type endured in seaside resorts and market towns, rather than in industrial cities where land was at a premium. In towns such as Bournemouth and Bognor Regis, both on the south coast, the façade of the corridor was treated as a light screen, set between two pavilions with lock-up shops on their ground floors and caretaker's accommodation above. The Back of Inns façade of the Royal Arcade in Norwich (1899; George Skipper), a particularly fine example of this kind of arcade (pl. 103), is faced in colourful Doulton Carraraware with art nouveau decoration.

101 The components of the Barton Arcade in Manchester were manufactured in Walter Macfarlane's Saracen Foundry in Glasgow in 1871. Despite its architectural splendour and central position, it is not a resounding commercial success.

Most arcades continued to be built with two-storey corridors, without galleries. First-floor rooms could be put to a variety of uses but, if they were connected to the shop units by staircases, they were now more likely to be showrooms than living accommodation. Basements provided storage space, and in later years some were fitted out as sales areas, or even opened up as trading levels. In many developments, however, the upper-floor rooms were nothing to do with the shops, and were rented separately as offices, which could be accessed through the entrance buildings. As the shops did not usually have yards or back doors, deliveries were generally made through the pedestrian corridor outside trading hours. For that reason, most arcade shops sold small, lightweight goods, such as jewellery or haberdashery.

A number of arcades had upper levels accessed by galleries. Both the Barton Arcade in Manchester and the Silver Arcade (1899; Amos Hall) in Leicester rose precipitously through four storeys, creating vertiginous spatial effects. While the Silver Arcade had a simple glazed pitched roof, the Barton Arcade had a barrel vault, perhaps the first of its kind in an English arcade. Also, while the galleries in the Silver Arcade housed shops, like

102 The Wayfarer's Arcade in Southport (1896) incorporates a central space which was originally filled with palm trees, seats and a bandstand.

103 The tiles decorating the Royal Arcade in Norwich (1899) were executed by W. J. Neatby, who was also responsible for the City Arcade of 1898–1901 in Birmingham, and the famous Meat Hall of 1902–3 in Harrods.

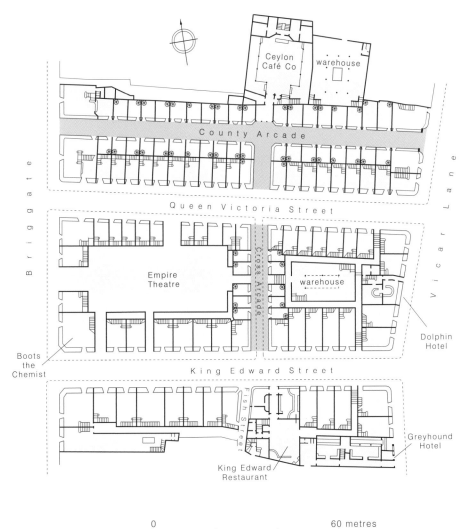

104 The Leeds Estate Company redevelopment plan (c.1897–8) for Briggate included the County and Cross Arcades. Harvey Nichols now occupies the space of the Empire Theatre, and Queen Victoria Street has been roofed over. Based on plan in Leeds City Library LQP 333.33 L517.

105 Of all the arcades in Leeds, the County Arcade of 1900 is probably the most ornate. It was designed by the theatre architect Frank Matcham, and is faced in Burmantofts faience. The glass barrel vault is carried on cast-iron arches and is interrupted by three domes with mosaic decoration.

106 The City Arcade in Coventry (1960–2) is obviously in a different class from the highly decorative arcades of the Victorian and Edwardian eras but, like them, serves as an important pedestrian thoroughfare within the townscape.

the great galleried arcade in Cleveland, Ohio (1888–90), those in the Barton Arcade gave access to offices. Galleries were usually constructed of cast iron, with wrought-iron railings, but only occasionally, for example in the Wayfarer's Arcade, was there space for a grand public staircase. Unusually, the Silver Arcade had a lift from the outset: most gallery shops were reached via dark and unwelcoming back stairs, and were never a commercial success.

The most ornate arcades, which rank alongside contemporary public-house and music-hall architecture, were built around 1900. The most elaborate of all, Frank Matcham's County Arcade in Leeds (1898–1900), formed part of an ambitious redevelopment scheme undertaken by the Leeds Estate Company on the east side of Briggate. The red brick and terracotta complex

(pl. 104), executed in an enriched Free Jacobean style, included two new streets, two arcades, two warehouses with internal galleries, two hotels and the Empire Theatre. The County Arcade (pl. 105) incorporated three circular or elliptical domes, with mosaic pendentives representing the Arts and Sciences. In 1989–90 this arcade network was extended when a stained-glass roof was erected over Queen Victoria Street, creating the Victoria Quarter.

Arcades in the Twentieth Century

Arcades had achieved such widespread popularity by the 1890s that they were even being built by local authorities as entrances

107　The spandrels of the central dome in the Exchange Row Arcade, Nottingham (1928), display historical scenes representing Robin Hood, the Danes arriving in Nottingham, Charles I and William the Conqueror.

to market halls, for example in Carlisle (1889) and Halifax (1891). Around the same time, multiple traders such as Boots started to occupy arcade shops. But arcades may have become too popular for their own good, as most of those built between 1900 and 1939 are rather disappointing in comparison with their exuberant Edwardian predecessors. They were usually only two storeys high, with utilitarian roofs. Few were now built with galleries, and they seldom attempted to stimulate upper-floor shopping by installing lifts. A typical example was The Arcade (1927; Goodey & Cressall), which ran between Long Wyre Street and Queen Street in Colchester, where the rooms over the shops were used as showrooms.[49] The Arcade did not have a long life, and was transformed into an open-air precinct (Kingsway, now Priory Walk) in 1969. In contrast, the prestigious Exchange Row Arcade in Nottingham (1928; Cecil Howitt) (pl. 107) remains an asset to the city centre. It was built on the ground floor of the imposing new Council House, which replaced the old Exchange and Shambles in the market place. A particularly unusual feature was the basement delivery level, complete with lorry lift, which helped to maintain the dignity of the street frontage.

Over the years, many arcades became marginalised as new shopping developments caused shifts in town centres. This process accelerated after the Second World War, when central area redevelopment and pedestrianisation wrought fundamental changes. The utopian projects of the Victorians were long forgotten, and arcades seldom figured in new schemes. A rare example was the concrete City Arcade in Coventry (pl. 106), which was built in 1960–62 to replace the City Arcade of 1932.

It incorporated a staircase that gave access to rooftop parking but, by and large, new arcades did little to modernise the building type. Appropriately, Leeds was one of the last cities to abandon the arcade, building at least two post-war examples: the Empire Arcade (1961) and Burton's Arcade (1974) (pl. 234), both on Briggate, which then boasted at least seven arcades. Burton's Arcade resembled contemporary shopping malls, although it did not have the same sealed environment. The difficulties involved in delivering goods to arcade shops, as well as the small size of the individual units, are amongst the reasons they dropped out of favour with town planners and developers.

Although many arcades have continued to trade, they rarely do so profitably, and it is ironic that some of the most lucrative commercial developments of recent years have imitated their appearance. A prime example is The Lanes in Carlisle (see p. 269) which, like many Victorian arcades, aspired to cover existing lanes with glass roofs and convert them into a shopping centre. The arcade also became something of a clichéd theme for mall designers, beginning with the so-called Georgian Arcade in the Merrion Centre in Leeds (see p. 269), and continuing with 'arcades' in the MetroCentre, Meadowhall and Bluewater (see Chapter 13). Several arcades have found a new lease of life by being integrated with mall developments: St Michael's Row in Chester is now attached to the Grosvenor Centre; the Cambridge Arcade in Southport is linked to Cambridge Walks; and the Westgate Arcade in Peterborough leads into the Queensgate Centre. Many, however, are located too far from the heart of the town centre for this kind of lifeline to be offered, and their future is far from assured.

6

Civilising the Centre:
Market Halls

IT WAS ONLY IN THE 1820s THAT LARGE, enclosed halls began to replace open-air markets, often as a prelude to sweeping urban improvements. Large numbers of halls were built in the Victorian era, followed by a lull in the first half of the twentieth century. Market halls, however, occupied important positions in the post-war redevelopment schemes of the 1950s and 1960s. At that time, several significant nineteenth-century halls were demolished. Today, if a market hall falls out of use it is more likely to be converted into a speciality shopping centre. Those that continue to fulfil their original purpose, usually under the auspices of the local authority, have succumbed to change to a lesser extent than other types of retail building.

Steps Towards Market Reform

The dirt, noise and congestion of the open-air market were condemned by those intent on improving the appearance of English towns and cities in the late eighteenth and early nineteenth centuries. As it grew wealthier, society became increasingly fastidious, and abhorred the idea of respectable housewives frequenting such uncouth places to buy food and other necessities. Indeed, the danger and confusion of the market place was compounded as towns grew in size and prosperity. Rather than offering a bucolic idyll, it attracted rough sports such as bull-baiting and cockfighting, as well as unsavoury characters like beggars, bookmakers, pickpockets, prostitutes and quacks. The ground was usually littered with refuse, including rotting debris from butchers' and fishmongers' stalls, while traders' carts and barrows obstructed neighbouring streets and lanes.

In small towns, traditional market buildings with open-sided trading areas continued to be erected, and used effectively, throughout the eighteenth and nineteenth centuries. Although they differed little in form and function from their medieval predecessors (see Chapter 1), they now aimed to elevate the homely image of marketing by adopting an exalted classical style, rather than the humble local vernacular. This can be seen, for example, in the grand Town Hall and Market Piazza in Berwick-upon-Tweed (1761). In fast-growing cities, however, these structures could shelter only a fraction of the stalls that now thronged the market. Some towns, such as Carlisle, tried to control market chaos by allocating different streets to different trades, while Manchester experimented with decentralisation over a greater geographical area.[1] Other towns, rather than disperse their market in this way, attempted to confine it within a walled enclosure, following the example of earlier metropolitan markets in London and Continental cities.[2] Enclosed complexes, like the Provision Market in Ipswich (1810), were usually surrounded by colonnades, or piazzas, and could encompass a variety of market structures. In a similar vein, the long, narrow markets built in towns such as Stamford (1808) contained a mixture of open spaces and covered stalls within the confines of ordinary burgage plots.[3] Ultimately, both the decentralised and the enclosed market failed to offer a practical solution to the problem of overcrowding, and it was realised that the most effective measure was to sweep the entire market into a large hall.

In a market hall, the movements and behaviour of traders and shoppers could be closely controlled, and extraneous activities excluded. Unlike the shambles and market houses of the past, a market hall could accommodate every species of trader. It established new standards of hygiene, with washable surfaces, a plentiful water supply and even ice houses for fishmongers. The provision of gas lighting and natural ventilation facilitated marketing at all times of day and in all weathers, although heating was considered inadvisable. With a well-equipped market hall, a town could concentrate on civilising its public spaces, particularly by paving, lighting, widening and policing its streets, furnishing them for vehicular traffic and the activity that we now regard as 'traditional' shopping. On one level, it might be argued that the middle classes were commandeering town and city streets from the lower orders, while at the same time deploying lofty halls as tools to reform the behaviour of their social inferiors.[4] Admittedly, the middle classes did occasionally visit market halls themselves, but they did so on different days and at different times from the workers. Market halls were always at their busiest on Saturday, as that was pay day, and at the end of each working day. It was then that they came alive as venues for social interchange.

Like co-operative stores, most market halls were built in the industrial conurbations of the North-West and Midlands, with a particular concentration in Lancashire. Although some resulted from private enterprise or philanthropic impulses, most were provided by local authorities, either the municipal body or improvement commissioners, who were beginning to wrest control of food distribution from manorial families. They were obliged to obtain their reformative powers, including powers of compulsory purchase, through private bills, until the Municipal Reform Act (1835) and other permissive legislation made it easier for them to borrow money to acquire market rights and finance rebuilding.[5] Occasionally a hall was built on the old market place, but there was usually a desire to keep that as a public amenity, and so a new site had to be found in as central a location as possible. In the nineteenth century it was still possible to acquire large residences with gardens in urban situations, as happened in Leeds, but it was more usual for authorities to clear tracts of slum dwellings. The displaced population was generally rehoused on the outskirts of town.

The nineteenth-century market hall was rarely a multiple-use building, like earlier market structures, but there were always exceptions. The Pannier Market in Barnstaple, Devon (1855), for example, accommodated a guildhall and corn exchange on its upper floors.[6] Like the arcade, the market hall served as a public thoroughfare during opening hours. Like the corn exchange, it was a symbol of civic pride, and was often adorned with mottoes, heraldry and appropriate statues, such as Flora or Plenty. And like town halls, its style and imagery sometimes attempted to establish links with local traditions, and outshine the efforts of neighbouring towns. In 1848, for example, Blackburn became the first town to erect a market hall with a prominent tower, and throughout the later Victorian period no self-respecting market hall was without its competitive array of turrets, spires and pinnacles. Today, the slender tower of Darlington Market Hall (pl. 113), erected in 1864, is perhaps the finest surviving example of these urban landmarks.

With the mid-Victorian market-hall boom, many small markets dwindled and vanished. It was in towns served by the railway that markets now thrived, and could offer the cheapest and most varied food supplies.[7] With their low overheads, market

traders initially faced little competition from shops. When co-operative stores and multiple grocers arrived on the scene in the 1860s and 1870s, they seldom sold perishable foodstuffs. Independent grocery shops usually targeted very different customer groups, who expected courteous counter service, and were consequently willing to pay higher prices. Nevertheless, to discourage local producers from selling fish or grain in bulk to stores, or sending their goods to other cities, many towns decided to erect a wholesale facility next to their retail market. In many complexes, the boundaries between retail and wholesale marketing were poorly defined, to the customer's benefit.

Early Market Halls

The first of the great nineteenth-century market halls was St John's Market (pls 108–9), built in Liverpool in 1820–22 to a design by the city architect, John Foster. Before then, large purpose-built market complexes had included a mixture of covered and open areas, but St John's was the first in the form of a completely covered general trading hall. The precise origins of this concept are unclear. Around 1820, France was a common source of new ideas for British architects and retailers, but Napoleonic markets had mostly been erected as enclosures incorporating open-sided market houses.[8] Tentative prototypes can be found closer to home, in London market houses with enclosed ground-floor trading areas (see Chapter 1). Most suggestively, some time before its demolition in 1829, the Fleet Market House (pl. 9) was enclosed.[9] To all intents and purposes that created a market hall, and may unwittingly have inaugurated a new building type. In comparison with the new St John's Market, however, the celebrated Fleet Market was declared to be little more than 'a miserable shed'.[10]

Before 1820 Liverpool market had clustered around St George's Church, but that area had become so overcrowded that secondary markets were set up elsewhere. St John's Market was built on a site formerly occupied by a rope works. It was a free-standing building with an oblong plan (approx. 74,000 sq. ft/6,874.6 sq. m), relatively plain in design and covered by five long, parallel, timber roofs, two of which were raised to provide clerestory lighting and ventilation. These roofs were carried by rows of cast-iron columns, 23 feet (7 m) high, which occupied a minimum of floor space and formed a 'beautiful perspective . . . in the evenings, when illuminated by successive rows of brilliant gas lamps'.[11] No less than sixty-two lock-up provision shops with open fronts, together with the market offices, were arranged around the interior, while the central space was divided into blocks of stalls and benches by five longitudinal and five transverse avenues. Four water pumps occupied strategic locations, and a large clock was suspended from the roof. Although this

109 (facing page bottom)   While the central space of St John's Market was laid out with various types of stall, the periphery was lined by small, open-fronted food shops. The building was demolished to make way for the St John's Precinct in the 1960s. Redrawn from plan published in Architectural Magazine, vol. 2, 1835, 132.

S. Austin.   Kelsall.

THE INTERIOR OF ST. JOHN'S MARKET, LIVERPOOL.

108 (*above*)   With its cast-iron columns, roof lights and regimented avenues of stalls, St John's Market in Liverpool (1822) was the first of the great nineteenth-century market halls. This tinted engraving dates from about 1832.

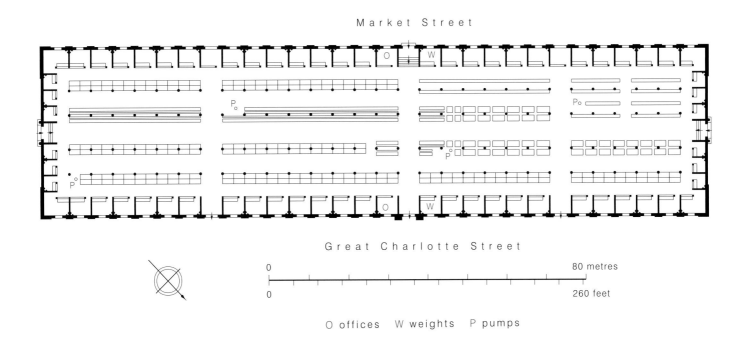

Market Street

Great Charlotte Street

0   80 metres

0   260 feet

O offices   W weights   P pumps

was the prototype for the great Victorian market halls, some time elapsed before this type of design was widely adopted; the main reason being the common perception, throughout the 1820s and 1830s, that stone pillars had greater architectural integrity than iron columns.

Betweeen 1828 and 1833 two greatly admired market complexes were erected in London to designs by Charles Fowler, whose recent work had included a small colonnaded market at Gravesend in Kent (1822), and the innovative 'Botanic Conservatory' at Syon House near London (1827–30). Fowler's Covent Garden Market (1828–30) and Hungerford Market (1831–3) were both indebted to earlier London markets. Covent Garden (pl. 282), which had become the main retail and wholesale market for fruit and vegetables in the city, occupied three parallel ranges surrounded by loggias. A section of the open courts between the buildings, destined for the wholesale fruit market, was covered by a cast-iron structure with an arched roof.[12] Similar shelters remained in favour with wholesalers for many years to come. Covent Garden had no hall for the retail trade: instead, retail shops, with living accommodation above, opened off a covered passage that ran through the central building and was lit by a clerestory. Although reminiscent of the much smaller structures in Oxford Market and Honey Lane Market (see Chapter 1), this was a cut above most market buildings, and seems to have aspired to arcade status: at one end stairs gave access to two conservatories and an exhibition room on a terrace, while at the other end they led to rooms where fruit and ices could be consumed.[13] In 1851 the passage was described as 'the favourite promenade

110   Charles Fowler's Hungerford Market (1831–3) had a short existence, being demolished in 1862 for the construction of Charing Cross Station. This view of around 1833 looks north from the balcony on the river front, across the fish market, towards the Central Market Hall.

A VIEW OF THE NEW HUNGERFORD MARKET.

of those who visit the market after the rougher business of the morning is over'.[14] People came chiefly to admire forced fruit and rare flowers.

Hungerford Market (pl. 110), which had become a general commodities and wholesale fish market, comprised open courts to either side of a central hall but, due to its steeply sloping site, the courts lay at different levels. As at Covent Garden, basement storage was provided throughout. While the upper court on the Strand was surrounded by a colonnade sheltering shops with living accommodation on their upper floors, the lower court by the riverbank (i.e. the wholesale fish market) was bordered by fish shops, and galleries for the sale of grain and flowers. In 1835 the fish market was covered by an innovative metal structure, designed by Fowler, with a ridge lantern and a cantilevered metal roof. Behind that, the monumental hall assumed the form of a basilica (approx. 23,000 sq. ft/2,136.7 sq. m), its central nave lit by a clerestory and flanked by aisles, beyond which were rows of shops with galleries fitted up as a bazaar. The combination of fashionable bazaar and lowly market must have seemed incongruous, but the Leeds Central Market of 1824–7 also had bazaar galleries, Kettlewell's Bazaar stood over the Leeds Shambles of 1826, and Glasgow built a Bazaar Market in 1817 (rebuilt 1843). Furthermore, when Hungerford Market failed, around 1850, the hall was converted into a bazaar, with a diorama and a theatre for displaying optical illusions.[15] It was probably around that time that many markets began to sell fancy goods, and especially haberdashery, which remains something of a market speciality to the present day.

Fowler went on to design the Lower Market (1834–7) in Exeter, a combined meat and corn market that was bombed in 1941. The central nave was notable for its wooden barrel vault, which greatly enhanced the sense of spaciousness within the hall. In other respects, the building adhered to the standard format of the long avenue lit by a clerestory, which was widely adopted for 1830s markets, including the т-shaped Brighton Market (1830), the Butchers' Hall in Newcastle's Grainger Market (1835), and even the much smaller Shambles in Devizes, Wiltshire (1835, extended 1838). The Birmingham Market Hall (1828–35) had a central avenue with a clerestory, flanked by aisles with skylights. More unusually, the central avenue of the Higher Market in Exeter (1835–8), designed as a fish, pork, poultry and vegetable market by George Dymond, was two storeys high, with an extensively glazed Horticultural Gallery on the first floor and skylights over the central well, which was described as an 'hypæthral opening'.[16] To either side of this were open halls, with roofs carried by iron columns that acted as drainpipes. The fish market, however, was self-contained, surrounded by a peristyle and equipped with a central fountain. A bazaar in the form of a short arcade was planned for the opposite end of the building, far removed from the smell of fish.

The largest and most ambitious market hall of the 1830s was undoubtedly the Grainger Market in Newcastle (1835; John Dobson). It was designed for the local builder-developer Richard Grainger, whose earliest works in the city included Eldon Square (1825–31) and the Royal Arcade (1832) (pl. 98). In 1834 Grainger embarked upon a radical scheme for the reconstruction of the city centre, inevitably displacing some traditional street markets.

111 One of the avenues of the Butchers' Hall in the Grainger Market, Newcastle upon Tyne (1835), photographed by G. B. Wood in 1943.

The old Flesh and Green markets were rehoused in a new building (approx. 80,000 sq. ft/7,432 sq. m), concealed on all four sides by ranges of three-storey houses with ground-floor shops.[17] Inside, the two markets occupied separate, but intercommunicating, halls that received very different architectural treatments. The Butchers' Hall (pls 111 and 236) was divided into four main avenues lit, in addition to the usual clerestory windows, by small skylights set into its coffered ceiling. A quite different method of top-lighting was used for Grainger's Vegetable Market, which was divided into a nave and aisles by rows of cast-iron pillars, and covered by a timber, hammerbeam roof with a continuous ridge lantern.[18] It was this open-hall design, with its light cast-iron arcades, that pointed the way to the future.

The Great Victorian and Edwardian Market Halls

A further technological advance was marked by the erection in 1845 of Birkenhead Market Hall, which claimed to have the largest cast-iron supported floor in existence, although the building (approx. 56,000 sq. ft/5,202.4 sq. m) was actually smaller than either St John's Market in Liverpool or the Grainger Market in Newcastle.[19] Its three naves were covered by wrought-iron roofs rather than timber ones, carried by cast-iron columns rather than masonry piers, and lit by a fully glazed ridge lantern rather than a clerestory.[20] The structure was by Fox & Henderson, who later designed the ironwork for Joseph Paxton's Crystal Palace (1851). An early addition to the basic template offered by Birkenhead was the landmark tower: that in Blackburn (1848) contained the residence of the market keeper, while later examples were generally used as combined clock and water towers, connected to fire hydrants throughout the building. Many halls continued to include galleries but, unlike the cast-iron galleries of contemporary bazaars (see Chapter 5), these were rarely major architectural features.[21] Like the more modest galleries of later arcades, they enjoyed limited commercial success.

The Crystal Palace, and possibly also the design for Les Halles Centrales (built from 1853 onwards) in Paris, inspired a handful of towns to erect market halls with glass rather than masonry walls, thus emphasising their progressive modern character rather than their civic respectability. The most notable example was the second Kirkgate Market in Leeds (1854–7; Charles Tilney), which was demolished fifty years later. The Leeds Market Committee had visited the market halls in Birmingham, Worcester, Manchester, Liverpool, Birkenhead and Newcastle, and received advice from Joseph Paxton himself. The influence of the Crystal

112   The market in Stockport spills out of the structure erected in 1860–61, and fills the triangular medieval market place. The building was originally erected with open sides and was a shelter rather than a hall.

113   Like Stockport, Darlington Market Hall in Co. Durham (1864, by Alfred Waterhouse) was originally open sided.

114   Preston in Lancashire is served by two open-sided market shelters, as well as a hall within the modern shopping centre. This shelter was erected – not without some technical problems – in 1870–75 to a design by Garlick, Park & Sykes.

116   Derby Market Hall was built 1864–6 and restored in 1989. Although impressive internally, the exterior is largely concealed by other buildings. From *The Illustrated London News*, 2 June 1866, 537.

Palace can also be seen in the façade of the Floral Hall in Covent Garden (1859–60; E. M. Barry), which was intended, as its name suggests, as a flower market, but proved a white elephant and now forms part of the revamped Royal Opera House.

It soon became evident that glass walls and roofs were not really desirable for buildings selling perishable produce, and so most market halls continued to be built with masonry walls and part-glazed roofs. Direct sunlight was controlled by aligning roofs east–west rather than north–south, sometimes with glazing on the north side only, and by using rough rather than polished plate glass. Proprietors often had to resort to whitewash or improvised blinds when an architect had incorporated too much glass. Ventilation could be admitted through entrances, grilles or the louvred sides of ridge lanterns, but a few markets were built as open-sided cast-iron shelters, like those designed by Fowler for the open areas of Covent Garden and Hungerford markets (see above). In 1860–61 a glass and iron shelter with open sides, described as a 'glass umbrella on stilts', was erected over Stockport market place (pl. 112).[22] Comparable open-sided structures were built in Manchester in 1853, in Darlington in 1864 (pl. 113)

and in Preston in 1870–75 (pl. 114). At Manchester, traders began to complain about undue exposure to the elements as early as 1854, and a glass screen was fitted to the tops of the arches.[23] Stockport's market shelter had been completely enclosed by glass by 1924, while that in Preston remains open to the present day.

One of the most ambitious market halls to be built in the aftermath of the Crystal Palace was in Bolton (1853–6). The architect, G. T. Robinson, was appointed after winning a nationally advertised competition.[24] Within his rectangular building (pl. 115), a central space was created at the juncture of two naves, which were each flanked by multiple aisles. This nucleus was framed by screen-trusses, with delicate openwork decoration, and supported a ventilation tower. The main roofs, with spans of 54 feet (16.46m), had light wrought-iron trusses and were lit by arched clerestorys and ridge skylights. The end result was unusually elegant and airy, but an even more spacious effect could be gained by adopting barrel vaults, with bands of skylights and ridge lanterns. One of the most impressive examples of this was Derby Market Hall (1864–6) (pl. 116), designed by the borough surveyor T. C. Thorburn, with ironwork by James Haywood of

115   Bolton Market Hall (1853–6) was refurbished in 1989, when a large new shopping centre and car park were erected against one side of the building.

117 (*above*) After Leeds received city status in 1893, much of the central area was 'improved'. Between 1901 and 1904, the leaky, glass-sided Kirkgate Market of 1857 was demolished and replaced by a much more solid, richly ornamented building.

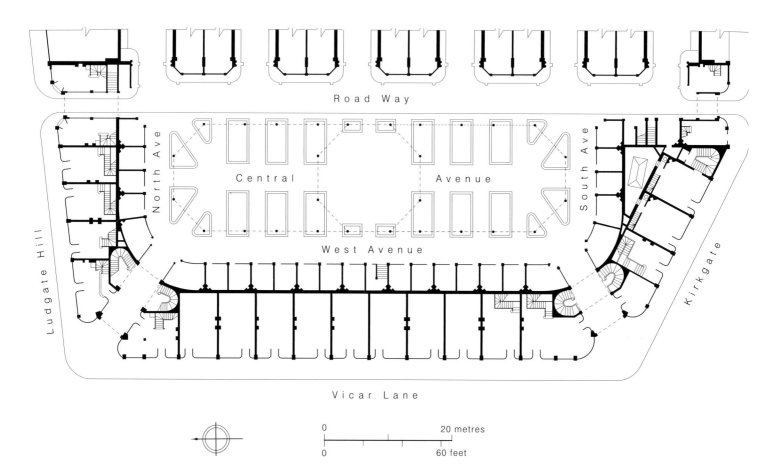

Road Way

North Ave

Central   Avenue

West Avenue

South Ave

Ludgate Hill

Kirkgate

Vicar Lane

0   20 metres

0   60 feet

the Phoenix Foundry and interior decoration by Owen Jones.[25] Although the hall was approximately half the size of Bolton Market Hall, the span of the roof, which has been compared with St Pancras Station, was 86 feet 6 inches (26.4 m).[26] Coventry Market Hall of 1867 had a roof span of 90 feet (27.4 m), while the three barrel vaults of Carlisle Market Hall, constructed in 1889, each spanned a distance of 70 feet 6 inches (21.5 m).[27]

While some of the largest market halls followed the example of the Grainger Market and were surrounded by multi-storey ranges with shops on the ground floor, others, like Bolton, were built with simple classical skins. That was the preferred option for small market halls, such as those built in Harrogate (1874) and Southport (1879), but, notwithstanding their modest proportions, these buildings still incorporated the obligatory tower. Some slightly bigger halls, such as Huddersfield (1880), had multi-storey front ranges with shops and, again, a tower, but had plain side and rear elevations. Whether built into a peripheral range of buildings or not, shops provided rental income which helped to pay for the construction and maintenance of a hall. Those in Carlisle (1889) and Halifax (1896) were even arranged in the form of an arcade, something that amounted to a middle-class affectation on a par with the earlier phenomenon of the market-hall bazaar.

In the last quarter of the nineteenth century some northern cities built market halls that were engulfed by elaborate multi-storey street ranges, often with showrooms, offices or flats above shops. These buildings, including Bradford (1878) and Halifax (1896), looked like grandiose railway hotels and gave no hint of the cathedral-like spaces concealed within. The grandest market hall of this type was undoubtedly Kirkgate Market in Leeds, which was designed by Leeming & Leeming, the architects of the Halifax market, and opened in 1904. Its construction coincided with the redevelopment of the east side of Briggate (see pl. 104) and the widening of Vicar Lane. The richly ornamented U-shaped ranges (pls 117–18) were wrapped around the ornate cast-iron structure of the hall, which still retains some of its original free-standing stalls (pl. 119), with their barley-twist columns and foliage capitals.

The internal arrangements of Victorian market halls were standardised to a great extent.[28] Halls were divided into long aisles, connected by cross-aisles, and with shops around the periphery. Stalls in the centre of the hall were usually of permanent wooden construction rather than cast iron. The vendors were sometimes provided with space behind the stall, but usually had to stand in front of it, in the aisle. Much thought was invested in equalising the value of stalls, and some large halls offered a variety of types. Darlington, for example, offered shuttered stalls, box stalls, open stalls and butchers' stalls.[29] Butchers' and fishmongers' stalls were often clad in white glazed tiles, but

other washable finishes, such as salt-glazed bricks and terrazzo, were also favoured. Fishmongers were usually allocated an enclosed area within the hall, to contain the smell, but some towns chose to provide separate buildings for fishmongers and butchers. In Barnstaple, for example, a Shambles was built across the road from the new Pannier Market in 1855–6. Halls usually included a clock, fountains, weighing machinery, offices for the market inspectors and clerks, and public facilities such as a restaurant and toilets.

119 Several of the cast-iron stalls in Kirkgate Market, Leeds, appear to date from 1904, while others are reproductions in the original style. The central octagon had to be rebuilt following a fire which broke out during restoration work in 1992.

118 (facing page bottom) This plan shows the new Kirkgate Market in Leeds (1901–4), with its double row of shops and cross-shaped avenues. To the rear, it abutted five detached blocks of fruit and vegetable stalls and two flanking rows of shops that had been put up in 1875. The open market square to the east of these was roofed over in 1901, and rebuilt after a fire in 1975.

While northern cities were being graced by magnificent market halls with modern amenities, Londoners resorted once again to their street markets. Covent Garden had gone over to the wholesale trade, and Hungerford Market, which had never been very successful, was demolished in 1862 to make way for Charing Cross railway station. Although great wholesale markets were built, such as Billingsgate (1852), Smithfield (1866) and Leadenhall (1881), all designed by the City architect, Horace Jones, London's few new retail markets were rarely successful. The most ambitious of all was probably Angela Burdett-Coutt's Columbia Market in Bethnal Green (1864–9), designed by H. A. Darbishire and described in later years by Nikolaus Pevsner as 'one of the great follies of the Victorian Age'.[30] It had a quadrangle containing a galleried and vaulted Gothic hall, imbued with strong ecclesiastical and moral overtones that befitted the philanthropic motives of its founder. Such enterprises were doomed because London's costermongers preferred the freedom of the streets, where market regulations and rents could not be enforced, although they had to be careful not to incur fines by blocking streets.

The absence of a great successful retail market in the capital was considered a matter of shame by some, who felt that London should build an equivalent to Les Halles, just as it had kept up with other Parisian shopping developments, such as the arcade and the department store.[31] Ambitious proposals for new markets were made by the Public Control Committee on London Markets in 1893, and plans for market halls were drafted by Arthur Cawston, the architect of Carlisle Market Hall.[32] Nothing came of that, however, and London's informal street markets have survived as one of its greatest charms to the present day. Since the Second World War, many of these, such as Brixton (Electric Avenue/Atlantic Road), Brick Lane and Ridley Road markets, have been injected with new vitality by immigrant communities, while others, like Camden Lock, have successfully targeted the youth market.

Twentieth-Century Markets

By the beginning of the twentieth century many working families preferred to buy their food in co-ops, which now sold meat and vegetables, or in multiple provision shops, which were slowly widening their stock. Several national chains, like Marks & Spencer (see Chapter 10), had started out in market halls, while others, such as Lipton, were not averse to occupying the better class of shop on market-hall peripheries. Occasionally, even co-operative stores were located in market halls. The few new halls that were built in the first half of the century were simpler and plainer than those of the nineteenth century. Some – for example those in Southport (1931) and Harrogate (1937) –

merely replaced older halls that had been destroyed by fire. At the same time, existing halls seemed to be in decline: unlike privately owned shops and stores, they were seldom modernised, and some were even truncated or closed. Wartime rationing dealt a big blow to markets, as people had to register with a particular shop for their food shopping, and the majority chose their local co-op.

Despite the growth of the supermarket as a major source of cheap food, the building of market halls resumed in earnest during the lean post-war years, often as part of redevelopment plans for bombed city centres. New halls often incorporated modern amenities, and were built as free-standing structures on marginal town-centre sites. The circular Coventry Market Hall (1958) had a rooftop car park with exit and entry ramps that interrupted the continuity of its frontage. The building was entirely of concrete, as was the Pannier Market (1959, approx. 33,000 sq. ft (3,065.7 sq. m)) in Plymouth (pl. 120), which had a shell concrete roof that enabled the cavernous central area to be unencumbered by supports. These halls had to follow more stringent hygiene regulations than their predecessors, and new shambles with glazed shopfronts were erected in many older halls, for example in Kirkgate Market, Leeds. Meanwhile, the first New Towns, such as Harlow in Essex, did not include market halls, but instead had open market squares adorned with public sculptures. It was only in 1973 that a market hall was built in Stevenage, Hertfordshire, on the ground floor of a multi-storey car park.

In the great central area redevelopment schemes of the 1960s, new market halls often formed adjuncts to precinct or mall developments, something that might involve the demolition of the old market hall. The first step of sweeping redevelopment in Blackburn was the erection of a new free-standing market hall (pl. 268). That actually comprised two market buildings, separated by a pedestrian way, and with an open area for wholesalers and market gardeners to the rear. The Daily Market had a curved roof, constructed with four bays of fourteen shells of curved 2-inch (5.08 cm) pre-stressed concrete, on tapering portal frames. A glass-fronted Chinese restaurant on the south front boasted 'a matchless view of the town's busiest traffic spot'.[33] Behind the Daily Market, the Two-Day drapery market and Three-Day food market were covered by a much more mundane concrete roof, coffered on its underside, and used as a car park which was accessed by ramps and detached Brutalist stair towers. The completion of this complex, in 1964, was followed by the demolition of the Victorian market hall of 1848, and the erection of a shopping centre on its site (see pl. 267). Market halls were soon being incorporated within urban malls, including the Bull Ring Shopping Centre in Birmingham (1964), the St John's Precinct in Liverpool (1968), the Kirkgate Shopping Centre in Bradford (1973) and the Manchester Arndale Centre (1979). A

120 Plymouth's spacious Pannier Market is located on the western edge of the post-war town centre. It was built in 1959, with a shell concrete roof.

new Green Market formed part of the Eldon Square Shopping Centre in Newcastle (1976) but, fortunately, the Grainger Market was allowed to survive. The new 'mall' halls possessed little charm. They were utterly utilitarian in design and excluded natural light as much as possible, relying instead on long fluorescent tubes suspended above the aisles. Ignoring the lessons learned by the Victorians, many had gallery levels with shops, cafés and offices: today, these are often disused.

Market-hall building diminished in the mid-1970s, by which time the character and social value of Victorian market halls were being appreciated by architects and planners. In the 1980s their appearance was aped by many superstore developments (see

Chapter 12), and some new malls even featured idealised themed 'market' areas rather than genuine market halls. A number of important halls, such as Bolton, Derby and Leeds, underwent expensive refurbishment programmes. In London, Covent Garden was reinvented as an American-style 'festival' mall (pl. 282) after the wholesale market had been moved to Nine Elms in Battersea in 1974. In Newark, the old hall of 1883 was successfully converted into a speciality shopping centre, but attempts to achieve something similar in Carlisle in 1991 ended in disaster: the market was severely truncated and the new shops remained empty until 1998 when, still pristine, they were dismantled.

121   The Meat and Fish Hall of 1999 in Bury, Lancashire, forms part of an extensive market complex, including a large modern market hall and an outdoor area.

Recent market buildings display great diversity in terms of their location, size and architectural style. At the smaller end of the scale, more symbolic than practical, is Brownsword Hall (2000) in Poundbury, a middle-class suburb of Dorchester, which was built by the Prince of Wales to challenge the principles underlying much post-war town planning. In keeping with his notion of traditional urbanism, Brownsword Hall was located in the heart of the community, and was designed in an attractive vernacular style, with an open-sided ground floor. In contrast, the Fish and Meat Hall (1999) in Bury in Lancashire (pl. 121), forms an addition to a much older market complex in a bigger

community and is a light, airy structure in a streamlined hi-tech style that seems eminently suited to its function. Rather more plodding is the Birmingham Indoor Market (2000; 55,000 sq. ft/ 5,109.5 sq. m), the first step in the redevelopment of the Bull Ring. It occupies the lower floors of a utilitarian building, with car parking on its upper levels, and is very much in the tradition of the post-war market hall, if marginally lighter and brighter internally. It boasts the largest refrigerated meat and fish counter space in Europe, complete with a state-of-the-art cooling system to monitor the food's temperature, and every stall is individually metered for water, electricity and gas.[34] Clearly,

122   Great Yarmouth market is still held in the long, rectangular medieval market place, but it has been partially covered by a shelter.

the form and design of the modern market hall is tailored to the size and nature of the community it serves, just as it always has been.

Today, many market halls, and especially those erected in northern towns after the Second World War, cater very much for the under-privileged, while older market halls in prosperous southern cities, such as Oxford and Bristol, have become fashionable places to shop, with stalls selling organic food, ethnic clothes and crafts. But some towns, particularly in the South and East, allowed the era of the market hall to pass them by, and never abandoned their open market places. The market places in Leicester and Great Yarmouth (pl. 122) now contain semi-permanent shelters, while those in King's Lynn, Salisbury and Cambridge are still open to the elements: a less practical approach, perhaps, but one that is eminently more picturesque.

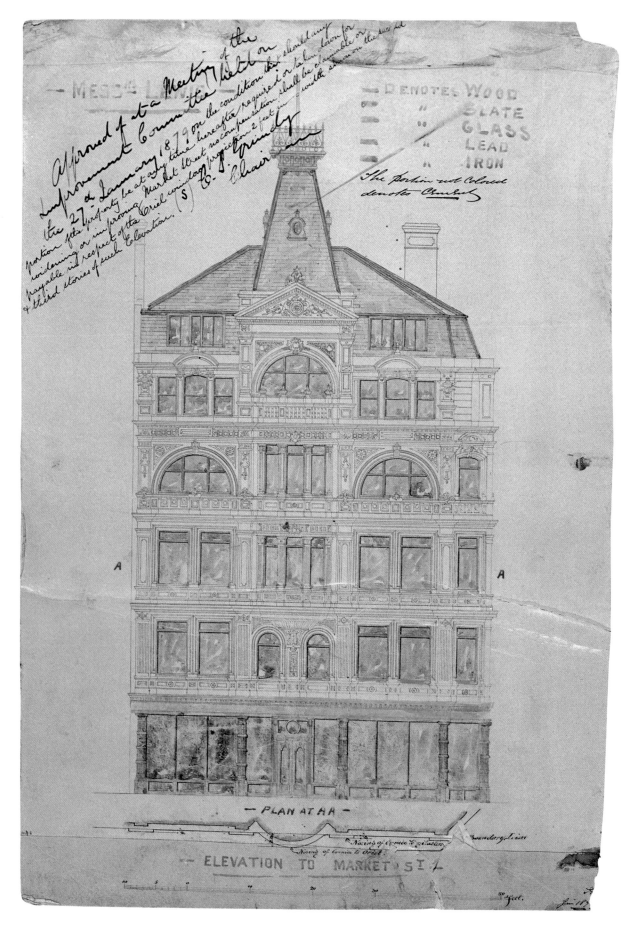

123 Horton & Bridgford's elevation drawing for David Lewis's store extension on Market Street, Manchester, dated 1879, revels in the growing fashion for French-style ornamentation and mansard roofs.

7

Shopping Palaces: Warehouses and Emporia, 1800–1900

DEPARTMENT STORES, WHICH EXISTED in a recognisable form from the mid-1870s, have dominated the study of nineteenth-century retailing.[1] Like bazaars (see Chapter 5), mid-nineteenth-century drapery, furniture and ironmongery warehouses tend to be treated merely as a preamble to the story of the department store, their historical significance assessed purely by the extent to which they anticipated that phenomenon. All of these developments, however, were highly influential in their day; they mirrored the rise of the middle classes and have left a deep impression on the face of English towns.

Ultimately, one cannot belittle the impact that the department store had upon the British retail landscape in the last decades of the century. Traders such as William Whiteley of Bayswater diversified beyond the dreams of earlier generations, and their establishments grew at a pace, and on a scale, that would have been unimaginable before the 1870s. Indeed, there was no language to describe them. Whiteley called himself the 'Universal Provider', and even in the 1890s the American term 'department store' was not used in this country. Instead, refined stores still traded under traditional titles, such as 'silk mercer', representing their main line of merchandise, while more popular stores continued to adopt the tag of 'warehouse' or 'emporium'. The term 'store' was in common usage only within the co-operative movement, and with grocery businesses that emulated their practices, such as Harrod's Stores.

Drapery Emporia, circa 1800–1850

Drapers expanded more than any other class of retailer in the first half of the nineteenth century. Around 1800, the typical draper occupied small premises and stocked a narrow range of goods, often limited to a particular type of cloth, which he purchased from the wholesale houses that congregated around St Paul's Churchyard in London, or from travelling salesmen. Lengths of material draped in the doorway and windows darkened the interior of the shop, which was lit by oil lamps. The draper shunned advertising, and granted long-term credit to his faithful clientele, whose families he had served for generations. He was content to make up for his slow turnover by charging high prices. Only metropolitan drapers' shops, which were being visited increasingly by strangers, had begun to operate a no-credit policy. One of the first to do so was Flint & Palmer's on London Bridge, where Robert Owen, the future mill-owner, obtained a situation in 1784.[2] Like most drapers' assistants and apprentices, he lodged with the owner's family above the shop and was expected to work very long hours. Owen clearly regarded Flint & Palmer's as an inferior establishment, and quickly moved on to greater things.

Many more drapers' shops had come into existence by 1850, largely to sell the products of the Lancashire cotton mills. Faced with intense competition, cheap drapers resorted to publicity gimmicks: the lettering on the frontages of their shops grew ever larger, discounted goods were sold under a variety of pretexts ('dreadful conflagration!', 'awful inundation!'), and the attention of the passer-by was seized by catchwords ('Look here!', 'Stop!', 'Down again!').[3] Such advertising was geared towards a new breed of urban consumer, whose forebears were more used to buying from itinerant pedlars or market stalls, and who might have been inhibited by the time-consuming etiquette of bargaining in a well-to-do shop. The application of fixed prices and an insistence on cash payments helped to demystify the art of shopping for those recently elevated to the middle classes, but it was also necessary for the shopkeeper, who could not rely on the bargaining skills of his growing band of assistants, and who now had little personal knowledge of his customers. Pushy tactics, a ready-money policy, a healthy demand for cloth and an improved distribution network by road and (increasingly) rail,

124 The front of Shoolbred & Cooke on Tottenham Court Road, London, in 1840. Shoolbred's became a major department store but went out of business in 1935 and was promptly demolished. From Whittock 1840, plate 4.

helped the draper to achieve a high turnover and, eventually, to amass sufficient capital to invest in expansion.

For successful drapers, expansion might mean stocking every line associated with the drapery, furnishings and furniture trade, including fancy goods and carpets, and even offering a funeral and undertaking service. For some, it might mean starting up a wholesale house, as the practice of giving trade discounts over the main counter tended to alienate retail customers. To house their new departments, drapers moved into larger premises or spread into neighbouring properties. Topographical views and panoramas of London streets reveal that even the largest drapery and furnishings warehouses of the 1820s and 1830s maintained a domestic style of architecture, with the presence of the shop indicated merely by a glazed shopfront at street level, lettering on the upper storeys of the façade and, in a few cases, a flag fluttering from a rooftop mast. This is not to say that upper floors were not devoted to business: some first floors were undoubtedly used as showrooms, and second and third floors as workshops, wholesale warehouses and staff accommodation. Living-in was compulsory, and dormitories, a dining room and a kitchen, if little else, had to be provided for dozens of male assistants and apprentices, as well as the female housekeeper who looked after them. In addition, rear wings may have housed additional showrooms, and cellars could have been used for storage.[4] But it is unclear how many thriving businesses were prepared to erect a

new building, planned to meet their precise needs. Regent Street had been built as the premier shopping street in the capital during the 1820s (pl. 44), with shops at street level and lodgings above, but nothing that might qualify as a store. Twenty years later, however, John Tallis's *London Street Views* depicted several warehouses that may have been constructed for or by retailers. Amongst these were: Rogers & Hitchcock, haberdashers, St Paul's Churchyard; Halling, Pearce & Stone, linen drapers, Cockspur Street; Jackson & Graham, upholsterers, Oxford Street; and Shoolbred, Cook & Co., furnishing drapers, Tottenham Court Road (pl. 124). One of the largest of all warehouses belonged to Harvey, Kingston & Co. of Westminster Bridge Road (pl. 125), a firm that was described as 'drapers, mercers, hosiers, haberdashers, carpet manufacturers and general furnishing warehousemen'. Unfortunately, detailed information about these large early nineteenth-century warehouses – let alone floor-plans showing the arrangement of their interior spaces – is extremely hard to come by.

Outside London, some successful drapers in industrial cities began to erect spacious new premises around 1840. One of the most impressive must have been Warwick House (pl. 126) on New Street in Birmingham, which was erected for W. Holliday, to a design by William Thomas, in 1839. Another intriguing building was Waterloo House in Ipswich, which was built for John Footman & Co. (later Footman, Pretty & Nicolson) in 1842, the name Waterloo House – very popular amongst early nineteenth-century drapers – being transferred from Footman's previous premises. Little is known about the interior. By 1858, however, Footman, Pretty & Nicolson were advertising as wholesale and retail linen and woollen drapers, silk mercers, haberdashers, hosiers, carpet and general warehousemen. Their large site included a purpose-built stay factory, which was later developed as a separate business by one of the partners.

As far as historians are concerned, the most significant provincial draper's shop of the early Victorian period is Bainbridge's, which was founded in Newcastle in 1838. It has been claimed that, with twenty-three separate sets of takings in 1850, Bainbridge's qualifies as the first true department store in Europe, and similar claims have been presented for Kendal, Milne & Faulkner, a drapery partnership established on Deansgate in Manchester in 1836.[5] Although both businesses departmentalised their stock, they kept within the conventional limits of the drapery trade until the 1870s, and did not breach product barriers more than many of their contemporaries. Unfortunately, little is known about the physical form of their premises. Bainbridge's original shop on Market Street was erected for the developer Richard Grainger rather than the firm, but in 1847 the old stables of the Turk's Head are said to have been converted into 'the most handsome suite of business rooms and galleries to be found at that time in the country'.[6] The architect

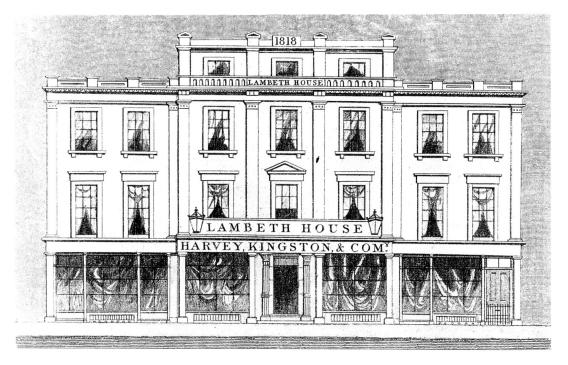

125 Harvey, Kingston & Co., Lambeth House, Westminster Bridge Road. Around 1839 the business was taken over by Joseph Harvey, whose younger brother Benjamin had set up shop (later Harvey Nichols) in Knightsbridge in 1831. Harvey obviously diversified as far as possible within the confines of the general drapery trade. From Tallis 1838–40, part 69.

126 Warwick House at 25–30 New Street, Birmingham, was one of the finest purpose-built drapery stores of the 1830s.

Thomas Oliver may have had this building in mind when, in 1851, he claimed that the interiors of the larger shops in Newcastle 'are judiciously constructed, and in the centre part formed with spacious galleries, which are lighted by elegantly ornamented domes'.[7] As for Kendal, Milne & Faulkner, they took over the bazaar that had been built in 1831 for their predecessor John Watts (see p. 95), and although they expanded into neighbouring properties, the firm did not rebuild on a large scale until compelled to do so by a municipal improvement scheme in 1872.[8]

Visual or documentary evidence for the interiors of drapery emporia – or, indeed, any kind of large shop – in the early to mid-Victorian era is scarce. The combined effect of mirrors and chandeliers had been exploited by top London shops since the eighteenth century, and in 1840 Everington's shawl warehouse on Ludgate Hill was praised for the 'blaze of light streaming from magnificent glass chandeliers, reflected on all sides by burnished mirrors, reaching from the floor to the ceiling'.[9] Everington's seems also to have been one of the first shops to be carpeted.[10] Although views of Harvey's on Ludgate Hill (pl. 46) reveal that it had a mezzanine gallery, it is clear that top-lit galleries of the kind that existed in Newcastle were still uncommon in drapers' shops, even those approaching the size of bazaars. Instead, there is some evidence that galleries were favoured by a new category of retailer, the outfitter who specialised in ready-made clothing and who was, perhaps, closer in spirit to the bazaar.

Ready-made clothing had been available as a minor line of merchandise in shops since the late seventeenth century, but it was only in the 1840s that shopkeepers began to develop large-scale establishments that specialised in ready-made garments – as yet catering almost exclusively for working- and middle-class men, rather than women. The most successful of these enterprising retailers, E. Moses and H. Hyam, were involved in manufacture as well as retailing, and were among the first to develop chain stores.[11] In 1843 Knight's *London* described Moses's 'extraordinary' shop on Aldgate: 'it may be said to reach from the ground to the roof, every storey being fronted by plate-glass and filled by goods'.[12] The shop was enlarged in 1846,[13] and drawings of 1847 (pl. 127) reveal that the ornate showrooms were spread over three floors, with a galleried well running through the top two floors. This space probably fell comfortably inside the limitation of 200,000 cubic feet (5,660 cu. m) imposed on divisions within warehouse-type buildings by the London Building Act of 1844, which was drafted principally with fire safety in mind.[14] Other mid-nineteenth-century outfitters' shops arranged around galleried, top-lit spaces included Clery's in Dublin (1853)[15] and Hyam's Birmingham shop of 1859, which sold workmen's clothing in the basement, ready-made clothes in the ground-floor shop, and had a bespoke department on the first-floor gallery.[16]

127 The showrooms of E. Moses & Son, tailors and outfitters, were located on the corner of Aldgate and Minories in London. This drawing by G. F. Sargent, dated 1847, shows the central well, which was lit by a large chandelier. Guildhall Library, Corporation of London.

Instead of having a lantern or skylight, Moses's well was illuminated by an enormous chandelier – or gasolier – which was suspended over the main counter, with secondary branches lighting the gallery level. Buildings that did not have a coal-gas supply continued to depend on lamps. A major improvement was the Bude light invented by Gurney & Rixon in 1839, which burned inflammable gas obtained by distillation from coal, oil and bituminous substances. It was used in many large stores, including Kendal, Milne & Faulkner,[17] while paraffin lamps were used in smaller shops throughout the second half of the century.

Furniture and Ironmongery Emporia, circa 1850–1900

It is not easy to pinpoint the precise impact that the Great Exhibition of 1851 had upon retailers, although it is intriguing to find that the vast iron and glass exhibition building, the Crystal Palace, was described by several contemporaries as a 'bazaar', or even 'the greatest bazaar of all'.[18] This is a reminder of the familial relationship among early museums, exhibition halls and bazaars, all of which encouraged the public to admire goods freely, whether for the purposes of education, amusement or direct consumption. The fact that William Whiteley visited the Great Exhibition is often cited as evidence of its contribution to the development of the department store, but the physical form of Whiteley's premises (pl. 136) had little, if anything, in common with the Crystal Palace.[19] It is indisputable, however, that the Great Exhibition fuelled the desire of the British middle classes to possess a wide range of domestic items, thus stimulating the turnover of furniture dealers and ironmongers as well as drapers and upholsterers. The number and size of these establishments grew enormously in the second half of the century. As *Modern London* claimed in 1888: 'there is not any department of social progress in which the effects of modern refinement, culture, and improved taste are seen at greater advantage than in the furnishing and general interior equipment of our nineteenth century homes'.[20]

The immediate influence of the Crystal Palace was limited because, in the early 1850s, iron and glass were still considered beneath the dignity of English street architecture. Across the Atlantic, Manhattan could already boast several prominent stores with thin cast-iron fronts which admitted abundant light. The earliest of these façades, designed and manufactured by James Bogardus in the late 1840s, may have inspired John Baird to design an arcaded iron frontage for Gardner's furniture warehouse in Glasgow in 1851–6.[21] Gardner's had no counterpart in central London, where expanses of glass were concealed inside such buildings as Owen Jones's London Crystal Palace Bazaar (pl. 97). Jones was also responsible for Osler's glass and china shop at No. 100 Oxford Street, which opened in 1859. Its long, single-storey showroom was covered by a glazed barrel vault of trefoil section, while mirrors were hung on the side walls to imply the lateral continuation of the space, and maybe even to suggest the presence of glass walls.

Although iron and glass façades were out of the question, the technological confidence expressed by the Great Exhibition may have persuaded both Heal's on Tottenham Court Road and Wylie & Lochhead in Glasgow to endow their new stores with light wells, in the bazaar tradition. Heal's old premises included a spacious mattress factory and a farmhouse where the family, and later the staff, were accommodated.[22] The firm specialised in bedding, but in 1852 it began to stock bedroom furniture, and soon afterwards James Morant Lockyer was engaged to design new showrooms in an Italianate style (pls 128–9). His building, which opened in 1854, resembled the Panklibanon (see pl. 96): the internal galleries were long and narrow, of undisguised cast-iron construction, with short bridges linking their long sides at first- and second-floor levels.[23] This would have appeared ultra-modern in comparison to other metropolitan furniture warehouses such as Atkinson's on Westminster Bridge Road and Maple's on Tottenham Court Road.

The limitations of the London Building Acts probably ensured that Heal's store lacked the theatricality of Wylie & Lochhead's Glasgow warehouse, which resembled the Pantheon and the great Parisian *bazars* and, in retrospect, seems prophetic of the *grands magasins* of the 1860s. Wylie & Lochhead had started out as feather merchants and undertakers, but by the 1850s had expanded into carpets, furniture and paper hanging. Their new cast-iron building of 1855 had a single vast atrium surrounded by three tiers of galleries and spanned by a glass barrel vault.[24] The customer could comprehend the layout of the entire establishment at a glance, and could reach the upper floors using the first passenger lift, or elevator, to be installed in a British store.[25] That was little more than a rudimentary hoist, but it seems to have pre-dated the first customer lifts to be installed in either American (for example, E. V. Haughwout's, 1857) or French (for example, Ville de Saint Denis, 1869) stores.[26] Wylie & Lochhead clearly understood that the lift endowed the multi-storeyed, galleried space with tremendous sales potential, and it is notable that London stores began to install lifts only in the late 1870s.[27] Eventually, the lift revolutionised the organisation of space within retail buildings, encouraging the development of upper-floor showrooms, and displacing staff accommodation into ancillary buildings.

Although neither Heal's nor Wylie & Lochhead's new building sported an iron and glass façade, each had an unusually high proportion of window to wall, and was decidedly commercial rather than domestic in appearance. It may not be coincidental that both the Italianate façade and the long, narrow galleries of Heal's resembled the Galeries du Commerce et de l'Industrie, which was built in Paris in 1837 and later became the Palais Bonne-Nouvelle.[28] Certainly, Heal's round-headed first-floor windows would have allowed light to pour into the showrooms that ran along the front of the galleries. Masonry or brick façades with close-set upper-floor windows – often separated by no more than pilasters – became popular for many kinds of business premises in later decades, but especially those selling furniture and ironmongery. Examples survive in every large town and city in the kingdom, and include the warehouse built by Henry Ogden & Son, cabinetmakers, on Deansgate in Manchester in 1862, and that of the manufacturing and furnishing ironmongers, W. & J. Woods, built on Cross Street in Ryde in the 1880s.

Complete iron and glass façades in the fashion of the Crystal Palace slowly gained popularity after 1860, particularly with provincial furniture dealers and ironmongers. Effectively, the shopfront extended the full height of the façade, producing a building in the form of a glass-fronted showcase, fitted with shelves. The glass façade had the advantage that it could be erected in front of an existing building, creating the appearance of new premises at minimal expense. Generally, wells were added

128 Heal's new furniture showrooms were built in 1854 on Tottenham Court Road in London. The arcaded cast-iron shopfront had low stall-boards which particularly suited the display of large objects. This photograph was taken by Bedford Lemere in 1897.

only if a store was particularly deep and thus required additional light.

One of the earliest surviving iron and glass façades dates from 1863, when Holmes & Son, engineers and agricultural machinery manufacturers, erected their new suite of showrooms on Cattle Market Street in Norwich (pl. 130). The glazing is divided into tall, narrow panels by tapering mullions with fillets that expand to form shaped bases and capitals. This has always been the only source of natural light for the shallow showrooms: there

are no other windows, and no roof lights. Perhaps the finest surviving all-glass front belongs to the furniture dealers Arighi, Bianchi & Co., who have occupied the converted Commercial Road Silk Mill in Macclesfield, Cheshire, since about 1883. Initially, a cast-iron façade was erected in front of the three-storey mill, on the site of the present-day car park, but in 1892 a four-storey extension was built on the right-hand side of the mill, dwarfing it.[29] The façade of that building (pl. 131), which still stands today, is divided into three bays by brick piers, between

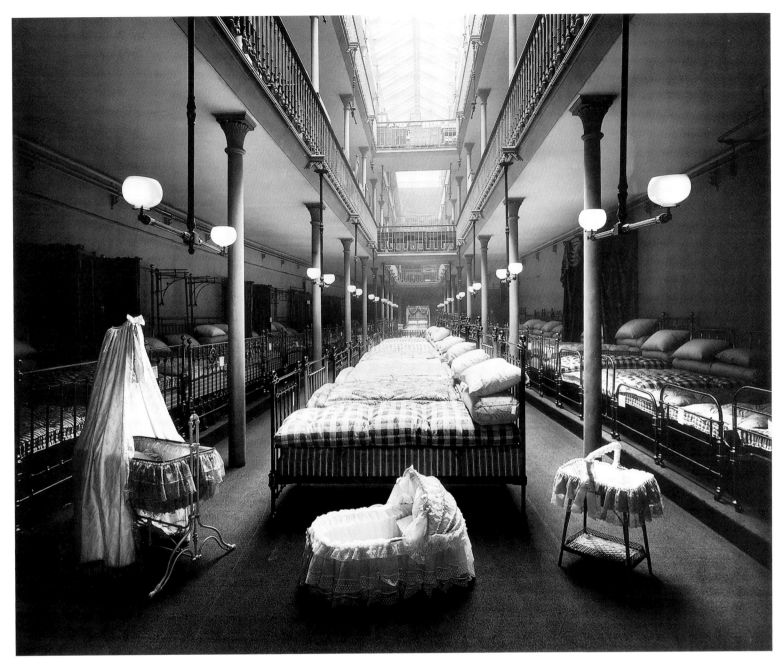

129 Behind the street range Heal's new premises comprised a series of top-lit galleries. Despite rebuilding in the twentieth century, a fragment of one gallery survives inside the present-day store. This photograph was taken by Bedford Lemere in 1896.

which are glazed arcaded panels of cast iron with openwork spandrels that matched the ironwork of *circa* 1883. The unusually deep interior contains a simple well which rises through four floors.

Several glass-fronted furniture stores were built in high street locations where, in contrast to Holmes & Son or Arighi, Bianchi & Co., they were hemmed in by more conventional buildings. These stores included 4–5 Feasegate, York (pl. 132), designed by W. Brown for the cabinetmakers Wilkinson, Brown & Agar in

1884–5, with ironwork by Thomlinson-Walker of York.[30] The much later frontage of Birchall & Son's ironmongery at 40 High Street, Whitchurch (Shropshire), was manufactured by Walter Macfarlane's Saracen foundry in Glasgow in 1904. While ironmongeries died out – or were transformed into general hardware stores – furniture stores with glass façades continued to be erected in the twentieth century. No English store, however, attempted to compete with the iron and glass art nouveau façades of prominent Continental department stores such as

130   Because of its glass façade, the showroom building of Holmes & Son in Norwich (1863) is dubbed 'Crystal House'.

Hermann Tietz in Berlin (1898), Jelmoli in Zurich (1899), Innovation in Brussels (1901) or Samaritaine Magasin 2 in Paris (1905).

London Drapery Stores, circa 1850–1900

The vast majority of London drapers eschewed light wells and highly glazed façades until the 1890s. Their conservative approach is often explained in terms of the London Building Acts, which had limited the size of compartments within ware-house buildings to 216,000 cubic feet (6,112.8 cu. m) since 1855.[31] But these Acts had not prevented the construction of the London Crystal Palace Bazaar or Heal's, and a much more significant factor must have been the tradition of housing staff and workshops above the shop: bazaar proprietors did not have to worry about accommodating these secondary functions, as the traders lived in their own homes and were responsible for the acquisition and storage of their own goods. Similarly, Heal's cabinetmaking workshops and staff accommodation lay behind, rather than above, the store, while provincial cabinetmakers and ironmongers did not, as a rule, live in.

for 150 years. Older English cities retained even more complex patterns of occupation, with narrow medieval plots, and even the new industrial cities had, at their hearts, old market towns with an inheritance of small plots in multiple ownership. Other than by the painstaking acquisition of contiguous properties, ambitious retailers could contemplate building a new store only by cooperating with a municipal improvement scheme. And even if a suitable site could be obtained, building a store was an expensive undertaking, usually funded out of profits. It was only in the late 1880s that owners began to raise capital for reconstruc-

131   Arighi, Bianchi & Co.'s furniture store on the outskirts of Macclesfield, Cheshire, has one of the best preserved cast-iron façades of the Victorian period. It was erected in 1892.

132   A typical high street furniture store of 1884–5 at 4–5 Feasegate, York.

Moreover, an exhibition-hall style building, designed to enhance interior display and invite customers to wander about – Emile Zola's image of the cathedral of consumption – did not suit the sales techniques that prevailed in English drapers' shops, techniques that subordinated the seductive potential of display to the persuasive skills of sales assistants. Into the first quarter of the twentieth century, English shoppers continued to be apprehended by shopwalkers, and seated in bentwood chairs at counters where they were attended by well dressed assistants.[32] They were even escorted ceremoniously from department to department, much to the annoyance of Continental and American visitors, who wished to walk freely around stores.[33] This ritual lingered even longer in the provinces: as late as 1930, W. Eaden Lilley's of Cambridge found it necessary to announce that customers could walk around the store, with no obligation to make a purchase, 'as obtains in the large London stores'.[34] With such ingrained formality, it is no wonder that drapers turned up their noses at the models presented by the galleried bazaar and the glass-fronted furniture emporium.

Until the 1890s, few London drapers were actually in a position to build a spacious, new store, whatever its form. It was extremely difficult to acquire a large site in a desirable location. The opportunities presented by Baron Haussmann's new street layout in Paris, by the colonisation of virgin terrain in Manhattan or by fire in Chicago, simply did not arise in central London, where the form of the West End had been established

tion by forming limited companies. Before then, the public showed little appetite for retail investment.

Under the circumstances, it was common for businesses to spread through an agglomeration of old buildings. The best surviving example of this in central London is Asprey's jewellery shop on New Bond Street. Although not a drapery establishment, and strictly speaking not even a store, the size and rambling character of Asprey's premises illustrates the developmental process through which many ambitious retail businesses passed in the second half of the nineteenth century. After moving to 166 New Bond Street in 1847, it expanded into no fewer than eight adjoining properties, rising to mezzanine or first-floor level only in three of these. Externally, the result is a cluster of buildings of different styles and dates, only partially united by the New Bond Street shopfront. Inside, the floor levels are uneven. Typically, some load-bearing walls have been stripped out of the main sales area and the weight of the upper floors is carried by slender iron columns. The centre of the shop, occupying an area that was originally a backyard, is lit by a glass rooflight. No large drapery premises of this type survived the twentieth century without rebuilding, but smaller drapers' shops in provincial towns can still convey an idea of their character (see pl. 73).

In the meantime, several vast iron and glass stores with picturesque names were being erected in Paris, such as the Ville de Saint Denis, Coin de la Rue, Belle Jardinière, Paix, Tapis Rouge and, most famous of all, the Bon Marché. Contrasting with these was the ultra-conservative new store erected on Conduit Street, Mayfair, in 1866 by the silk mercers Lewis & Allenby. Designed by James Murray, the building was nine bays long and five storeys high, with a ground-floor sales-room and four storeys of staff accommodation.[35] The layout, with its small proportion of public space, simply imitated the configuration of non-purpose-built stores, as did that of the drapery establishment of J. Alderson & Co. on Westminster Bridge Road, also built in 1866.[36] By the mid-1870s, however, the first generation of *grands magasins* was known to London retailers, and their influence could be perceived to a limited degree in the building erected by another firm of silk mercers, Marshall & Snelgrove, on Oxford Street in 1875–8.[37] At the time, this was the most ambitious drapery emporium ever erected in the capital, and probably the first to occupy the full width of a block, which had been acquired over a twenty-year period. It was profit from silks purchased at Lyons during the Franco-Prussian War that eventually supplied the necessary capital for a new building.[38] Perhaps in homage to that French expedition, or in acknowledgement of the new Parisian stores, a French Renaissance style was adopted, with pavilion roofs and classical detailing (pl. 134). Inside, in typical English fashion, retailing was restricted to the ground floor. The counting-house was in the basement, the warehouse and wholesale business on the first floor, and accommodation for 250 staff

on the three upper floors. Two floors – probably the ground and first floors – were of 'fireproof construction' with riveted wrought-iron girders and rolled-iron joists carried on cast-iron columns, all encased in concrete. From 1880 the store even had its own fire brigade.

While Marshall & Snelgrove's prestigious new premises were being built, James Smith of Tooting was creating what has been hailed as the first purpose-built department store in London, the Bon Marché on Brixton Road (pls 134–5), with money won on Newmarket racecourse.[39] According to *The Builder* it was being 'erected and internally arranged on the principles of some similar establishments in Paris'.[40] The most famous of these was Aristide Boucicault's Bon Marché, which was built between 1872 and 1887 and quickly became a byword for department stores throughout the western world.[41] Like bazaars, the Bon Marché was a place of entertainment: concerts were held on the ground floor, and there were a reading room and an exhibition hall on the second floor. Billed as 'one of the sights of Paris', in 1872 it was even possible to take a guided tour of the building, with peeks behind the scenes.

The Bon Marché of James Smith could not compete with that of Aristide Boucicault. Externally, its appearance was still thoroughly domestic, and internally there was no great gallery or spectacular glass roof.[42] Nevertheless, the interior introduced some important innovations, particularly in its vertical separation of sales areas and staff accommodation, and in the open plan of the showrooms, with departments flowing into one another without the intervention of walls or partitions, other than those created by fixtures and fittings.[43] The front block on Brixton Road accommodated sales departments on four floors, including the basement, with the mail-order department and other offices situated to the rear at ground level. The first floor was reached via a grand staircase that projected from the back of the building and was lit by a stained-glass window. The two-storeyed rear range along Ferndale Road housed sales departments on the ground floor, and carried a mansard roof containing a huge water tank. Staff accommodation was concentrated in a five-storeyed domestic block to the rear of the store, and included separate dining rooms for male and female employees, day rooms, visitors' rooms, a library, a billiard room, managers' apartments and more than fifty bedrooms.[44]

The exact arrangement of the sales departments in Smith's Bon Marché remains unclear. In 1876 *The Builder* announced that the ground floor would be devoted to food, with a meat market at the front and a fruit and vegetable market to the rear.[45] When the store opened in April 1877, *The Builder* merely noted that the establishment sold 'almost every imaginable article in food, furniture, and dress'.[46] By 1885, however, food was no longer sold.[47] Around 1888, when a eulogistic account of the Bon Marché featured in *Modern London*, it boasted a total of

133   In 1888 Marshall & Snelgrove's Oxford Street store was described in *Modern London* as 'the most perfectly equipped and arranged establishment of its kind in London'; at that time it accommodated 700 of the firm's 2,000 staff. This photograph was taken by Bedford Lemere in 1909.

thirty-one departments, including men's outfitting, cycles and toys in the basement, drapery and fancy goods on the ground floor, costumes and mantles on the first floor and furniture on the second floor.[48] One of the departments on Ferndale Road, where the original display windows and entrance survive to this day, was the Auction and Estates Department, which specialised in furniture removals, house decoration, sanitary engineering, general plumbing, house repairing 'and even, if necessary, house building'.

The opening of Smith's Bon Marché seems to have encouraged London retailers to diversify more than ever beyond traditional trade boundaries. Diversification was stimulated by mass production, extensive urbanisation and improvements in trans-portation, which facilitated the movement of both goods and people. For large stores to succeed, however, location was paramount. Those in the West End (pl. 159) were concentrated around Oxford Street and Regent Street, which became increasingly accessible from the burgeoning suburbs with the building of the underground railway. The largest West End stores included Marshall & Snelgrove, Dickins & Jones, Peter Robinson, Swan & Edgar, Debenham & Freebody, Fenwick, Liberty, D. H. Evans and John Lewis, all of which were affiliated with the drapery trade. In addition to Marshall & Snelgrove, the only ones to indulge in major building work before the twentieth century were Debenham & Freebody (*c.*1883), John Lewis (*c.*1890) and Peter Robinson (1890–1).[49] Many of the largest purpose-built

West End stores of the 1880s and 1890s belonged to specialist retailers, such as Henry Heath, a hatter on Oxford Street (1887), and Thomas Goode, a china and glass dealer on South Audley Street (1875–6; 1889–90, pl. 49). The West End, however, did not have a monopoly on large-scale retailing in the capital.

Gamage's ('The People's Popular Emporium') on High Holborn was one of the few stores that grew to large proportions in the City, which had steadily lost ground to the West End. It catered for men as well as women, owing to its location, and concentrated on toys and sports. The City was also the birthplace of the middle-class co-operative, a type of store established for specific professional groups at a time when there was considerable outrage at the high prices charged by tradesmen.[50] Of the many societies that existed before 1890, only three enjoyed durable success.[51] The first of these, the Post Office Supply Association, was set up in 1865 by a group of clerks at the General Post Office, but membership was soon extended to all civil servants, and the name was changed to the Civil Service Supply Association (CSSA). Premises were taken on Queen Victoria Street and the Strand. A rival society, the Civil Service Co-operative Society Ltd (CSCS) was founded on Haymarket in 1866. Initially, these stores sold mainly groceries, with affiliated traders supplying members with other categories of goods, but, like working-class societies (see Chapter 8), they soon opened their own non-food departments. In the early days, store interiors were austere. Customers filled departmental invoices with their requirements, added prices from a list, then paid their bill at the cashier's desk. They then had to wait at a counter while their order was assembled.[52] In 1868 The Builder reported that even peeresses had been seen at the CSCS store, 'making out their own invoices, and taking away their own parcels'.[53]

More successful than the civil service societies was the Army & Navy Co-operative Society Ltd, which was established in 1871 for the benefit of officers of the army and navy, and their families. The store occupied part of Vickers' distillery on Victoria Street, a Gothic-style building that looked nothing like any other emporium, as it lacked display windows of any kind until 1922.[54] Indeed, its interior is said to have resembled a club.[55] Like working-class co-ops, the Army & Navy undertook a great deal of manufacturing, and opened numerous branches, both overseas and in service towns. Various offshoots were created: the Junior Army & Navy Stores was established in 1879 in York House on Waterloo Place – another building without show windows – and the Army & Navy Auxiliary Co-operative Supply Ltd opened on Victoria Street in 1880. Like the CSCS, the Army & Navy came to resemble other middle- and upper-class emporia, eventually discarding its co-operative trappings and becoming part of the House of Fraser group (see Chapter 9).

Middle-class co-operation was undoubtedly an innovative and influential form of retailing, with stores that, although of limited architectural interest, have been described with some justification as 'the first major department stores in England'.[56] Certainly, as early as 1870, the CSSA sold 'anything from a blotting-pad to a bicycle or a billiard table – from ginger beer to carte blanche champagne'.[57] That was before the Brixton Bon Marché was even conceived, and before William Whiteley became the 'Universal Provider'.

Whiteley was the most successful shopkeeper of his generation to set up in one of London's fashionable inner suburbs, in his case Bayswater. As the city expanded, and outlying areas were connected by the metropolitan railway, several secondary shopping centres developed. Brixton, where Smith built his Bon Marché, never managed to compete with Kensington High Street or Brompton Road, but Clapham, Edgware Road, Holloway, Lewisham, Stratford and Streatham all sustained large stores (Arding & Hobbs, D. B. Johnstone's, Jones Brothers, Chiesman's, Robert's and Pratts, respectively). The major suburban shopping centre remained a London phenomenon.

Whiteley's shop grew piecemeal, rather than being formed outright like the Bon Marché. It began as a ribbon and fancy goods shop, which opened at 31 Westbourne Grove in 1863. At that time the street was nicknamed 'Bankruptcy-avenue', but its fortunes were about to change thanks to the opening of the nearby Bishop's Road underground station, and it soon became known as 'the Bond Street of the West'.[58] In this choice location, Whiteley's emporium grew by accretion at an astonishing rate. By 1867 he had become a general draper with seventeen separate departments, and he began to snap up any shop that became available within the terrace lining the south side of the street. Soon he was opening men's departments, such as tailoring, boots and hats, but the crucial step was taken in 1872 when he began to sell goods and offer services that went well beyond the scope of the traditional draper. These included an estate agency, an ironmongery, a hairdressing salon and, to howls of protest, a butcher's shop. By the time Smith opened his Bon Marché in Brixton, the unpopular Whiteley could justifiably style himself the 'Universal Provider', selling everything from a pin to an elephant, or as The Builder put it, 'from a wife to a box of matches, a babinette to a hearse'.[59] There was one crucial difference, however, between the two establishments. While

134 (facing page top) To all intents and purposes, the Bon Marché in Brixton (1876–7, by H. Parsons & W. H. Rawlings) was the first purpose-built department store in the U.K. It closed about 1975 and the building now houses a pub and offices.

135 (facing page bottom) This view of the ground floor of the Brixton Bon Marché probably exaggerates its height, but illustrates how the departments flowed into one another rather than being constructed as individual shops. From Modern London, c.1888, 141.

GROUND FLOOR PLAN

136 This layout plan of Whiteley's in Bayswater, London, has been redrawn from a diagram that fronted the store's catalogue. It reveals how the premises were still divided into small shops, in contrast to the openplan Brixton Bon Marché. Redrawn from Whiteley's catalogue of 1885, City of Westminster Archives Centre 726/14.

Smith had built a modern emporium, Whiteley's empire remained little more than a string of separate shops (pl. 136), with doorways knocked through party walls to create somewhat tortuous circulation routes for customers. Various salons had been built over gardens to the rear, and staff dining halls were set up in basements.[60] The shops had to be rebuilt on several occasions in the 1880s, following a spate of suspicious fires, and with each rebuilding they were modernised and improved. The most notable additions were perhaps the dormitory block for 300–400 men and the block of thirteen shops, which were both erected on Queen's Road (now Queensway) in 1881.[61] The store, however, was not comprehensively rebuilt on a centralised plan until after Whiteley's dramatic demise in 1907, at the hands of a gunman claiming to be his illegitimate son (see p. 167).[62]

In 1870 one of Whiteley's silk buyers, John Barker, left to establish his own business on Kensington High Street, occupying two shops that had been built under the Kensington Improvement Scheme of 1868–70, not far from the recently opened underground railway station.[63] By 1894 Barker's premises were dispersed throughout thirty-three separate shops, the most interesting of which was the furniture shop erected on the corner of Kensington High Street and Young Street in 1885–7.[64] That building was differentiated from the rest of Barker's property by having continuous plate-glass windows at both ground- and first-floor levels, giving the impression that the staff accommodation, with its conventional fenestration, was floating in the air. Arding & Hobbs adopted a similar design for its new store at Clapham Junction in 1885. That elevational treatment (see pl. 171) remained popular with drapers right up to the First World War, although it was severely criticised in the architectural press. Two of Barker's main competitors on Kensington

High Street were Derry & Toms (est. 1870) and Ponting's (est. 1873), which both spread into neighbouring properties as they added new departments throughout the 1870s, 1880s and 1890s.

Brompton Road and Knightsbridge became a flourishing shopping thoroughfare in the final quarter of the nineteenth century. This was fortunate for Charles Henry Harrod, a wholesale grocer and tea dealer from the East End, who had taken over a grocery shop on Brompton Road in 1853. The business expanded and diversified in the 1860s and 1870s, in the hands of his son, Charles Digby Harrod, who combined co-operative prices with a superior level of customer services.[65] By the early 1880s Harrod's Stores was approaching department store status, although it still lacked the crucial drapery and outfitting departments. After a fire in December 1883, a new building (pl. 137) was designed by Alfred Williams, the assistant district surveyor of Kensington. The exterior remained unpretentious, with a single-storey projection on the frontage, on the site of Brompton Road's original front gardens. The food departments, still the mainstay of the business, were arranged around a circular counter in the centre of the ground floor, and a broad staircase led up to a wide variety of other departments on the first, second and third floors.[66] This vertical development of sales floors was possible because Harrod's staff did not live in. After the business went public in 1889, it mushroomed in the hands of Richard Burbidge, an ex-employee of the Army & Navy Stores and Whiteley's, who became Harrods' managing director in 1891. It was he who undertook the task of building the enormous present-day store, beginning on Basil Street and Hans Crescent in the mid-1890s, and moving round to Brompton Road in the early 1900s (see pl. 164).[67] From the start, in 1894, the upper floors of the new building contained flats. Another London

137 Harrod opened his grocer's shop at 105 Brompton Road in 1853 and spread into 101–103 in 1879. The premises (i.e. the block with six windows at third-floor level) had to be rebuilt in 1884 after a fire. This photograph was taken about 1900, just before the main frontage was rebuilt.

grocer, Morel Brothers, Cobbett & Sons Ltd, had done something very similar on Piccadilly a few years earlier (pls 79 and 181) and the idea was taken up by several other retailers in later years. Between 1902 and 1905, for example, Barker's adopted this format for its new furnishings store on the north side of Kensington High Street.[68] Barker's architect, Philip E. Pilditch, is said to have consulted Richard Burbidge, and even visited Paris to study apartment blocks.[69] But Knightsbridge and Kensington were rare in being fashionable residential neighbourhoods where exclusive mansion blocks could exist cheek by jowl with commerce.[70]

Several stores in Knightsbridge and Kensington began to rebuild in earnest in the 1890s, with some new structures, such as Woolland's (1896–1900; Henry L. Florence), incorporating structural steel.[71] Despite the constraints imposed by the London Building Acts, most of these stores had two sales floors pierced by modestly sized light wells surrounded by galleries, their balustrades often draped artistically with shawls, rugs or carpets. Galleries existed in Harvey Nichols (1889–94; Charles William Stephens), Peter Jones (1889–90; Perry & Reed), Ponting's (1899–901; Arthur Sykes), Derry & Toms (1901; F. E. Williams) and the front range of Harrods (1900–5; Charles William Stephens).[72] They were smaller and less dramatic than the central halls of contemporary French and Scottish stores (e.g. Printemps, or Wylie & Lochhead's new building of 1885), and while it is tempting to suggest that this resulted from the continuation of living-in on the upper floors of English drapery establishments, it is worth noting that Jenner's in Edinburgh, the only Scottish store with live-in staff, had a vast central hall, while Harrods, whose staff never lived in, was highly compartmentalised. Living-in remained common despite protests by reformers who con-

sidered it exploitative. Although some firms, such as Woolland's, now accommodated staff in outside houses, the upper floors of Ponting's new building had bedrooms for 120 assistants and in 1900 the new John Barnes store at Swiss Cottage opened with beds for no less than 400 members of staff.

They may have lacked magnificent vistas, but London store interiors at the end of the century could be extremely opulent, with a heavy emphasis on customer comfort, including passenger lifts. Although Burbidge of Harrods disapproved of lifts, his customers enjoyed a futuristic experience in 1898, when England's first escalator was installed in the store. That contraption (pl. 138) had a continuous flat belt rather than steps, and was manufactured by a French company, Piat & ses Fils.[73] An assistant stood at the top with smelling salts and cognac in case 'travellers' were upset by their new experience.[74] As it turned out, escalator technology did not become sufficiently cheap, silent or efficient for general usage until the 1930s (see p. 179).

As the century drew to a close, large stores gradually switched from gas to electric lighting. In Glasgow, three different types of electric lighting were installed in the Colosseum in 1882, and in London, Liberty's 'Eastern Bazaar' was lit by electricity in 1884.[75] In Manchester, Paulden's bought the electric lighting equipment from the Jubilee Exhibition of 1887, and used it in their popular store.[76] Jones Brothers' store extension in Holloway, built in 1892, was lit throughout with electric arc lamps, as was Peter Robinson's at Oxford Circus, which, in 1896, offered a 'dark room' where customers could inspect the effect made by either electric or gas lighting on various materials.[77] One year later Peter Robinson's became one of the first great London stores to introduce yet another technological advance: a motor parcels van.[78]

138 Having seen an escalator in a Paris store (Les Magasins du Louvre), Harrods' general manager, Richard Burbidge, installed England's first moving staircase in the grocery department in 1898.

Although improved cash registers were available, many stores now installed overhead cash-ball railways, wire-line carriers or pneumatic tube systems, which connected the individual sales counters with a central cashiers' office (see pls 75 and 150).[79] These mechanisms were developed in America in the 1870s and 1880s, and were thought more secure than cash registers. One of the first London stores to install an overhead system was the Bon Marché in Brixton, which had a cash railway by 1888.[80] In Britain, the most popular systems were probably Lamson's pneumatic tubes and their 'Rapid' wire-line carrier; the latter continued to be sold into the 1950s but was eventually displaced by cash registers.[81]

In recent years, Victorian and Edwardian department stores, especially in London, have been viewed as a significant factor in the emancipation of women, although it can also be argued that they prospered as a consequence of female freedom. The success of department stores was certainly helped by the fact that, by mid-century, respectable women could frequent the West End unchaperoned. Despite this, some (male) social commentators complained that large stores actually fostered female immorality, not just by encouraging them to spend their fathers' or hus-

bands' money, but by bringing respectable women into contact with their more disreputable sisters. Setting aside the moral rhetoric, which contained a strong element of self-interest, the most tangible contribution made by department stores to female emancipation was the provision of refreshment rooms, writing rooms, rest rooms and other services. These had been provided in bazaars, and so it is strange that when Whiteley opened a refreshment room in 1872 it was denounced in *The Graphic* as 'dangerous in the highest degree', as if it was something quite new and threatening.[82] Such articles spoke of the female shopper as if she were a child who required constant supervision. According to *The Graphic*, the opportunity to relieve her fatigue would prolong the shopper's spending spree, while the chance to imbibe wine might cause her male companions to lower their guard and condone rash purchasing. In spite of the controversy surrounding Whiteley's restaurant, other stores soon followed his example. The highly respectable Army & Navy Stores, for example, opened a tearoom in 1877. At the end of the century, there was a fashion for decorating tearooms in Moorish style (pl. 139), a trend that may have started when Arthur Liberty opened his 'Arab' tearoom on the first floor of Chesham House, one of his Regent Street shops, in the mid-1880s.

The peripheral activities undertaken by big stores in the late nineteenth century should not be forgotten. While most kept their costs low by buying in bulk from wholesalers, or even developing separate wholesale businesses, others bought direct from manufacturers or – like co-operative societies – entered the manufacturing process themselves. That usually involved dressmaking, tailoring, upholstering or cabinetmaking, activities that could be housed on the premises or in a nearby building, although there was a growing tendency to establish separate manufacturing plants in cheaper locations. More unusually, Whiteley owned farms and a jam-making factory. Mail order and home delivery services depended on large warehouses, despatch departments and stabling; from the late 1880s stores also accommodated telephone ordering services, and the Army & Navy Stores was even printing and binding its catalogues in its own workshops. In this way, large-scale retailing had a significant impact on the environment far beyond the confines of the high street.

Provincial Drapery Stores, circa 1850–1900

From the middle of the nineteenth century the largest provincial stores were established in industrial and manufacturing centres with burgeoning middle-class populations. Initially, few of these stores tried to appeal to the working classes. Labourers and their families still had limited spending power, although skilled workers were now buying many goods from co-

139   This Moorish-style tearoom occupied the fourth floor that was added to the corner of Derry & Toms' building at 99–101 Kensington High Street, London, in 1892.

operative stores, rather than from markets and pedlars. The gentry and aristocracy in the counties seem to have patronised the great London stores, which they visited during the season, taking advantage of their increasingly efficient mail order services for the remainder of the year. As a result, few attempts were made to emulate the magnificence of London's top drapery establishments.

One of the most prosperous cities of the day was Liverpool where, in 1865–7, Compton House (pl. 140) was erected on

Church Street for the drapery establishment of J. & W. Jeffery & Co. The building replaced premises that had grown by accretion since 1832, but were destroyed by fire in 1865.[83] Even as the new store was rising from the ashes, the young assistant who started the blaze was being sentenced to ten years imprisonment at Liverpool Assizes. Like its London contemporary, Lewis & Allenby's, the new building had an extensive ground-floor shop and upper-floor staff accommodation, but as an architectural conception it was much more ostentatious. It sported a mansard

140 When it first opened, Compton House in Liverpool (1865–7) was one of the largest purpose-built stores in the country. The main occupier is now Marks & Spencer. Beyond Compton House, on the extreme left, is a building erected by H. Samuel, the jewellers, in the 1960s.

roof and two corner towers, inviting comparison with the Magasins Réunis of 1865–7 in Paris.[84] Indeed, this was one of the first signs that English drapers might be looking across the Channel for influence. The capital outlay on the construction of Jeffery's (£150,000) seems to have proved too much for the business, which closed in 1872. The building was then converted into a hotel, with a row of shops on the ground floor. It later became a furniture store, and its main occupant is now Marks & Spencer.

Liverpool is also significant as the city that gave birth to the first English department store chain, Lewis's, which originated in 1856 when David Lewis, the son of a Jewish London merchant, opened a men's outfitters shop on Ranelagh Street. Lewis had served his apprenticeship in the local branch of Hyam & Co., one of the first tailoring chains in the country. He opened his first branch on Basnett Street in Liverpool in 1859, but his original Ranelagh Street store proved the more successful, gradually consuming its neighbours, and eventually being rebuilt after a fire in 1886.[85] Lewis's first venture outside Liverpool, the Manchester store of 1877, was built as a men's outfitters along the lines of Hyam's, but quickly evolved into a department store, with French-style extensions erected in 1879 (pl. 123) and 1885.[86] The latter was topped by a tower with a clock and the motto

'Use Time Wisely'. In contrast, the Birmingham store of 1885 was conceived as a department store from the start.[87] It was stocked with every imaginable item of female clothing and offered a second-floor refreshment buffet.[88] A hydraulic passenger lift 'in the shape of an ornamental cage, richly upholstered' served the first and second floors, augmenting the double staircase.[89] Like Lewis's other stores, the roof carried a mast festooned with flags, and at the top was a revolving electric light, a symbol of modernity. David Lewis had become the first department store owner to follow the multiple route: when Marshall & Snelgrove had opened seasonal branches in Scarborough and Harrogate in the 1840s, and when Clark & Debenham had opened branches in Cheltenham (1823) and Harrogate (1843), these firms had traded as drapers, not department stores.[90] They had chastely announced their arrival in local newspapers, while Lewis trumpeted his new stores by the most flamboyant means at his disposal, such as the release of balloons with attached lists of merchandise. Moreover, Lewis's stores occupied purpose-built premises, and sold cheap goods to the lower middle classes, eventually using techniques such as self-selection.

Lewis's main rival in Liverpool was George Henry Lee, whose store grew steadily on a site next to Compton House. In Manchester, Kendal, Milne & Co. were flourishing: they had dropped the title 'bazaar', developed a strong trade in drapery and furniture, and proudly advertised themselves as 'agents for Pollock & Schmidt's sewing machines, and for the patent metallic sanitary coffins'.[91] A rather conventional new store was built in 1872–3, by E. J. Thompson, as part of the Deansgate improvement scheme. In Birmingham, Lewis faced competition from Holliday, Son & Co. in Warwick House (see above, p. 126), and from Rackham & Matthews on Temple Row. Meanwhile, Bainbridge's supremacy in Newcastle was being challenged by J. J. Fenwick, who established an upmarket draper's shop on Northumberland Street in 1882, and opened a London branch – something that gave him tremendous cachet – in 1891. The people of Leeds seem to have preferred shopping in arcades, but Sheffield had a number of sizeable drapers, including Cole Brothers, T. B. & W. Cockayne, and John Walsh, whose premises were rebuilt as part of a street improvement scheme between 1896 and 1899.[92] In Bradford, a fine new drapery establishment was erected for Illingworth, Son & Co. in 1868. It adopted a French Renaissance style and had a circular well, 45 feet (13.7 m) high, with an office on the mezzanine floor.[93] A few years later, in 1871, Brown & Muff rebuilt their extensive Bradford premises as part of an improvement scheme, but had to remodel them again in 1878 after a fire.

Large drapery establishments in traditional county and market towns tended to have a different character from those in industrial cities. Genteel stores such as Brown's in Chester depended much more on personal connections, and were slower to adopt modern retail methods and diversify their stock. Their customers, who tended to belong to the gentry or to prosperous farming communities, expected to be treated quite differently from the bourgeoisie of Manchester or Liverpool. Different yet again were the stores set up in seaside towns to capture the transient holiday trade, such as Beale's in Bournemouth and Bobby's in Margate. Few small-town drapers erected new buildings before the 1890s, unless enabled to do so by improvement schemes or, more frequently, fire.

Tragically, most store fires occurred at Christmas, when they were bursting at the seams with extra stock. At Christmas 1884, for example, Jermyn & Perry's, a draper's shop on King's Lynn High Street, burned down when an assistant set fire to the cotton-wool decorations.[94] The store was quickly rebuilt, together with its neighbour, Jermyn & Sons, a furniture and upholstery warehouse. The contrast between these two buildings (pl. 141) is instructive. The furniture store had very large plate-glass windows on both floors and looked decidedly utilitarian alongside Jermyn & Perry's, now titled the Victoria Phoenix Bon Marché, which had much smaller first-floor windows, in ornate surrounds, and a fancy parapet topped by urns. This new building did not last long, as on Boxing Day morning, 1897, an assistant in Jermyn & Perry's started another fire whilst lighting the store's 220 gas jets, reducing the premises – and those of the Lynn Drapery Emporium across the road – to rubble. A new building designed by Herbert J. Green provided a more unified frontage to the High Street, while allowing the furniture store large windows along its side elevation on Victoria Parade.[95]

Inside Jermyn & Sons, a line of very plain iron columns ran down the centre of each showroom, carrying floors fitted with basic tongue-and-groove ceilings. These were typical Victorian furniture showrooms, relying on extensive windows that formed, to all intents and purposes, a glass wall along one side. The interior of Jermyn & Perry, on the other hand, contained a huge top-lit well, surrounded by a decorative cast-iron gallery with fluted columns and openwork spandrels. Three smaller octagonal wells pierced the southern section of the store, and a gracious showroom – sensibly fitted with sliding fire doors – ran along the front. Although buried under the trappings of the modern store, now Debenhams, this interior survives remarkably intact. Neither Jermyn & Sons nor Jermyn & Perry accommodated staff: very wise, considering their history.

By the end of the 1890s many shops and stores incorporated steel girders, or even full steel frames. In 1928, 1929 and 1930

141   The differences between Victorian furniture and drapery stores are amply illustrated by this engraving of Jermyn & Sons' and Jermyn & Perry's premises in King's Lynn, Norfolk, which were both rebuilt following a fire in 1884. Typically, the roof of Jermyn & Perry's shop adds a French touch. King's Lynn Library.

W. Basil Scott of the engineering firm Redpath, Brown & Co. made various claims that he had designed the frame of a furniture warehouse in either West Hartlepool or Stockton-on-Tees, in either 1896 or 1898.[96] That was, to the best of his knowledge, the first English steel-skeleton building. Although the building in question is frequently identified as 'Robinson's Emporium' in West Hartlepool,[97] it is much more likely to have been Mathias Robinson's branch store in Stockton-on-Tees, known as the Coliseum. At this date none of Robinson's West Hartlepool buildings had a steel frame, and Robinson's first store in Stockton-on-Tees, built in 1896, combined steel girders with cast-iron columns.[98] After it was destroyed by fire in December 1899, Barnes & Coates of Sunderland designed a new building with a steel skeleton clearly expressed in the three broad bays of the main façade.[99] Like Jermyn's of King's Lynn, it survives as a branch of the Debenhams department store chain. At the beginning of the new century, such buildings held the promise of expansive, well-lit interiors, unencumbered by a forest of structural supports, and offering greater resistance to fire than their Victorian predecessors.

A "VITROLITE" SCHEME IN
TANGO EGGSHELL AND BLACK

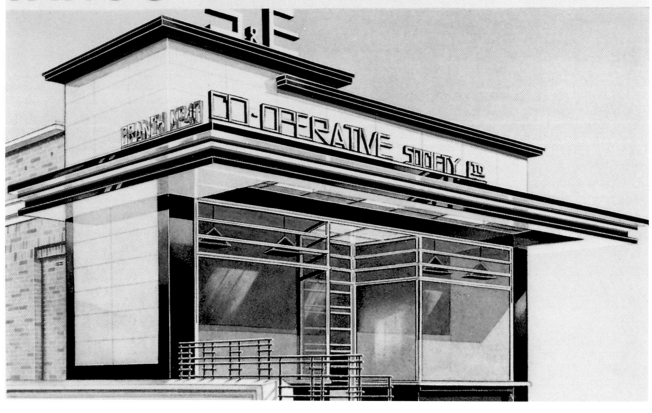

142   An advertisement of 1936 for The British Vitrolite Company, illustrating the Midhill branch of the Sheffield and Ecclesall Co-operative Society. From *Architectural Review*, July 1936, xxv.

8

From the Cradle to the Grave:
Co-operative Stores

THERE IS LITTLE TO DISTINGUISH the present-day co-op from other shops, but it was not always thus. For many years, co-operative stores developed as strings of shops on the ground floors of buildings that were designed to accommodate a wide range of co-operative activities. These stores have a robust character that is all their own, and they can be distinguished from their contemporaries as much by their peripheral positions and piecemeal construction as by the symbols of manufacture and industry that are emblazoned on their façades. As such they are a highly visible manifestation of the English tradition of utopian socialism, and form a distinct element in the English townscape even though they rarely belong to the architectural avant-garde. The importance of individual co-operative stores must not be assessed simply by comparing them with the independent grocery, drapery and department stores of their age, which will always seem more advanced and more ornate, but by locating them within the context of the co-operative movement and its buildings, both at a local and a national level.

Co-operative retailing thrived from the mid-Victorian period until the 1960s, when it experienced a sharp downturn. Since then its share of the grocery market has dwindled from 25 per cent to 5 per cent,[1] and many small local societies have been subsumed by large regional societies. Efforts have been made to revitalise the co-op, largely by tapping into public sympathy for ethical businesses, and by reviving the 'divi' (see below). If these moves fail, many unprofitable co-op retail outlets may close.

Beginnings

The first experiments in co-operative trading were carried out in the late eighteenth century, but it was the publication of George J. Holyoake's *History of the Rochdale Pioneers* in 1858 that triggered the widespread establishment of co-operative retail societies.[2] The Rochdale Society of Equitable Pioneers had been founded by a group of working men on 15 August 1844, and was inspired by the ideas of the mill-owner and socialist Robert Owen, who has been called the 'Father of Co-operation'.[3] Its key activity was to buy and sell provisions on principles of fair trading,[4] and to divide profits amongst members of the society in direct proportion to how much they spent. This was the co-op dividend, or 'divi'.[5] In subsequent years, numerous co-operative societies were founded on Rochdale principles, predominantly in the industrial towns of the North and Midlands, where new working-class housing was poorly served by independent traders. As well as running shops, these societies engaged in diverse social and educational activities, designed to improve the lot of their members. They built houses, offered mortgages and savings schemes, provided libraries and reading rooms, and entered production by establishing corn mills, abattoirs, bakeries, dairies and farms. Their stores are the most tangible legacy of these varied activities.

The first stores opened by co-operative societies were makeshift arrangements in existing buildings. The Rochdale Society, for example, began business with a capital sum of £28 (raised from the issue of £1 shares), in the ground floor of an adapted late eighteenth-century warehouse at 31 Toad Lane, Rochdale in Lancashire.[6] Only once sufficient capital had been amassed could societies set up small branch stores and build new central premises, which included meeting rooms and reading rooms as well as shops. Goods could be delivered to members by horse and cart from the central stores and principal branches, and if deliveries to a particular area proved popular, a new branch store was established there. Societies thus expanded in ever increasing circles, but without impinging upon one another's territory. In some areas societies encountered considerable opposition (pl. 143), especially from independent retailers, who had hitherto enjoyed trading monopolies, and from the

143   Independent traders tried to discredit the co-operative movement in the early twentieth century, but without much success. This anti-co-operative cartoon dates from about 1910.

landed classes, who regarded co-operators as dangerous revolutionaries.

To ensure a steady supply of reasonably priced goods of acceptable quality, most societies eventually joined the Co-operative Wholesale Society (CWS), which was founded in Manchester in 1863 and began to manufacture goods ten years later.[7] By the end of the century, its holdings included tea plantations in Ceylon, a butter depot in Denmark and British factories producing a wide variety of consumer goods. Its Architects' Department was established in 1897, and regional architects' offices opened in Newcastle in 1903 and in London in 1916. Until the 1920s, it was more common for a retail society to employ a local architect than to engage CWS architects, but that situation changed once societies began to erect modern department stores requiring particular expertise. The CWS eventually became a massive retail society in its own right and must be regarded as the keystone of the co-operative movement.

One of the best ways to understand the development of co-operative stores is to take a close look at those erected by a specific society, and much of the information in this chapter derives from a study of the Lincoln Co-operative Society. Founded by a group of working men as the Lincoln Equitable Co-operative Industrial Society in 1861,[8] it has managed to retain its independence to the present day. Its activities are well documented: three society histories have been published and a complete run of quarterly reports survives.[9] In most respects, Lincoln's experiences mirror those of other retail societies up and down the country, but it is of especial interest because it quickly expanded beyond the boundaries of the city, into its rural hinterland, thus benefiting both industrial and agricultural labourers.

The Early Years of Lincoln Co-operative Society: Central Stores

The first stores of the Lincoln Society were established

in the First Place, to secure *Un-adulterated Food, Goods of Pure Quality and Guaranteed Weight, at the regular Trade Prices*: in the Second Place, *to enable the Working Classes to improve their circumstances and position*, BY ADDING THE LEGITIMATE PROFITS OF TRADE TO THE WAGES OF LABOUR.[10]

The shop was set up in a double-fronted house at 1 Napoleon Place, with a capital of £40. The storekeeper lived rent-free on

144 (*above*) This engraving showing the Central Stores of the Lincoln Co-operative Society was printed in the Society's Quarterly Balance Sheets, and shows the store as it was between 1889 and 1910.

145 The Central Stores of the Lincoln Co-operative Society steadily expanded throughout the late nineteenth and early twentieth centuries. The buildings along Silver Street were redeveloped in the 1960s.

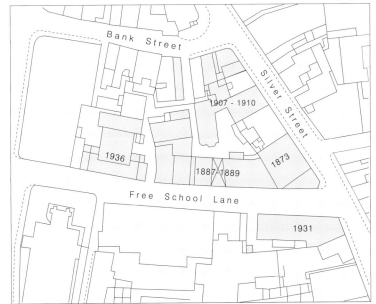

the premises, and opened the shop for the sale of a limited range of non-perishable provisions between 7 a.m. and 8 p.m. Initially, committee members made deliveries in the evenings and at weekends, but before long the Society employed a boy with a handcart, and eventually maintained a fleet of horses and carts.

In 1864 the store moved to 1¾ Waterside South, part of an old riverside warehouse, and arrangements were made for independent traders to sell drapery goods and coal to members. The Society went from strength to strength and, eight years later, purchased a site on the west corner of Silver Street and Free School Lane, to the north-east of Lincoln's main shopping streets. The

146 Ipswich Co-operative Society's Central Stores line one side of Carr Street. The building glimpsed on the far right is the original store of 1886. It is connected to the drapery department of 1908 by a bridge that spans Cox Lane. Beyond that are the furnishings and boot and shoe departments of 1928, and the grocery and tearoom of 1915.

new Gothic-style building of 1873 (pls 144–5), by the local firm of Bellemy & Hardy, accommodated three separate shops: a grocery, a drapery and a boot and shoe shop. This arrangement did not differ hugely from that of contemporary proto-department stores, such as Whiteley's in Bayswater (pl. 136). On the upper floors, however, were business rooms and a hall which could hold 1,200 people, and to the rear was a bakery. Numerous alterations and additions were made to this building throughout the remainder of the nineteenth century, as new departments were added (a penny bank in 1874; patent medicines in 1880; furniture in 1884) and existing departments outgrew their space. Carts had to be washed down in the street until 1881, when stables, a cart shed, a hayloft, a warehouse and workshops were built around an open yard behind the store. When stabling was removed to a separate site in 1885, the old stables were converted into a confectionery bakery. Soon afterwards, in 1887–9, the first of several large extensions was erected, adjoining the original store on Free School Lane. That housed furniture, crockery, tailoring and boot and shoe departments, as well as storerooms, fitting rooms, workshops, a library, reading room and conversation room. Again in a Gothic style, it was designed by F. Smith of Manchester,[11] and was built by a local contractor.[12] A relief depicting a beehive, a favourite co-operative motif, was displayed over the entrance. In 1907–10 a smaller extension was built by the Society's own Building

Department, which had already erected a mill, slaughterhouses and speculative housing for the Society, and had even undertaken projects for private clients.[13] The architect, however, was R. Worcester of the CWS Architects' Department, which had been approached for advice. The building was separated from the original store on Silver Street by the Lincoln General Dispensary,[14] and included a café, offices and a new tailoring department. As in 1889, the opening of this extension inaugurated a period of considerable disruption, as departments were repositioned and revamped within the old building.

By 1914 Lincoln's Central Stores resembled those of successful societies throughout the country. This was not surprising, as societies regularly visited one another's premises and could read of one another's progress in The Co-operative News, a periodical that ran from 1871 and featured illustrated articles about new buildings. Paradoxically, 'central' stores were not sited in the heart of town or city centres, but on the periphery, where property prices were not at a premium yet custom could be attracted. As buildings, their chief characteristics were their phased construction, which reflected the steady commercial progress of the movement, and their division into individual shop units. The oldest premises commonly resembled civic institutions: many were erected in the 1860s and 1870s, when the Gothic style was in vogue, and had turrets, or even towers, topped by finials and weather vanes. Extensions were seldom designed to match original builds, either in terms of materials or style. The resultant strings of buildings adhered to the true spirit of English street architecture, but seemed unsatisfactory to post-1945 generations, which frequently replaced them with monolithic structures (see below). Despite this, some remarkable central stores still stand, for example in Ipswich (pl. 146), which has an uninterrupted run of buildings dating from 1886, 1908, 1915, 1928, 1934 and 1955. While the distinct retail units typical of early stores rarely survive, they can be appreciated at the Beamish Open Air Museum in Co. Durham, where a branch store of the Annfield Plain Industrial Co-operative Society, complete with grocery, drapery and hardware shops, has been reconstructed. It even has an operational Lamson Paragon Cash System, with overhead rails.

The Early Years of Lincoln Co-operative Society: Branch Stores

Co-operatives were not the first retailers to set up shops in working-class residential areas. Large villages had been equipped with independently owned general shops since the seventeenth century, and by the mid-Victorian period many of these combined groceries and provisions with hardware, stationery and a post office, or whatever lines might be in demand locally. Shops

147   The Winn Street/Florence Street branch of the Lincoln Co-operative Society was built in 1900 in an area of housing that had been developed by the Society, providing a ready-made customer base.

selling essentials were also needed in outlying districts of towns and cities that were far removed from central shopping facilities and markets. Strings of small specialised shops lined major through-roads, often in the form of uniform terraces with single-storey, flat-roofed shop projections, occupying what might otherwise have been front gardens. Away from main roads, tracts of terraced housing were laid out with provision for shops on corner sites. These shops usually had a canted corner entrance with a window on either side, and sold a wide variety of goods. The shopkeeper invariably lived over the shop. While co-operative societies sometimes followed that familiar formula, their branch stores were usually designed to be more conspicuous than the average independently owned corner shop.

To supplement its Central Stores, the Lincoln Society soon opened branches throughout the city, keeping pace with the construction of new working-class housing, much of which was erected by the Society itself, to be sold to its members. Eleven city branches, mostly established in converted premises on corner

sites, opened between 1876 and 1897. One or two of these (for example, the Newport branch) were unsuccessful, and closed within a few years. Others, such as Shakespeare Street, continued to operate from terraced houses, at first rented and later purchased, but most were eventually rebuilt with red brick walls, slate roofs and modest shopfronts with central lobbies. The earliest of these, the Bracebridge branch (1879), closely resembled adjacent terraced housing, but displayed the name of the Society prominently on a parapet dominating its salient shopfront. This was the first indication that the Society was keen to distinguish its shops from ordinary corner shops.

Numerous branches were rebuilt after 1898, once the Society's Building Department was up and running. These stores, including Ripon Street (1900), Winn Street (1900; pl. 147) and Burton Road (1901; pl. 148), incorporated terracotta bands displaying the name of the Society, the branch number and, sometimes, the date of construction. Typically, both Ripon Street and Burton Road included two shops (one of which was a butchery), an upper-

manager's house

yard

manure

stable

stores

office

butcher's shop

shop

yard entrance

ground floor

manager's house

granary

hoist

stores

stores

bacon chamber

first floor

148 Co-operative branch stores had similar layouts and often included a house for the manager. This is the Lincoln Society's Burton Road branch of 1901. Based on Lincoln City Council Plan 3341.

staff   customers   goods

0   60 metres

0   200 feet

floor warehouse and a three-bedroom manager's house. In addition, Burton Road had a small stable yard, access to which was through a narrow vehicle entrance. Motor transport did not replace the Society's horse-drawn vehicles until the First World War. Indeed, a central depot for sixty-seven horses was built behind the branch store on Gresham Street as late as 1912, only two years before the animals were requisitioned for the Army and had to be replaced with motor vans.

Lincoln opened its first rural branch in 1878, in the village of Welbourn (population: 500), with a manager and a horse and cart to work the district.[15] By 1900, nine more had opened, including Saxilby (pl. 149), Bardney, Horncastle, Sleaford and Market Rasen. Once again, most began in rented premises, which were eventually purchased and rebuilt. The earliest of these new buildings were designed by private architects (for example, Market Rasen, 1897; W. Mortimer & Son),[16] while later examples were entrusted to the manager of the Society's Building Department (for example, Saxilby, 1907; John G. Hedley).

In layout, rural stores closely resembled urban branches. Both Sleaford and Market Rasen were large enough to have two separate shops: one for groceries and provisions; the other for drapery, boots and shoes. In general, the interiors of co-operative branch stores (pl. 150) seem to have been laid out in a very similar manner to independent shops, and often remained untouched until the 1950s, when they were thoroughly modernised. At least one rural bakery belonging to the Lincoln Society has survived, that added to the Bardney branch in 1897. It is lit by skylights and a ridge lantern, and has brick walls lined with white glazed tiles with a brown border. While rural branches usually hired church or school rooms for meetings, local opposition ensured that no such venue was available to co-operators in Bardney. As a result, in 1888 the committee was obliged to erect a small hall to the rear of the store. In later years that was transformed into a warehouse, augmenting the original upper-floor storeroom. Storage space was particularly generous in these rural stores, which undertook extensive delivery services. At Welbourn (extended 1885), the shop occupied two parallel ranges, above which was a vast storeroom, with a row of cast-iron columns supporting the valley between two open king-post roofs. Goods were loaded through a hatch in the floor over the

vehicle entrance of the front range, and through loading doors in the gable of the older rear range. Air was admitted through a row of cusped triangular roof vents, and by simply opening the windows. Now a light industrial unit, Welbourn appears to be the only rural Lincoln Society store to retain its original shopfront; in Lincoln itself, original shopfronts survive on Monks Road (pl. 151) and Winn Street (pl. 147). All of these are well proportioned, but appropriately plain.

Although few new rural stores were founded by the Lincoln Society in the early twentieth century, many new shops opened in the city. In addition to new branch stores, a couple of colonial meat shops opened in 1908–9,[17] milk shops appeared during the First World War,[18] and, after years of special arrangements with local chemists, the first pharmacies opened in the mid-1920s. Similar steps were taken by many other societies coun-

149 This view of the Lincoln Society's Saxilby branch of 1907 clearly shows the manager's house to the right of the shop.

150 (*below*) This branch co-operative store on Victoria Road, Darlington, was photographed in 1953. At that time it still had its solid Victorian counter, grocery drawers and overhead cash railway.

151   The Lincoln Society's Monks Road branch of 1911 was a typical 'bungalow' store. It still has its original shopfronts (with butchery on the right) although it is no longer occupied by the co-op. Hartley Street, to the left, was built by the Society and named after a co-op official.

trywide. In Lincoln, new branches tended to be established on streets that had been developed by the Building Department, a policy that provided managers with convenient housing in the close vicinity of their shop. As a result, managers' houses were omitted from the plans of new stores. One of the first without a house, the Winn Street branch, was a two-storeyed building, but later stores, such as Gresham Street (1907) and Monks Road (1911), took the form of single-storeyed or 'bungalow', premises, with storage in the roof space, or in a rear range.

   Faded advertisements for Pelaw Polish can still be read on the windows of the Winn Street store, testifying to the fact that

the Lincoln Society was a faithful customer of the CWS. By the early twentieth century, however, the Society produced much of the foodstuffs sold in its own shops. The first step had been the purchase of a mill for barley meal in 1877. Then, in 1884, a large block of buildings on Waterside North was acquired and converted into a corn mill and bakery. The Society's first farm, at North Hykeham, was bought in 1889, and in 1892 slaughter-houses were purchased on Sincil Bank.[19] In addition to selling produce from its own mill, bakery, farms and slaughterhouses, surplus farm goods such as butter and eggs were obtained from rural members for resale in the Society's shops.

Throughout the country, branch architecture of the 1920s and 1930s tended to be conservative. One stunning exception was the Midhill Road branch of the Sheffield and Ecclesall Society (1936; J. W. Blackhurst) (pl. 142). It was stylish in the extreme, with chromium window frames, a cantilevered canopy carrying square, chromium-plated lettering, and an asymmetrically stepped parapet.[20] Unfortunately, this shop, like most of its ilk, has been demolished. Nothing like it was erected by the Lincoln Society, although the two-storeyed Newport Arch grocery store had considerable merit. Designed by the CWS Architects' Department in 1938, it was faced in Ancaster stone and had a steep pantile roof with a ridge turret which ventilated a meeting hall large enough to hold 200 people. Halls were an increasingly common feature of new branch stores,[21] and warehouses in older stores were now frequently hired out to local people for concerts and meetings. This may have been because reduced delivery services meant that the co-op's vast storage facilities were becoming superfluous.

The Age of the Co-operative Emporium

Co-operative central stores experienced an acute problem throughout the late nineteenth and early twentieth centuries: how to fit rapidly expanding departments into the restrictive shop units provided by their buildings. Society quarterly reports reveal a process of constant reshuffling and adaptation, as new departments were created and existing departments, such as boots and shoes, grew beyond expectation. In the 1910s some radical co-operative societies began to reorganise their stores along the more flexible lines of modern department stores, with open-plan sales floors and unified shopfronts. The Lincoln Co-operative Society took its first tentative step in this direction in 1912, when the Tealby Street store was built with integrated drapery and grocery departments 'on the large providers' store principle'.[22] Elsewhere, other societies applied this principle on a much larger scale.

When the Birmingham Industrial Society erected a new store with a two-storeyed 'arcade' shopfront and a small central well for £10,000 in 1914–16, critics feared that it was 'too grand for the Co-op', yet only ten years later enlargements were being contemplated.[23] The neighbouring Metropole Hotel, purchased in 1927, was eventually rebuilt as a modern extension, proving that the co-operative tradition of piecemeal addition was not dead, merely being carried out on a larger scale than ever before. Many societies followed Birmingham's lead by erecting new emporia in the 1920s and 1930s, including Ashton under Lyne Co-operative Society in Lancashire which, in 1928, proudly opened 'Arcadia', where 'all your shopping can now be done under one roof in the atmosphere of an Exhibition building'.[24]

152   The Central Stores of the Gateshead Industrial Co-operative Society on Jackson Road, Gateshead, were enlarged by the erection of this building in 1925–6.

Different societies favoured different styles: the Ashington store of 1924–6 and the very similar Gateshead store of 1925–6 (pl. 152), both combined a Selfridges-style central elevation with heavy end pavilions in an Edwardian baroque idiom, while the neo-Georgian Ashford store of 1928 resembled some of Marks & Spencer's buildings. Other societies, such as Walsall & District (1934), opted to remodel existing premises, making efforts to convert suites of shops into open-plan stores by removing party walls.[25] The Lincoln Society, however, embraced the notion of the emporium rather late in the day.[26] After extending its Central Stores twice in the 1930s,[27] plans for total reconstruction, laid in July 1938, had to be shelved at the outbreak of war. This was a great shame, as co-operative architecture had come into its own in the 1930s, with the construction of many fine department stores.

The architectural achievements of the co-operative movement in the 1930s were largely the responsibility of two CWS architects, Leonard G. Ekins (Chief Architect, London) and William A. Johnson (Chief Architect, Manchester). At the instigation of Ekins, they visited the Netherlands and Germany in 1930 in the company of T. Gray (Chief Architect, Newcastle upon Tyne) to study modern architecture.[28] Ekins had designed the West Hartlepool co-operative store of 1915, which was one of the first

NEWCASTLE CO-OPERATIVE SOCIETY LIMITED.   CENTRAL EMPORIUM.

153 (*above*) The Newcastle Co-operative Society opened this department store in the city centre in 1929. Colour drawing from frontispiece of H. Townley, *A Survey of Interiors of Modern Co-operative Stores*, 1932.

154 A detail from the handrail of the staircase in Newcastle's central emporium.

155 (*facing page*) The central premises of the Bradford Co-operative Society were built in 1935–6 to a Modern design by William A. Johnson. Today, the Yorkshire Co-operative Society has twelve department stores that trade under the 'Sunwin' name.

to reveal the influence of Selfridges and Whiteley's. He went on to design a number of departmental stores for London societies in the 1920s, and was also responsible for the handsome central premises in Newcastle (pl. 153), erected just before his Continental sojourn, in 1929. It may be described as a tentative exercise in art deco, and included many fine ornamental touches, such as the crouching figures on the handrail of the main staircase (pl. 154). By the mid-1930s, however, the impact of contemporary European architecture was evident in Ekins's work.

The brick-faced store that he designed for the Gravesend Society in 1938 was evocative of Dutch Modernism, although the interior was divided into three discrete shops, in traditional co-operative manner.[29]

William A. Johnson expressed a dislike of historicising styles and embraced International Modernism more readily than his colleagues.[30] Johnson had a long career in the CWS, joining in 1899 and continuing in its employ until 1950.[31] After 1930 he was clearly inspired by the work of the German emigré architect Erich Mendelsohn (see p. 180). His most striking building was the store of the City of Bradford Co-operative Society (1935–6), which featured alternating bands of windows and York stone, the latter masking the edges of the floors (pl. 155).[32] A *moderne* touch was contributed by two cylindrical towers, with glazed bands separated by projecting sills rather than solid facings. Like contemporary department stores in London's West End, the interior of the Bradford store was arranged on the 'open-store' principle, with no voids, and with all staircases and lifts tucked around the edges of the building in fireproof compartments. It had the first two escalators ever to be installed

in a co-operative store. Sadly, none of its progressive character is preserved in the present-day Sunwin House store, which is about to be refurbished.

Johnson's influence can be seen in stores designed by other architects for the co-operative movement in the late 1930s. The Dudley Emporium of 1939, by the local architects Webb & Gray, was faced in faience, had a horizontal emphasis and sported a circular corner turret in true Johnsonian style.[33] Both Johnson and Ekins strongly resisted calls for a standard co-operative style of architecture, although Ekins proposed a co-op logo, many years before one was finally introduced.[34]

Co-operatives in the Post-War World

Co-operatives were amongst the first retailers to convert to self-service in the 1940s and to build supermarkets in the early 1950s (see p. 276). Throughout the 1950s, the huge shopfitting and shopfront department of the CWS dispensed advice to societies, as their grocery shops were transformed for self-service. This

springing up on the edges of towns and cities were served by temporary shops, usually huts, which were replaced by permanent premises only when an estate was fully populated and building restrictions had been lifted. Estate branches could take the form of shops under flats, as on Queen Elizabeth Road in the Ermine Estate, Lincoln (1956–7), or small, detached, single-storey blocks. Co-operative building resumed in town centres in the mid-1950s: the Lincoln Society erected a small store in Holbeach in 1954, and its first self-selection dry-goods store in Spalding in 1959.

Most of the large stores erected by co-operative societies in the 1950s were in New Towns and rebuilt town centres, such as Coventry. These stores usually followed the current fashion for glass curtain walls, and some incorporated artworks. The façade of the Letchworth, Hitchin & District Co-op in the Central Square of Stevenage New Town (1958–9) is adorned with a ceramic mural depicting 'the spirit and activities of the Co-operative Movement as a whole and in relation to Stevenage' (pl. 156).[35] Inside, these stores generally comprised self-selection dry-goods showrooms, self-service supermarkets, a restaurant and offices. The 'Starlight Room' restaurant of the Hounslow branch of the London Co-operative Society, completed in 1958, was surrounded by mirrors sand-blasted with the Signs of the Zodiac, and the restaurant/ballroom on the fifth floor of the Hull Co-op (1959), by the CWS Chief Architect George S. Hay,[36] was spanned by a shell concrete roof.[37] Elements of the 'contemporary' interior design of these stores can still be glimpsed on occasion, despite the later refurbishment of premises and the general elimination of colour. In particular, staircases often survive, including the cantilevered spiral staircase of the Sheffield Co-op, which rises from the basement to the second floor; it is adorned by a metallic sculpture of a bird, and topped by a shallow dome set with circular glass bricks (pl. 157).

Co-operative stores had always been recognisable, and this visual identity was enhanced in 1962 by the adoption of a distinctive co-op logo and turquoise colour. But co-operative unification took a much more concrete form throughout the 1960s and 1970s, as societies faced increasingly fierce competition from national multiples.[38] Many amalgamated to form large regional organisations: the Lincoln Society expanded by taking over the Newark, Grimsby and Gainsborough Societies, but remained small compared to United Norwest, which incorporated no less than 150 former societies, including Rochdale.[39] Today, only forty-eight retail co-operative societies survive in Britain. Amongst these, the CWS claims to be 'the world's biggest consumer co-operative', largely due to its amalgamation in April 2000 with the troubled Co-operative Retail Society, which had been forced to sell off its non-food outlets.[40] The CWS now runs 1,100 food stores in three formats: convenience stores ('Welcome'), market town stores and superstores.[41]

156   The Stevenage store of the Letchworth, Hitchin & District Co-operative Society was built in 1958–9. The ceramic mural by G. Bajo of the CWS Architects' Department represents 'the architectural atmosphere of the town' [top left], transport, industry, commerce, science, technology and agriculture [bottom]. Since this photograph was taken, the store has been taken over by Primark.

involved the removal of old wooden shelving and counters to make room for new island display units and cash desks, and the replacement of tongue-and-groove wall cladding with new hygienic finishes. At the same time, societies began to replace their old shopfronts with flush aluminium-frame frontages.

Until the mid-1950s, government restrictions on building work forced societies to modify their expansion strategy, by running travelling shops and purchasing existing small businesses, rather than erecting new stores. Echoing events after 1918, the new local authority and co-operative housing estates that were

Small societies have found it difficult to make a success of superstores. The Lincoln Society, like many others, first experimented with edge-of-town superstores in the 1980s. Its Moorland Centre (1986–9) sold a wide range of goods in a converted metal-clad industrial unit of 44,500 square feet (4, 134 sq. m), and was augmented by a restaurant and a 350-space surface car park. Despite the fact that it was situated close to a residential area which had been constructed as a co-operative 'colony' in the mid-twentieth century, the centre suffered from the proximity of large national multiples, such as Sainsbury's, which gradually stole its market. Since the early 1990s, the Society has concentrated on small local supermarkets.[42] In rural areas, these shops (such as Bardney and Metteringham) take the form of simple, single-storeyed boxes with tile (or imitation tile) roofs and blind brick walls punctuated only by sliding glazed entrance doors and a delivery bay. Outside, they are served by a small surface car park, and inside they contain an artificially lit shop, a stockroom, a staffroom, a manager's office and toilets. In Lincoln itself, the few older shops that have been retained (for example, Burton Road) have been given blind shopfronts, largely in response to ram raiding, while their upper floors have been converted into flats.

Today, co-operative societies still manage diverse property portfolios, including stores, banks, housing, dairies, petrol stations, car showrooms, pharmacies, travel agencies and funeral parlours. In this way they have continued to cater for the needs of the independent working classes in time-honoured fashion, from the cradle to the grave.

157　Some of the best surviving examples of Contemporary styling from the 1950s and 1960s can be seen in co-operative stores. This cantilevered staircase belongs to the Sheffield Co-op store on Angel Street, which was designed by G. S. Hay and opened in 1964.

158   D. H. Evans' new store of 1934–7 was the first in England to have an escalator system that served every floor. The installation, by J. & E. Hall, attracted a great deal of attention in the architectural press. House of Fraser.

9

The Big Store in the Twentieth Century

THE MOST EXCITING AND INNOVATIVE STORES to be built in England in the first half of the twentieth century were in London. They were conceived on such a lavish scale that provincial stores of the same period pale in comparison. The most advanced structural techniques, the most modern architectural styles and the newest forms of internal organisation could all be found in London stores, and especially those of the West End (pl. 159), which were served by an expanded and electrified underground railway system.

The most ambitious new stores of the 1950s were erected outside London, where John Lewis at Oxford Circus was the only major store to require rebuilding as a result of wartime bombing. Store building slowed down in the mid-1960s, as it became increasingly common for large-scale retailers to abandon their high street premises for outlets in malls, and eventually retail parks. It has been notable in recent years that, rather than rebuilding or extending, surviving town-centre stores have concentrated on refurbishment and modernisation, while new uses have had to be found for many that have closed. Intriguingly, some of the most promising new projects at the start of the twenty-first century have been initiated by Selfridges, which is where this story begins.

The Selfridges Revolution

At the start of the twentieth century, the 'Big Store' was entering its heyday. Many of the great London establishments were in the throes of rebuilding, or could already boast magnificent premises which offered a high level of customer comfort. Their proprietors, however, were quite unnerved in 1906, when the American retailer Harry Gordon Selfridge declared his intention to erect a progressive new department store at the west end of Oxford Street.[1]

The roots of Selfridge's store lay in Chicago. There, Selfridge had served as Marshall Field's retail manager before, briefly,

becoming proprietor of the newly built Schlesinger & Mayer store (later Carson Pirie Scott). He would have been familiar with Daniel Burnham's design for Marshall Field's (1900–07), and would have appreciated the principles underpinning the layout of Schlesinger & Mayer's, which had been designed by Louis Sullivan in 1898, but was completed in 1906 under Burnham's supervision. Both buildings had open-plan sales-floors, but otherwise their interiors were very different: while Marshall Field's had a vast central hall covered by a Tiffany vault, Schlesinger & Mayer's had unbroken floors and depended heavily on electric lighting. Selfridge would have appreciated the pros and cons of these alternative approaches, which balanced the benefits of daylight and sheer effect against those of capacious floor space.[2] Selfridge also had extensive experience of modern advertising and display techniques, including sophisticated graphics, mannequin tableaux and night-time window illumination. These ideas were promoted by men like the Chicago retailer L. Frank Baum, the author of *The Wonderful Wizard of Oz* (1900), who encouraged shopkeepers to replace cluttered windows with more artistic displays through his magazine *Show Window*. Now, Selfridge stood poised to introduce American-style retail theatre to Oxford Street.

The initial design for Selfridge's store was drafted by Burnham's office, but the American architect Francis Swales claimed that Selfridge employed him to add 'the French touch' to the elevations.[3] Burnham's design was based on high-rise building technology,[4] and failed to satisfy the requirements of the London Building Acts, which made no allowance for the fire-proofing qualities of steel skeletons and reinforced-concrete floors. These Acts still restricted the area that could be contained within each cellular compartment of a 'warehouse' to 250,000 cubic feet (7,075 cu. m), although that figure could be raised to a maximum of 450,000 cubic feet (12,735 cu. m) in special cases. Other stipulations affected the number and size (maximum 7 × 8 ft/2.13 × 2.44 m) of openings within internal walls, the overall height of buildings (maximum 80 ft/24.4 m) and the

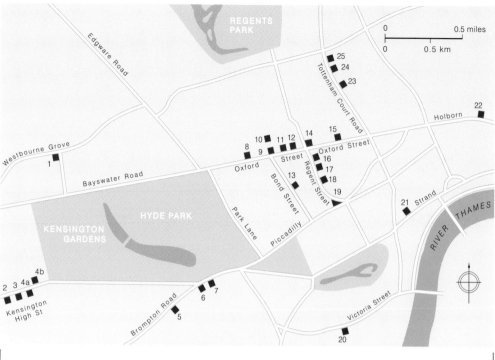

159 This map indicates the position of the 'Big Stores' of central London around 1914. West End shopping had been concentrated on Oxford Street and Regent Street since the early nineteenth century.

1. Whiteley's	9. Marshall & Snelgrove	18. Robinson & Cleaver
2. Ponting's	10. Debenham & Freebody	19. Swan & Edgar
3. Derry & Toms	11. D H Evans	20. Army & Navy Stores
4a Barker's	12. John Lewis	21. Civil Service Co-operative Stores
4b Barker's furniture store	13. Fenwicks	22. Gamages
5. Harrods	14. Peter Robinson	23. Heals
6. Harvey Nichols	15. Waring & Gillow	24. Shoolbred's
7. Woolland's	16. Dickins & Jones	25. Maple's
8. Selfridges	17. Liberty	

thickness of external walls (variable, depending on height).[5] Selfridge reacted by hiring an English architect, Robert Frank Atkinson, whose task was to petition the Building Acts Committee and rework the designs.

Atkinson, still at the beginning of his career, had just completed a store for Waring & Gillow, furnishers and decorators, further along Oxford Street. When it opened, in June 1906, that building (pl. 160) represented the cutting-edge of English store design.[6] Its Shaw-inspired Wrenaissance elevations contrasted with the extreme simplicity of contemporary American stores, which were generally too large to support such exuberant ornamentation. Internally, it was divided into sections by party walls, in typical English fashion, but it had a dramatic central space, surrounded by galleries and topped by a part-glazed dome. With a diameter of 54 feet (16.5 m) and a height of 85 feet (25.9 m), this well was undoubtedly the largest yet built in a London store. Selfridge would have visited Waring & Gillow's building and must have encountered Atkinson through his erstwhile business partner, Samuel J. Waring. On Selfridge's behalf, Atkinson successfully campaigned for larger windows, larger internal compartments (450,000 cu. ft / 12,735 cu. m) and larger openings in dividing walls (12 × 12 ft / 3.66 × 3.66 m), but he had to be content with an overall height of 80 feet (24.4 m).[7]

Once the design was approved, Selfridges (pl. 162) rose rapidly in the hands of Waring's construction firm, Waring & White Ltd, whose chief engineer, Sven Bylander, had extensive experience of steel-frame construction.[8] The completed structure, which opened amidst a blaze of publicity on 15 March 1909, was by no means the first British store to employ a steel frame (see p. 143). Selfridges, however, was built on an unprecedented scale, and with unprecedented speed. It adopted a 22 by 24 feet (6.71 × 7.32 m) grid, a spacing that remained standard for decades to come.[9] Two bays contained light wells, faced with Ionic columns,[10] but there was no vast central court or sweeping staircase. The desired effect was one of expansive, open-plan floors.

160 This photograph, taken by Bedford Lemere in 1917, shows Waring & Gillow's eye-catching Oxford Street store of 1906.

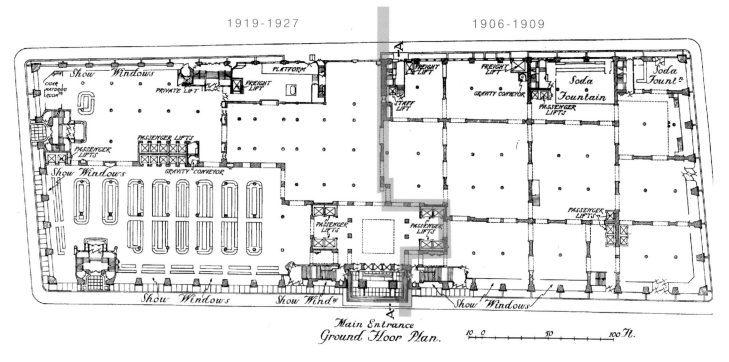

161   Selfridges' 1920s extension was designed with much larger compartments than the original building. Based on *Building*, June 1929, 261.

The most widely influential aspect of Selfridges was its elevation, which would have looked quite different had the two upper floors, designed as a mansard roof, been built. Although the bulky masonry walls were load-bearing, they permitted large amounts of glazing and revealed, rather than concealed, the internal steel cage. They adhered to the Italian *palazzo* tradition, featuring strong horizontal bands at ground-floor (podium) and fourth-floor (attic) levels. The attic was designed as a massive entablature, with windows in the frieze, and was topped by a balustrade. Most significantly, the middle band contained a giant order, with three-storey cast-iron and glass panels set between massive Ionic columns of Portland stone. This type of façade had already appeared overseas, for example at Printemps (1881–9; Paul Sedille) in Paris and Siegel Cooper (1896; Dehemos & Cordes) in Manhattan. While Selfridges introduced this elevational system to England, its heavy Beaux Arts classicism – the contribution of Frank Swales – was generally pared down in later examples, notably in Sir John Burnet's Kodak Building, which was erected on Kingsway in 1910–11.

The internal layout of Selfridges (pl. 161) benefited from the fact that the 1,200 staff did not live in. The entire building, representing the nine-and-a-half easternmost bays of the present store, was devoted either to selling goods or to indulging customers. Starting at the top, the innovative rooftop tea garden was deemed pretty by *The Builder*, although the writer clearly found it somewhat surreal, commenting that 'the chimneyscape seen through the jalousies of green matting is rather an abrupt tran-

sition from an Italian pergola'.[11] Also on the top floor were luncheon halls and a smokers' lounge. Below that, on the third floor, were 'patriotic rooms' for foreign visitors, a picture gallery, a hairdressing salon, a library, a first-aid ward, a silence room, a bureau de change, ticket-booking offices and a post office; in short, everything the customer could possibly want. The sales areas on the lower floors were light and bright, with white walls, olive-green carpets and low mahogany fixtures that contributed to the sense of spaciousness.[12] Here, shoppers could browse without being apprehended by frock-coated shopwalkers, aided by an information desk on the ground floor and served by a cashier in every section. To the rear of the basement were the staff lockers and stock forwarding department. The stockrooms and services were consigned to the sub-basement and lower basement. Access between floors was provided by five staircases, nine passenger lifts and two goods lifts; in addition, the store was served by a gravity package conveyor.

In 1909 most of the big London stores concentrated on middle- and upper-class female shoppers, and supplied them with comforts they would normally seek in a private club. Selfridges followed this convention, but attracted a wider social spectrum after opening an American-style bargain basement in 1911, although that also served as a mechanism for keeping lower-class customers apart from the mainstream clientele.[13] The store environment was overwhelmingly feminine, but men were not entirely neglected, having their own clothing departments in a corner of the ground floor, following current American

162   When it opened in 1909, the year in which this Bedford Lemere photograph was taken, Selfridges was much smaller than it is today. This view shows the corner of Oxford Street and Duke Street.

practice.[14] An American Soda Fountain was a particular draw for children, and in 1913 a crèche – probably one of the first of its kind – was provided.

The immediate impact of Selfridges was somewhat diluted by the antics of its competitors: Harrods (est. 1853) decided to commemorate its Diamond Jubilee the very week that Selfridges opened, while Dickins & Jones (est. 1803) celebrated its centenary six years late. Selfridge countered with a series of crowd-pulling stunts. Most famously, he displayed Louis Blériot's monoplane the day after its pioneering cross-Channel flight, in July 1909.[15] Selfridges never stole Harrods' mantle as the largest London department store, but its rivals took note of its American methods. It generated further improvements in customer amenities, a more open attitude to browsing and a

163 Harrods' new frontage was completed in 1905, but building work continued along Hans Road (on the right) until 1912. Since 1959 the store has been lit at night by strings of electric light bulbs.

more sophisticated approach to display. Furthermore, after a short lull, the design of its façade was adopted as a template for commercial buildings throughout the British Isles for the next quarter century or more.

★ ★ ★

Selfridges' London Rivals

The Draper's Record portrayed the furore surrounding the opening of Selfridges as 'The Battle of the Trade Giants'.[16] The most titanic of all was Harrods, a remarkable achievement given its quasi-suburban location and mundane origins. By now, it had adopted the motto *omnia omnibus ubique* ('Everything for Everyone Everywhere'), and the telegraphic address, 'Everything, London'. In the hands of its manager Richard Burbidge, the

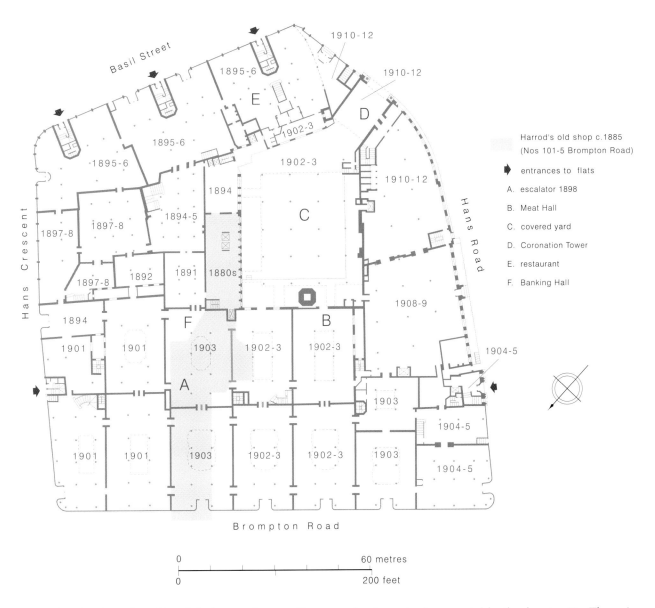

164   This plan shows how Harrods had grown by 1912. The green tint shows the site occupied by the shop in 1884. The main change since 1912 has been the reconstruction of the range on Basil Street in 1929–30 to a Selfridges-inspired design by Louis Blanc.

business had put on a spurt of growth, and added drapery goods to its departmental list. Successive share issues and profit plough-back funded the ambitious rebuilding programme undertaken between 1894 and 1912 to a design by Charles William Stephens, the architect of Harvey Nichols. The famous pink terracotta Brompton Road frontage (pl. 163) was erected between 1901 and 1905, then work continued in an anti-clockwise direction along Hans Road. The interior was divided into a series of inter-connected showrooms (pl. 164), most of which incorporated a central two-storey void, in the fashion of the 1890s. In 1906 a manager with Wanamaker's observed: 'Harrods is totally unlike American stores in construction being simply a series of sepa-rate stores side by side connected by archways'.[17] The opulent

showrooms (pl. 165) were designed by Frederick Sage & Co. Ltd, and featured ornate stucco ceilings and thick carpets. The best surviving showroom is the restored Meat Hall of 1902–3, which is adorned with tiles by W. J. Neatby.

Gordon Selfridge once declared: 'I should think if I were Peter Robinson or D. H. Evans, I should chuckle with glee at the prospect of Selfridge opening up in my street'; it was neverthe-less widely feared that he would pit American ideas against English, 'in a fight to the death'.[18] Positioned in the front line of battle, in terms of their locations, were Debenham & Freebody on Wigmore Street and D. H. Evans on Oxford Street, which both had new buildings. In each case, a grandiose façade con-cealed a modern steel and reinforced-concrete structure, but

165 Harrods' new showrooms, decorated by Frederick Sage & Co. Ltd, had opulent plaster ceilings, some of which survive. This photograph of 1919 shows the ladies' boot and shoe department on the first floor.

while the popular D. H. Evans had a plate-glass shopfront with slender pillars and an island display window, the more exclusive Debenham & Freebody had windows with solid arched surrounds.[19] Selfridges took a middle path, having large windows framed by fairly substantial piers. It would seem, therefore, that the style of the shopfront was some indication of the class of customer a store expected to attract.

Debenham & Freebody's building (1906–7; Wallace & Gibson) was essentially conservative, with a compartmentalised interior arranged around small wells. D. H. Evans' new West Block (1906–9; John Murray) (pl. 166) was more modern: it had been designed 'after careful study of numerous large trade buildings in Paris, Vienna and Berlin', and, although it did not quite dare to imitate Continental art nouveau store design, it featured a large central well and curvaceous staircase.[20] Like Selfridges, it was equipped with all modern conveniences. Its pneumatic tube system communicated with a cash desk located in a subway linking the new building with the older East Block, and two 'glissoires', or spiral chutes, conveyed parcels to the basement, where they were discharged on to a conveyor belt and carried to a revolving sorting table. A chute of that type is still used in Samaritaine Magasin 2 (1905–7; F. Jourdain) in Paris.

166 Like most large stores, D. H. Evans' West Block on Oxford Street was built in phases to enable the business to continue trading without a break. When this photograph was taken, in 1909, a third of the premises had been rebuilt.

In the years leading up to war, the fear of fire that dictated so many aspects of store design seemed justified by a number of major conflagrations, for example at Arding & Hobbs in Clapham in 1909 and at Barker's in Kensington in 1912. One store with a notorious history of fires was Whiteley's (see p. 138), but when that establishment was rebuilt on a monumental scale in 1910–12, fire safety was subordinated to spectacle. John Lawrie, the managing director, had admired Marshall Field's store when he visited America in 1909, and he determined to adopt a similar 'central hall scheme'.[21] Despite the strict building laws, the architects, Belcher & Joass, together with the engineer Alexander

Drew, contrived to arrange the interior around two vast four-storey wells, one circular and the other octagonal, covered by domes with double skins (both 67 ft/20.4 m in diameter), out-doing Waring's and creating England's closest equivalent to Paris's breathtaking Galeries Lafayette (Phase 2, 1910–12; Ferdinand Chanut).[22] The impact of the central rotunda (pl. 167), which was served by a double staircase with an elliptical balcony at first-floor level, could be fully appreciated from the restaurant on the upper gallery. This enormous, but potentially dangerous, space was made permissible only by the installation of elaborate safeguards that allowed the interior to be divided into seven sec-

On the outside, Whiteley's (pl. 168) took Selfridges' giant order and transformed it into a giant arcade by the introduction of spandrels. Taking this idea further, the giant order became a solid masonry arcade on the façade of Walter Cave's new Burberry store, which opened on Haymarket in 1913.[23] Instead of developing a further variation on this theme, Barker's new block of 1913–14 on the south side of Kensington High Street was virtually a Selfridges clone. This is explained by the involvement of Atkinson, who seems to have been commissioned to design the external wrap of the building, while the interior was the responsibility of Barker's house architect, H. L. Cabuche.[24]

In many ways, the most modern store to be erected in early twentieth-century London was Heal's extension on Tottenham Court Road (pl. 169), which was built next to the Victorian store (pls 128–9) in 1912–16.[25] The proprietor, Ambrose Heal, was a skilled furniture maker, responsible for establishing the firm's Arts and Crafts style. Cecil Brewer, his cousin, had already designed exhibition room-settings and a house for Heal, and so his firm, Smith & Brewer, was entrusted with the new store. The Portland stone façade incorporated Heal's chequered border motif, bold lettering by Percy J. Smith and cast-iron plaques depicting heraldic trade signs by Joseph Armitage. Inside, four floors of showrooms were lit by enormous windows, in true furniture-store tradition, and were connected to the rear by a spiral staircase. On the fifth floor was the latest ploy to entice cus-

168 (*above*) Whiteley's elevation was much criticised for appearing to rest a giant order of columns on jointed lintels with 40-foot (12.19 m) spans: an obvious physical impossibility. This photograph, by Bedford Lemere, was taken in 1917.

169 (*right*) As Heal's shopfront (1912–16) was in the form of a protected arcade, the design of the façade managed to be aesthetically pleasing without the shopkeeper sacrificing an inch of glass. This clever solution to one of the main problems besetting Edwardian store architects was popular with the critics, but not taken up by many retailers.

167 (*facing page*) This rotunda inside Whiteley's department store (1910–12) in Bayswater was refurbished when the building was converted into a shopping centre in the 1980s. Although the columns were of 'Siena' scagliola marble, and the capitals and bases were bronzed with pure copper, all surfaces have now been painted white.

tions, separated by thick brick walls, which could be thoroughly sealed off in the event of fire. Apertures were filled with bronze doors between pairs of steel roller shutters. In addition, the store had fireproof hollow-tile floors, a Grinnell sprinkler system, alarms, escape stairs, hydrants and fire-resisting copper-framed ('Luxfer') glazing.

tomers upwards: the Mansard Gallery. Dedicated to art and design exhibitions, this opened into a winter garden and a small paved court with a fountain, around which were room-sets in Heal's country style. When the store was extended in the same style by Edward Maufe, whose wife ran the Mansard Gallery, in 1936–8, the senior partner of Smith & Brewer sued for breach of copyright in architectural drawings and plans, and won his case.[26]

By 1914 the heavily criticised living-in system had fallen out of favour with London drapers. Some stores had abandoned it some time ago (for example, Woolland's), while others (for example, Derry & Toms) kept it for women but not for men, and a few built hostels, located within easy walking distance of the store. Bourne & Hollingsworth, for example, erected Staffordshire House on Tottenham Court Road for its female assistants in 1907. Outside London the system endured for longer, ensuring that much provincial store architecture remained decidedly old-fashioned.

★   ★   ★

170   Adderley's in Leicester (*c.*1900) was typical of provincial drapery emporia in the early twentieth century. The store was rebuilt in the 1920s but has since been demolished.

Although provincial stores were rarely as large as those of London, less rigid building regulations made it easier to dispense with party walls, creating open-plan floors that were usually pierced by small light wells or areas.[27] The interior of John Walsh's seven-storey building in Sheffield (1899; Flockton & Gibbs), for example, consisted of six 'shops', each 25 feet (7.62 m) wide and 200 feet (60.96 m) long, separated only by steel columns, which carried cast-iron joists.[28] That store may have been quite advanced in terms of its structure and layout, but undoubtedly Walsh's customers were still seated on bentwood chairs at heavy mahogany counters, where they were treated to one-to-one service, as they would have been in drapery stores up and down the country (pl. 170). Walsh's also adhered to the tradition of providing abundant staff accommodation on its upper floors, with men and women carefully segregated. Naturally, the circulation routes for staff and customers never overlapped.

One of the most up-to-date provincial stores of the early twentieth century must have been William McIlroy's in Reading (1900–03; Joseph Morris & Son) (pl. 171).[29] As it was constructed with a steel frame, the show windows on the two lower floors took the form of a continuous glass wall, without the intrusion of any brick or masonry piers. 'Floating' above the shop windows were three fancifully rendered upper floors, largely devoted to staff accommodation although part of the building, perhaps uniquely, housed a hotel. G. J. Keddie's (1908) in Leigh-on-Sea, Essex, found another unusual use for upper floors, laying them out as two houses, each with its own roof garden.[30]

While many provincial stores had small wells, few featured a central hall. Whittaker's in Bolton (1906–7) had a two-storey half-timbered well topped by a dome with a modest diameter of 17 feet (5.18 m). Much larger than that was the central hall of Blackler's Stores in Liverpool, which opened on an island site in 1909.[31] Although again only two storeys high, the rectangular hall seems to have been remarkably wide. It was covered by a glass barrel vault and surrounded by galleries served by a central staircase which bifurcated mid-flight, in French fashion. The arrangements for despatching goods at Blackler's were quite novel: the store kept a fleet of motor cars behind the store, and whenever one was required it was backed into an electric lift and lowered to the basement for loading. An alternative method was used for deliveries and despatch at McIlroy's, where a ramped road took vehicles down to the basement and around a loading platform, before rising once again to street level. Both Blackler's and McIlroy's solutions, designed to accommodate motor transport, would have greatly eased congestion at street level.

The architectural style of the great London stores had limited influence in the provinces before the 1920s, although the style

171 William McIlroy's fantastical store in Reading (1900–03) was considered the largest in the South, outside London. Although the store closed in 1955, the building still stands, sadly stripped of its fairytale corner turret and many of its picturesque gables and chimneys. Tinted postcard, c.1905.

of Harrods' shopfront was widely emulated. The giant order made a tentative appearance on the façade of Bunting's (1911–12; Augustus F. Scott) (pl. 172), a drapery and furnishing emporium in Norwich, which is thought to have been one of the first stores in the country with a reinforced-concrete frame,[32] although there are more likely contenders, such as Mathias Robinson's Coliseum furniture store in West Hartlepool (1906–7; Harry Barnes & Charles F. Burton).[33] Another ferro-concrete store in West Hartlepool, built by the Hartlepools Co-operative Society

172 Although Bunting's in Norwich (1911–12) had a central well which rose through three floors, the top floor of the two street ranges included twenty-one staff bedrooms.

in 1915, borrowed much more overtly from Selfridges and Whiteley's while incorporating a neo-baroque central feature. That popular stylistic combination could also be seen at Fenwick's in Newcastle (1914; Marshall & Tweedy). In these years, the building that most closely imitated Selfridges was undoubtedly Clery's new building in Dublin, which was designed by Atkinson, together with the firm of Ashland & Coleman, after its predecessor had been destroyed in the Easter Rising of 1916.[34] Due to the war, however, the store did not open until 1922.

Meanwhile, Lewis's of Liverpool – still in the forefront of mass retailing outside London – had begun replacing its Victorian stores with larger buildings, both in Liverpool (1910–23; Gerald de Courcy Fraser) and Manchester (1912–15; J. W. Beaumont & Sons). When completed, the Manchester store was the largest in the group, and one of the largest stores outside London. It was divided into three compartments separated by fire walls, and the circular well in the centre rose through six floors, with a restaurant at fifth-floor level, just under the dome (36 ft/10.9 m in diameter), as at Whiteley's. Lewis's installed electric lifts, which were distributed throughout the building. It had the largest soda fountain outside the USA and a sprung dance floor of marble.[35]

The interior was heated by 200 thermostatically controlled radiators: the first to be seen in Manchester.

Mainstream Store Design in the 1920s and 1930s

Independent retailers continued to do good business during the First World War, but began to encounter serious competition from co-operatives and chain stores in the economically troubled years that followed. Department stores reacted by increasing the range of services available to their customers, and making a determined effort to appeal to a broader social spectrum. Many were subjected to takeovers, and several large groups, including Debenhams and Selfridges Provincial Stores, came into being.[36] Stores taken over by Selfridges included Whiteley's and the Brixton Bon Marché. Store groups usually retained, even cultivated, the individual identities of their outlets but, in 1923 Lewis's became one of the first to adopt the central purchasing methods of the chain stores.

Despite their struggles, the numbers of department stores swelled from an estimated 150 to 200 in 1910, to between 475 and 525 in 1950, a growth partly attributable to the spread of

173   The new Dickins & Jones (1920–22) and Liberty (1924–5) stores can be seen on the left in this 1930s view looking down Regent Street.

suburbia and improvements in public transport, which greatly increased store catchment areas.[37] Between the wars, more people enjoyed a better standard of living than ever before, and hire purchase brought a wide range of consumer goods within their grasp. Realising this, department stores greatly expanded their stocks of furniture, carpets and household appliances.

Few new stores were erected between 1918 and 1923, but once building resumed store architects were faced with two alternative approaches. They could either create stores with spectacular wells that provided customers with dramatic views of the establishment and admitted daylight to the interiors of sales floors, or they could adopt the American 'horizontal' system, and build open-plan stores. Open-plan interiors were made viable by improvements to electric lighting and by the availability of good mechanical ventilation systems. They had the advantage of providing a great deal of extra floor space, something that was becoming more valuable than either natural lighting or theatrical spectacle. This was particularly true for businesses that had begun to switch from formal counter service, where the movement of customers was closely controlled by sales assistants and shopwalkers, to a system that encouraged customers to circulate freely amongst the goods, and browse to their hearts'

content. With old-fashioned counter service, only a small proportion of stock was on open display, most being stowed away in cabinets, drawers or shelves where it was inaccessible to shoppers without the intercession of an assistant. Once browsing was allowed, most of the merchandise had to be brought into the open, where it was attractively displayed in glass-topped counters or on stands. What this required, above all else, was floor space.

In the early 1920s stores with an exclusive clientele tended to be the most conservative and individualistic in outlook, both in terms of their internal planning and the treatment of their façades. Three such firms were affected by the redevelopment of Regent Street: Swan & Edgar's, Dickins & Jones and Liberty's. The Crown Estate dictated the design for the façade of Swan & Edgar's (1925–6; Sir Reginald Blomfield), on the southern tip of the Quadrant, and instructed other tenants to build classical façades in Portland stone.[38] For Dickins & Jones (1920–2) (pl. 173), Sir Henry Tanner drew indiscriminately on Egyptian, Roman and modern French sources. A contemporary critic declared: 'this building with its ornate details, its black balconies and attics above attics, is like the finale of some old-fashioned musical comedy when all the company collected on the stage

174 One of the wells in Liberty's Tudor Block, which was built in 1922–4. Such features of early twentieth-century stores seldom survive.

and waved flags and kicked legs and climbed rostrums while the orchestra rose from din to din'.[39] In contrast to Dickins & Jones, Liberty's East India House (1924–5; E. T. & E. S. Hall) (pl. 173) looked like an imposing financial institution. Its concave classical façade was topped by an imperialist frieze celebrating the wealth of distant countries being borne by camel, elephant and ship to Great Britain, with the figure of Britannia as a centrepiece. Designed by the same architects, Liberty's neo-vernacular Tudor Block (1922–4) on Great Marlborough Street was so different from anything on Regent Street itself that it may be regarded as a protest against the aesthetic dictatorship of the Crown Estate. The building reflected Liberty's image as a reputable firm that was no longer in the avant-garde, but specialised

in traditional country-house style.[40] It was designed in accordance with the principles of the ageing Arts and Crafts movement, and was built using timbers from HMS *Hindustan* and HMS *Impregnable*, excluding steelwork as much as possible.[41]

As light wells were no longer a practical necessity, their wastefulness in terms of space now carried connotations of luxury, and implied the preservation of traditional service. Liberty's Tudor Block was arranged around three wells (pl. 174). These vertical spaces were evocative of old English inns, and were surrounded by cosy galleries, fitted with fireplaces and wall panelling, emitting an aura of intimate domesticity. A longer and lower well ran through the centre of Swan & Edgar's narrow building, which was designed internally by J. J. Joass. Over the well, Joass introduced a flat weatherproof and fireproof ceiling, one of the first of its kind, made of amber-coloured 'Cristol' glass which was moulded in light relief.

Elsewhere in the country, a number of smaller stores and store extensions continued to be built with galleried light wells, for example Bobby's in Southport (1923–4) and W. Eaden Lilley's in Cambridge (1928). By the mid-1920s, however, variety stores and some metropolitan department stores were adopting open-plan floors and encouraging browsing as a means of attracting new custom. There was no technical reason why they should not do this. With peripheral stairwells enclosed by fire walls, the maximum permissible cubic capacity could be concentrated horizontally rather than vertically, thus complying with the demands of the most stringent building regulations. Amongst the first post-war stores to adopt the horizontal system were Peter Robinson's men's store (1924; T. P. Clarkson) on Oxford Street and Barker's new furniture and men's store of 1924–6, on the north side of Kensington High Street, which had exteriors by Blomfield and interiors by H. L. Cabuche.[42] Inside Barker's, the main stairs were located within the entrance halls, in accordance with standard practice, but the seven lifts stood in a single bank, opposite the main doors. This placement of lifts was a ruse to draw customers through the main sales area, encouraging impulse purchasing, and had originated in pre-war American stores, such as Filene's in Boston.[43] A very similar layout was adopted for the new Derry & Toms store (1929–33), now in Barker's ownership. Its sophisticated *décoratif moderne* interior was designed by a Chicago architect, C. A. Wheeler. The onyx and black marble lifts were adorned with gilded chevron grilles and reliefs, and the elegant restaurant ('The Rainbow Room') and fashion theatre (pl. 175) were lit by snaking tubes of coloured light concealed within curving cornices. The conventional way to light store interiors in the 1920s was by electric bulbs of 200 to 500 watts, contained in open bowls or opaque globes, suspended from the ceilings. The less direct effects achieved in Derry & Toms were soon being imitated throughout the country.

175 The new Derry & Toms store of 1929–33 in Kensington High Street was equipped with this stylish mannequin theatre.

Open-plan floors did not go hand in hand with a particular elevational treatment, although the first stores to experiment with the system tended to opt for a giant order that permitted large windows with a vertical emphasis, in the Selfridges tradition. Selfridges itself was greatly extended in the 1920s (pl. 161), beginning with the block on the corner of Orchard Street and Oxford Street (1920–24), followed by the central entrance hall (1926–8), which was built after only attempts to gain approval for a gigantic tower (pl. 176) or dome had failed.[44] Its continuous building activity kept Selfridges to the fore, and its elevations inspired additions to a number of established Knightsbridge stores, including the Sloane Street and Seville Street sections of Harvey Nichols (1922–8; Williams & Cox), which had mansard

roofs, suggesting how Selfridges might have looked if its upper storeys had been permitted.

Bernard George, the architect of the new Derry & Toms (1929–33) and Barker's (1936–9 and 1955–8) stores, was a former pupil of R. Frank Atkinson. As well as looking back to Selfridges, George may have been impressed by Heal's pre-war store, as in each case he simplified the giant order and elaborated it with bas-reliefs. Meanwhile, retail buildings with colossal orders were being erected on high streets the length and breadth of the country, not just for department stores, but also for furniture stores, chain stores, co-operative stores and speculative developments. Somewhat later, in the 1930s, several Modern stores were built with a verticality achieved through the use of slender, con-

176 Numerous designs were produced for a massive dome or tower that would crown the centre of Selfridges in Oxford Street, including this proposal by the architect Philip Tilden. There was never any realistic possibility that the scheme would receive approval. From Tilden 1954, fig. 37.

177 Kendal Milne's new Manchester premises of 1938–40 were designed by J. S. Beaumont, whose firm produced several Modern stores with a pronounced vertical emphasis in the middle years of the twentieth century. Upon completion, this building was requisitioned for the Civil Service and it did not open to customers until after the Second World War.

tinuous mullions rather than classical pilasters or columns. The most prominent examples of that approach were D. H. Evans (1934–7) on Oxford Street, by Harrods' former house architect Louis Blanc, and Kendal Milne's (1938–40; J. S. Beaumont) (pl. 177) in Manchester.

There were alternatives to the vertical modernity of the Selfridges' model. A neo-Georgian style was adopted for the new Fortnum & Mason store, built in that bastion of traditional shopping, St James's, in 1923–5, and by the late 1920s a rather dull Georgian idiom, executed in Portland stone, was being espoused by a number of large provincial stores. These included Lewis's branches in Birmingham (1926–7) and Leeds (1929–32), and an extension to the firm's Manchester store (1929), which was now enormous. A few years later, Lewis's in Leicester (1935–6; G. de

C. Fraser and John Sheridan) was also built in a severe style, relieved merely by a frill marking the setback of the upper storey, and a prismatic tower which was illuminated at night.

A red brick neo-Georgian style was chosen for several stores with apartments on their upper floors. These included Gamages (1929–30; Messrs Joseph with Sir Edwin Lutyens), at the west end of Oxford Street, and Welwyn Department Stores (1938–9; Louis de Soissons) (pl. 178), in Welwyn Garden City, Hertfordshire, which had sixty-two flats on its upper floors and a Masonic Suite with badminton and squash courts on the roof.[45] Another pre-war store with flats was John Barnes at Swiss Cottage, London, which had been taken over by Selfridges in 1926, and was rebuilt in 1936 by the architects T. P. Bennett & Son.[46] The building combined a three-level store with five floors of flats

178 Welwyn Department Stores (1938–9), the largest commercial premises in Welwyn Garden City, Hertfordshire, was designed in a neo-Georgian style, with flats on the upper floors. This photograph was taken by H. Felton in the late 1930s.

known as St John's Court, and rather than attempting to integrate these two elements – which was the approach at Gamages and at Welwyn – the architects chose to emphasise their distinctness. The store was faced in white ashlar and, at first-floor level, had a continuous window band which curved around the corners. Above this, the U-shaped block of flats was set back from the building line. It was of brick with stone dressings, and had canted bays which opened on to curved balconies. To some extent, this anticipated tower-and-podium designs, combining shops or stores with office or apartment blocks, which became so popular in the 1960s.

One crucial innovation of the 1930s was the continuous cantilevered canopy or marquise, which had been a feature of Continental stores for many years, but was not permitted in London, where even Selfridges' canopy had been restricted to the area directly in front of the main entrance. In 1930, however, a new

Building Act gave the London County Council discretionary powers to approve permanent canopies. The first existing store to take advantage of this, five years later, was Bourne & Hollingsworth, which installed canopies that projected 8 feet 6 inches (2.59 m) over the pavement, but were kept 2 feet 6 inches (0.76 m) from the kerb, in case people leaned too far from the upper decks of omnibuses.[47] The first new London stores to incorporate canopies from the outset were Peter Jones (pl. 184), D. H. Evans and Simpson's (pl. 181).[48] As well as providing shelter for window-shoppers, canopies had the aesthetic advantage of drawing a line between the ground-floor show windows and the superstructure of a building. They often incorporated glass lenses or bricks, to shed light on the area immediately in front of the window displays.

Store interiors were now streamlined. Bulky radiators had interfered with internal arrangements, and from the mid-1920s

ceiling heating panels offered a viable alternative. These were used in Harvey Nichols in the 1920s, and in John Barnes in the 1930s. Fittings were now required to be flexible and mobile, enabling departments to be expanded or contracted with ease. At D. H. Evans the fittings were on the interchangeable unit principle, but were a different colour on each floor. As well as organising goods by type, stores were now embracing the idea of the 'shop within a shop', for example at Kennard's of Croydon, which leased its wireless and grocery departments to outside interests. The visual impact of these 'shops' was imitated in conventional departments, such as Kennard's 'Bonnet Box', as a means of introducing variety to sales floors, and bringing privacy to departments such as corsetry and lingerie.

Lifts and, increasingly, escalators were the key elements in manipulating the circulation of customers within stores, and increasing the value of upper floors. Although lifts had to be operated by attendants (pl. 179) and required large lobby areas to obviate pockets of congestion, they were still preferred to escalators. Until the 1930s, the use of escalators was restricted to the lower floors of the largest stores. In the late 1920s, for example, a double-width escalator was installed to link the two levels of Selfridges' bargain basement, which was now virtually a self-contained store within a store, with its own food department and tea room.[49] The more high-status upper floors were served by lifts. In America, however, stores such as Macys already had sets of escalators seamlessly integrating five or more floors.[50] The first British store with that facility was D. H. Evans (pl. 158). The Building Acts forced these escalators, which were of the cross-over type and travelled both up and down, to be enclosed within their own hall, against the side of the building. In contrast, beyond the reach of the Building Acts, Bentall's in Kingston upon Thames (1930–35; Sir Aston Webb) installed superimposed escalators on the long sides of a vast central atrium.[51] This ingenious arrangement meant that customers could look at the merchandise as they travelled, but it also meant that they had to walk around each sales floor to get to the next escalator, and might be tempted to make impromptu purchases *en route*. Another unusual escalator installation could be seen in John Barnes, which received a special dispensation to combine the ground and first floors to form a space of 500,000 cubic feet (14,150 cu. m), with central escalators without fire doors. These escalators were unique in London, as they were continuous, rather than superimposed: very convenient for the customer, whose journey was greatly hastened, but not so lucrative for the retailer. Different yet again, but equally convenient, were the two separate sets of parallel continuous escalators in Kendal Milne's, which were located in their own hall to the rear of the sales floors (pl. 180). Most pre-war escalator services outside London took customers up but not down, and were of single width. Not only was this more economical, but it took customers upstairs

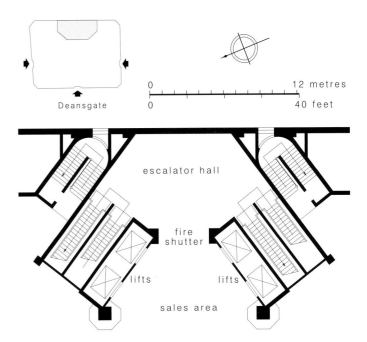

Deansgate

0   12 metres
0   40 feet

escalator hall

fire shutter

lifts   lifts

sales area

180   The escalator hall in Kendal Milne's was located to the centre rear of the sales floors, together with the main staircases and lifts. Based on Manchester Building Plan 24938, 1938.

quickly, then obliged them to find their way down at a much slower pace. However they were arranged, escalators did more than grand staircases or lifts had ever achieved in releasing the sales potential of upper floors, enabling retailers to exploit spaces at an increasing distance from the street frontage.

Restaurants were usually located on upper floors so that food smells did not permeate sales areas, and were often served by express lifts, which did not stop on intermediate floors. Their kitchens could be shared with staff canteens. Most offered table service, but some self-service cafeterias or luncheonettes appeared in the mid-1930s. Rooftop restaurants were still in vogue. The most splendid, added to Derry & Toms in 1936–8, had live flamingos. Even some co-operative stores had a roof garden: the East Ham store of the London Co-operative Society, which opened on 4 May 1935, had a 'cafeteria, flower beds, crazy walks, rookery nooks, lily pond, fountain, kiddies' playground, giant telescopes, and many other attractions'.[52] The 'other attractions' included mannequin parades, pony rides and an orchestra.

As always, the circulation of staff and goods was kept as separate from that of customers as possible. Sales, restaurant and office staff worked in different parts of the building, but usually shared the same entrances, stairs and common rooms. Goods were received in a dock which could be sealed by rolling shutters; they were checked and then sent via goods lifts either to stockrooms or sales areas. Despatch and mail order departments were usually kept separate, to avoid confusion. Towards the end of the 1930s, the LCC and other local authorities were empow-

179   This contemporary photograph shows a bank of lifts, with uniformed operators standing to attention, in Selfridges' 1920s extension.

ered to insist that all loading and unloading took place within store premises, rather than in the street. Many stores already had large loading docks on their rear or side elevations, which lorries could reverse into. On an island site, however, loading bays destroyed the continuity of the shopfront and interrupted pedestrian flow on the pavement. An ingenious, if expensive, solution to this problem was produced for Owen Owen in Coventry (1938; G. de C. Fraser), where the delivery entrance was approached through an underground tunnel, entered some distance from the store itself. That building was still brand new when it was bombed on two occasions, in 1940 and 1941, but the service arrangements were retained in its post-war replacement (see pl. 185).

Big stores of the 1930s aspired to be much more than shops. Selfridges declared itself to be 'infinitely more than a Store – it is the meeting-place in London of the peoples of the World, and we are proud to claim it as "London's Civic Centre"'.[53] Even outside London, stores pulled out all the stops to attract customers. Bentall's, for example, had a Palm Court Orchestra, fashion shows, bonny baby competitions, a circus – the lion was housed overnight in the lift shaft – and even hired a female Swedish diver to plunge 63 feet down the escalator hall into a tank of water.[54] Some store services were quite bizarre: Selfridges offered a free wart-removing service, while Kennard's 'removed shoppers of one of their burdens' by setting up a corn-removing department.[55]

Avant-Garde Store Design in the 1930s

During the 1920s English architects had not participated in the formation of the International Modern style, which was roundly criticised by the old guard of the architectural establishment. Its appeal became harder to resist in the early 1930s, when a number of well-known architects and designers fled the Continent to work in Britain. Foremost amongst these émigrés was the German architect Erich Mendelsohn, who had designed a number of highly influential Modern stores in the late 1920s.[56] These displayed awareness of the Carson Pirie Scott store in Chicago, especially in the pronounced horizontality of their elevations and their rejection of internal voids. Mendelsohn's first important store was the controversial C. A. Herpich Sohne, a furrier's store on Leipzigerstrasse in Berlin (1924–8). That was followed by Deukon House in Berlin (1927) and the Schocken department stores in Nuremberg (1926), Stuttgart (1926–8) and Chemnitz (1928–9).[57] Alternating bands of window and wall, in varying proportions, characterised the main façades of these stores. At one extreme, the Herpich frontage was virtually a glass curtain wall, while the Schocken store at Nuremberg had narrow ribbon windows because the patron, Salman Schocken, had

insisted that their sills be placed above the internal cabinetry, and that the interior ledges be deep enough to hold displays. The windows in Mendelsohn's stores admitted a great deal of light, which was diffused through tulle curtains and augmented by illuminated ceiling panels (at Herpich) or more basic globe light fittings (in the Schocken stores).

Apart from their bold horizontality, one of the most influential aspects of Mendelsohn's store façades was their architectonic fusion of lettering and light, designed to advertise the premises by day and night.[58] The projecting vertical signboard of Deukon House, for example, served visually to separate the narrow stair bay from the main section of the façade, and was folded at its base to create a canopy over the doorway. Whole façades, as well as signage, were illuminated at night. The Herpich store had external lighting troughs, but for his later stores Mendelsohn placed lights inside the window soffits, so that the interiors appeared to blaze with electricity. All of this was far in advance of store design in England, where the straightforward flood-lighting of Selfridges and the Army & Navy Stores attracted great attention.[59]

Mendelsohn's buildings did not have an immediate impact on English store design, although they were very well known. Some critics thought them aggressively functional, and with surprising foresight Howard Robertson of *The Architect and Building News* questioned the practicality of piercing store façades with such large windows, as 'wall space seems to be a greater desideratum than floods of natural light'.[60] As a case in point, he reported that the glass front of the Beijenkorf (Beehive) shop at The Hague (1924–6; Piet Kramer) was 'largely blocked up internally'. Despite these reservations, in the course of the 1930s several English stores were erected with extensive glazing, and even pure curtain walling. One building in particular, Simpson's men's store on Piccadilly (1935–6), was directly inspired by Mendelsohn's work.

Simpson's was designed by Joseph Emberton, the architect of Olympia (1929–30) and one of the first buildings in London to have a glass curtain wall, Universal House in Southwark (1932–3). Emberton had to adopt a different approach at Simpson's – his first opportunity to produce a unified store on a grand scale – because the ground landlord, the Crown, insisted on a Portland stone façade.[61] The result was an innovative Modern design, with horizontal bands of windows and stone, probably more indebted to C. A. Herpich Sohne than any other Mendelsohn store.

The Piccadilly façade of Simpson's (pl. 181) was divided by horizontal strips of metal-framed windows and given additional interest by 'glascrete' canopies at ground-floor and sixth-floor levels. It was designed to be illuminated by coloured neon strips after dark. The use of coloured light as an architectural element had been a key feature of Emberton's work since he visited the Paris *Exposition* in 1925, but the use of lighting troughs may have been directly inspired by the Herpich store. The application of coloured light to store façades was not entirely new in England. From 1921 the Victorian façade of the 'His Master's Voice' (HMV) shop on Oxford Street provided a backdrop for a huge illuminated electric 'motion' sign, manufactured by the Franco-British Sign Company, featuring 1,300 lamps.[62] It featured a man 9 feet 6 inches tall playing a revolving record on a giant gramophone (pl. 182) and paid no heed to the underlying façade. Emberton's approach at Simpson's was altogether more sophisticated, with coloured light treated as an integral component of the architectural design.

When Simpson's opened in 1936, the concept of the general men's store had been gestating for some time. Large multi-storeyed tailors' and outfitters' stores had existed since the mid-nineteenth century (see p. 128), but the notion of stepping upmarket and stocking a wide range of masculine products probably originated in America when Marshall Field's built a six-storey annexe for men in 1914.[63] Several London department stores aped this on a smaller scale. Selfridges' men's shop opened in the newly completed store extension in June 1922, and had a separate entrance.[64] Two years later, Peter Robinson's opened a free-standing multi-storey shop for men, to the east of the main store, replacing a building that had originally been erected to house its men's outfitting departments in 1890–91. The shirt-maker Austin Reed went one step further with his Regent Street shop of 1926, which absorbed ideas picked up by Reed and his architect, Percy Westwood, during visits to New York and Chicago in 1920. The store was superior to Peter Robinson's, offering services such as a barber's shop (pl. 183) as well as various outfitting departments. The interior was fitted out in a spectacular art deco style by Westwood and Emberton, and the centrepiece was a great oval hall, which reached the ceiling of the third floor and had balconies in the shape of wing collars. Ten years later, Alexander Simpson deliberately placed his store in the heart of St James's, where he could compete not just with Austin Reed, but also with the stalwarts of Jermyn Street and Savile Row. At Simpson's, men's (and eventually women's) clothes, accessories and services were distributed over seven sales floors, each divided into three departments. This expanded many of the ideas contained in Austin Reed's store, and smacked of a desire to outdo an arch rival: Simpson insisted on having at least one more barber's chair than Reed. Although Reed had a national chain of shops, and Simpson sold his DAKS brand through provincial outfitters, the concept of the men's store, as opposed to the outfitter's shop, remained a London phenomenon. Elsewhere, it became common for department stores to establish separate men's shops, with their own discreet entrances and typically masculine ambience. That arrangement occasionally survives, for example in the end bay of Bullough's, a small independent department store in Carlisle.

181 Simpson's (1935–6), designed by Joseph Emberton, was the most modern building on Piccadilly. The corner building glimpsed on the extreme left was built for the grocers Morel Bros., Cobbett & Son Ltd, around 1890 (see fig. 79).

Emberton went on to design the HMV shop on Oxford Street, which was rebuilt following a fire in 1936 and reopened by Sir Thomas Beecham in 1939. It occupied a narrow, tapering plot and was much smaller than Simpson's. Like Drages' and Marks & Spencer's buildings on the same street, the sleek façade was clad in polished black granite but, more unusually, the casement windows were set in bands of glass bricks. This created high sills, which meant that displays could be arranged beneath the windows of the upper sales floor, and that office staff could not gaze out of the windows. That type of fenestration remained rare, although something similar was attempted in the Plymouth co-op (now Derry's) after the war.

Soon store architects throughout the country were discovering the advantages of a streamlined *moderne* style, featuring long, narrow window strips with high sills that permitted interior displays. Many now argued that this horizontal style was a more natural expression of steel framing than the verticality typified

182 Before the opening of Simpson's, the façade of 'His Master's Voice' (HMV) on Oxford Street – originally erected as a men's outfitters – was one of the most sophisticated examples of neon signage to be seen in London. The building was rebuilt to a design by Emberton following a fire in the late 1930s. EMI Recorded Music.

by Selfridges. *Moderne* stores included the Bradford Co-operative Society store (pl. 155) and an extension to Fenwick's in Newcastle. The style was particularly apt for shops selling the products of modern technology, such as radios, refrigerators or televisions, and for furniture stores and car showrooms, both of which were shifting from town centres to suburban sites as a result of increased middle-class car ownership. A typical furniture store of this period was Randall's in Uxbridge (1938; William L. Eves), which was faced in faience and incorporated a strongly contrasting vertical accent in the form of an asymmetrical tower with a clock and flagstaff.[65] Utility showrooms could be similar, if smaller. The brick façade of the Urmston Gas Showroom (1938; Percy Howard) was set with rather small *moderne* windows, producing an elongated effect which was enhanced by a shaped canopy.[66] Such buildings usually had a ground-floor showroom and an office, as well as an upstairs lecture theatre which would have been used to demonstrate household appliances.

In the late 1930s the only store to make use of more advanced structural techniques than Simpson's was Peter Jones on Sloane Square, which belonged to the John Lewis Partnership.[67] When it opened in 1939, it was voted best modern building in a survey by the *Architectural Review*, receiving twice as many votes as any other candidate.[68] The architect, William Crabtree, was relatively inexperienced but would have seen Mendelsohn's stores when he toured Germany in 1930. He had also worked with Raymond Hood in New York and with Emberton on the design for Olympia in London. At Peter Jones (pl. 184), working with Slater & Moberly and C. H. Reilly, he produced one of the earliest examples of curtain walling to be seen in England. Its predecessors, such as the Daily Express Building on Fleet Street (1929–33; Ellis & Clark with Owen Williams) and Emberton's Universal House, had windows set in concrete walls, supported by cantilevered floors. Glass had been applied to the concrete as a veneer rather than a curtain. At Peter Jones, the windows were

arranged in a similar manner, but the glass stood proud of the concrete walls and floors, now forming a true curtain. Crabtree also introduced seemingly continuous mullions, which interrupted the inherent horizontality of the underlying structure without imposing a dominant verticality. Like Simpson's, the building had tiered or zoned upper storeys: something that quickly became a standard feature of English stores.

Surprisingly, aspects of the internal design of Peter Jones were rather conservative. By now, many new stores had been erected with open-plan floors, and some establishments, such as Whitaker's in Bolton, were even beginning to floor over their existing wells. Peter Jones none the less incorporated a large well, but with steelwork arranged in such a way that it could be floored over at a later date. A similarly tentative approach was revealed by the decision to install stairs and lifts rather than escalators. Once more anticipating future alterations, the east staircase was constructed of pressed steel, so that it could be

183   Joseph Emberton and his partner, Percy Westwood, designed the interior of Austin Reed's 'flagship' Regent Street store of 1926. The wavy light fitting and other aspects of the basement barber's shop are amongst a handful of original features to have survived to the present day.

easily removed and replaced with an escalator if need be, something that was, indeed, carried out after the war.[69]

Another well-publicised store built with a curtain wall in the late 1930s was Kingstone's (1937–8; Raymond McGrath), which was located on the periphery of Leicester city centre and sold furniture, radios and cycles. The façade dispensed with intervening mullions and, like Universal House, expressed the floor structure.[70] The continuous window strips held prismatic glass, and the panels beneath them were clad in 'shell-pink rolled opal glass', a type of Vitrolite which was fixed by copper strips and dabs of putty. As at Simpson's, a canopy with a cradle track for window cleaning ran along the top of the façade, whereas at Peter Jones the windows opened on pivots and could be cleaned from the inside.

Within the British Isles, the boldest Modern store of the 1930s was perhaps the furniture store erected by the St Cuthbert's Co-operative Association in Edinburgh in 1938. Designed by Thomas P. Marwick & Son, the centre of the façade contained a vast screen of plate glass, behind which the rectilinear structure of the building, the floors and stanchions, was clearly revealed. The glass was arranged in large square panes, with no horizontal or vertical emphasis, and had a thin ashlar surround. The St Cuthbert's Co-op, Peter Jones and Kingstone's were greatly influential in the 1950s, when stores of all descriptions were built with curtain wall façades, or glass walls within masonry frames. It was not long, however, before the doubts which Howard Robertson had expressed about glass-fronted stores in 1928 began to take hold, with dire consequences for the British high street.

The Post-War Store

After the Second World War, the biggest department store group was Debenhams, although House of Fraser began to catch up by acquiring several stores from Debenhams in 1952, and shortly afterwards buying the Binns, Barker's and Harrods groups.[71] But the market share of department stores, which were spending huge sums rebuilding war-damaged buildings, was dropping. Chain stores were increasing in number, and many had already reached the size of small department stores (20,000–30,000 sq. ft/1,858–2,787 sq. m). As multiples traded up, so department stores realised the savings to be made from standardisation, and traded down. In 1957–66 even Debenhams switched to central buying, bringing corporate awareness to the sales floor and shopfront for the first time. This trend established a broad middle market, and helped to produce a rash of somewhat dull buildings.

In the 1950s steel was still the preferred building material for stores but, as it was in short supply, many were built with reinforced-concrete frames. Owen Owen's new store in Coventry (pl. 185) used the 'mushroom' method of construction, characterised by columns with splayed heads.[72] This produced smooth, beamless ceilings and spacious open-plan sales floors on a grid of 27 feet 6 inches (8.38 m). The elevations of the store were discontinuous: one side had a curtain wall, another had strips of window alternating with brick bands, and a third had a blind wall pierced only by porthole windows. To a degree, this reflected the arrangement of functions within the building: the offices occupied a mezzanine gallery, while the stockrooms filled a vertical tranche of the building, rather than a basement floor. As they required a lower floor-to-ceiling height than salesrooms, this corner of the building contained seven, rather than five, floors.

185   As a result of bomb damage, Owen Owen's Coventry store had to be rebuilt after the war. The new building of 1951, by Rolf Hellberg and Maurice H. Harris, experimented with a number of different elevational treatments. It has recently been taken over by Allders.

New stores in historic towns often combined framed expanses of glass with regular fenestration which could still, at a push, be described as pseudo-Georgian. Such stores, usually faced with Portland stone, rose from the rubble of central Plymouth, Portsmouth and Southampton. In New Towns and industrial cities, architects were encouraged to produce more modern designs. Working in the tradition of D. H. Evans and Kendal

184   The Peter Jones store on Sloane Square was undoubtedly one of the most influential Modern buildings of the pre-war period. This photograph was taken around 1936 while building work was still in progress.

186 Tyrrell & Green's in Southampton was erected in 1954–6 to a design by Yorke, Rosenberg & Mardall (YRM). It was heightened and extended to the left at a later date.

Milne's, the Manchester firm of Beaumont & Sons produced several stores with continuous vertical mullions, such as Walsh's (1952–3) and Cockayne's (1957) in Sheffield. A more popular stylistic choice, however, was the glass curtain wall, continuing where Peter Jones and Kingstone's had left off. An example of this was Tyrrell & Green's store in Southampton (1954–6; pls 186–7) by the Modernist architectural practice of Yorke, Rosenberg & Mardall (YRM). The bays were defined by mullions faced in Portland stone, but the brickwork beneath the aluminium sash windows was masked by panels of Westmorland slate (front), fluted asbestos (side) or concrete aggregate (rear), rather than a glass product or YRM's signature white tiles. It was already clear, however, that such façades admitted more daylight than retailers desired, and modifications were introduced to remedy this. At Cole Brothers in Sheffield (1963; YRM), the central part of each window bay was blocked by a salient panel of brown glass mosaic tiles, and in later years stores used an opaque blue film to mask unwanted vision glass.[73] When curtain walling was juxtaposed with a solid wall the opportunity was seized to use the latter as a field for the display of artworks (pl. 156), bold lettering or logos.

Open-plan floors were now the norm, but a few stores were still built with wells. A major example was John Lewis's on Oxford Street (1955–60), which was designed by Slater & Uren. But now that wells were consigned, by and large, to the past, store layout was considerably simplified and standardised.

first floor

roof level

d

f f

j

g

h

i

h

second floor

A b o v e   B a r   S t r e e t

ground floor

b

a

c

basement

a. receiving & dispatch
b. boiler room
c. staff cloakroom
d. delivery
e. hairdressing
f. workroom

g. restaurant
h. staff canteens
i. kitchen
j. offices
k. plant room

staff   customers   goods

| 0 | | 20 metres |
| 0 | | 60 feet |

187   The open-plan sales floors and distribution of secondary functions within Tyrrell & Green's was typical of stores built in the 1950s and 1960s. The store relocated to West Quay mall in 2000, and was renamed 'John Lewis'. Based on *The Architect and Building News*, 11 October 1956, 483–4.

188   This drawing depicts the scheme by Sydney Clough, Son & Partners to provide Selfridges with an underground delivery bay and multi-storey customer car park (1957–8). Selfridges' logo, seen on the side of the building, combined the dollar and pound signs.

Armour-plated glass doors added to their sense of openness. Inside, suspended false ceilings concealed wiring and ducting that had previously been trailed through floors, and 'egg-crate' louvres or opaque ceiling panels shielded fluorescent light fittings and housed spotlights. Escalators or stairs rose through the middle of the floors; lifts were used less and less, and were rarely operated by attendants, unless their mechanisms were particularly Byzantine in their workings. As well as enclosed fire-escape stairs, stores often featured attractive free-standing staircases with tubular balusters, open risers and wooden treads. The rails of these staircases have usually had to be raised for safety, and the treads resurfaced. Sales areas increasingly adopted the display methods of the variety stores, with open-topped counters for fancy goods, and self-selection rails for clothes.

It has been claimed that the first department store in the country to display all of its merchandise on self-selection lines was the Landport Drapery Bazaar in Portsmouth, which opened in 1954.[74] Self-selection in such stores can be viewed as part of a wider campaign to attract working-class customers. Another tactic was the simplified interior, although an austere modern style did suit the enforced frugality and rejection of traditional-

ism that characterised the immediate post-war period. Even the most elitist stores were now attempting to attract the multitude by flooring wells, encasing columns and inserting false ceilings. They were also expanding the idea of the shop-within-the-shop, some geared especially for young people, such as 'Younger London' which opened in Dickins & Jones in 1947, Miss Selfridge, launched by Lewis's in 1966, and Harrods' Way In boutique, which opened in 1967.

Offices were now smaller in size, partly because cash tills were replacing complex overhead cash systems. They tended to be placed on the top floor, side by side with the staffrooms and restaurant. Delivery areas were increasingly provided within buildings, feeding stockrooms in a basement or on an upper floor. Several big stores constructed underground delivery roads. From the late 1950s, delivery vehicles entered Selfridges' basement via a ramp on Orchard Street, then re-emerged at street level in the middle of the Duke Street elevation, breaking the line of show windows. Few smaller stores, then as now, could afford the engineering costs inherent in such systems.

Motor cars were now within reach of the masses, and several stores offered customer parking facilities.[75] This trend had started in the early 1930s, when Bentall's built a huge hangar-like car park, shared by delivery vans and customers' cars, across the road from the store.[76] Before long Kennard's opened a car park with a quick snack counter for owner-drivers or chauffeurs, and Welwyn Department Stores offered a free car park over an underground air-raid shelter.[77] The idea did not spread far, however, until easy kerbside parking became a thing of the past. The 1,000-space multi-storey garage built behind Selfridges in 1957–8 (pl. 188) included a petrol station, an accessory shop, motor-car showrooms, cloakroom facilities and seven parking floors accessed by double ramps, with turntables for manoeuvrability on each level.[78] A few years later, in 1963, the car park of Cole Brothers in Sheffield took the form of a continuous ramped parking floor that could accommodate 400 cars.[79] As in Selfridges, each level communicated directly with the store, and corresponded with lifts. Cole Brother's architects, YRM, were also responsible for Keddie's in Southend, Essex, a tile-clad tower-and-podium store and office complex, which provided 150 parking spaces. The first phase, completed in 1963, incorporated two storeys of car parking above three sales floors, but the lower parking floor was converted into a sales area in the second phase, completed in 1972, by which time there was an extensive rooftop car park.[80] Rather laboriously, however, the parking floors were served by car lifts, rather than ramps, and vehicles were conveyed to parking spaces by trolleys. C&A adopted yet another method of integrating parking with shopping, when its store in Wembley High Road, London, was built with a basement car park. This varied approach to customer parking mirrored the experiments taking place in conjunction with precincts and malls in the same period (see Chapter 11).

Aided by air conditioning, stores began to shift from the transparent to the solid elevation, dispense with natural light and adopt peripheral stock layouts. In truth, the curtain wall had proved wholly unsuitable for stores; even that in Peter Jones was screened off from the inside shortly after it was completed. In 1956 Ellis Somake and Rolf Hellberg commented: 'the mid-20th century has learnt to appreciate the all-glass façade but cannot yet handle the unpierced wall, which is the more logical development for the department store'.[81] America had already embraced the closed wall, for example at Foley's in Houston, Texas.[82] Blind façades were also appearing in Europe, for example at De Klerks in Rotterdam. Soon stores like Keddie's in Southend and Burton's in Leeds (pl. 234) were being built with façades in which windows were reduced to thin slivers, and before long chain stores, in particular, were being designed with no windows at all above the shopfront. As a cheaper expedient, some proprietors even faced 'ugly' Victorian buildings with unbroken expanses of cladding. By the 1970s the detrimental impact of such buildings had become painfully plain to all.

Apart from Heal's extension (1962, now Habitat), Peter Robinson's on the Strand (1957–9) and Marshall & Snelgrove's on Oxford Street (1970), few prestigious new stores were built

189 The drapers John and Daniel Heelas opened their shop in Reading in 1853 and soon developed a strong furniture trade. The agglomeration of buildings that housed the store was reconstructed in 1979–85 in three phases, increasing the sales area by 50 per cent. The store was renamed 'John Lewis' in 2001.

in London in the 1960s and 1970s. One particularly high-profile project was the Army & Navy Stores on Victoria Street, which was rebuilt in 1973–7 with bronze-tinted boxed-out windows. When Debenhams rebuilt the old Footman Pretty & Co. store in Ipswich in 1977–80, the architects Ketley, Goold & Clark chose a similar style, with dark brick walls and boxed-out windows with opacified glazing. This overpowering building was supposedly 'produced to blend with the surrounding conservation area'.[83] While most post-war stores had flat roofs, the new Heelas store in Reading (1979–85) (pl. 189) was topped by a huge pagoda-style roof. Inside, it had a four-storey well lit with 'Tivoli' lights and equipped with glass-sided lifts. This marked a U-turn in department-store design, which was paralleled by similar developments in malls.

Department stores began to move into malls in the early 1970s. The John Lewis Partnership led the way: Jessop's of Nottingham moved into the Victoria Centre in 1972, Bainbridge's of Newcastle moved into Eldon Square in 1976, and new

190 The elevations of Selfridges' store in the Trafford Centre, Manchester (1998), clearly refer directly to its parent on Oxford Street.

Bentall's and Bourne & Hollingsworth's, were converted into malls, while Woolland's and Lewis's of Leicester were demolished. With a surfeit of unwanted store property on the market, the new high street department store, or even the store extension, became a rarity. The greatest activity was now the renovation of old buildings. Most spectacularly, Mohamed al-Fayed undertook the refurbishment of Harrods in 1987, with an Egyptian-style scheme (pl. 192) that aimed to revive some of the glamour of the store's Edwardian past. In 2000 Selfridges underwent an expensive revamp featuring new escalator wells and a profusion of coffee bars sited close to the merchandise. Many other stores have been refurbished to produce a light, bright atmosphere (pl. 167). Since the rediscovery of the old perception that daylight adds to the pleasure of the shopping experience, it has become normal for modern refits to incorporate light wells and/or glass fronts. One particularly prestigious example of the latter is Harvey Nichols in Leeds (1995; Brooker Flynn Architects) (pl. 191), which was slotted into the site of the former

191 The restrained glass façade of Harvey Nichols in Leeds is typical of late twentieth-century retail architecture; it does not try to compete with its Edwardian neighbours.

John Lewis branches opened in Brent Cross in north London in 1976 (pl. 303) and in Milton Keynes in 1979. These 'anchor' stores were positioned at the ends of mall walkways, and although they were physically distinguished from the remainder of the complex, they were little more than exercises in American-style big-box retailing. In the 1980s Debenhams became a major player and helped to popularise the 'galleria' (central well) format and the return to natural lighting.

Furniture chains, like Maple's and Habitat, moved to retail parks in the 1980s, but department stores remained on the high street and in the mall. In Lincoln, Debenhams found a location in a pedestrianised area midway between the main shopping street and a retail park (see p. 292), something reflected in the colourful postmodern design of the building which, with its warehouse-style hi-tech touches, is typical of neither high street nor mall stores. Stores attached to out-of-town shopping centres can also be fanciful. The Trafford Centre, on the outskirts of Manchester, is anchored by a Selfridges store (pl. 190) with an elevation that clearly refers to the London 'flagship' (pl. 162).

With the move to malls, high street department stores plummeted in number from 818 to 580 between 1971 and 1989.[84] Former giants like Barker's, Derry & Toms, Gamages, Swan & Edgar's and Peter Robinson's closed their doors for good. Several redundant department store buildings, such as Whiteley's,

192 Mohamed al-Fayed's refurbishment of Harrods began in 1987. This shows the ground-floor Egyptian Hall of 1991. The spectacular Egyptian Escalator Hall behind this was unveiled in 1997.

Empire Theatre on Briggate. In many stores, as in malls, the environmentally friendly face of capitalism is superficially celebrated in veneers of natural wood, glass and metal, generally within a limited palette of buff, green and grey. Within these minimalist interiors, elliptical shapes are ubiquitous, often outlined in the floor or suspended from the ceiling. More cutting-edge styling is offered by the new Selfridges store in Manchester (2002), which occupies part of a building originally designed for Marks and Spencer (pl. 249). Each floor has been designed by a different architect: Future Systems, David Adjaye, Stanton Williams, Aldo Cibic and Vincent van Duysen. Future Systems is also responsible for the most unusual and dramatic new store in the pipeline, Selfridges in the new Bull Ring shopping centre in Birmingham, which is due to open towards the end of 2003. Its extraordinary shape has been described as 'billowing curves drawn together at a waist'.[85] The concrete shell will be clad in aluminium disks, while the interior will be arranged around a

naturally lit atrium, or 'urban canyon'.[86] No less than the Oxford Street building of 1906–9, it promises to attain landmark status.

When Harry Gordon Selfridge first arrived in England, all drapery and department stores prized their individuality, but the sector is now dominated by a small number of powerful groups which, despite their inheritance of a heterogeneous building stock, have imposed centralised buying policies and house styles that affect the signage, the interior design and even the names of their branches. In 2001 House of Fraser rebranded the historic D. H. Evans as 'House of Fraser', following a refurbishment programme of £16 million,[87] and John Lewis has renamed most of its outlets, including Bainbridge's of Newcastle and Jessop's of Nottingham. Inside, concessions have taken over, with goods grouped by brand, rather than by type. With so many counters rented out to other retailers, it is as though the modern department store has returned to the format of the early nineteenth-century bazaar.

IO

Kings of Commerce:
Multiple Shops and Chain Stores

Britain has one of the most monopolistic retail markets in the world, with power concentrated in the hands of groups such as Dixons and Arcadia. The inexorable rise of multiple retailing is blamed for the demise of the independent shopkeeper, and unlike many of its European competitors the country certainly seems to lack a well-developed, small-scale, entrepreneurial culture. In Britain, independent shopkeepers have been pushed to the margins of town centres, and into increasingly specialised and localised sectors of the market. In contrast, high-rent properties in malls and high streets are crowded with the eye-catching liveries of national multiples, which can be recognised in an instant. The proliferation of these shops, with their standardised, branded goods, has made shopping easier and, in relative terms, cheaper, but critics of multiple retailing claim that this has been achieved at the expense of local distinctiveness, consumer choice and the human touch.

Most multiple retailers prefer to rent their premises, relying on the superficial impact of colour and signage to proclaim their presence. Only a minority elected, at some point in their history, to own and build their own stores, thus leaving a permanent stamp on the face of the high street. In adopting that approach companies visibly expressed their size and strength, honed their image and enhanced their recognisability. They discovered that they could make the most efficient use of space in a purpose-built store, and also that property was a sound investment, which could be exploited to raise capital in times of hardship.

Unlike independent drapers and co-operative societies, national multiples rarely employed local architects or building suppliers. It is, therefore, not surprising to find that their buildings trampled rudely upon local architectural traditions, and as early as the 1920s they were being denounced as the 'worst enemies of architecture'.[1] Despite this, many twentieth-century chain stores have considerable appeal. They survive in great numbers, but those that retain their original shopfronts, not to mention fenestration, signage and internal fittings, are becoming increasingly rare. These ephemeral aspects of national chain stores evoke experiences that were shared by entire generations, regardless of where they lived, and are capable of arousing great nostalgia.

The Early Development of Multiple Trading

Circumstances converged to encourage the development of multiple retailing, at first regionally and then nationally, in the last quarter of the nineteenth century.[2] In particular, improved transportation made the supervision of widely separated branch shops and centralised warehousing practical possibilities for the first time. Initially, multiples targeted concentrated working-class populations and, like co-operative retail societies, were assisted by the poor service offered at that level of society by independent traders. They offered a narrow range of products at cheap prices in a clean environment, aimed at a high turnover with a low profit margin, and generally sold only for cash. Their no-frills approach encouraged standardisation and hastened the development of pre-packaged branded goods.

By virtue of its railway book stalls, W. H. Smith's could claim to be the first multiple retailer in Great Britain (see p. 201), but it was a special case rather than part of a broad trend. The same can be said for upmarket London drapers, such as Marshall & Snelgrove, which opened seasonal outlets in spa resorts in the 1830s and 1840s.[3] By then a number of prominent retailers had opened second or even third branches in London itself. Hewetson's upholstery warehouses on Oxford Street and Tottenham Court Road (pl. 194) are particularly interesting, because they demonstrate an attempt to make two separate premises as alike as possible, right down to the method of hanging the curtains.[4] By the 1870s the oil and colourman George

193   A general view of Woolworth's flagship store on the Promenade in Blackpool (1938), which survives today as a discount shop and nightclub.

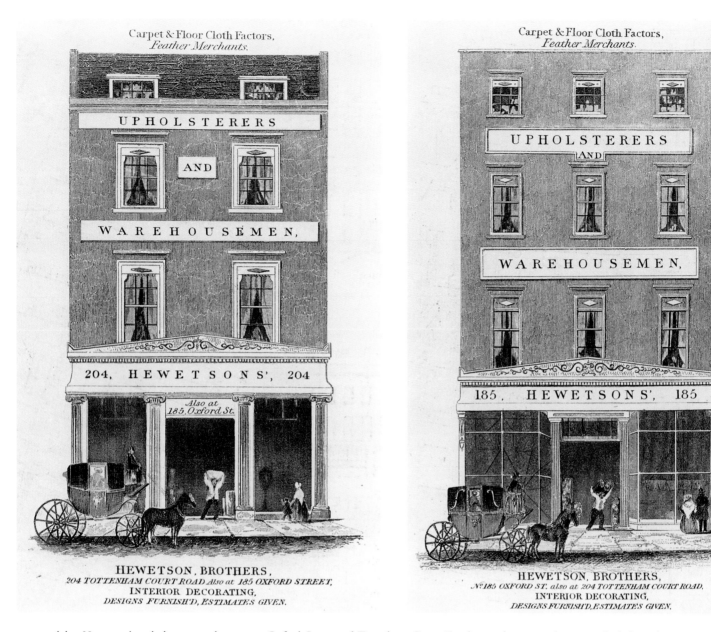

Carpet & Floor Cloth Factors,
Feather Merchants.

UPHOLSTERERS

AND

WAREHOUSEMEN,

204, HEWETSONS', 204

*Also at
185 Oxford St.*

HEWETSON, BROTHERS,
204 TOTTENHAM COURT ROAD Also at 185 OXFORD STREET,
INTERIOR DECORATING,
DESIGNS FURNISH'D, ESTIMATES GIVEN.

Carpet & Floor Cloth Factors,
Feather Merchants.

UPHOLSTERERS
AND

WAREHOUSEMEN,

185, HEWETSONS', 185

HEWETSON, BROTHERS,
N.º185 OXFORD ST. also at 204 TOTTENHAM COURT ROAD,
INTERIOR DECORATING,
DESIGNS FURNISH'D, ESTIMATES GIVEN.

194a and b   Hewetson's upholstery warehouses on Oxford Street and Tottenham Court Road must be counted as a particularly early occurrence of a retail house style. From Tallis 1838–40, parts 48 and 52.

Mence Smith had more than twenty branches in the London area, and by 1877 Singer, the sewing-machine manufacturer, had a more widely distributed chain of 160 branches.[5]

With the necessary transport infrastructure in place by 1870, multiple retailing flourished. One sector in which chains found swift success was the grocery trade (pl. 195), including provision shops and tea dealers. In 1880 only two grocers had twenty-five branches or more, but by 1910 forty-four had twenty-five or more.[6] By the turn of the century, the largest firms included Home & Colonial Stores, Maypole Dairy and Lipton's. Initially, these chains funded expansion by reinvesting profits, but by the 1890s many were raising finance by becoming limited compa-

nies and issuing shares. Despite this, individual shops remained very small and carried limited lines of merchandise. Before long, other types of food shop were treading in the grocer's footsteps. In particular, butchery chains began to develop in the 1880s as a result of the importation of frozen meat, and by 1900 there were an estimated 2,058 branch shops in the meat trade.[7]

Another area in which multiple retailing grew apace was the boot and shoe industry (pl. 196). This was associated with improvements in manufacturing processes which increased factory output. By 1870 ten firms had more than ten branches, selling mainly machine-made footwear, but twenty-one existed by 1880.[8] The market in men's clothing, especially ready-made

clothes and 'wholesale bespoke' tailoring, was also quickly entered by multiples. E. Moses & Son had three London branches by 1860, and Hyam & Co. had established a small chain of large stores in major cities by the early 1850s. They were followed by many who soon became household names, such as Joseph Hepworth (tailors), Austin Reed (shirts), G. A. Dunn (hats) and Charles Mackintosh (outerwear). By the time that Montague Burton arrived in England in 1900, no less than twenty-two specialists in men's clothing had ten or more branches, and Hepworth's alone had more than one hundred.[9] Women's clothing was still dominated by independent drapers and department stores, although Fleming Reid & Co. had more than seventy-five wool shops by 1895 and a number of chains specialised in furs.[10] By the end of the century the only conspicuous department store chain was Lewis's (see p. 142), which had originated as a men's outfitters rather than a draper's.

While most chains colonised a particular city or region before contemplating further expansion, W. H. Smith's was unique in establishing a national chain of newsagents virtually overnight in 1905, as a result of very special circumstances (see p. 201). In England, Smith's had few competitors in the newspaper trade. The principal tobacconists were Salmon & Gluckstein of London and Finlay's of Newcastle, while Maynard's of London was the largest confectioner and H. Samuel of Manchester the

195 This small grocer's shop in Sherburn Hill, County Durham, photographed around 1900, proudly proclaims its status as a branch of Walter Willson's 'colossal business'.

196 (*below*) The style of lettering on the fascias of Cash & Co.'s shoe shops (which belonged to the boot and shoe manufacturers Manfield's) cleverly imitated that of Boots Cash Chemists. This particular branch, photographed in the 1920s, was at 11 High Street, Wisbech, Cambridgeshire.

197   The store erected on Northumberland Street in Newcastle by C&A in 1932 was demolished in the early 1970s.

leading jeweller. Most of the variety stores or 'penny bazaars' that emerged in the 1890s and early 1900s were regional, although both Marks & Spencer and Woolworth enjoyed a national presence by 1914, and had clearly become leaders in their field.

One last sector in which multiples enjoyed success before the First World War was patent medicines and pharmaceuticals. Boots was probably the first multiple to specialise in drugs, but by the 1890s several other companies had developed strong regional chains. These included Taylor's in Leeds and Timothy White's in Portsmouth. Boots was one of the few national multiples to cultivate a middle-class clientele before 1914, without losing sight of its working-class roots. It was also one of the first to erect buildings that may be regarded as chain stores, beginning in the 1890s. At that time it was still rare for multiple firms to invest in property: their shops had remained small, with the manager and his family living on the upper floors. None the less, the majority erected distinctive shopfronts, produced either by their own shopfitting department or, more commonly, by an outside specialist.

★   ★   ★

The Golden Age of the Chain Store

Multiples came to dominate urban retailing in the inter-war period, when the number of companies with more than one hundred branches rose from forty-nine in 1920 to eighty-two in 1939.[11] It is probably no coincidence that this was paralleled by the rise of the commercial estate agent.[12] One important new area in which multiple retailing now thrived was women's clothing, with the appearance of firms such as Cresta Silks, Evans Outsize and Dorothy Perkins, which was named after the popular climbing rose to suit the cottagey design of its shops, with their gabled windows and 'crinoline lady' logo. Large furniture multiples were also appearing, such as The Times Furnishing Company, which erected impressive stores with faience façades, mostly designed by Cecil J. Eprile, one of which still stands on the edge of Birmingham's Bull Ring Centre.

By the mid-1920s Boots, Marks & Spencer, Woolworth, W. H. Smith's and Burton were all erecting chain stores (see below). They were not alone. The clothier C&A (Modes) arrived from the Netherlands in 1922 and set up its first branches in London (1922), Liverpool (1924), Birmingham (1926) and Manchester

198 Newcastle's overpowering new C&A store of 1973–4, now occupied by Primark, was of reinforced concrete, faced in dark chocolate-coloured bricks, with an exposed frame clad in mosaic tiles. A few bays of the 1932 building survive to the right.

(1928). Many of its early stores were inherited from Hyam's (see above), which it bought in 1925, but others were designed for the firm by North, Robin & Wilsdon (later North & Partners). Although C&A never developed a coherent house style to the same degree as Marks & Spencer, a small group of buildings was erected in a distinctive style, reminiscent of Burton stores, in the early 1930s. The largest of these included the art deco stores that brought echoes of Manhattan to Newcastle (pl. 197) and Sheffield in 1932.[13] In Newcastle, one wing was rented out to British Home Stores (BHS), which had been launched in Brixton in 1928 as a 3d. to 5s. variety store, in an attempt to fill the middle ground between Woolworth and Marks & Spencer. One other significant chain to arrive on the scene before the war was Littlewoods, which was founded by Sir John Moores and opened its first variety stores – including those in Brixton and Blackpool – in 1937.[14] The company's shopfront and diamond logo, still to be seen at its pre-war branch (renamed Hitchens) in Morecambe, Lancashire, clearly imitated Woolworth's, while C&A favoured the arcade fronts that were then so beloved by department stores. Such features acted as signals to attract different customer groups.

As will be seen from the case studies below, the uniformity of chain store architecture between the wars has been overstated by their critics. Most of the big national multiples built shops and stores of varying formats to suit different sites, headed by a flagship store in a prominent location that sometimes also accommodated the company's main office. Many flagship stores – including those of C&A, Dolcis and Lilley & Skinner – were sited on Oxford Street, the best-known and most popular shopping street in the country. At the other end of the scale, many companies opened outlets in suburban shopping parades. Sainsbury's even built parades under the auspices of its development company, Cheyne Investments Ltd, always taking the central shop for itself.[15] Just like modern malls, parades built by private developers needed to attract well-known multiples to draw other occupants and ensure their success. George Cross, the developer of a row of twenty-one shops beside the new Edgware Road station in Marylebone in the early 1920s, used Sainsbury's and W. H. Smith's as bait.[16] To ensure their cooperation, Cross made concessions: he granted Sainsbury's request for a piece of land on which it could build its own shop, and allowed W. H. Smith's to buy the largest unit in the centre of the parade, at a very favourable price. Other developers were prepared to grant multiples a rent-free period, sometimes as much as five years, if they would deign to grace parades with their presence. Another tactic was to assist the expansion of new chains to guarantee tenants. Edward Lotery, for example, persuaded Jack Cohen to open the first Tesco shops in his north London parades by offering free shopfronts and fittings.[17] Lotery's parades appear to have been similar in design, having a herringbone pattern in the brickwork above the shops.[18]

Clearly, businesses that built on a national scale required considerable amounts of capital. The value of high street sites rocketed between 1918 and 1939, and even exceeded store development costs.[19] The mere presence of Marks & Spencer or Burton made neighbouring properties more desirable and, just as particular trades had clustered together in the past, now national chains congregated on specific streets (for example, Northumberland Street in Newcastle upon Tyne). As prime locations became scarcer, property values appreciated all the more quickly. This phenomenon squeezed out old-established resident shopkeepers, who moved to peripheral areas where retail property values were declining. The process was self-perpetuating: by placing a premium on sites occupied by multiples, the property investment market enabled them to raise capital on their assets, which was ploughed into further expansion. Capital could be raised through mortgages, bank overdrafts or, most profitable of all, 'sale and leaseback' arrangements, which were often calculated to include rebuilding and shopfitting costs as well as the initial purchase price. Leaseback was adopted by Burton in the mid-1930s and, a few years later, by Woolworth. Woolworth and BHS also exploited a related financing technique, by which a site was acquired by a financial institution, redeveloped, then handed to the retailer on a long lease.

The drawback of 'sale and leaseback' was a loss of freedom with regard to extensions and structural alterations. This made it unattractive to Marks & Spencer which, once its chain was established in the 1920s, tended to enlarge its existing stores in preference to opening new branches. The company liked to own the freehold to its premises or, at the very least, to hold 99-year leases. To raise capital for expansion, Marks & Spencer launched itself as a public company in 1926; in later years, it raised further finance through mortgage debentures, and by increasing ordinary share capital. Although they pursued different methods, Simon Marks and Montague Burton became renowned as property entrepreneurs, and Burton was one of the first to set up a subsidiary company to hold retail premises in order to minimise tax liabilities.

The economical image of the earliest multiple shops was now changing, and more were appealing to the middle rather than the working classes. Some even commissioned established architects to design their shopfronts and fittings. In the late 1920s

Joseph Emberton, with his then partner Percy Westwood, worked for Austin Reed and went on to produce striking designs for Lotus & Delta shoe shops (pl. 77). In the same decade, E. Vincent Harris, architect of numerous imposing civic buildings, designed shopfronts for Mac Fisheries, a rare example of a fishmonger's chain, set up by Lord Leverhulme after the First World War to sell the catches of Lewis and Harris fishermen.[20] In the 1930s Wells Coates designed shops in London, Bournemouth and Brighton for Cresta Silks, and the émigré architect Fritz Landauer was, briefly, employed by both Boots and Burton.[21]

Multiples in the Post-War World

Amalgamation was largely responsible for the existence of twelve firms with more than 500 branches each by 1939.[22] The merger process continued after the war, with the expansion of large umbrella groups such as Allied Suppliers, Great Universal Stores and the British Shoe Corporation. Power and influence was, therefore, concentrated in fewer hands. Nevertheless, in determining the architectural form and style of shopping centres in bomb-damaged cities and New Towns, it was the local authorities and development corporations who, at first, called the shots.

Much post-war redevelopment involved the compulsory purchase of commercial property, and caused many sites that had previously been occupied by independents to fall into the hands of multiples. But, as the aesthetics of new buildings were dictated by local authorities, throughout the 1950s it remained rare for multiple house styles to extend beyond the superficies of colour and logo; even their lettering was controlled to some extent. This began to change in the 1960s and 1970s, when private developers took over the reins, and multiples once more had the chance to develop individual sites in a singular style. Many reacted against the monotonous uniformity of 1950s developments by producing buildings that paid little heed to their surroundings. Indeed, their scale and style often seemed deliberately aggressive. This charge could be levelled at C&A's new development of 1973–4 in Newcastle (pl. 198),[23] although it must be admitted that the firm's chief competitors were erecting equally unsympathetic buildings on the same street at the same time. BHS continued to rent space in C&A's building, although it had recently erected numerous new stores of its own, designed by G. W. Clark. Littlewoods' Construction Department was also very active throughout this period (pl. 199), with generally unimpressive results.

By the mid-1970s high street developments by multiple firms were slowing down. Possibly the proliferation of precinct and mall developments in the late 1960s and 1970s had accustomed the major national multiples to accept a shell from a developer rather than erect their own premises. This was a new way of

199 Monolithic chain stores like this Littlewoods in Sunderland exemplify the architectural insensitivity of the great national multiples during the 1960s and 1970s.

doing things. Architecture now played a lesser role in the branding exercise, while design became all-important. Some retailers managed to exercise considerable influence in that sphere, setting trends for others to follow. Particularly prominent were Terence Conran's Habitat, and Next, established by George Davies in 1982. In the 1980s these companies promoted a fashion for light, bright, glass-fronted shops, which is still with us today. Some Conran-trained designers, such as Rodney Fitch, went on to work for other clients, including Woolworths and Marks & Spencer.

Since the war, many new sectors have been colonised by multiples, from young fashion in the 1960s and 1970s (for example, Topshop) to mobile phone and computer shops in the 1990s (including Phones 4U). Some highly specialised areas have also been identified and cornered (for example, Sock Shop), and novel forms of retailing have been developed by firms such as Argos, with its over-the-counter catalogue shopping, and Matalan with its club membership. Following in the steps of the Italian retailer Benetton, many recent arrivals – such as IKEA (Swedish), the Disney Shop (American), Zara (Spanish) and

Sephora (French) – originated in other countries, and are symptomatic of global retailing. Over the years, many British chains have tried their luck abroad, with mixed success. Laura Ashley, Mothercare, the Body Shop, Early Learning Centre and Boots all failed in attempts to expand abroad, especially in North America, Western Europe and South-East Asia.[24]

Since 1945 increasing numbers of chains have appealed to middle-class rather than working-class tastes, but many still focus on the high streets of run-down northern towns, whose industrial infrastructure has been destroyed. 'Your More Store', Poundstretcher, Poundland and countless variations on that successful formula, have adopted a 'pile it high and sell it cheap' philosophy to suit areas where unemployment is high and wages are low. These successors to the penny bazaar coexist with charity shops, such as Oxfam, which are themselves chains, and are even developing own-brand merchandise. In recent years, discount multiples have managed to take over some ground formerly occupied by middle-of-the-road retailers, and have moved into large stores in high street locations. One example is Primark, whose one hundred outlets now include sixteen acquired from BHS, ten from C&A (which withdrew from the UK in 2001), ten 'Living' stores from the co-op, and Lewis's defunct Manchester department store.

At the opposite end of the spectrum are upmarket fashion shops, designed by such well-known architects as Branson Coates (Jigsaw, pl. 62), Rasshied Din (Next and French Connection) and Eva Jiricna (Joseph). These shops might be described as the retail expression of a brand. Shops such as Gap and the Body Shop have particularly strong house styles and sell a limited range of own-label products in an environment that reflects and enhances their brand image. Gap, with its faintly military emphasis on khaki and chinos, which are stacked on shelves and surfaces, has something of the quartermaster's store about it, while the Body Shop constantly reminds the customer of its environmentally friendly and socially responsible product sourcing. A few other retailers have expended a great deal more on interior design to create a 'brand cathedral', something that is a temple to the brand and not just a shop.[25] Amongst these can be counted Dr Marten's Dept Store in Covent Garden, with its industrial ambience, and the altogether more sophisticated and complex NikeTown, which attempts to construct an alternative version of London – Nike London – within part of the former Peter Robinson store at Oxford Circus (pl. 200). Having crossed two vestibules, the Nike shopper enters the inner sanctum, a circular atrium dominated by a large central cylinder: not a lift, but a curved screen on to which films and images are projected. On the upper levels can be seen a row of fictive Georgian façades in London brick, and these prove to be departments dedicated to various sports. Within each one, shoes and shirts are displayed as museum objects: Nike athletes appear in the form of photographs, text

200 Shoes are displayed with great care in the first-floor 'running pavilion' in NikeTown London. The interior design (by BDP/Nike Retail Design, 1999) evokes not just a running track, but a sense of speed. Merchandise is delivered to the sales floor via the transparent tubes that can be seen in the background.

and video; sound is controlled department by department and usually involves commentaries of relevant sporting events. From the upper storeys there is access to the interior of the central cylinder, which contains pseudo-educational displays about the manufacture and design of sports shoes and shirts, as well as photographs of ordinary people involved in sport, all displaying the 'swoosh' logo on their clothes or shoes. It remains to be seen whether this type of shop has a future beyond the main shopping avenues of the world's greatest cities.

The following case studies examine how five of Britain's best-known multiple retailers changed the face of the country's high streets in the course of the twentieth century.

★   ★   ★

I W. H. SMITH & SON LTD

W. H. Smith's became Britain's leading wholesale newspaper distributor in the early nineteenth century, and its foremost high street newsagent and stationer in the early twentieth.[26] After the Second World War, the company made great efforts to extend its appeal beyond its traditional middle-class customer base, and broadened its horizons by entering new areas of retailing, such as DIY. In recent years, Smith's has refocused on the sale of books, newspapers and stationery. In the sale of magazines it remains particularly influential, with the ability to make or break new publications. Today, the company has 532 high street shops in the UK, and more than 240 outlets in stations and airports.[27]

Britain's First Multiple Retailer?

The story of W. H. Smith & Son Ltd begins in 1792, when a small 'news walk' (i.e. paper round) was established in Mayfair by Henry Walton Smith. The business was continued and enlarged by Henry's widow, Anna, and when she died in 1816 it passed to her sons, Henry Edward and his more competent brother, William Henry (W. H.; 1792–1865). By 1818, when the Smiths moved to 42 Duke Street, they were described as 'newspaper agents, booksellers and binders'; soon they were also wholesale stationers.[28] Two years later they opened an office at 192 Strand. By then the newspaper trade was blossoming. Production had profited from the invention of the steam printing press in 1812, and circulation was boosted by rising literacy levels, encouraged by an abundance of reading societies, literary institutions and newspaper rooms. Before long, Smith's was undertaking the wholesale distribution of newspapers throughout the country, at first by coach and then by rail.

The spread of the railway system presented many new business opportunities, and in 1848 Smith's won the contract to run bookstalls for the London & North-Western Railway. Contracts with other railway companies followed, and the company's bookstalls steadily increased in number, from 35 in 1851, to 290 in 1870, and 1,242 in 1902,[29] figures that lend credence to the claim that Smith's was England's first national multiple retailer.[30] Smith's stalls sold books, magazines and newspapers and, from 1860, even offered library facilities, enabling customers to borrow a book at one station and return it at another. Meanwhile the wholesale side of the business continued to grow, and provincial warehouses were opened to supply newsagents with merchandise that had previously been sent direct from London. The London headquarters moved to 136 Strand in 1849, then into imposing new offices at 184–187 Strand, designed by H. R. Abraham, in 1855.[31] This building's main feature was the 'English and Foreign' department, complete with gallery and dome.

Shops for the Literate Classes

Smith's opened a handful of high street shops in the late nineteenth century, but it was in the early 1900s that it began to establish shops as a matter of policy, usually by taking over existing businesses. The first of these were in Clacton (1901), Gosport (1902), Paris (1903), Southport (1903), Reading (1904) and Torquay (1904), revealing a strong concentration on the British holidaymaker as a core customer.[32] The establishment of a Shops Department in 1904 demonstrated the company's intention to continue its expansion into high street retailing, but such plans were hastened by the 'great upheaval' of October 1905.[33] For some time the Great Western Railway and the London & North-Western Railway had been attempting to raise book-stall rents; Smith's refused to cooperate, and lost its contracts to run 250 stalls. To compensate for this, a Shopfitting Department was promptly formed under Frank C. Bayliss, who managed to fit out 150 newly acquired shops, located mostly on approaches to stations, by January 1906. These shops proved just as popular as the bookstalls.

Bayliss, who became a fellow of the Royal Institute of British Architects in 1925, remained in post until his death in 1938. The wide-ranging activities of his department, renamed the Estate Department in 1919, concerned the identification and development of new sites, the design of new and converted buildings, maintenance and repair, decoration, lighting and heating. Occasionally Bayliss commissioned local architects to design major schemes, and employed outside companies to install shopfronts and fittings to the company's specifications. His department also supervised the erection of Smith's wholesale warehouses, and its new head office, Strand House in Portugal Street, which was designed by H. O. Ellis in 1913.[34]

From the beginning Bayliss favoured a neo-Tudor or neo-Elizabethan style for Smith's shops. That was a natural choice, as medievalising styles had been embraced by stationers and booksellers since the early Victorian period. In 1840 Nathaniel Whittock had published a Gothic design for a bookshop, and in 1855 a Chester bookshop was reported to have a half-timbered façade and an 'Elizabethan' interior.[35] Many later examples could be cited, such as the shop built in 1877 for the stationers Anderson & Co. on King Street in Manchester, which displayed a range of motifs of late Gothic inspiration.[36] Smith's shops, therefore, attached themselves to an established stylistic tradition that was recognised by the cultured habitués of booksellers and stationers throughout the country. The addition of neo-Georgian bow windows to Smith's repertoire may have been inspired by Hatchard's new Piccadilly shopfront of 1912.

In the first half of the twentieth century Smith's undertook less new building work than Boots, Marks & Spencer or Woolworth, but when it did build anew it did not impose a rigid house style on façades, but tried to ensure that they were well adapted to their environs.[37] The branch erected on Cornmarket in Oxford in 1914–15 was faced in ashlar, and had a college-like appearance, with an oriel window at first and second floor levels. In contrast, the Stratford-upon-Avon shop of 1922 (pl. 202) was a mock-timber structure in a Tudor style, 'like nearly all of the best old buildings of Stratford'.[38] The neo-vernacular Winchester branch of 1927 was designed by Blount & Williamson, a firm of outside architects employed by the company, and exhibited many of the decorative details (pl. 203) for which Smith's was so well known.

Over the years, Smith's undertook a number of interesting conversions. Between 1906 and 1922 the Stratford branch occupied an early seventeenth-century building, thought to have

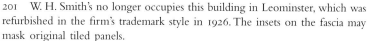

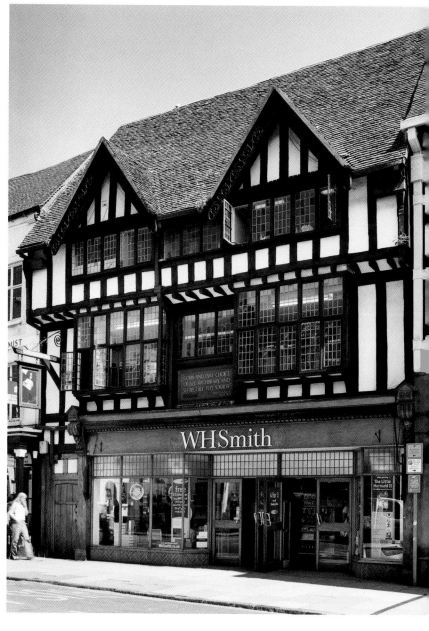

201 W. H. Smith's no longer occupies this building in Leominster, which was refurbished in the firm's trademark style in 1926. The insets on the fascia may mask original tiled panels.

202 W. H. Smith's Stratford-upon-Avon branch was built in 1922 and is one of the company's best-preserved pre-war shops.

been the home of Judith Shakespeare, the playwright's daughter. Although the company quit these premises in 1922, Smith's restored the building in 1923, complete with a shopfront in their own house style which still survives. Between 1918 and 1925, the company also set about restoring the Assembly Rooms in Salisbury, which had been purchased in 1914. When completed, the building offered rooms for public meetings and readings above the shop, but the clock turret clearly branded it as Smith's. The company's signature was also stamped upon the brick corner building that was acquired in Leominster around 1926 (pl. 201).

From the outset, Smith's shops were classified 'A' or 'B'. Generally speaking, the 'B' shops were the equivalent of the former railway bookstalls: they were located on station approaches, and their buying was undertaken by head office rather than a local manager. The 'A' shops had much more independence, and occupied more prominent high street locations. The frontages of major shops, regardless of whether they were 'A' or 'B', were treated lavishly. First-floor showrooms or tea rooms frequently had small-paned glazing, incorporating bullion glass. Above the entrances of the shops on Kingsway in London (1907) and Stratford-upon-Avon (1922) was the Shakespeare

203 This decorative rainwater head, on the side elevation of W. H. Smith's Winchester branch, displays a ship motif, the WHS monogram and the date of the shop (1927).

restored branch in Newtown in Powys. The main display windows invariably flanked a splayed entrance lobby with a bookstall on one side, for the quick sale of newspapers, magazines and penny-edition books. Because it was used in this way, the lobby was sheltered by a glazed weather screen. Its mosaic floor was decorated with the firm's 'egg' logo, involving a WHS monogram within an ovate frame, designed by the illustrator R. P. Glossop. Projecting from either end of the shopfront were pier cases for the display of books. Above this, the earliest fascias were painted green with cream-coloured lettering in a Roman face specially designed for the company by Eric Gill in 1903. Gill painted many fascias by hand until 1905, when Bayliss's staff took over. After the First World War, most fascias were tiled, with white lettering on a green ground, but by the 1930s many were of natural oak with incised lettering. 'Newsboy' lanterns, run on either gas or electricity, were suspended above the shopfront, to light displays after dark. The image of the newsboy, conceived by the artist Septimus Scott, also figured on metal hanging signs, which occasionally survive (see pl. 204). By 1930 Smith's shopfront was established to such a degree that it was being imitated by independent newsagents and booksellers, many of whom were clients of Smith's wholesale houses.

The internal layout of Smith's shops depended on the shape and size of the site, and the individual requirements of each branch. At the smaller end of the spectrum, the shop in

204 Several W. H. Smith shopfronts survive from the 1920s, including this example in St Albans, which was erected in 1929. At one time all of Smith's shops displayed a newsboy sign.

quotation, 'come and take choice of all my library',[39] while Cheltenham customers were treated to Wordsworth: 'Dreams. Books are each a World and Books we know are a substantial World both pure and good' (pl. 205).[40] The stone façade of the Birmingham shop (1921) was adorned with the heads of Dante, Chaucer, Scott and Shakespeare, and a frieze of children playing.[41] Similar imagery had been used by Victorian booksellers. For example, the stone façade of Southeran, Baer & Co., a bookshop erected at 36 Piccadilly in 1872, displayed the names of several great authors, busts of Shakespeare, Newton and Michelangelo, and *opus sectile* panels depicting historical scenes, including the dream of Guttenberg.[42]

Bayliss had established a standard shopfront design for Smith's by 1907,[43] and maintained it, subject to minor modifications, into the mid-1930s.[44] By then, the main components were low Cotswold stone stallrisers, and oak-framed display windows which frequently took the form of shallow bows composed of small square panes of glass, including random panes of bullion glass. Examples can still be seen in Stratford-upon-Avon (1922), Winchester (1927) and St Albans (1929; pl. 204), and at the

205 Cheltenham had an important branch of Smith's, with an ornate two-storey shopfront. This photograph was taken in 1955.

Richmond, Surrey (1921–2), was restricted to a single floor.[45] The lobby opened into the book department, which had glass-fronted bookshelves behind a counter to the left of the entrance. Typically, the fittings were of oak, and customers were provided with chairs and tables so that they could peruse books before buying. Beyond the book department, the shop widened into a top-lit stationery department, with a single sales counter on the left and the manager's office on the right. To the rear was the lending library, and a small, yard with a despatch room where boys collected newspapers for delivery rounds. Of the same date as Richmond was the larger Birmingham shop. It occupied three floors, with the book and stationery departments taking up the entire ground floor, and the Book Lovers' Room, for serious literature, in the basement. The mezzanine floor was lit by two large windows and light wells, ensuring good natural light for reading. It housed a balcony library, a children's book room, a seasonal stationery department and a fancy goods department. Smith's libraries tended to be located to the back of single-storey shops, or upstairs in larger shops, which had rear stairs to encourage a flow of customers through the ground floor. Similar strategies were deployed by Boots (see p. 216 and pl. 223), which also had a popular lending library.

When Smith's occupied a particularly large building, the upper floors could accommodate the manager, or staff involved in the early morning sorting of newspapers.[46] Some upper floors were sub-let or, at the discretion of the manager, used as a tea room.[47] While the ground floor of the purpose-built Winchester shop was laid out like that at Richmond, a hall on the first floor (pls 206–7) was originally used as a dance hall and tearoom. It had an impressive timber roof, and decorative plaster panels depicting historical scenes including, most appropriately for a tearoom, King Alfred burning the cakes.[48] Together with the branch on the Rue de Rivoli in Paris, this remains one of the best preserved early twentieth-century W. H. Smith's interiors in existence. Archive photographs (pl. 208) show that most shops were lavishly decorated with plasterwork and wood panelling but, alas, only fragments of these schemes survived the modernising zeal that gripped the company after 1945.

★   ★   ★

a. library

b. packing room

c. box office

d. tea room / dance hall

e. supper room

f. lounge & crush hall

g. kitchen

second floor

first floor

ground floor

Parchment Street

basement

staff   customers   goods   public

206   Floor plans and elevation of W. H. Smith's Winchester branch, as originally designed by Blount & Williamson in 1927. Based on Hampshire Record Office W/C11/2/2195.

Shops with Popular Appeal

Bayliss undoubtedly produced some of the most attractive multiple architecture of the early twentieth century, but in 1928 his superiors informed him that they considered his work too elaborate, and expressed the hope that he would make future shops simpler in design.[49] Initially, such remarks may have been prompted by financial difficulties, and especially the huge death duties occasioned by the demise of Freddy Smith in 1928, but the firm clearly wanted to broaden its appeal by embracing a less elitist approach. In 1929 P. R. Chappell of the Advertising Department observed: 'there is a limit to the amount of business to be obtained from the cultured classes to whom our handsome shops mainly appeal'.[50] He recommended opening a subsidiary to supply books to new 'Cheap Book Shops' that would operate on the 'Woolworth standard'.[51] Although his proposal was seriously considered, it was never implemented.

207   The first-floor tearoom of Smith's Winchester branch, now a modern sales-room, retains its open roof and original decoration, including 'King Arthur and the Table Round' in the end gable.

208 This view of the ground floor of Smith's Leeds branch, dated 19 November 1926, looks through the book department in the foreground to the stationery department at the rear. The interiors of Smith's Newtown branch were restored in a similar style in 1975.

Smith's erected few new buildings during the 1930s. Some railway contracts had endured, and much of the Estate Department's work now focused on bookstalls. Shops were also installed in the Southampton liner terminal in 1934, on the *Queen Mary* in 1936, and at London airports. Around 1937, the company launched a new design of shopfront, in marble and bronze, with neon signage. The clean Modern style was maintained after Bayliss's death in 1938, but by the outbreak of war only major shops in London and other cities had received face lifts.

In the hands of its next chief architect, H. F. Bailey, Smith's new shopfront design was slightly modified, with Vitrolite

often used as a substitute for marble. By the late 1950s lobby bookstalls were being eliminated, and many old oak shopfronts replaced. Typically, the shopfronts of Crawley and Eastbourne in Sussex (pl. 209), both erected in 1957, had great expanses of glazing and rows of glass doors, within green marble surrounds. The introduction of self-service, for example in Eastbourne, brought about many internal changes: counters and shelves were removed, and Vizusell island fittings were installed so that customers could browse.[52] The Vizusell range was manufactured by the shopfitters Eustace & Partners Ltd, and retailed to other newsagents by Smith's.

209   In 1957 Eastbourne became one of the first of Smith's branches to sport this new style of shopfront. It was also one of the first to adopt the self-service system, termed 'Simplified Selling' by the firm, using 'Vizusell' fixtures manufactured by Eustace & Partners. The shop itself was designed by Smith's chief architect, H. F. Bailey.

In the course of the 1960s Smith's shops dropped in number from 376 (1961) to 319 (1971),[53] a decline offset by the creation of larger shops, referred to as 'super-stores'. This involved a great deal of modernisation and rebuilding.[54] The first 'super-store' opened in Bradford in 1960, with 12,000 square feet (1,114.8 sq. m) of retail space, a size comparable with Marks & Spencer stores of the 1930s. It included innovations such as a conveyor belt that transferred stock from the reception dock in the loading bays to the stockrooms, and electronically operated blinds. As well as the largest W. H. Smith's gramophone record department to date,[55] the three selling floors included departments for camping,

china and fancy goods. These lines were soon scrapped, however, when the Central Buying Group decided to concentrate on core merchandise, namely books, stationery, newspapers and magazines. In 1961, facing competition from cheap paperbacks and free public libraries, the lending libraries finally closed.

Externally, the ground floor of new stores was glazed, while the upper floors were virtually blind. The stores in Southend (1965), Leicester (1970) and Peterborough (1973; pl. 210) merely had a narrow band of lights running between the first and second floors. Internally, the Peterborough branch traded solely on its 15,000 square foot (1,393.5 sq. m) ground floor, with

210 Despite its bulky form and limited fenestration, the use of red brick and minimal arcading in Smith's Peterborough branch – built in 1973 on the site of the Angel Hotel – were signs that mainstream high-street architecture was swinging away from the Modern movement. The building to the left of W. H. Smith's was erected by Marks & Spencer in 1932.

offices and stockrooms of equal area above. The Birmingham 'super-store' (1973) traded on three floors (basement, ground and first floors), with 29,000 square feet (2,694.1 sq. m) of selling space, making it Smith's largest store at the time.[56] It was one of the first to adopt a new brown and orange livery, which was said to 'reflect the company's new approach to design'.[57] Modern features included lifts and escalators, and a travel agency.[58] A network of underground roads enabled delivery vehicles to drive into a service bay where a conveyor system carried goods to the stockroom's unpacking area, located in the sub-basement.

In the late 1970s Smith's reacted to opposition from new specialist chains by diversifying and buying up its competitors. It purchased LCP Homecentres (later Do-it-All) in 1979, Paperchase in 1986, Our Price in 1986, and became the major shareholder in Waterstone's in 1989. In the mid-1990s, however,

Smith's decided once again to concentrate on its core businesses, and disposed of these interests.[59] In 1998 the company bought John Menzies to consolidate its high street position. More radically, in 2001, the historic wholesale division, with its fifty-one warehouses, was put on the market.

Since the 1970s many W. H. Smith's shops have opened in malls rather than on the high street, and in recent years the company has tentatively begun to open stores in retail parks. New high street shops are generally smaller than the 'super-stores' of the 1960s and 1970s, although many still trade on two levels. The current house style, introduced in 1997, is largely confined to a plain blue and white fascia and a logo comprising a small 'WH' over a large 'S'. This is far removed from the style adopted by Bayliss, under the influence of the Arts and Crafts movement, in the early 1900s.

Boots the Chemists has dominated pharmaceutical retailing in England since the late nineteenth century, and now occupies shops on every high street and in every shopping centre throughout the country.[60] Its position, however, is not unassailable. In recent years, new specialist chains such as Superdrug and supermarkets such as Tesco have stolen a large part of the health and beauty market. The company has retorted by announcing numerous new initiatives, including a trial scheme to open Boots counters in Sainsbury's supermarkets.

Humble Beginnings on Goosegate

The founder of the Boots company was John Boot, an agricultural labourer from Radcliffe on Trent in Nottinghamshire. In 1849 he opened the British and American Botanic Establishment, a wholesale and retail shop, at 6 Goosegate, Nottingham. Customers were invited into the back parlour for consultations on Mondays, Wednesdays and Saturdays, and were sold herbal remedies prepared by John and his wife, Mary.[61] Mary ran the shop after John died, and when their son Jesse (1850–1931) reached the age of 21 he became a partner. For a while the business traded under the name M. & J. Boot, herbalists, but in 1877 Jesse took sole control. That summer he launched a hugely successful promotional campaign, aimed at working-class customers, with newspaper advertisements listing more than 100 patent medicines at discount prices.

The old family shop could no longer contain the growing business, and in 1878 Boot leased 16 Goosegate.[62] Soon afterwards, numbers 18–20 were acquired, and in October 1881 a local architect, Richard Charles Sutton, was engaged to alter the extended premises.[63] It was envisaged that the ground floor would house a retail shop (no. 16), a wholesale shop (no. 18) and stores with a workshop to their rear (no. 20), with Boot's office occupying a central position. On the first floor there would be four stockrooms, and on the second floor living accommodation comprising two sitting rooms, two bedrooms and a kitchen. This compact scheme may not have progressed far when, in March 1882, Boot decided to rebuild.[64] Sutton now designed a large four-storeyed building (pl. 211) with a spacious open-plan shop, and offices were added to the rear as an afterthought.[65] Extensive stockrooms on the first and second floors indicate that the wholesale side of the business was burgeoning, and the layout of the domestic accommodation, now split between the second and third floors and equipped with seven bedrooms, suggests that it was designed as a staff hostel rather than a family home, although directories indicate that Boot lived here for a few more years.[66] The most striking aspect of the new building was its two-

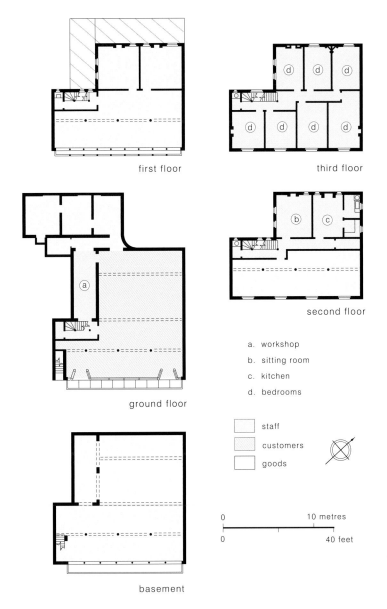

a. workshop

b. sitting room

c. kitchen

d. bedrooms

staff

customers

goods

0   10 metres

0   40 feet

211   The layout of Jesse Boot's shop on Goosegate, Nottingham, as designed by R. C. Sutton in 1882. Based on City Building Plans, 542, 1 March 1882, Nottinghamshire Archives.

storeyed cast-iron shopfront (pl. 212), which still survives today.[67] Although this shopfront hints at the presence of a first-floor showroom, this did not materialise until 1885, when Boot moved his stockrooms into a converted row of houses behind the shop.[68] The new showroom could be reached by a hydraulic lift– probably the first passenger lift to be installed in any Nottingham retail establishment–but working-class customers refused to use it, preferring the stairs.[69]

In 1883, the year the new Goosegate shop opened, the business became a private limited liability company (Boot & Co. Ltd), with Jesse Boot as chairman and managing director.[70] This enabled Boot to offer a legitimate dispensing service in his shop,

212 The splendid cast-iron shopfront of Boot's Goosegate shop was manufactured by Goddard & Massey and installed in 1882. Since that time the positions of the doorways have been altered.

and introduced a period of phenomenal expansion. Between 1881 and 1893 Boot opened seven new branches in Nottingham,[71] and in 1884 he opened his first shops outside the city, in Sheffield and Lincoln. An architectural house style was first adopted in the late 1890s, when a number of new branches were designed by Albert Nelson Bromley, an architect who ran a successful private practice in Nottingham, and whose relationship with the company was to span thirty years.[72] Amongst his first Boots stores were Bedford (1898), Burton upon Trent (1897) and Grantham (1899; pl. 213), all of which adopted an eclectic Jacobean style, with elaborately shaped gables, and were not greatly different from much street architecture of the day.[73]

By the turn of the century Boot controlled a network of no less than 181 branches which were concentrated in the Midlands and North, and included a strong presence in seaside towns. Many of these were located in sub-central positions, and were conversions rather than new buildings, with a house style restricted to signage and, from about 1900, the signature logo known as the Boots scroll.[74] Meanwhile, the manufacturing and wholesale side of the company was expanding in parallel with its retail outlets and, around 1890, moved into a former cotton mill on Island Street, Nottingham.[75]

Pelham Street and the 'Black and White' Stores

In the mid-1890s Boot and his wife, Florence, began to pursue a middle-class clientele. As well as erecting imposing new stores on central sites, they extended the range of merchandise sold in their largest branches to include books, stationery, fancy goods, artists' materials and toiletries. These departments were usually on the first floor, as was the Boots Booklovers' Library, a subscription library which was established in 143 branches between 1898 and 1903. Meanwhile, some key branches, such as Brighton and Nottingham, were fitted out with cafés in the fashion of fully fledged metropolitan department stores. Many of these innovations originated with Florence Boot, whose family ran a bookseller's and stationer's shop in St Helier, Jersey, but others may have been suggested to Jesse during a trip to America in 1889.[76]

Between 1900 and 1914 the number of Boots branches more than trebled, to 560, partly through the acquisition of regional chains such as William Day's, which had sixty-five shops in London and the South, and J. H. Inman's, which had twelve outlets in the North. Expansion was also achieved through the construction of new branches, and Boot showed a keen interest in the design of new stores. As an acquaintance observed: 'My private opinion is that nothing in life gave Mr Boot so much pleasure as building and, if it could not always be new buildings, then alterations.'[77] The artistic Florence Boot was closely involved in the interior design of the shops, and her ideas were developed by the company's own Building and Shopfitting Departments. The Building Department had been created in 1884, when Boot bought out his builder, Alf Fisher of Red Lion Square, Nottingham. The Shopfitting Department evolved more gradually, beginning with the employment of two joiners in 1883, but employing thirty men by 1900.[78] In 1898 an architect, James Young, was appointed manager of the merged department. After Young's dismissal in 1900 it was managed by M. V. Treleaven.[79]

In 1903–4 Boots rebuilt its existing store on the corner of Pelham Street and High Street, Nottingham (pls 213, 214, 216),

213 This illustration from Boots Scribbling Diary 1905 shows the shops falling within the remit of Boots Cash Chemists (Eastern) Ltd. Those in Bedford and Grantham, as well as the 'flagship' Pelham Street store, were designed by A. N. Bromley.

214 The cast-iron gallery in Boots' Pelham Street store (1903–4) appears to have been retained from the earlier shop on the site. Today, the columns can still be seen inside the building, which no longer belongs to Boots.

retaining a cast-iron galleried well that had been erected ten years earlier.[80] The architectural design owed a great deal to the smaller stores that Bromley had designed for the company in the late 1890s, but was immeasurably grander. The building stands three storeys high, with an attic partly concealed behind a balustrade, and is expensively faced in terracotta. Jacobean and classical elements mingle on the ornate façades, but the wooden shopfront is wholly art nouveau in style, with curvaceous glazing bars in the transom lights of the display windows and on the mirrored soffit of the deep entrance lobby (pl. 216). The interior (pl. 214) has been greatly altered, but traces of the original gallery, with its crocket capitals, can still be seen.

Clearly, the Pelham Street store was much more than a simple provincial chemist's shop. It revealed aspirations to departmental store status, and indicated a serious attempt to woo middle-class custom. Its Jacobean style, its domed corner tower, the lavish use of terracotta and the galleried interior were all evocative of modern London department stores such as Harvey Nichols. It served as the model for numerous Boots branches throughout the country, including Birmingham (Bull Street, 1915–16), Lytham St Anne's in Lancashire (1906), and Southend (c.1915) (pl. 215).[81] The shopfronts of these stores were generally more sober than that of Pelham Street, but Bromley's elaborate art nouveau design was reproduced by the company on several

215 Boots' branch in Southend, Essex, of 1915 – photographed when new by Bedford Lemere – was designed by Bromley & Watkins and faced in Doulton Carrara Ware. The building still stands, shorn of its original shopfront and signage.

It is generally thought that 'black and white' Boots stores were inspired by a seventeenth-century building in St Albans, which was restored by the company in 1900.[86] This theory is doubtful, as the building in question did not have exposed timber framing. The 'black and white' stores belong to a fashion of English street architecture that produced a number of mock timber-frame stores, including Goodall's in Manchester (1899–1902) and Whittaker's in Bolton (1906–7), which incorporated 'old oak obtained chiefly from buildings erected 200 to 400 years ago in

216 The ceiling of the entrance lobby of the Pelham Street branch was lavishly decorated with curvaceous glazing bars and mirror glass in an art nouveau style.

occasions, for example at Lytham St Anne's, Buxton and Southampton.[82] A popular variant was employed at Cambridge and Scarborough. Even some independent chemists adopted this style, for example, a shop at 11 George Street in Bath.

Around 1903 a 'black and white' style was introduced for the façades of important Boots branches, especially those located on prominent sites in historic centres. This style featured gabled façades with mock-timber framing, decorative bargeboards, 'Venetian' oriels, leaded casements, stained glass, pargetting and statuary depicting ecclesiastical figures or local worthies. Despite assumptions to the contrary,[83] the concept may have originated with Treleaven, rather than Bromley. Treleaven was certainly the author of two particularly early exercises in this style: a simple design for King's Lynn, dated 1903, and the more ambitious Winchester store of 1905.[84] At least sixteen 'black and white' stores were erected, including Lichfield (1909), Peterborough (1911) and Shrewsbury (1906–7; pl. 217).[85] Their shopfronts, none of which is known to survive intact, had leaded transoms set with bullion glass, much in the style of W. H. Smith's, and for a short time the company even adopted a mock-Tudor logo. It is unclear to what extent this medievalising style was carried through to the interiors of the stores, all of which were subsequently modernised.

217 Boots' 'black and white' Shrewsbury branch was built in 1906–7, and was extended at a later date in a matching style (i.e. the bay on the right).

the Bolton district'.[87] This trend was preceded by, and probably inspired by, the large-scale rebuilding of commercial medieval properties in Chester in the mid to late Victorian period. From 1896 Boots had leased just such a property, at 24 Eastgate Street, Chester, now occupied by Evans (pl. 24).[88] Unlike the St Albans branch, that building incorporated specific features, such as 'Venetian' oriels, later used to great effect by Treleaven.

The eccentric London architect Percy R. Morley Horder is sometimes credited with the decorative aspects of the 'black and white' Boots stores, including the statuary and glass.[89] Horder is better known for his houses and churches, which are in the tradition of the English Vernacular Revival, than for his commercial work. His involvement in the 'black and white' stores is open to question, as he does not seem to have worked for Boots before 1914.[90] During the First World War he designed several branches: Eastbourne and Bristol in a classical style,[91] Windsor in neo-Georgian. The Windsor store, although small, appears to have marked a stylistic watershed for the company.

Not all large new Boots stores of the early 1900s were built by the company. In Leeds, for example, the company moved into a prominent corner unit in Frank Matcham's Empire Theatre development (pl. 104), and the main London store occupied a handsome new building at 182 Regent Street. In contrast to such relatively upmarket city-centre stores, many smaller branches occupied converted terraced houses, often with huge billboards masking the upper storeys and proclaiming the presence of the largest retail chemist in the world. Line drawings of shops published in Boots Scribbling Diaries for 1905 (pl. 213) reveal the huge variety of Boots buildings and shopfronts at that time.[92]

Boots between the Wars

In 1920 Jesse Boot, who was suffering from poor health, sold the company to Louis Liggett of the United Drug Company of America for £2.25 million. Liggett retained Jesse's son John as a director and in 1933, after experiencing huge losses in the stock market crash of 1929, sold out to a syndicate of British bankers, led by John Boot, for £6 million. Throughout these years the most important event for the company was the relocation of its manufacturing arm to a site in Beeston, near Nottingham, where Owen Williams's well-known factory (D10) was built in 1933. In the same year, the company opened its thousandth store, in Galashiels in Scotland.

Boots abandoned the 'black and white' style after the First World War. From around 1919 the Architects' Department was headed by F. W. C. Gregory, the former partner of Ernest R. Sutton, whose father had designed the Goosegate store in the 1880s.[93] Much of Gregory's energy, in the early 1920s, was directed into the revamping of existing business premises that

had been acquired by the company. In the mid- to late 1920s, however, Gregory designed a number of new stores in a neo-Georgian idiom (for example, Hull and Mansfield). His standard shopfront (as at Hertford, 1919), which he repeated until he left the company in 1927, had a stepped fascia, a reeded surround and transom lights with x-shaped glazing and margin lights.[94]

The grandest new Boots buildings of the 1920s were designed by either Horder or Bromley, rather than Gregory. One of the most impressive was Horder's neo-Georgian Lincoln store (1923–6; pl. 218),[95] which occupied a corner site at the top of the High Street. The delivery entrance on King's Arms Yard was flanked by a store for staff bicycles and a single-van garage. A goods lift was situated close to the entrance, and served all four floors. Goods were delivered to the basement, unpacked in a special area and then stored in one of several stockrooms, which were probably organised on a departmental basis. This floor also included separate mess-rooms for the male and female shop staff. The ground-floor shop was large enough to contain island counters, and was served by a small dispensary, discreetly located at the rear, close to the delivery entrance. Both the large first-floor showroom and the second-floor 'dancing and tea room' could be reached by lift or stairs. A small supper room opened off one corner of the tea room, and customer facilities included tele-

218 Percy Morley Horder designed several neo-Georgian stores for Boots, including this branch in Lincoln (1923–6), which is now a Job Centre. The Boots monogram can still be seen in the wrought-iron work of the second-floor balcony.

219 In the 1920s Bromley & Watkins designed several stores for Boots in this sober classical style. This branch was built in Cheltenham in 1924–6.

phone booths, as well as the usual ladies' and gentlemen's lavatories. Amongst the kitchen and restaurant staffrooms on the third floor was a special 'cakemaker's room'.

Bromley, with his partner H. G. Watkins, was now responsible for an extraordinary group of Boots stores, including Cheltenham (1924–6; pl. 219), Leicester (1926–8) and Brighton (1927–8), with grandiose neo-classical façades fronted by porticos and topped by full pediments. These monumental ashlar buildings resembled venerable financial institutions rather than shops. Indeed, Bromley & Watkin's design for the National Provincial Bank in Nottingham, published in 1926, sported an identical centrepiece.[96] It does not seem fanciful, therefore, to suggest that the Boots stores evolved from the architects' experience of bank buildings. In the context of chain-store architecture, the closest comparisons are Marks & Spencer's Winchester, Peterborough (pl. 210) and Canterbury stores, all of which date from the 1930s. Perhaps, in this instance, Marks & Spencer was inspired by Boots. There is, after all, ample evidence that the major multiples kept a constant eye on one another's building activities.

In 1927 Percy J. Bartlett took over from Gregory as head of Boots Architects' Department, and in 1928 Bromley ceased to work for the company.[97] From now on most new Boots stores were designed by Bartlett, rather than outside architects, although Henry Tanner was responsible for the rather dull

Bournemouth branch of 1933.[98] The change in personnel was not accompanied by a stylistic revolution, as Bartlett clearly continued where Gregory had left off. Indeed, the fact that Bartlett entered partnership with Gregory after retiring from Boots in 1949 is some indication of how closely the two men might have collaborated in earlier years.[99] In the early 1930s Bartlett stated that it was the firm's policy to design buildings to suit their context and, true to these words, he produced 'free Georgian' stores for towns such as Colchester and Norwich, a Tudor style for Cambridge (1931) and a 'frankly modern' treatment for large industrial towns such as Coventry (1932), Liverpool (c.1935) and Leeds (c.1935).[100]

Some of Bartlett's earliest shopfronts, for example that at Eastleigh in Hampshire (1927), were almost identical to those designed by Gregory throughout the 1920s. By 1930, however, he had developed a streamlined Modern design, with close-set horizontal glazing bars in the transoms, and art deco metal doors (as at Wilmslow, 1930). Even the neo-Georgian Reading branch (1935) had a Modern shopfront, incorporating a long island showcase. The streamlined travertine shopfront of the Leeds branch wrapped around an acutely angled corner site and was crowned by an illuminated cornice. The branch on Ranelagh Place, Liverpool, had an even more Modern look, as it combined travertine with stainless steel doors and window surrounds, rather than teak, as at Leeds.

Bartlett returned to the medievalising style of Boots's past for at least one new store of the 1930s: Farnham in Surrey (c.1930).[101] Both this store, and the genuinely medieval building restored by the company in Canterbury in 1931, were given neo-Georgian shopfronts, with curved bows under jetties. The Canterbury shopfront, actually more typical of W. H. Smith's than Boots, is one of the few surviving pre-war Boots shopfronts in England. The shopfront of the Georgian Chichester branch (c.1930) was surprisingly old-fashioned, with leaded transom lights and a central canted lobby. It was deliberately finished in an 'old' green colour.

In large Boots stores of the 1930s, the subscription library was positioned above the main showroom and dispensary. Most shops, however, were long and narrow, with a single-storeyed showroom lit by a roof lantern to the rear. In these, the dispensary stood behind the sales area, with the library beyond, drawing users through the shop, where they might pause to make an impromptu purchase. Stockrooms and 'empties' sheds occupied a yard to the rear. After the No7 cosmetics range was introduced in 1935, beauty parlours were added to top stores, including that on Regent Street in London.

★　★　★

Boots after the War

The demand for drugs was accelerated by wartime conditions, the inauguration of the National Health Service (1948) and significant medical advances. Not surprisingly, Boots continued to expand. After the war, rather than buying private chemists' businesses, the company concentrated on establishing large 'departmental' stores in prime locations, and big chemists' shops in secondary centres. The manufacturing facilities at Beeston were greatly enlarged, additional factories were established, and the agricultural division of the company flourished.

Thirty-three Boots stores had been destroyed by bombing, including those in Manchester, Plymouth and Portsmouth. The job of rebuilding these, and designing stores for New Towns, fell to Colin St Clair Oakes, who took over from Bartlett in 1949.[102] More than ever, each individual store and shopfront was designed to suit local circumstances, if not local traditions. The elevations of new stores were relatively conventional, some adhering to the neo-Georgian formula preferred by the company between the wars (as at Plymouth), some having a high proportion of wall to window (St Helens), some having glass curtain walls (Rotherham), and others compromising by surrounding glazed areas with blank walling (Hanley). Shopfronts were similarly varied: those installed in new stores used modern materials such as mosaic tiles, perspex, aluminium and neon, while those in older buildings (Oakham) had traditional wooden surrounds. Interiors were arranged around rows of island counters (pl. 220), but were adapted to partial self-service from 1956, and since then most Boots stores have remained part self-service and part counter service.

In the 1960s and early 1970s, in common with other large multiples, Boots erected new stores with elevations that paid no heed to the style or materials of older buildings in the vicinity (pl. 221). Harsh modern cladding, such as concrete aggregate, was used a great deal, and many elevations were completely blind above street level. Occasionally this approach was tackled with aplomb (as in Cardiff, 1967), but it usually made little positive contribution to the ambience of the high street. Inside stores, the main change was the phased closure of all first-floor Booklovers' Libraries (pl. 223) in 1965–6. In 1968 the rival chain of Timothy Whites & Taylors was acquired, and its 622 stores were integrated into the Boots organisation. It was also in 1968 that a new head office was built at Beeston, designed by Skidmore, Owings & Merrill of Chicago.

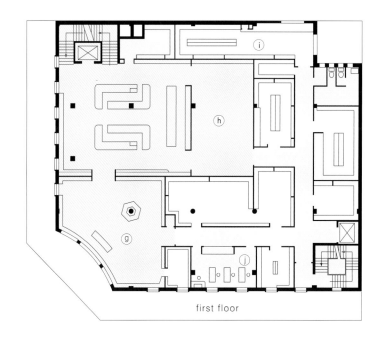

first floor

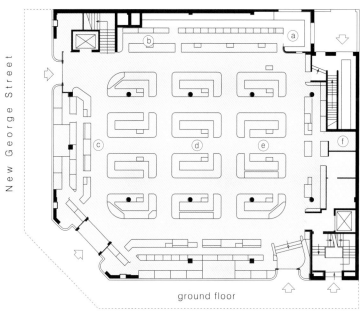

New George Street

ground floor

Armada way

staff	a. dispensary	f. surgical fitting room
customers	b. photographic	g. library
goods	c. toiletries	h. seasonal
	d. stationery	i. chemists store
	e. fancy goods	j. cashiers

0   20 metres

0   60 feet

220   These floor plans show the layout of Boots' Plymouth store, which was erected to a design by the company architect C. St C. Oakes in 1951–2. Based on plan in the Boots Company Archives.

221 The Boots branch at 27–28 Bridge Street, Swindon, Wiltshire, designed by Oakes about 1965, was typical of chain-store buildings of that era. Note Dunn's hat shop just visible on the left.

222 A recently completed Boots store (Oxford, 1999–2000) in a contemporary style.

Oakes was succeeded as Chief Architect by I. V. Mitchell in 1967, followed by J. H. Gant in 1972–3. Gant reorganised the Architects' Department as a multi-disciplinary team, on the model developed in the 1960s by Building Design Partnership (BDP).[103] Around 1980 Gant handled a major store expansion programme. As ever, not all new stores were designed by the company: in many cases the structure was provided by an outside developer, and occasionally Gant engaged the services of a well-known architectural practice (at Preston it was BDP). Fitch & Co. were commissioned to produce designs for two types of store: large stores (over 6,450 sq. ft/599.2 sq. m), which were departmentalised, and small shops (under 6,450 sq. ft/599.2 sq. m), which concentrated on health and beauty products. Each type had a slightly different shopfront, but both were characterised by

the company's blue and white colour scheme and scroll logo, which was now set within an oval frame. In the mid-1980s the company launched Boots Opticians and Children's World; the latter was developed by Fitch & Co. as a stand-alone brand, and was later sold to Mothercare.

The late 1980s saw great changes. Between 1987 and 1990, through a series of departmental mergers, the Architects' Department became part of a new department, Store Planning (later renamed Property and Planning), which also encompassed shopfitting, retail engineering and estates. Gant resigned in 1989, and Alan Cooper was appointed Chief Architect until 1995.[104] The new department was responsible for overseeing the company's first forays into retail parks, and for developing a new design for high street stores, which was first applied at West Bridgford,

223 Boots' Booklovers' Libraries closed in 1965–6. This library was situated on the first floor of the Plymouth branch of 1951–2.

Nottingham, in 1995. Since then, several different store concepts have been launched, referred to as 'Concept 1' (for example, at Peterborough), 'Concept 2' (Bluewater) and 'Integrated Customer Offer' (Watford).[105] Over and above this, some of the most interesting work of Boots Properties PLC in recent years has been the erection of shopping centres (for example, The Land of the Prince Bishops in Durham) and retail parks for the purpose of capital investment.[106]

Boots the Chemists remains one of the most respected names on the English high street, to which it contributed such a fine array of historicising buildings at the beginning of the twentieth century. In most towns, the chances are that Boots has quit these buildings for more modern premises (pl. 222), and except for the occasional cursive 'B' on a sill or pilaster, there is nothing to indicate their true origin to the unsuspecting passer-by.

III BURTON

From the 1920s until the 1960s Burton was the most successful high street tailor in Britain, a veritable national institution. Then fashions changed, and the demand for made-to-measure suits plummeted. Although it suffered greatly, Burton survived by capitalising on its immense property portfolio and diversifying into more casual clothing. The firm (known as Burton Menswear) now belongs to the Arcadia Group, which includes numerous other chains, such as Topshop/Topman and Dorothy Perkins. In 1999 Arcadia acquired several major 'fascias' from Sears, making it one of the largest clothing retailers in the UK. Philip Green, who was responsible for the break-up of Sears, and who made a fortune though his purchase of BHS in 1999, bought Arcadia in 2002

The Early Years

Evidence for the early years of the Burton chain is sparse, and many of the 'facts' are open to question.[107] The story begins in 1900, when Meshe David Osinsky (1885–1952) emigrated from Lithuania to Britain and assumed the name Montague Burton.[108] Like Michael Marks, he is said to have started his career as a pedlar, but by 1904 he had opened a small shop at 20 Holywell Street in Chesterfield. That was soon followed by a second shop in the same town, then a third in Mansfield. Initially, Burton's shops concentrated on the sale of cheap, ready-made clothing for working-class men and boys. He first offered a 'wholesale bespoke' tailoring service in 1906, but contracted out the manufacture of suits until 1908–9, when he opened his own factory.[109] By 1912 bespoke tailoring had superseded the sale of ready-made suits in Burton's shops. He was now entering an established field of commerce, pioneered by manufacturer-retailers such as Joseph Hepworth in the 1880s, when innovations in factory production and rising disposable incomes first enabled working-class men to ape their betters by wearing suits.

In 1909 Burton married Sophia Amelia Marks and the couple moved to Sheffield, where they opened a Burton & Burton store at 101–103 The Moor, sandwiched between Boots and Home & Colonial Stores. Success was swift, and by 1914 Burton had a chain of fourteen shops, mainly located in the North. All of these occupied leased premises, on the ground floors of ordinary buildings, and little is known about their internal arrangements.

During the First World War, Burton was excused from military service and concentrated on developing his business. He won a contract to supply uniforms to the armed forces, and by 1916 his factories were employing 400 staff and producing 48,000 garments a year. A year later, Burton & Burton became a private limited liability company, named Montague Burton Ltd: Burton held all of the shares, except for one, which was owned by his wife.[110] His factories were kept busy making 'demob' suits in the immediate aftermath of the war, but thereafter had to rely on shop trade to keep going.[111] In 1919 there were thirty-six shops, scattered throughout the country. Twenty years later, the chain comprised 595 shops, lauded by the firm as 'modern temples of commerce'.[112]

'Modern Temples of Commerce'

Between the wars, suits were worn by men of all classes, for all social occasions, in the boardroom and on the football terrace. Burton profited from this sartorial conformity, despite fierce competition from other multiple tailors, such as Alexandre, Hepworth, Jackson the Tailor and Prices (The Fifty Shilling Tailor), most of whom charged a standard sum of 50s. for a made-to-measure suit, compared with Burton's base price of 55s. Burton stayed ahead of his competitors by launching a series of advertising campaigns and mail-shots, by posting men with sandwich boards outside his shops, and by erecting impressive stores in central locations. He was not alone in building imposing new premises, since Horne Brothers was erecting large stores, designed by its own architect, S. N. Tacon, as early as 1923.[113] Most of Burton's rivals preferred to rent premises, although Hepworth owned 156 shops by 1929 and Prices owned 260 by 1932.[114]

The manufacturing and retail sides of Burton's business enjoyed a symbiotic relationship, expanding in tandem throughout the 1920s and 1930s. Manufacturing was concentrated at Hudson Road, Leeds, a site that was purchased from the clothing firm Albrecht & Albrecht in 1920, and subsequently enlarged, making it one of the largest clothing factories in Europe. In 1937 the company built the Burtonville Clothing Works at Worsley, which was conceived as a 'garden factory'. By then Burton owned four factories, in Lancashire and Yorkshire, which fed the growing chain of stores.

In the early 1920s most Burton shops still occupied converted premises, but they had a distinctive appearance (pl. 224). Their most prominent feature was a lunette-shaped, or segmental, green glass fascia with the name 'Burton' executed in white lettering, edged in gold, and with the slogan 'The Tailor of Taste' incorporated within an underscore. Beneath this, the shopfront had plate-glass windows divided by slender wooden colonnettes. The glazing bars of the transom lights formed garlands that encompassed the words 'elegance', 'taste', 'economy' and 'courtesy'. Signage adorned the upper parts of façades, sometimes masking windows. Far from being unique to Burton, this blatant advertising was highly characteristic of tailors' shops at that time (pl. 238).

In 1923, when the chain comprised 200 shops, Burton began to erect new stores on freehold sites for the first time. He engaged the estate agents Healey & Baker to identify suitable property for redevelopment, but remained personally involved in the process, frequently assuming the alias 'Mr. R. J. Pearson, Estates Manager' and, on one occasion, being detained as a prowler when inspecting a property incognito.[115] Buildings were often bought through a nominee to ensure that the company did not pay too much.[116] From the beginning, Burton held a strong preference for prominent corner sites in urban centres. Adjoining properties were acquired gradually, until a site could be redeveloped or converted to create a large store. Smaller stores were built in less central locations, often very near one another. In the market town of Newark, for example, two stores were built close together within a year: Stodman Street in 1934 and Market Place in 1935. In most cities Burton shops were care-

224   This typical Burton shop of the early 1920s was located on Hessle Road in Hull. The addresses of major metropolitan branches were often, confusingly, displayed on the fascia to enhance the company's image.

LET
MONTAGUE
BURTON
THE TAILOR OF TASTE
DRESS YOU
TO LET
APPLY
MONTAGUE
BURTON
THE TAILOR OF TASTE
87-89. OXFORD ST. LONDON.
18-19. PRINCES ST. EDINBURGH.
ELEGANCE
TASTE
ECONOMY
COURTESY
LET
BURTON
THE TAILOR OF TASTE
DRESS YOU
45/
45/

constructed by the Furniture Department, while the Building Department carried out structural work.

The earliest Burton stores, such as that at Great Yarmouth (*c*.1927; pl. 228), were in a plain neo-classical style, but from the late 1920s façades were usually enriched by art deco motifs. The

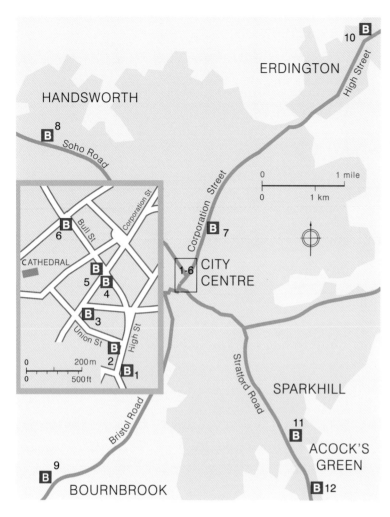

225 By the late 1930s, Burton shops had opened in six outlying districts of Birmingham, supplementing the six stores in the city centre. Outlets were similarly distributed in other large cities.

226 Elephant-head capitals, and other angular art deco motifs, featured on several Burton façades in the early 1930s. This store in Halifax (1932) is now a McDonald's restaurant.

227 (*below*) Parapets were removed from many Burton stores in post-war years, because they had become structurally unstable. This example, complete with original lettering, is located in Tunbridge Wells, Kent, and was erected about 1930.

fully distributed throughout secondary shopping centres (pl. 225). The cluster of stores in central areas is explained by Burton's belief that the average British man was too lazy to cross a street!

The first purpose-built Burton stores were designed by the Leeds architect Harry Wilson, who was employed by the company from about 1923.[117] Occasionally outside architects were employed, for example Fritz Landauer, the German émigré architect who worked on Burton stores in London and Glasgow around 1930. After the company's own Architects' Department was formed around 1932, it maintained the house style that had been established by Wilson. Indeed, it seems likely that Wilson set up the Department, and was employed as chief architect until he was replaced by Nathaniel Martin around 1937. Both architects were obliged to seek Montague Burton's approval for any scheme.[118] They worked with the Shopfitting Department, which designed shopfronts and internal fittings.[119] Fittings were

228   The first large stores built by Burton in the mid-1920s generally adopted a neo-classical style and occupied a prominent corner site. This branch in Great Yarmouth, Norfolk, faced the large market place, and was located close to other major multiple retailers.

largest stores, usually on corner sites, were three or more storeys high. The steel-framed windows of the upper floors were contained within narrow vertical bays, with moulded cast-metal panels masking floor levels.[120] Between the windows were columns or pilasters, sometimes with high volute capitals in an Egyptian style or, as at Halifax and Wolverhampton, in the shape of elephant heads (pl. 226). At the top, usually in a parapet, was the slogan: 'Montague Burton The Tailor of Taste' (pl. 227). Ornamentation, concentrated around the windows, included a variety of classical or geometric motifs, such as urns, palmettes,

overlapping semicircles, chevrons and sun-bursts. Façades could be clad in Portland or Empire stone, emerald pearl granite or faience. The most stylish of these materials was probably emerald granite, which can still be seen to full effect at Hull (1934; pl. 229), where it is teamed up with gold-coloured metalwork.[121] A similar range of materials and ornamental motifs was applied to the façades of smaller stores, while unadorned rear and side elevations were faced in brick.

In the early 1930s some Burton stores were erected in a neo-Georgian style, with frontages of red brick with ashlar dressings,

229 The Hull store of 1934, with its black granite facing and gold metal-work, was one of Burton's most glamorous properties. Overlapping cusping recurred on Burton façades throughout the 1930s, becoming something of a leitmotif.

230 Although the shopfront of this Burton store (now a day centre) on Goosegate, Nottingham, survives, it has been greatly altered and has lost its dated foundation stone. This archive photograph shows how it looked in the late 1930s. The glazing pattern in the transom lights represents a popular alternative design to that at Newark.

and with small-paned windows. A favourite composition involved giant pilasters, executed in a white stone that stood out against the brickwork. The store in Newark Market Place (1935; pl. 231) was of this type, and survives complete with its original shopfront.

Burton shopfronts invariably had black granite surrounds, with at least one plinth inscribed to commemorate the laying of the foundation stone by a member of the Burton family. The stall-risers sometimes incorporated bronze vents bearing the company's name. The fascia displayed the name 'Burton', flanked by the addresses of the main stores, or mottos such as 'The Palace of Fashion' and 'Student of Harmony'. The entrance lay within a deep lobby, usually with a mosaic floor. The mosaic pavement on one corner of the Hull store still pleads: 'Let Burton Dress You'. Customers entered through double doors, often fitted with an elongated hexagonal area of etched glazing, which resulted in

their being nicknamed 'coffin doors'. A late example of these can still be seen in Huntingdon, Cambridgeshire (1951). Occasionally, the entrance lobby was enclosed by a wooden gate with a sun-burst motif, providing some security at night.

The surviving Burton shopfronts on Market Place, Newark (1935), and Goosegate, Nottingham (c.1938; pl. 230), illustrate the two principal transom designs that were produced by the Shop-fitting Department in the 1930s, representing the company's 'chain of honour'. At Newark, the transom lights were decorated with pairs of horizontal bands filled with chains of lozenges, between which were inscribed the names of cities where major stores were located.[122] At Nottingham, the glazing bars formed a chain of elongated hexagons, each framing the name of a city.[123]

Parts of the ground floor of many Burton buildings (pl. 232) housed lock-up shops which were let to other retailers. Such

231 This building on Newark Market Place, built in 1935, is one of the most complete Burton stores to survive from the inter-war period.

shops provided the company with an opportunity for expansion as well as an income: they were always let on short leases, and could be recovered quickly if Burton's own shop needed to be enlarged. Burton's shops featured larger display windows and smaller sales-rooms than most retail premises, partly because they carried little stock. The large display windows had wooden panelled backs, with access doors decorated with etched glass. As he entered the shop, the customer faced a screen which was generally 7 feet 3 inches (2.21 m) high, and fitted with three leaded lights above timber panels. It provided a degree of privacy. Inside (pl. 233), the oak-panelled walls, wood-block floor and oak or mahogany fittings created the feel of a gentleman's club, making the shops particularly impressive to their lower-middle-class and respectable working-class clientele.[124] Contemporary descriptions frequently stressed their 'refinement' and 'taste', something that gave them an edge over their competitors.[125] Sales areas were quite free of clutter: the main fittings were mantle-cases for hanging garments and fixtures for displaying bolts of cloth, both of which lined the shop's walls, although there would also have been a couple of free-standing counters. Toilets and staffrooms were located to the rear of the shop. Due to the nature of the business, there was no need for large delivery entrances or yards.

The customer followed a set procedure when buying a suit. First of all, assistants helped him to select a style from a catalogue, and to pick a fabric from samples. Then his measurements were taken and he paid a cash deposit to the cashier, who was the only woman on the premises. His measurements were sent to Burton's factory, which usually manufactured the suit within a week and despatched it to the branch, where the customer would try it on in a private fitting room and complete his payment.

Because the upper floors of Burton buildings were rarely needed for retail or storage space, they were provided with independent access (pl. 232) and leased out in order to generate revenue.[126] Montague Burton, who espoused the temperance movement, recommended that upper floors be used as billiard halls, which would provide an alcohol-free environment in which working-class men could enjoy themselves. Furthermore, he was aware that men visiting a billiard hall would pass the shop display windows and consider making a purchase. To encourage the use of upper levels for billiard halls, dancing schools or ballrooms, the floors were constructed of 6-inch (15.24 cm) reinforced concrete covered with wood-block. Many snooker halls survive on the upper floors of Burton shops to this day, even when the shop has long passed out of Burton's hands. An alternative use for upper levels was as offices. In Hull these were occupied by the Head of Customs, on Newark Market Place by the local tax office, and in Stafford and Kendal by the County Court. Occasionally, flats for employees were provided over the shop.

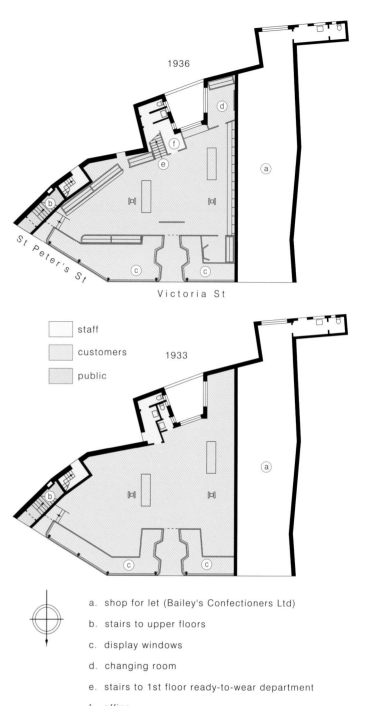

a. shop for let (Bailey's Confectioners Ltd)

b. stairs to upper floors

c. display windows

d. changing room

e. stairs to 1st floor ready-to-wear department

f. office

232   These plans show the Burton store on the corner of St Peter's Street and Victoria Street in Derby as it was when it first opened in 1933, and after alteration in 1936 to incorporate a first-floor ready-to-wear department and fitting rooms. The display windows took up a great deal of the floor area. Based on plans held by Arcadia Group PLC.

Ready-to-wear departments reappeared in Burton shops in the mid-1930s. The Derby shop, for example, was altered to include a first-floor ready-to-wear department and ground-floor fitting rooms in 1936 (pl. 232).[127] Ready-to-wear soon began to take over. This can be seen in the changes made in 1938 to the 'flagship' store on the corner of Tottenham Court Road and New Oxford Street in central London (1930; Harry Wilson). The basement was converted into a new bespoke department, while the more lucrative ground and first floors were fitted out for ready-to-wear.[128]

★ ★ ★

Adaptation to Change

Sir Montague Burton died in 1952, having established a business empire that claimed, with 635 shops, to be largest tailoring multiple in the world. Men's fashion was changing, however, and the abandonment of the suit as a uniform for all occasions soon began to have an adverse effect on the company. Burton's successor, Lionel Jacobson, instituted a programme of refurbishment, and by 1956 almost half of Burton's branches had been modernised.[129] At the same time, new buildings were much less ostentatious than their predecessors; they occupied less prominent sites, and were more austere in style.

Burton shops were slow to switch from suits, because they were tied to the company's own factories. In the early 1960s,

233   This photograph shows Don Bradman and the Yorkshire cricket team being measured for suits in Burton's flagship store at 118–132 New Oxford Street in the early 1930s. In the 1920s Burton issued a memorandum urging staff to 'avoid the severe style of the income-tax collector and the smooth tongue of the fortune teller. Cultivate the dignified style of the "Quaker tea blender" which is a happy medium'.

however, the popularity of Italian suits seems to have briefly boosted sales. Certainly, around that time Burton built numerous new high street stores in a very masculine Modern style. These buildings were usually two or three storeys high, with a high proportion of wall to window and asymmetrical, geometric façades. Shopfronts now had pale grey granite stallrisers and pilasters. Red perspex letters illuminated in red neon were set on mosaic tile fascias. Above this, like contemporary stores designed by YRM (see p. 189), walls were clad in white mosaic or oblong tiles, and scored by dark, recessed bands of long, narrow windows which ran into larger, square windows. Inside, the shops often occupied two floors, and included both bespoke and ready-to-wear departments. In addition to the traditional counters, mantle cases and cloth fixtures, sales areas were furnished with self-selection hanging rails and display units. Some shops retained an entrance screen, now modified to incorporate a ledge at the front, for the display of mannequins, and a pattern rack at the rear. Rather than being leased out, upper floors were used by the company as stockrooms, retail space and offices. Burton's 1960s stores are amongst the most recognisable of all post-war multiple architecture, even when the tiles have begun to fall off and façades have been rendered, as in Harrogate. The company adhered to this style into the 1970s (pl. 234).

234   Burton's house style in the 1960s and 1970s was very different from that of the 1930s. This Modern tile-clad building on Briggate, Leeds, incorporated an arcade (to the left), and was located just down the street from another major branch. While the latter is still a Burton store, this outlet has been converted by Burton's parent company into Topshop/Topman.

The erection of modern stores failed to stem Burton's decline, since young men demonstrated an increasing preference for casual clothes. The days of made-to-measure were over, but it was only some years after its competitors had decreased their dependence on suits that Burton began to stock ties (1969) and shirts (1974), lines that had previously been the preserve of the outfitter rather than the tailor. In the course of the 1970s most of the company's factories closed. Despite belated adaptation to change, in 1974 the firm's profits were described as 'an unmitigated disaster'.[130] The Architects' Department, which had been renamed the Design and Construction Department in 1971, closed in 1975, and a design company was brought in to revamp Burton's image. A new fascia was introduced that could be constructed from a variety of contemporary materials, such as fibreglass or brown oblong tiles.[131] From this time, many Burton shops were disposed of by Montague Burton Property Investments Ltd, which had been set up in 1972. Its valuable property portfolio undoubtedly cushioned the firm during the disastrous years of the mid- to late 1970s.

To compensate for the poor performance of Burton shops after the war, the Burton Group (named in 1969) concentrated on women's wear. It bought Peter Robinson's in 1946 and developed it into a chain. Its manager, Ralph Halpern, launched the highly successful Topshop, designed by Fitch & Co., in 1968.[132] Evans Outsize was purchased in 1971 and Dorothy Perkins in 1979. In 1984 the Group launched Principles for Women and, in 1985, Principles for Men. Debenhams and Collier Holdings were acquired in 1985, and the home shopping brands Racing Green and Hawkshead in 1996. Following the demerger of Debenhams, the Group was renamed the Arcadia Group in 1998. In 1999 it purchased several women's wear chains from Sears Ltd, including Richards (the successor to Richard Shops), which it promptly closed down, as well as the more successful Miss Selfridge and Wallis.[133]

Burton shops now form a small part of Arcadia's portfolio. They have often been reduced in size to occupy half of the ground-floor sales area of a former Burton store, the remainder being given over to another Arcadia brand. Sometimes the entire building has been handed over to other Arcadia shops. The co-location of Arcadia brands looks set to continue, as the company continues to strengthen its position through a programme of closures and disposals.

★   ★   ★

A decade ago, Marks & Spencer was the best-known British retailer, with an international reputation for inexpensive clothing and high quality foods. Its Marble Arch store attracted hordes of tourists, and the company had opened outlets worldwide. Then, in the late 1990s, Marks & Spencer's dominance of the British high street was very publicly questioned when its percentage of the women's clothing market, and its stock market price, fell sharply. This caused a crisis of faith amongst its loyal following, and some heart-searching within the company, which desperately sought to revitalise its image. Remedies have included the closure of all thirty-eight Continental stores, the sale of the leases of many British properties and an expensive store refurbishment programme. So far, this policy seems to be working.

The Penny Bazaars

Marks & Spencer was founded by Michael Marks (1859–1907), a Jewish immigrant from Russian Poland, who began his career as a pedlar. By 1886 Marks had set up a stall in Kirkgate Market, Leeds, with a loan of £5 from a local wholesaler, Isaac Dewhirst.[134] He sold a wide variety of goods, such as cotton reels and buttons, with the slogan 'don't ask the price, it's a penny'.[135] This popular strategy enabled Marks to open additional stalls, now named penny bazaars, in Castleford and Wakefield markets. In order to expand further afield, to Birkenhead (1887) and Warrington (1890) in Cheshire, Marks employed sales assistants, allowing him to concentrate on buying.[136] In the early 1890s he moved to Lancashire, eventually settling in Manchester, where he lived over his shop on Cheetham Hill Road. One year later, in 1894, he entered into partnership with Dewhirst's cashier, Tom Spencer (1851–1905), and the firm of Marks & Spencer was born.[137]

By the end of 1900 Marks & Spencer had twenty-four penny bazaars in market halls, and twelve in shops, located on streets or in arcades.[138] Shops proved more lucrative than stalls and, by the time of Marks's death in 1907, their number had increased to thirty-four, while that of stalls had dwindled to fifteen.[139] The shops imitated the style of the market stalls. Their open fronts were closed by roller shutters at night, and were surmounted by 'ADMISSION FREE' signs, indicating that the public could enter without an obligation to buy. By the early 1900s the words 'originators of penny bazaars' had been added to the bright red signboard, to distinguish Marks & Spencer shops from their imitators. Some goods spilled on to the pavement, but inside each shop the merchandise was displayed in baskets on counters arranged in a horseshoe shape around a long gangway,

rather than being stored on shelves behind the assistants in the traditional manner. Customers were thus encouraged to browse, and an element of self-selection was introduced to the buying process. Money was kept in simple drawers, without locks, located under the counters.

In the period following the founders' deaths, the company was run by William Chapman, an executor of Spencer's will. In Chapman's hands, the bazaars increased in number, drawing on funds from a General Reserve,[140] but their character changed little. Woolworth's arrival in 1909 seems to have persuaded Marks & Spencer to improve the appearance of its premises. Minute books of that year make numerous references to repainting and redecoration,[141] and one year later the company erected its first purpose-built bazaars, in Portsmouth and Sunderland.[142] These buildings had identical brick frontages, each displaying a stone plaque inscribed 'M&S 1910'. The slightly grander Reading shop (pl. 235) was built in 1912–13, by which time the company had appointed its own architect, Ernest E. Shrewsbury, and a building department of a dozen men.[143] Reading was one of the first

235   Marks & Spencer's Penny Bazaar at 12 Broad Street, Reading (1912–13), had one of the company's new-style 'penny' shopfronts. Some of the upper-floor rooms were clearly surplus to requirement, and were rented out to a dentist.

shops to boast shopfront design featuring a prominent penny logo, which remained in use until the penny price policy was abandoned during the First World War.[144] This new shopfront incorporated plate-glass sashes, which provided staff with a measure of protection against bad weather. In addition to their sales area, bazaars now housed a mess room with a gas stove on which the staff could heat food,[145] and a small stock-room capable of holding a six-week supply of merchandise, which was delivered from one of the company's three regional warehouses.[146]

Shortly before the outbreak of war in 1914, the company consolidated its position by purchasing the Arcadia Bazaar Company and the London Penny Bazaar Company.[147] With these acquisitions, the geographical focus of the company shifted to the London area, where there were now fifty-six branches.[148] The swing from stalls to shops had continued: there were now only 10 stalls, but 133 shops. While no pre-war shop has survived, Marks & Spencer still trades from the stall it opened in the Grainger Market, Newcastle upon Tyne (pl. 236), in 1895.

'Super-Stores'

Following a prolonged power struggle, resolved through legal action, Michael Marks's son Simon (1888–1964) assumed the chairmanship of Marks & Spencer in 1916. Marks realised that he must mount a vigorous challenge to Woolworth, which had made extraordinary inroads in Britain since 1909, but it was some years before he drafted a coherent plan for the future development of the company.

In the meantime, the freeholds of many bazaars were purchased and the shops began to evolve into stores. The first that were wide enough to hold island counters were Darlington and Wakefield (pl. 237), both conversions of 1922. An even larger store opened, again in converted premises, in Blackpool in 1923. Middlesborough (1923) (pl. 238) was one of very few premises to be purpose built at this time.

In 1923 Simon Marks was informed that a group of Woolworth directors had visited a Marks & Spencer store and described the goods as 'lemons'.[149] This spurred Marks to visit America in 1924, in search of fresh ideas, and he returned with the conviction that success depended upon the erection of 'imposing, commodious premises'.[150] Two years later he raised capital for an ambitious rebuilding programme by floating the company on the stock exchange, and in the same year Hillier Parker May & Rowden prepared a report on the company's 135 shops.[151] Marks & Spencer then spent the next five years replacing these existing shops with buildings that resembled popular emporia, and were referred to as 'super-stores'. The company declared:

We are developing a new type of store, and incorporating architectural features which will make them a landmark in their respective towns. We believe that a beautiful building is a constant advertisement, which must result in increased trading.[152]

The pace of reconstruction was extraordinary. Between 1926 and 1930, fifty-six stores were built or rebuilt (including Portsmouth and Sunderland), and another forty (including Reading) were extended. The Depression did little to hinder progress, and by 1932 most of the company's old shops (including Middlesborough) had been replaced, enabling it to 'advance into fresh territories'.[153] Between 1931 and 1939, 162 stores were built or rebuilt and many more extended. There were now 234 stores, all substantially larger than the earlier bazaars, and all occupying prominent urban sites.

Marks & Spencer's building process was very systematic. From 1926 until his retirement in 1942 Mr Shrewsbury dealt with private architects, engineers and surveyors, and with a single contracting firm, Bovis.[154] Most of the design work was distributed amongst three architectural firms, whose schemes were submitted to the Board of Directors for approval. These were: W. A. Lewis & Partners (later Lewis & Hickey), Norman Jones & Rigby and Monro & Partners.[155] Other architects who occasionally worked for Marks & Spencer included Alfred Batzer and W. Braxton Sinclair.[156] These different architects adhered to a standard formula under the vigilant eye of Mr Shrewsbury.

From the mid-1920s Marks & Spencer's shopfronts (pl. 238) were filled with plate-glass windows and had recessed entrance lobbies with double doors, just like Woolworth's. The windows had quadrant corners, and their light sources were masked by shaped pelmets decorated with an 'M&S' monogram. The name 'bazaar' was dropped in favour of 'stores', and in 1924 a green and gold fascia was introduced, to enhance the distinction between Marks & Spencer and Woolworth. Above most shopfronts, classical pilasters or columns divided a Portland stone façade into vertical bays containing steel casements with margin lights and, sometimes, 'o' and 'x' glazing patterns (pl. 239).[157] Metal panels masked the floors, and a stepped parapet displayed the name of the company. Unlike Burton's, stores built on corner sites (for example, Sheffield, Bedford and Lewisham, all 1929) had low turrets with cupolas, but most Marks & Spencer stores were hemmed in, to left and right, by other multiple retailers. At this date few stores had rear façades or entrances, other than loading bays.

Several Marks & Spencer stores did not conform to the standard formula. In 1927, for example, Batzer designed a decidedly old-fashioned Edwardian baroque façade for the branch in Gravesend.[158] Then, in the early 1930s, the company erected a number of stores in a neo-Georgian style, with red brick façades

236 This photograph of Marks & Spencer's Penny Bazaar, Grainger Market, Newcastle upon Tyne, was taken in December 1906, just after the stall had been extended.

237 Marks & Spencer's Wakefield store – shown here in 1922 – was one of the first that was wide enough to accommodate island counters. Toys, many imported from Germany and Austria, were a major line for the company at this time.

involved the exact duplication of the 1913 design. The addition of another matching bay in 1934 rendered the attic storey asymmetrical, and so that was removed. More typically, the Portsmouth store was completely rebuilt in 1927, extended by one bay to the left in 1931 and by one bay to the right in 1936–7.

Inside Marks & Spencer 'super-stores' (pl. 241), customers would find few of the luxuries or services associated with contemporary department stores. As in most Woolworth stores, the open-plan sales area was restricted to street level. While the sales area of pre-war bazaars had occupied under 1,500 square feet (139.4 sq. m), those of the earliest super-stores might measure 3,500 square feet (325.2 sq. m), rising to 10,000 square feet (929 sq. m) by the early 1930s. Floors were of bare oiled hardwood, walls were plastered above wooden dados, and pressed-steel ceilings were traversed by sturdy steel beams carried on steel columns.[159] Electric and gas light fittings with opaque glass shades were suspended from ceilings by chains, the gas lamps being for emergency use, in case the electricity supply failed. Goods were laid out on mahogany counters, held in place by low glass screens and ticketed with 'stem showcards'. Assistants stood in small wells in the centre of the counters and operated manual tills. Upper floors housed offices, staffrooms and stockrooms. The stockrooms were served by hoisting mechanisms until goods lifts were introduced in the late 1930s. As stores were now supplied direct from manufacturers, the company's three warehouses were closed in the course of the 1920s.

Gradually, the unorthodox jumble of household goods, toys, stationery and confectionery that had filled Marks & Spencer's counters in the early 1920s was replaced by textiles and pre-packaged foods, now sold with a 5 s. price ceiling. The company

238 Marks & Spencer's Middlesborough store was photographed just after rebuilding, in December 1923. It was typical for Marks & Spencer's stores to be flanked by other national multiple retailers, in this case Alexandre the tailor and Dunn & Co the hatter.

and hung-sash windows. The grandest of these, at Canterbury (1930), Peterborough (1931–2; pl. 210) and Winchester (1934), had full pediments; others, such as Lincoln (1931; pl. 240) and Cambridge (1934), were more modest. Different yet again was the façade of the Derby store (1933), which had a strong horizontal emphasis, and Brixton (1931), which was overtly Modern.

Unlike co-operative societies, which extended stores at a comparable rate, Marks & Spencer took great care to maintain uniform frontages. The enlargement of the Reading store in 1927

239 (right) Marks & Spencer's store on Gallowtreegate in Leicester opened in 1930 and was extended in 1937, and again in 1964.

240 (facing page) The Marks & Spencer store on Lincoln High Street adopted an unusual classical design. The three left-hand bays were built in 1931. When the store was later extended to the right, care was taken to maintain a symmetrical facade.

241 The interiors of Marks & Spencer's 'super-stores' were very like those of Woolworth, which also sold goods on self-selection lines. This unidentified store was photographed around 1929–30.

thus became more specialised than Woolworth. Bypassing the wholesaler, it dealt directly with British manufacturers, often proscribing stringent rules for its producers, and introducing the reputable St Michael own-brand in 1928. A significant innovation in the 1930s, again emulating Woolworth, was the introduction of tea bars, fish bars and cafés (pl. 242). Between 1935 and 1938 twenty-one stores were equipped with a café: the number rose to eighty-two during the war, but later declined, and the last two closed in 1961.[160] Coffee bars did not reappear in Marks & Spencer stores until the late 1990s.

In 1934 Robert Lutyens, son of Sir Edwin Lutyens, was appointed consultant architect to Marks & Spencer.[161] To further the uniformity of store façades, he devised a grid system based on a module of 10 inches (25.4 cm). At least forty stores were built to that system, with façades clad in square tiles of artificial stone. Although occasionally almost Cubist in treatment, these façades usually seemed very flat, with ornamentation limited to paterae and shallow rustication. In most cases, the stone cladding varied in colour from pale cream to orange, creating an irregular chequered effect (as at Bradford, 1935; pl. 243), but two stores (Leeds, 1939–51, and the Pantheon, London, 1938) were faced in shiny black 'ebony' granite, a fashion introduced to London by the National Radiator Building of 1929, and much favoured by Burton's Architects' Department.[162] With Lutyens's system, which promised to simplify extensions, Marks & Spencer took the idea of the standardised store façade further than most other national multiples.

The culmination of Marks & Spencer's inter-war development programme was the Pantheon (pls 244–5), a highly prestigious new store that attempted to woo middle-class customers.[163] The store featured an 'arcade' shopfront with free-standing island showcases, and had more upmarket interiors than other Marks & Spencer stores, with walnut counters and wall panelling, teak doors, oak block floors and coffered ceilings without visible beams. The main departments on the ground floor, occupying 20,000 square feet (1,858 sq. m), were foods,

242 Cafés were established in eighty major Marks & Spencer stores between 1935 and 1942, including that in Watford, Hertfordshire. shown here.

clothing and footwear, with a café-bar to the rear. The food department had white enamelled counters, a refrigerator-showcase and a fruit counter with rails for customers' baskets. Many of the clothes were displayed on garment rails. The café, which was inspired by Wanamaker's luncheonette in America,[164] could seat 150, mainly on upholstered red leather stools arranged around three curved bars with wells for waitresses in the centres. The walls were clad in primrose and black Vitrolite. Although there was a ladies' rest room and writing room on the first floor, the store had no comparable services for men, reflecting the fact that most of Marks & Spencer's customers were female. With the exception of management, the staff was also all-female, and the company took pride in providing its employees with up-to-date facilities.[165] These included a cloakroom on the first floor, a

243 Marks & Spencer's Bradford store of 1935 was designed according to Robert Lutyens's modular system.

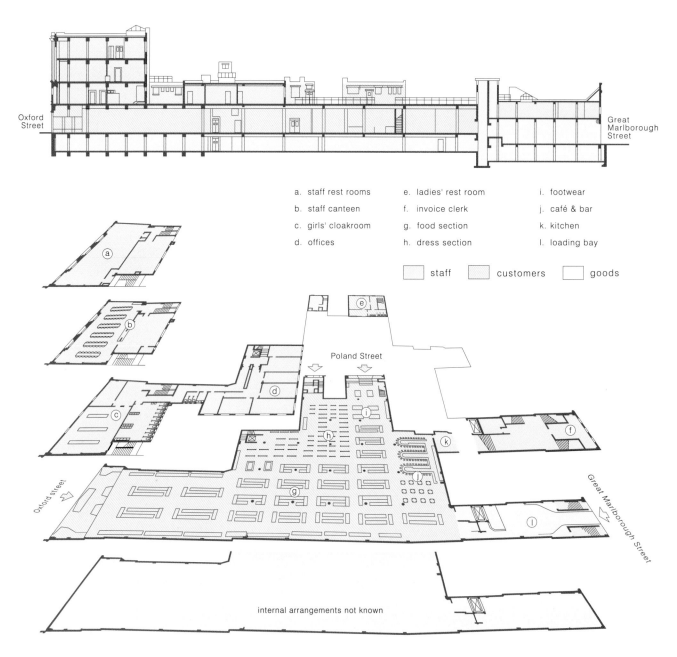

a. staff rest rooms   e. ladies' rest room   i. footwear

b. staff canteen   f. invoice clerk   j. café & bar

c. girls' cloakroom   g. food section   k. kitchen

d. offices   h. dress section   l. loading bay

staff   customers   goods

Oxford Street

Great Marlborough Street

Poland Street

Oxford Street

Great Marlborough Street

internal arrangements not known

244   The layout of The Pantheon store. Based on *The Architect and Building News*, 28 October 1938, 106.

dining room and kitchen on the second floor, and a rest room furnished with Lloyd Loom furniture and a radiogram on the third. In addition, the third floor housed a training room.

Post-War Reconstruction and Store Development

Soon after the war had ended, Marks & Spencer began to replace sixteen stores that had been destroyed by enemy action. Once this was completed, the company concentrated on rebuilding or enlarging its existing stores, rather than expanding the chain, a process that continued into the 1970s, when expansion resumed.

By 2000 the company had 287 UK stores which were, typically, much larger than its pre-1939 stores.

During the 1950s Marks & Spencer stores demonstrated considerable continuity with the past. Although Robert Lutyens's system was used only four more times,[166] the company maintained a close relationship with the architectural firms that had worked for it between the wars, with the result that many façades bore a strong similarity to their pre-war counterparts.[167] The neo-classical façade of the rebuilt Birmingham store (1956), for example, had a central panel filled with five vertical window bays separated by shaped piers resembling columns. In other new stores (for example, Exeter, 1951), the curtain walling that filled

245   Putting the final touches to Marks & Spencer's Pantheon store at 173 Oxford Street, London, the day before it opened, on 19 October 1938. Appropriately, it occupied the site of the Pantheon Bazaar, which had housed the showrooms and offices of W. A. Gilbey, wine merchants, from 1867 to 1937.

the central panel of the façade retained an inherent verticality, often with tripartite divisions. In its essential components, this design survived into the early 1960s, being used for the York store in 1961 (pl. 246). As in the 1930s, alternative designs were chiefly in a neo-Georgian idiom (such as Great Yarmouth, 1952; pl. 228). By 1960 many stores had become urban thoroughfares with front and rear entrances and integral loading bays. Store interiors were lit by fluorescent lights in square ceiling panels and were centrally heated and ventilated. Most goods were still displayed on counters, but increasing amounts of clothing were hung on rails (pl. 247). The cafés had been converted to self-service during the war, and now general foodstuffs were sold on

246 (*left*) A typical post-war Marks & Spencer store in York, dating from 1961.

247 (*below*) The interior of Marks & Spencer's Eastbourne branch, photographed in the late 1950s.

248   This extremely large Marks & Spencer's store was erected in Bolton in 1968.

a self-service basis. Indeed, the first full-fledged version of self-service in the UK opened in Marks & Spencer's store in Wood Green, north London, in January 1948 (pl. 285; see p. 276).[168] With more frozen and chilled foods being sold, stores now accommodated extensive cold stores and refrigeration plant behind the scenes.

In the 1960s, 170 of the company's 245 stores underwent major building works, although only 30 were built anew.[169] Extensions, however, were no longer designed to match original stores. By 1968 eighteen of the company's stores had over 35,000 square foot (3,251.5 sq.m) of selling space, often including a second sales floor served by escalators. The huge

Newcastle store (1965–7; 58,000 sq. ft / 5,388.2 sq. m), was one of the first to be clad with pre-cast concrete aggregate panels. Many façades now featured continuous, vertical window strips separated by fins or pilasters, and a favourite veneer was polished grey granite (for example, Bolton, 1968; pl. 248).

According to P. Hickey, one of Marks & Spencer's architects, new stores of the 1970s and 1980s demonstrated 'a new more liberal expression'.[170] Certainly, the traditional Marks & Spencer verticality was abandoned, together with all notions of a homogeneous architectural style. Throughout this period the company opened numerous branches in malls, and many of its older stores were linked to new shopping complexes by being given rear

extensions and mall frontages. Where there was no room for expansion, specialist satellite stores opened. The erection of large distribution warehouses freed up space originally devoted to stockrooms, enabling basements and upper floors to be converted to sales areas. The London stores at Marble Arch (1987; 96,000 sq. ft/ 8,918.4 sq. m) and the Pantheon (1988; 126,000 sq. ft/11,705.4 sq. m) were the first to have four sales floors.

In the 1990s the company kept up with modern shopping developments by opening in retail parks and engaging in joint-venture shopping centres with other retailers. The large new store in the Bluewater shopping centre (1999) adopted the 'galleria' layout favoured by contemporary department stores, with galleries arranged around a central light well. The most prestigious new store of recent years, however, is the Manchester store (pl. 249), designed by BDP to replace a building destroyed by a terrorist bomb in 1996. It occupies an island site and its façades are fitted with thick laminated glass that afford maximum views into and out of the building. When this store opened in December 1999 it was the largest Marks & Spencer store in the world, but the company was already in trouble, and before long it was announced that Selfridges would share the building (see p. 191).[171]

After 1998, in the context of falling sales and general customer disaffection, Marks & Spencer was forced to scrutinise its image. Dozens of new initiatives were announced, including, in March 2001, the closure of foreign branches, the scrapping of its catalogue operation and a renewed concentration on its core home market. Its *fin-de-siècle* crisis seems to have proved a catalyst for the most thorough remodelling of Marks & Spencer's stores since the 1950s: the pine-effect cladding that has characterised store interiors for the last three decades has finally had its day.

V   WOOLWORTHS

The character of Woolworths has scarcely changed since F. W. Woolworth opened his first variety store in Liverpool in 1909, selling a similar range of goods to that on sale today.[172] The company thrived throughout the middle years of the twentieth century, even outperforming its American parent, but it struggled through the recession of the 1970s, and was sold in 1982. Since then, Woolworths has done well in the face of determined competition from new discount chains, such as Poundstretcher. It has launched several different retail 'concepts', including Woolworths Local (1995), Big W (1999) and Woolworths General Stores (2000; abandoned 2002). In August 2001 the company was demerged from its parent company,

Kingfisher, which decided to concentrate on its more lucrative DIY and electricals businesses.[173] As part of that deal, Kingfisher sold numerous Woolworths properties, including the Marylebone Road headquarters.

The Americans Come to Town

Frank Winfield Woolworth (1852–1919), a farmer's son from Jefferson County, New York, established a successful chain of 'five-and-dime' stores in America during the 1880s. In these lowly but remunerative stores, goods were displayed on counter tops and could be perused freely by customers, without an obligation to buy. The closest English equivalent was the penny bazaar, but Woolworth was not very impressed with these, or with any other English shops, when he visited the country in 1890. He wrote from London:

> They may have some fine stores here but we have not yet found them. Those we have seen are nothing but little shops and the way they trim their windows is new to me. They trim them close to the glass from top to bottom, and it is impossible to look into the store. The stores themselves are very small and are called 'shops' and not much like our fine stores. I think a good penny and sixpence store run by a live Yankee would create a sensation here, but perhaps not.[174]

Despite his initial doubts, by 1909 Woolworth had resolved to compete with the English penny bazaars – of which Marks & Spencer was now one of the largest – by founding a chain of 'bright, commodious, well-stocked red fronts', modelled on his American establishments.[175] As a first step, he travelled to England with a scouting party, to identify likely sites for 3d-and-6d stores in manufacturing centres.[176] Before long he settled on a building at 25 Church Street in Liverpool, which opened on 5 November 1909 as the first branch of F. W. Woolworth & Co. Ltd, the British arm of the Woolworth company. Behind its old-fashioned Italianate façade, 25 Church Street was no ordinary shop: it had belonged to the glover Henry Miles, who had recently remodelled the interior along lavish lines, with a grand staircase, a gallery and a Lincrusta ceiling by Waring & Gillow.[177] It was a world away from Woolworth's American stores, and from British penny bazaars, which must have viewed this development with fear and trembling. A rival retailer is supposed to have quipped that 'the Americans are opening in Liverpool to be near the boat for 'ome', but the prophets of doom were wrong: success came quickly, and before long other Woolworth branches were opening in the North.[178] In 1910 the first London branch opened in Brixton, opposite Marks & Spencer, and within two years the company had twenty-eight stores. These included a

249   The north façade of Marks & Spencer's Manchester store (2000, by BDP), with the Arndale Centre in the background. This section of the building, fronting Exchange Square, was handed over to Selfridges, which opened its second provincial store here in September 2002.

250   Woolworth erected this landmark store on Church Street, Liverpool, in 1923, just across the road from its first ever British shop. It no longer belongs to the company.

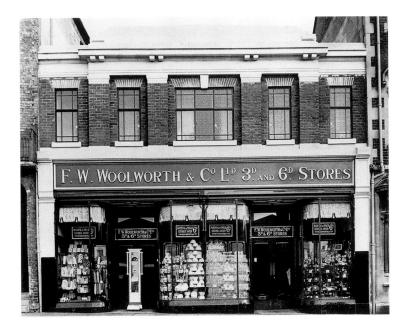

251 The branch in Andover, Hampshire, was typical of small Woolworth stores erected in the 1920s and 1930s.

(1926–9) on the corner of Oldham Street and Piccadilly in Manchester.[184]

Throughout the inter-war period, most new Woolworth stores were built of red brick with ashlar or cement render dressings; they were generally two storeys high and either three or five bays wide. If a larger store was required, this formula could be expanded either laterally (for example, Colchester) or vertically (for example, Whitby), to fit the available site. Two different styles were adopted: neo-classical or Modern. Neo-classical façades were produced from the early 1920s to the late 1930s. They incorporated motifs such as pediments or Venetian windows, and had hung-sash windows containing 'cathedral' (rough plate) glass. The Modern approach was adopted in the late 1920s. Now the central bay was wider than the flanking bays, the windows contained metal-framed (Crittall) glazing with margin lights, and the composition was topped by a solid, stepped parapet. Classical ornamentation was reduced to an absolute minimum, or eliminated altogether. This unobtrusive design (pl. 251) was reproduced in hundreds of English towns, and can still be readily identified. As well as building its own stores, Wool-

shop in Manchester with a shopfront by the upmarket shopfitters F. Sage & Co., already in the classic Woolworth style (described below).[179]

Woolworth died in 1919, and was succeeded in England by Fred M. Woolworth, followed in 1923 by W. L. Stephenson. Under these directors, the company set about expanding its chain of 'domestic bazaars' with buildings designed by its own Architects' Department, headed by William Priddle, and erected by its own Construction Department. Several of these were large structures in high-profile locations. The Liverpool store (pl. 250) of 1923 formed part of a large development, on the site of St Peter's on Church Street.[180] The central block was occupied by Woolworth while the lateral ranges, added in 1924, housed Burton and C&A. The centre of Woolworth's five-storey elevation contained a huge recessed panel, three storeys high and three bays wide, fitted with metal-framed windows within a framework of bronze panels. This 'complete metal front', executed by Crittall,[181] took ideas inherent in Selfridges' design further than any other British retail building of the 1920s, but was criticised by contemporaries. The architect C. H. Reilly described it as a 'howler', complaining that the recessed central feature was 'big enough to drive the *Queen Mary* through'.[182] The Woolworth store erected at 311 Oxford Street, London, in 1924, and that erected on Briggate in Leeds in 1928, were both very similar to the Liverpool store, but in each case the central feature was subdivided by pilasters. The Leeds store was designed by B. C. Donaldson, who had succeeded Priddle as Woolworth's Chief Architect.[183] He was also responsible for the major branch

252 The Woolworth store in Hertford retains its original shopfront and first-floor glazing.

253 'Tin' ceilings stamped with this pattern survive in several Woolworth stores, including this branch in Saffron Walden, Essex (c.1930), but most are concealed by modern suspended ceilings.

worth often took space in speculative developments (as at High Holborn, London, 1924), and converted several older buildings for its own use (for example, the Spread Eagle Hotel, Lincoln, 1923).

Woolworth shopfronts were highly standardised throughout the 1920s and 1930s, and several have survived, including Hertford (pl. 252), Ludlow and Ilkeston. Customers entered through double doors – of natural wood, part glazed, with brass push and kick plates – within small lobbies.[185] A weighing machine was habitually positioned within one of these lobbies outside opening hours. The plate-glass display windows had quadrant corners and were held in place by bronze colonnettes of square section. They were hung with pelmets and with notices that read 'nothing in these stores over 6d.'. Above them were bronze ventilation strips studded with rosettes; below were pearl granite risers incorporating circular ventilation grilles. Mosaics in the lobby floors at Ludlow still depict a 'w' in a plain lozenge, the so-called 'diamond w'.[186] This replaced an earlier logo, current from around 1923, comprising a lion mask with a shield suspended from its mouth.[187] The geranium-red signboard was mounted with gold letters (gold leaf on mahogany), reading 'F. W. WOOLWORTH & CO. LTD. 3d. AND 6d. STORE'.[188] All that usually survives of these fascias are the end consoles.

The open-plan interiors of Woolworth stores were, like their shopfronts, very similar to those of Marks & Spencer, with goods displayed on longitudinally arranged mahogany counters, with wells in the centres for assistants.[189] Unlike Marks & Spencer's stores, however, some early Woolworth stores have never been

enlarged or substantially remodelled.[190] On occasion, one can still see the hefty transverse beams of the floor structure. These were usually encased in moulded plasterwork, but the ceilings were of pressed-steel panels, popularly referred to as tin (pl. 253).[191] Tin ceilings, stamped with a floral design to imitate Lincrusta, were a common feature of American stores from the late nineteenth century onward, and can still be seen in commercial premises throughout the USA.[192] They appeared in British shops at the beginning of the twentieth century and by the 1920s were being installed on a regular basis by Woolworth, Marks & Spencer and J. Lyons. The primrose-coloured walls of Woolworth stores were enriched by pressed-steel friezes, with panels containing a red 'diamond w' under gold swags, topped by a fleur-de-lis.[193] Apart from the ground-floor sales area, Woolworth stores included first-floor stockrooms and a staffroom. These were usually accessible from an enclosed staircase or a lift, located at the rear of the store, close to the delivery and staff entrances. Some stores (such as Manchester) had first-floor cafés as early as 1913.

In the early 1930s, when Woolworth had more than 400 branches, the company experimented with different styles of building. Several new stores resembled contemporary Burton premises (for example, Carlisle, 1933; Harrogate, 1931),[194] while the new Plymouth store of 1930 was more like Marks & Spencer's buildings. The restrained neo-Georgian branch in Bath (1928–9) and the mock timber-framed stores in Kingston upon Thames (1931), and Lincoln (1931) may represent efforts to produce sympathetic designs for historic town centres.[195] In Lincoln, however, it is interesting to note that a local draper named Bainbridge had poached Woolworth's standard house style a few years before the firm decided to rebuild on the site of the Spread Eagle Hotel.[196] As Bainbridge's was located only a few hundred yards from Woolworth's store, this may have clinched the firm's decision to build something out of the ordinary.

By the mid-1930s, under the stewardship of Donaldson, Woolworth had settled for a gloriously over-the-top art deco style that rivalled the efforts of Burton's Architects' Department, not to mention contemporary cinema architects. The architectural press took greater notice of these stores than of any previous Woolworth buildings, and it was with the art deco style that the company became associated, in the public mind, for decades to come.

Montague Burton was greatly intrigued by Woolworth's new buildings, which must have seemed ostentatious and extravagant in comparison to their older stores. On 30 August 1937 he wrote to his architect, Nathaniel Martin:

Messers Woolworth have adopted a new type of elevation for their super store – a kind of horizontal [sic] pillar design, which looks remarkably effective. It has three floors above. In

244

254 From a distance Woolworth's Lewisham store in south-east London (1937) could be mistaken for a cinema.

255 Faience was the favourite cladding material for chain stores in the 1930s because of its clean, modern appearance. As in Ilkeston, Derbyshire (1938), it has not always weathered well.

256 Woolworth's store, Blackpool, interior view.

some cases the top floor will probably be a dummy for effect only. . . . It looks very impressive, for it gives the impression of metropolitan immensity. I believe it is American sky-scraper architecture. . . . Probably this is a retort to Marks & Spencer's attractive buildings.[197]

Surviving stores in this style include Blackpool (pl. 193), Brixton, Dudley, Edgware Road in London, Morecambe, Preston, Southend and Sunderland, but none was more Odeon-esque than Lewisham (1937; pl. 254).[198] Smaller stores, such as that in Ilkeston (1938), were essentially art deco reinterpretations of the standard red-brick store type. Regardless of size, the façades of these buildings were articulated by vertical 'fins' which resembled clustered shafts, sometimes equipped with notional capitals and bases. The favoured facing material was cream or white faience, and leitmotifs included fluted borders, voluted scrolls, cable mouldings and guilloche (pl. 255). The tall, narrow window bays incorporated bronze panels and either metal-framed glazing with margin lights or glass bricks, but their vertical effect was often marred in later years, when much of the metalwork was painted white. In contrast to these façades, side and rear eleva-

tions were faced in cheap bricks. When these were visible, for example on Coldharbour Lane in Brixton, the fenestration was often given a horizontal emphasis.

Burton thought it worth commenting to his architect that Woolworth's shopfronts had been 'improved' by introducing bronze door frames and bronze lettering over the door but, on the whole, the design was unchanged, with lobby entrances alternating with display windows along the frontage.[199] It is significant, however, that entrances were proportionally wider than in the 1920s, and display windows shorter. Transom lights, manufactured by the London Sand Blast Co.,[200] were etched with horizontal bands superimposed with the 'diamond w', and sometimes edged with chevron.[201] The gilt letters on fascias were neonised and façades were lit at night. Illuminated letters spelled 'WOOLWORTH'S' at the top of the façades of the new Lewisham and Brixton stores, and the corner tower of the Blackpool store displayed an illuminated sign reading 'WOOLWORTH'S CAFÉ' (pl. 193).[202]

By the late 1930s some new stores incorporated the latest structural innovations, including pre-cast concrete floors manufactured by Truscon. Inside, display and sales tactics remained unchanged, but sales floors were more expansive, and more often spread on to an additional floor level. There was also a greater emphasis on customer services and staff facilities. At Blackpool (pl. 256), the largest Woolworth store, the ceilings were now of plaster rather than tin. The walls of the cafés were finished in pale green and primrose Vitrolite, and were hung with peach coloured mirrors; the chequered linoleum was in two shades of green, with black borders.[203] While Marks & Spencer's cafés still had waitress service, Woolworth's cafés were now 'designed on the American cafeteria self-service principle'.[204] That in Blackpool (pl. 257) claimed to be the biggest self-service cafeteria in the country. It occupied two floors, and could seat a total of 1,679 customers at 432 tables. To cope with this multitude, the store had large public lavatories for both sexes, extensive kitchens and a rooftop bakery (pl. 258).

Woolworth in the Post-War World, 1945–1982

Woolworth's art deco house style was abandoned after the war, as was the firm's standard red brick front, probably because it suddenly looked old-fashioned. Architectural uniformity was no longer a desideratum – styles dated too quickly – and Woolworth now erected buildings in a wide variety of contemporary styles (see pl. 122). The Building Department seems to have been headed by William Sherrington until the mid-1960s, when Doug Hardy took over. Under these managers were four regional teams, each with its own architects, quantity surveyors and builders.[205] Like many other national chains, the company participated in the redevelopment of bomb-damaged centres, and the creation of New Towns in the 1950s. It also undertook the gradual modernisation of store interiors, with suspended plaster ceilings, fluorescent lighting, Formica walls and terrazzo floors. Nevertheless, many older premises remained untouched, and old-fashioned counter service was maintained into the mid-1960s, when it was at last superseded by full self-service. By then Woolworth had become one of the first retailers to occupy large anchor units in malls, beginning with the Bull Ring in Birmingham and Elephant & Castle in South London (see pls 270 and 271). In 1967 the company launched Woolco (see p. 278), a precocious chain of out-of-town hypermarkets. It bought B&Q in 1980 and Dodge City, another chain of DIY stores, in 1981.

Between 1945 and 1982 Woolworth shopfronts were constantly being updated, and the degree of uniformity attained between the wars was never recaptured. The first new Woolworth stores to be erected in the 1950s included Southsea (Hampshire) and Plymouth, both of which replaced bombed stores. Each had a continuous canopy with an illuminated soffit, and an internally lit white fascia with red letters. Beneath the

257 The Blackpool store was equipped with a vast self-service cafeteria which took up the first and second floors of the building. The walls were clad in green and yellow Vitrolite.

fascia, the shopfront still comprised a series of lobbies and display windows, now with shiny stainless-steel surrounds. In the mid-1960s new shopfronts had polished red granite pilasters and fascias with neon tube 'Embassy' letters (as at Edgware Road, 1965). Around 1970 some new shopfronts were given red mosaic fascias bearing the single word, 'WOOLWORTH'. Mosaic tiles were also used to clad structural columns, which had originally been concealed within display windows but were externalised as display windows shrank and entrances expanded. It was also around this time that some stores dispensed altogether with fascias: at Walthamstow in east London (pl. 259), for example, square panels spelling the name 'WOOLWORTH' were affixed to the

258 (*above*)   The bakery on the roof of the Blackpool store, with the Blackpool Tower just behind it.

259   The style of Woolworth's buildings changed dramatically after the war. The Walthamstow branch of 1972 closely resembled the company's suburban Woolco hypermarkets.

profile metal cladding rather than the shopfront, which still had the traditional alternation of recessed lobbies and projecting display windows. The 'basket logo', in the form of a looping w, was introduced around 1973, as part of a new corporate image.

Woolworths, 1982–2000

By the late 1970s Woolworth was performing badly, and fewer new buildings were being erected. In 1982 the failing American company sold its UK arm to a consortium called Paternoster Stores, which then assumed the name Woolworth Holdings, and later became Kingfisher PLC.[206] Food retailing immediately ceased, and the Woolco outlets were sold off. The new company also disposed of many high street stores, including some of the most profitable (for example, Church Street, Liverpool, and Oxford Street, London), in order to raise capital to improve the remainder of its portfolio. The Architects' Department was wound down but, in 1985, a new look designed by Rodney Fitch was launched at the Edgware Road store. Store fascias were now sprayed with buff-coloured Wallglaze and given acrylic red-faced, gold-edged lettering; shopfront surrounds were clad in white oblong tiles; and the aluminium frames of doors and windows were powder-coated in pale blue. The pale blue colour scheme extended to signage inside the stores, the 'basket' logo of the 1970s was dropped, and the 'diamond w' revived. This new design proved successful, and by the late 1980s the company was, once again, thriving. Fitch's design was, nevertheless, abandoned in 1992 for a much simpler look which has endured to the present day.

Success in the late 1980s and 1990s encouraged the company to develop three variations on the traditional Woolworths concept. To begin with, between 1995 and 1999, around 300 Woolworths Local conversions were made throughout the country. Then, in 1999, the company launched 'Big w', huge retail warehouses with eye-catching blue, orange and white liveries which sell Comet, Superdrug and B&Q brands, as well as Woolworths merchandise. The company had steered clear of retail parks since the Woolco debacle, and so this marked a significant new direction. Finally, in 2000, the first Woolworths General Store opened in Palmers Green, north London. Loosely modelled on American drug stores, the General Stores offered basic foodstuffs, services such as a pharmacy and photographic processing, and opened late. The formula was dropped, however, in 2002.[207] Meanwhile, the number of high street stores stands at around 800, and continues to rise. New outlets are no longer purpose-built by the company, which prefers to take on existing units,[208] or a new shell offered by private developers. This approach is now near-universal amongst national multiple retailers.

Building a Better Tomorrow:
Urban Precincts and Malls

Pᴸᴀɴɴᴇᴅ ᴍᴀɴᴀɢᴇᴅ ꜱʜᴏᴘᴘɪɴɢ ᴄᴇɴᴛʀᴇꜱ did not emerge in this country until the 1950s, yet the notion of gathering a diverse group of retailers together in a restricted area, or under a single roof, is very ancient. The bazaars and souks of the Arab world and the fairs and markets of Western societies demonstrate its extensive history. In England, entrepreneurs have been leasing out stalls and shops within buildings to assortments of retailers since the medieval period: selds, exchanges, bazaars and arcades all operated along those lines.

What differentiates modern shopping centres from earlier developments is the fact that they are designed for the motor age, with a sophisticated segregation of pedestrian and vehicular traffic.[1] As well as shops, they have to accommodate car parks and loading bays. Whether the distinct activities of shopping, parking and loading are arranged horizontally or vertically has crucial implications, not just for the layout of the development, but also for the quality of its surroundings, which are often char- acterised by historic or landmark buildings and complex patterns of land ownership. In the 1960s and early 1970s developers were permitted to ride roughshod over that heritage, but an increased appreciation of the built environment has ensured that recent schemes are more integrated with their context, and are recon- ciled with broader urban design agendas.

The planning issues concerning town-centre malls are quite different from those affecting off-centre malls, so the latter are discussed separately, in Chapter 13.

Open-Air Pedestrian Precincts

The problem of traffic congestion in urban centres was recog- nised before the Second World War, but rather than the aerial pedestrian bridges proposed in 1936–7 (pl. 261), or the precincts open exclusively to business traffic suggested in 1942,[2] it was the fully pedestrianised open-air precinct that played a central role in the reconstruction of bombed city centres, and in the crea- tion of the New Towns that were erected to relieve metro- politan crowding during the 1950s.[3] The perception that traditional town centre streets, shared by pedestrians and motor vehicles, were outdated was heightened by the appearance of their buildings, which were dirty and ill-maintained after six years of war. Blitzed centres and New Towns seemed blessed with a unique opportunity to develop alternative models, for which inspiration was found in the modern pedestrianised precincts of Dutch towns, such as the post-war Lijnbaan in Rotterdam (1951–3; van den Broek & Bakema).[4] Closer to hand, but perhaps less relevant, was the example of Sicilian Avenue (1906–10) in London, which was closed at either end by Ionic screens, or indeed The Pantiles in Tunbridge Wells, created in the late seventeenth century.[5] Precincts sheltered shoppers from the danger, noise, fumes and dirt generated by streams of delivery vehicles, refuse lorries and private cars. In addition, their con- tinuous canopies offered protection from rain and sun.[6] One of the first pedestrian precincts in Britain, the Chrisp Street Shop- ping Precinct in Poplar, east London, was displayed as part of the Festival of Britain in 1951.

The devastation of war presented the chance to create a brave new world, yet in some heavily bombed centres, such as Exeter and Bristol, the rebuilding respected existing street patterns and successfully incorporated surviving structures. Elsewhere, notably in Plymouth (pl. 262a) and Coventry (pl. 262b), a more radical approach saw old layouts swept away to accommodate new streets that balanced the contradictory requirements of pedes- trians and motor vehicles. The centre of Plymouth, like that of the earlier Welwyn Garden City, comprised a series of island blocks with delivery yards and car parks concealed within their centres, arranged to either side of a grand central shopping avenue. Coventry also featured a central axis, with a vista that

This suggestion for widening streets in order to alleviate traffic congestion in the shopping centres of large cities should be considered in the light of 1940 conditions, when there will be a million more motor vehicles to congest our already crowded streets. Something will have to be done; this method provides a free flow for traffic and complete safety for pedestrians.

Cantilever construction of the concrete and glass promenades would entail the minimum disturbance to property. Parliament could give municipal authorities the necessary powers to proceed with this plan.

THE CEMENT AND CONCRETE ASSOCIATION, 52 GROSVENOR GARDENS S.W.1

261 Traffic congestion was already causing problems in town centres in the late 1930s, when this vision of the future was published by the Cement and Concrete Association. From *Architectural Review*, April 1937, liii.

a

Corporation Street

Burges

Smithford Way

P

P

Owen Owen

Broadgate

Lower Precinct

Upper Precinct

Market Way

Market

P

P

P

P

P

P

Hertford Street

City Arcade

P

Queen Victoria Road

Warwick Row

b

P

P

Danestrete

Queensway

Park Place

PH

Bus Station

Market

Town Square

PO

P

Market Place

St George's Way

Queensway

The Quadrant

P

Southgate Road

c

Cobourg Street

P

P

Mayflower Street

Western Approach

P

P

Market

Cornwall Street

P

P

P

New George Street

P

P

P

Royal Parade

Armada Way

P   multi-storey car parks

P   roof-level car parks

P   surface car parks

⬜   old buildings

⬜   new buildings

▨   pedestrian precinct

0 ———————————— 200 metres

0 ———————————— 600 feet

262   Three post-war town centres: Coventry (a) and Plymouth (c), which were rebuilt following bomb damage and Stevenage (b), a New Town built on a greenfield site. The plans show each town centre as it was by the mid-1960s.

263   The view from the upper level of Coventry's Lower Precinct (1957–60), looking east towards the cathedral.

was stopped by the cathedral spire to the east (pl. 263), and by a tower block, Mercia House, to the west. Here, pedestrianisation was a major feature of the plan. In the original design a cross-route for traffic (Market Way/Smithford Way) divided the Upper Precinct from the Lower Precinct, but in 1955 full pedestrianisation was implemented.[7] By then, extensive precincts were also taking shape in New Towns. While the centre of Harlow retained a vehicular road separating the Market Square from Broad Walk, traffic was completely barred from Stevenage town centre (pl. 262c) from the outset. In these New Towns, as in Coventry, shops were serviced from rear yards, with direct access

from inner ring roads. This introduced an aesthetic problem that had not arisen in Plymouth: namely, the high visibility of back elevations and delivery yards. Invariably, as architects concentrated their efforts on pedestrian frontages, the vehicle sides of precincts were treated as second-class environments.[8]

The walk to and from the car became 'the inescapable seamy side of everyone's shopping experience'.[9] When the centre of Welwyn Garden City was designed after the First World War, it had been assumed that kerbside parking in Parkway and Howardsgate, two particularly wide streets, would suffice for those few residents who might use their cars to go shopping. In

264   The architecture of the Tricorn Centre (1963–5) in Portsmouth, with its detached stair towers and elevator columns, has a strong masculine character.

the 1950s, however, it became clear that mass car ownership was expanding the catchment areas of shopping centres, and that designated parking areas must be provided. Although multi-storey car parks had a long history in Britain, stretching back to the early years of the twentieth century, they were not widely adopted outside London until the early 1960s, when cheap, open-deck systems became available. The possibility of building underground car parks beneath town squares was generally dismissed because of excavation costs, although these would certainly have offered the most economical solution in terms of space. Instead, post-war planners opted for the simple, surface car park: wasteful of land and devoid of aesthetic value, but cheap. In many English towns, cleared bomb sites were used for that purpose, but in planned town centres such as Stevenage, new surface car parks were tucked around the edges of the central zone, with direct access from a ring road. That was the original intention in Coventry,[10] but as space was at a premium the city planners soon decided to direct cars to the flat roofs of the shops via a series of ramps. These car parks were interconnected by aerial bridges which spanned the pedestrian ways, and although they presented a somewhat surreal, modernistic spectacle from the roofs themselves, they were largely concealed from shoppers by solid parapets.

Because the provision of town-centre parking stimulated demand, the single-level car parks of the early 1950s had to be supplemented by multi-storeys. When roof parking was incorporated into central area redevelopment schemes of the 1960s and 1970s, as at Blackburn and Rochdale, it was usually in conjunction with a multi-storey. An alternative solution was the rooftop multi-storey car park, entered via a vertiginous spiral ramp. These were built over compact shopping precincts in Portsmouth (The Tricorn Centre, 1963–5; Owen Luder), Gateshead (Trinity Square, 1964–7; Owen Luder) and Southend (Victoria Circus, 1968; Bernard Engle & Partners) (pl. 260). While the central court of Victoria Circus was relatively airy, the middle of the Tricorn Centre was traversed by a roadway and overshadowed by concrete stair towers and lift shafts, which were imbued with a powerful, even sinister, sculptural quality (pl. 264). The Tricorn was one of the first retail developments in England to have roof servicing, with ramps bringing vehicles up to delivery bays above the shops.

Having attended to the needs of delivery vehicles and private cars, planners and architects set about creating a pleasant environment for shoppers. What is so striking about new town centres of the 1950s is their architectural uniformity, which contrasts sharply with the heterogeneity of unplanned historic centres. The heights of the buildings, their style and materials, were all decreed by development corporations or local authorities, and no retailer or developer was given free rein. While Portland stone lent some monumentality to the new centres of

Bristol, Plymouth and Southampton, brick and curtain walling featured heavily in Canterbury, Exeter and Coventry, as well as in the New Towns, where building budgets were relatively small. The traditional arcade played a very small role in this, possibly because of the difficulties it presented in terms of vehicular access. Shops and stores were arranged in straight lines, preferably with a north–south orientation, with banks and large stores allocated corner sites. The average unit was between 18 and 22 feet (5.49 and 6.71 m) wide and 60 to 100 feet (18.3 to 30.5 m) deep, with a small office or stockroom and a shared yard to the rear. Shopfronts were invariably sheltered by cantilevered canopies, or recessed behind colonnades. Theoretically these protected window-shoppers from the elements, but their heights were not always ideal to meet that purpose. They also helped shoppers to focus on the shops and disregard what existed above them. In town centres this was more likely to comprise storage facilities or office space than flats or maisonettes, because 'the ideal conditions for shopping and for living are diametrically opposed: in the former bustle and movement and in the latter quiet and rest'.[11] The debate about whether or not first-floor storerooms should have windows raged into the 1970s: the architect Owen Luder recommended blind walls because cartons and cases 'grin through the obscured glazing in a most disconcerting and unattractive way'.[12] The same problem still besets the high street today.

Some attempts were made to give each section of shopping precincts its own character and sense of identity. In Harlow, Frederick Gibberd attempted to create a series of open-air rooms by closing the views along the streets and by assigning individual blocks to different architects.[13] Ultimately, decorative coloured paving, public sculpture and trees played the most significant part in generating a distinctive sense of place. In both Stevenage (pl. 265) and the Lansbury Estate, Poplar (1951), a clock tower provided the focus for the design. That in Lansbury, supposedly modelled on the famous sixteenth-century double staircase at the Château de Chambord, comprised two concrete staircases arranged in scissor formation, leading to a viewing platform.[14]

Post-war planners in several towns, especially where space was at a premium, experimented with two-level shopping. The most notable example was Coventry, where the Upper Precinct (1951–4) and Lower Precinct (1957–60; pl. 263) each incorporated a spacious square with two shopping levels connected by ramps and staircases. The circular Lady Godiva Café in the Lower Precinct was accessible from both levels, and superimposed shops could be combined vertically to create a single retail unit, if so desired. Rather differently, The Rows, which occupied one side of the Market Square in Harlow, was directly inspired by The Rows of Chester. It incorporated a recessed shopping gallery at first-floor level, accommodating a dry cleaner, optician, hairdresser and others who did not depend on window display

265   Town Square in Stevenage, Hertfordshire, with fountain and clock tower, was built in 1957–8.

to attract trade. This perennial problem of enticing shoppers to upper levels encouraged some intriguing solutions. At Victoria Circus in Southend, the lift serving the multi-storey car park stopped on the upper shopping level, forcing people to continue their descent via stairs and escalators in the middle of the open square.

In the early 1960s funding became available for redevelopment schemes in towns that had not necessarily suffered much damage during the war, but which required adaptation to the age of the motor car. The Merrion Centre (Phase 1 1962–4; Gillinson, Barnett & Partners) (pl. 266) on the northern edge of Leeds city centre was erected by private developers on a cleared local authority site, and incorporated a cluster of elements that received different architectural treatments.[15] The shopping centre at the heart of the 'city within a city' was originally open, but

pedestrian bridges or decks if necessary, and with 'urban rooms' replacing streets.[17] Of the major urban surgery that ensued, the architect Keith Scott of Building Design Partnership (BDP) wrote: 'we really did think we were embarking upon the first major overall review of the urban fabric since the days of Haussmann and L'Enfant'.[18] In many towns, street after street was flattened to construct inner ring roads, leaving the centre truncated and isolated. Within centres, planners created pedestrianised areas and, using powers of compulsory purchase conferred by the Town & Country Planning Acts, displayed a ruthless approach to historic fabric in their desire to provide modern shopping centres, market halls and multi-storey car parks.[19] Demolition was undertaken on a huge scale, and redevelopment generally failed to acknowledge the character of the locality. One of the most dramatic examples of this approach was Blackburn

266 Shortly after it opened in 1964, the Merrion Centre in Leeds was roofed over, converting it from a precinct into a mall. This shows the main entrance.

267 A typical open-air precinct of around 1970, Bell's Court in Stratford-upon-Avon.

its north–south alignment made it extremely windy, and soon it had to be enclosed.[16] The development was remarkable in several ways, especially for its large multi-storey car park and its basement servicing, but also for its integration of shopping with a wide range of entertainments, such as a bowling alley, a night club, a dance hall and a cinema. Although these amenities were not always open at the same time as the shops, their presence demonstrates that the concept of retail-with-leisure is not simply a modern American importation.

Comprehensive redevelopment received a great boost from Colin Buchanan's Report, *Traffic in Towns* (1963), which strongly advocated the separation of traffic and pedestrians, by building

(pl. 268), where 15 acres (6 ha) of the town centre were cleared to create a 500,000 square foot (46,450 sq. m) shopping centre and market hall. Within the hybrid shopping centre, enclosed malls disgorged shoppers into open squares with upper galleries, accessed by ramps and detached tile-clad stair towers.[20]

The principles of pedestrianisation were extended to numerous existing town and city streets in the 1960s and early 1970s, usually in conjunction with new parking facilities and traffic routes. Sometimes brand new precincts were inserted as compact developments, but often these related poorly to existing shopping facilities (pl. 267). Large precincts continued to be built, however, particularly in towns earmarked for expansion

268   This view of Blackburn town centre shows the market hall (1964) in the foreground, with the shopping centre beyond.

under the Town Development Act of 1952 to house overspill populations from London, Birmingham, Bristol and other cities. This expansion was often on such a scale that the shopping centre had to be redeveloped, and the precinct offered a cheaper solution than the covered mall, which was still in its infancy. Typically, at Basingstoke in Hampshire, an elongated pedestrian precinct called The Walks (1968; Ian Fraser; 500,000 sq. ft/ 46,450 sq. m) was built on a platform spanning a service road.[21] The platform maintained the level of the older shopping streets of Basingstoke, which were thus linked with the new centre to a greater degree than those adjoining earlier developments, including the Merrion Centre, where an American-style Speed-

ramp had conveyed shoppers up to the main shopping level. Like the Merrion Centre, The Walks was a mixed-use development, with a library, a sports centre, offices, flats and multi-storey car parks distributed amongst the shops.

Basement servicing was a feature of most large 1960s precincts, such as the Whitgift Centre (1969; Fitzroy Robinson Partnership) in the London suburb of Croydon, which was transformed into a mini-Manhattan as businesses relocated there from central London.[22] The 12-acre (460,000 sq. ft/42,734 sq. m) precinct occupied a sloping site behind a row of established stores on the main shopping street, North End.[23] The complex had the appearance of classic backland development, but in fact the site had just been vacated by the Trinity School of John Whitgift. The open malls and squares were edged by shops on two levels and served by a two-storey pub (The Forum); five office blocks and a multi-storey car park towered over them. From the point of view of the shopper, the design of this development clearly owed a great deal to Coventry, but the existence of a number of stores (for example, Marks & Spencer, Woolworth and Allders) that wished to dovetail with the new development introduced complications that were largely overcome by the subterranean service road. Clearly, great advances had been made in the organisation of parking and servicing since the 1950s, and in the integration of new developments with existing high streets, even if North End did remain choked with traffic for many years to come.

By the early 1970s the optimism that had pervaded radical post-war town planning was evaporating. Although pedestrianisation had worked for some existing streets, for example King's Lynn's narrow High Street, a disregard for natural topography and a tendency to build over-wide precincts gave many new schemes the character of 'windy deserts'.[24] 'Nooks & Corners' in *Private Eye* commented with irony on King's Lynn's new Vancouver Centre in 1973:

> Everything that the shopper could want lends itself in this tasteful development – rubbish spirals daintily across the windy expanses of concrete pavement – small bricked pig troughs display miniature shrubs at a convenient height for dogs and a set of gay flag poles pierce the Norfolk sky to give a yacht-club ambience. White plastic purpose-built interlocking fencing is supposed to surround the car park but most of it

lies splintered on the ground due to fierce sea breezes and runaway supermarket trolleys.[25]

Moreover, exposed rear elevations and delivery yards remained an aesthetic problem since it was only in high cost, high rental situations such as Croydon that underground or rooftop servicing were practical options. Precincts really were becoming the poor relation of the mall, and without restaurants or cafés many became no-go areas after nightfall, the hangouts of vandals and muggers.

In an attempt to redress the social and aesthetic failings of post-war precincts, many were converted into malls in later years. This has been the fate of the Merrion Centre, The Walks and the Whitgift Centre, while redevelopment is proposed in King's Lynn. Mall conversion usually involves the removal or refurbishment of projecting canopies and the installation of pitched glass roofs, through which one can often glimpse the superstructures of the original buildings. Conversion also involves the renewal of floor and wall finishes, to create an obviously indoor environment.

A more successful generation of open-air precincts, with more enclosed plans, emerged around 1980. The furore surrounding the development of the Chequer Street site in St Albans reveals how public opinion was beginning to influence developers and local authorities.[26] It also demonstrates how protracted the planning process can be for shopping centres. The Chequer Street site was earmarked for a shopping development as early as 1965. By the early 1970s the council had acquired much of the land and was lending its support to a scheme drafted by Samuel Properties. That involved the wholesale redevelopment of unlisted eighteenth- and nineteenth-century buildings lining Chequer Street, and the erection of a modern-style mixed-use development with an air-conditioned mall. Only public outcry – which came to a head in summer 1978 – made the council reconsider, and eventually opt for a smaller, open-air development, which preserved existing buildings. Phase 1 of the new development (The Maltings), built in 1982–3, was in a neo-vernacular style, of brick with pitched, tiled roofs.[27]

Architects and planners were now taking great pains to reconcile open precincts with the irregularities of their urban context, an approach exemplified by Coppergate in York (1983; Chapman Taylor Partners) (pl. 269), which was inserted into the core of the historic city, close to the castle and adjoining St Mary's Church. The site, hemmed in by existing buildings and the river, was an awkward shape, and – as was discovered during preparatory excavations – contained important Viking remains. The approach was lined by buildings on a domestic scale, with flats on their upper floors. From there, the view of the central square was partially obscured by a skewed building which, like those around the square itself, was given an industrial character

269   The Coppergate precinct (1983) in York. The industrial-style windows above Allders conceal a car park.

to suit its riverside setting. The upper two floors around the square concealed car parking decks, accessible from the far corner of the site. Opposite these was the entrance to the Jorvik Viking Centre, which became a major tourist attraction. Another particularly well-integrated open shopping centre is Orchard Square in Sheffield (1987; Chapman Taylor Partners), which is conceived as a group of individually designed blocks, suggestive of organic urban growth and harbouring a mixture of uses.

Since the 1980s, several tiny open-air precincts have been developed in small market towns, accommodating low-rent speciality shops rather than national multiples. Such sites often represent long narrow medieval burgage plots, built up over the centuries with cottages, stables and workshops, which are now being converted into shops, with matching structures erected to fill the gaps. As with Meadow Walk and Cornwall Walk in Buckingham, these precincts often form thoroughfares between main shopping streets and superstores or car parks, providing a continuous flow of potential customers. As key routes within the modern town, such precincts perform a similar role to that of the arcade within the Victorian townscape.

Enclosed Shopping Centres

The high street shopper is exposed to the rain and cold, has to dodge traffic and street furniture, and confront poverty and urban decay. Precincts are not much better. In contrast, sealed, air-conditioned malls offer a sheltered, safe and predictable shopping experience. As well as a range of familiar multiples, they contain restaurants and leisure facilities. But despite their convenience, malls can have a sterile environment. They also have a detrimental effect on the economic viability of high streets, both locally and regionally. This problem is set to grow, as the current veto on out-of-town shopping developments has brought about the resurgence of the giant urban mall, particularly in the south of England where large malls have been absent in the past.

Following the tenet that form follows function, the first enclosed malls, built in the mid-1950s in America, were little more than cheaply constructed boxes which relied on artificial lighting and air conditioning. Because they were built on greenfield sites outside towns they could be served by extensive surface car parks and delivery yards. When malls eventually appeared in Britain, they were adapted to less spacious urban locations, necessitating more compact parking and servicing arrangements. The introverted character of American malls was, however, retained.

The seminal malls in England, which anticipated the influential Buchanan Report (see p. 258), were the Elephant & Castle Shopping Centre in Southwark, London (1965; Boissevain & Osmond; 202,000 sq. ft/18,765.8 sq. m) (pl. 270) and the Bull

Ring Centre in Birmingham (1964; Sydney Greenwood and T. J. Hirst; 350,000 sq. ft/32,515 sq. m) (pl. 271). Both were peripheral to established city-centre shopping facilities: Elephant & Castle was optimistically touted as 'the Piccadilly Circus of South London', while the Bull Ring occupied the site of the former market hall on the edge of Birmingham's main shopping district.[28] As with the contemporary open-air Merrion Centre in Leeds, they each formed part of a multi-use development, expressed as a tower, or towers, and a podium. The towers housed offices and had glass curtain walls, while the shopping and entertainment facilities below were windowless. In each case, the concrete mall was stranded in a sea of traffic, with pedestrian access through unfriendly underpasses and up shuttered-concrete ramps. Elephant & Castle had a two-level basement car park, but the Bull Ring was served by a mechanical multi-storey car park,[29] which failed to cope with demand and closed down within weeks of the opening ceremony. Neither offered a hospitable environment for the car-borne shopper. Both complexes had basement servicing and, in addition, the Bull Ring included an underground bus station and a lower-level market hall. Inside, both shopping centres operated on three levels, with galleries and atria. Although the atria were covered by serrated roofs that admitted some daylight, the malls were heavily dependent on artificial lighting and air conditioning. It was precisely these technological advances that had encouraged the adoption of the windowless wall for pre-war American department stores and post-war American malls, and which were now having a similar impact in Britain.

The near-blind exteriors of Elephant & Castle and the Bull Ring set a standard that was followed by large mall developments throughout the 1960s and early 1970s. The favourite external finish for this new building type was shuttered concrete, which was lauded for its strong and honest architectural expression until the streaking effects of atmospheric pollution became manifest. By the late 1960s aggregate or textured concrete panels were being used increasingly, for example at the Victoria Centre in Nottingham (1972). Another popular veneer was oblong cream, orange or brown tiles, but these proved problematic as they eventually fell off, necessitating recladding. But whatever materials were used, fenestration was kept to a minimum.

Pedestrian access to the pioneer malls was highly awkward, and their successors attempted to remedy this by setting the entrance at street level and introducing ramped floors to cope with gradients. It was only in the late 1960s, however, that double-swing aluminium-frame doors were replaced by automatic sliding doors or powerful air curtains. Once inside, galleries remained underused, since utilitarian staircases and the occasional escalator failed to encourage upward movement.[30] One strategy was to position escalators within department stores rather than within concourses, but the best opportunity to

270   The main entrance to the Elephant & Castle Shopping Centre (1965) in south London.

produce an even footfall was offered by steeply sloping sites, such as those of the St George's Shopping Centre in Preston (1964) and the Kirkgate Arndale Centre in Bradford (1973; pl. 272), which permitted direct pedestrian inflow on two levels. Most developers, however, preferred to build low-risk single-level malls.

Following the example of the pioneers, most 1960s malls admitted some daylight at clerestory or roof level, but by the early 1970s even this was being omitted, in favour of a totally artificial environment having no visual contact with the outside world (pl. 273). Increasingly, low lighting levels and dark wall, ceiling and floor finishes gave deliberate prominence to brightly lit shopfronts. Ceilings of 'egg-crate' louvres, metal strips, acoustic tiles or fibrous plaster served to conceal suspended ducting. Wall surfaces were faced in terrazzo, tiles, granite or marble. Malls were wide and straight, occasionally opening into square courts which could be used for shows or exhibitions, and which served to effect changes in direction, whether horizontal or vertical (pl. 278a). Seating areas enabled shoppers to rest and enjoy the array of planting, fountains, big clocks and sculptures that compensated, in the largest city-centre malls, for low levels of daylight, and softened their rigidly geometric architectural forms. Sound was crucial: terrazzo floors produced a high noise level, which gave an impression of life and activity, while piped music aspired to create atmosphere. The interior environment was closely controlled. Heated or cooled air was usually blown directly into the malls, passed through the shops and extracted via the service areas, but large stores had their own systems. As

271   Birmingham's Bull Ring Shopping Centre (1964), which was demolished in 2001.

with Victorian and Edwardian department stores, fire precautions also had an impact on the design: ceilings were fitted with louvred vents and sprinkler systems, while shutters enabled malls to be divided into smoke reservoirs in the event of a fire.

The first large malls included one big store, usually Woolworth, and a supermarket: Elephant & Castle had Tesco and the Bull Ring had Fine Fare. In the Sandwell Centre, West Bromwich (1971; pl. 278a), the main outlets were occupied by Tesco, Sainsbury's and Boots. Smaller shops were occupied by a mixture of multiples and independents, many of which dispensed with shopfronts from the outset. These were interspersed with restaurants and coffee bars, including the ubiquitous Wimpy Bar. In later malls, an American dumb-bell plan was adopted, with an anchor or magnet store at either end, to encourage pedes-

trian flow past smaller shops. The Victoria Centre in Nottingham was one of the first to include a department store (Jessop's), rather than a large multiple, as an anchor tenant. Throughout the 1970s the John Lewis Partnership was to the fore in relocating department stores from the high street to the mall (see p. 189).

One of the most successful commercial property developers of the 1960s was Arndale Property Trust Ltd, a company founded by a Yorkshireman, Sam Chippindale, whose early years as an estate agent seeking sites for chains such as Marks & Spencer, made him aware of the crucial importance of 'location, location and location'.[31] Although Arndale's first venture, in Jarrow, comprised an open precinct, a visit to America in 1960 convinced Chippindale that covered shopping represented the way forward. The first British Arndale Centre opened in 1967, on the sub-

urban high street of Crossgates, three miles from Leeds city centre and close to an existing Gem supercentre.[32] It had taken Arndale no less than six years to acquire the 9-acre (3.64 ha) site, which was in more than forty different ownerships and included cheap backland as well as expensive frontages. Unlike big city-centre malls, Crossgates had surface-level servicing and parking, and the shops (158,000 sq. ft/14,678.2 sq. m) were on a single level. The wide L-shaped malls were air conditioned, but admitted copious daylight through clerestorys. Their main feature was 'a weirdly beautiful complex of lighted tubes, shining like a myriad of phosphorescent stalactites'.[33] Crossgates was followed by another fourteen developments, whose progress was unimpeded by the takeover of the company by Town & City Properties Ltd in 1968.[34] Although the company claimed, like so many other developers over the years, that these malls were 'separately designed to suit the area in which they [were] situated', the very name 'Arndale' quickly became derogatory, the very embodiment of the concrete-bunker mall.[35] Wandsworth's Arndale Centre has even been described as 'one of London's great architectural disasters'.[36]

The most ambitious mall projects of the mid-1970s were undoubtedly Eldon Square in Newcastle (1976; Chapman Taylor Partners), which was integrated with existing fabric to an unprecedented degree, and the Arndale Centre in Manchester (1972–9; Sir Hugh Wilson and Lewis Womersley), which was a late exercise in comprehensive urban redevelopment. Their different approaches were expressed in their footprints: while Eldon Square wove through the city centre, becoming part of its communications network, the Arndale Centre occupied a regular site that eliminated several backstreets and lanes (pls 274–5). Today, much of Eldon Square seems to overpower the older components of Newcastle city centre, but in the 1970s it seemed highly innovatory.[37] A study of its exterior reveals a hierarchy of elevations, ranging from oppressive expanses of dark brown brickwork on the rear (Prudhoe Street, Percy Street and Newgate Street), to the careful retention of historic façades (Nelson Street) facing the town centre. The canted mall entrance on Northumberland Street, the main shopping street in the city, and the curved end of the Blackett Street elevation (pl. 64), were both clad in tinted mirror glass which attempted to effect assimi-

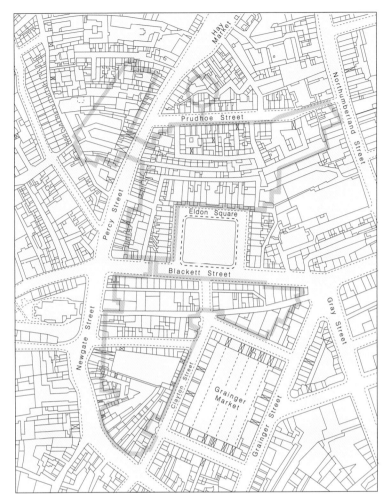

273 (*above*)   The interior of the Victoria Centre in Nottingham (1972) featured a water clock by Roland Emett and was artificially lit throughout.

272 (*facing page*)   A brutalist shopping centre imposed on a Victorian townscape: the Kirkgate (Arndale) Shopping Centre in Bradford, of 1973.

274–5 (*right top and bottom*)   These maps emphasise the different approaches adopted for Eldon Square in Newcastle upon Tyne (*top*), which weaves through the city centre, and the monolithic Arndale Centre in Manchester (*bottom*).

276   The exterior of Manchester's Arndale Centre (1972–9): 'the longest lavatory wall in Europe'.

lation by reflecting older buildings. Less successfully, two sides of Eldon Square and most of Blackett Street were dressed in severe brickwork articulated by recessed panels filled, in places, with lead. Eldon Square was a commercial triumph, proving that a high degree of integration could be achieved without sacrificing economic gain. A similar approach was adopted in Peterborough, where the Queensgate Centre opened in 1982.

Manchester was a different matter. It was the most complex and ambitious of all Arndale Centres, occupying a 15-acre (6.07 ha) site with a 'rabbit warren of ownership' which Sam

Chippindale had begun to acquire in 1952.[38] With 1,200,000 square feet (111,480 sq. m) of shopping (compared with 961,000 sq. ft/89,276.9 sq. m at Eldon Square) it was the largest shopping centre in the country, and aspired to draw custom back to the city centre and away from Stockport's Mersey Way Centre. The forbidding exterior was tiled, producing an effect that has been described as 'the longest lavatory wall in Europe' (pl. 276).[39] Chippindale responded to such criticisms by maintaining that 'one day the Manchester Arndale Centre may even be listed'.[40] Instead, following refurbishment in the 1980s, it was damaged by a terrorist bomb in 1996, and is currently undergoing substantial 'improvements'.[41]

Milton Keynes Shopping Centre (1979; pl. 277) was roughly contemporary with Eldon Square and the Manchester Arndale Centre, but the absence of an established urban context meant that it was compromised neither by demands that it incorporate secondary functions, nor by the presence of much-loved historic buildings. Milton Keynes, designated a New Town in 1967, was built as a low-rise, low-density city which, like Los Angeles, was utterly dependent on the automobile. The rectilinear grid of the city centre was zoned by function, with shopping concentrated in a single-level mall spanning two blocks.[42] That was designed as a door-less complex which would remain open to pedestrians twenty-four hours a day but, for reasons of security, it has been locked at night since the late 1980s, transforming a would-be thoroughfare into an obstacle. Externally, the walls of the Shopping Centre were faced in oblong panels of mirror glass, echoing the long, low proportions of the building. While mirror glass had been used at Eldon Square to reflect surrounding historic buildings, here it reflected plane trees and surrounding surface car parks, softening the rather severe geometry and seemingly endless elevations of the windowless structure.[43] Servicing took place on the roof, rather than in a basement, but was well concealed from shoppers. Inside, the straightforward layout (pl. 278b) comprised two parallel malls (Midsummer Arcade and Silbury Arcade) running between two anchor stores and linked by two cross-malls, with an open courtyard and a covered hall in the centre. The main malls received natural light through clerestorys, and featured trees and plants surrounded by marble benches.

Milton Keynes Shopping Centre more closely resembled the North American model than any other British development.

277 The long side elevation of Milton Keynes Shopping Centre (1979), its uniformity broken only by the occasional entrance canopy, stretches into the distance.

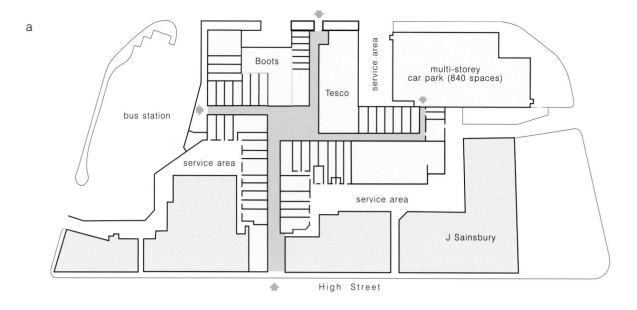

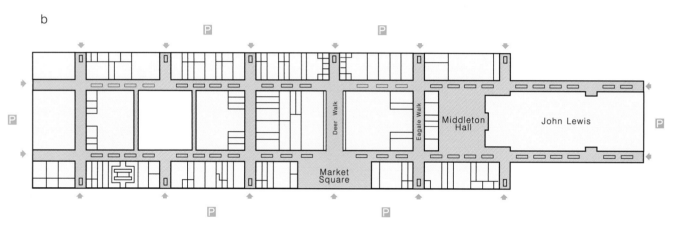

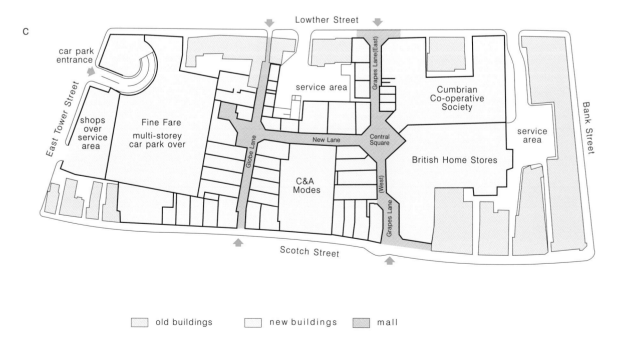

old buildings   new buildings   mall

278a–c   Plans of three very different English malls: the Sandwell Centre in West Bromwich (1971), Milton Keynes Shopping Centre (1979) and The Lanes in Carlisle (1984).

With its long, 'prairie effect' malls and clerestory lighting, it embodied the principles that had governed shopping centre design in England since the mid-1960s, even if its surface parking and smooth elevations brought it closer than usual to its suburban transatlantic roots. Indeed, although the atmosphere of Milton Keynes is somewhat bland, together with its off-centre contemporary at Brent Cross (see pl. 303) it must be perceived as the apogee of the Modern phase of mall development in England.

By the late 1970s attitudes in existing urban centres were changing rapidly. Conservation agencies were now persuading developers to produce schemes in traditional materials, with a hint of vernacular style. Phase 1 of the Millburngate Centre in Durham (1974–6; BDP) was on a similar scale to surrounding buildings, and had brown brick cladding, sparse fenestration and pitched roofs.[44] It was described, in a RIBA commendation of 1977, as 'a model of self-effacing modesty'.[45] Many of the neo-vernacular schemes that followed Millburngate espoused a generic heritage style of architecture, rather than being of specific relevance to the area in which they were built.

While British architects were discovering a new vernacular language for the exteriors of shopping centres, they were turning to America for fresh ideas concerning interior mall design. American architects had rediscovered glass in a big way, beginning with the 'galleria' malls of the early 1970s (for example, The Galleria, Houston, 1971). One of the earliest English 'gallerias' was the Plaza Building in the Brunel Centre (1975–7; Douglas Stephen & Partners with BDP; 574,000 sq. ft/53,324.6 sq. m) in Swindon. By the early 1980s glazed entrance bays, often with coloured anodised aluminium frames, had become ubiquitous.[46] They have remained popular because they make it easy to spot mall entrances from the street or the car park. At the same time, atria were increasingly being topped by polygonal glass roofs with hi-tech innards, and some malls were given continuous glass roofs, for example The Ridings in Wakefield (1983). The design of these roofs became increasingly complex as the decade progressed, and by the early 1990s malls with glazed external walls as well as glass roofs were being erected, for example the St Stephen's Lane section of the otherwise neo-vernacular Buttermarket in Ipswich (1992; BDP). Their transparent qualities allowed such buildings to sit happily in a historic urban setting without becoming too dominant or introspective.

A second crucial American development of the 1970s was the staggered or irregular mall (e.g. Woodfield Mall, Illinois, 1971), which created interest and variety for the shopper. This was adopted in many British designs from the late 1970s. American architects were also beginning to devise subtle strategies to attract shoppers to upper levels: shaped atria were flooded with light, creating attractive vistas, while glass-sided lifts and dramatic escalators, sometimes spanning two floors in one flight, trans-

formed the upward journey into an adventure. Soon, the 'scenic lift', twinkling with 'Tivoli' lights, became an indispensable feature of UK malls, giving upper levels economic parity for the first time.

Throughout the 1980s and 1990s, the standard of interior wall and floor finishes was upgraded (pl. 279), with shiny surfaces such as marble, brass and mirror glass, replacing the dull terracottas or glazed tiles of the 1970s. In general, glazed roofs and matt white fibrous-plaster walls made interiors much brighter, enabling planting to flourish as never before, and giving prominence to the shops. Lighting was also revolutionised. In place of undifferentiated fluorescent lighting, malls were lit by subtle combinations of floodlights, low-voltage spotlights and up-lighters concealed in cornices, an arrangement with a decidedly art deco touch. One particularly sophisticated example was the atrium of the Bentalls Centre in Kingston (1992; BDP), which was claimed as the largest covered space in Europe. Throughout the day, white perforated metal panels diluted the daylight that streamed in through the glass barrel vault but, after dark, up-lighters shining on these panels made the vault appear white rather than black. In addition, fibre-optic lights twinkled all over the vault's surface.

Another American concept imported in the 1980s was the food court. That was often located on a different level from the shops, encouraging vertical movement. One of the earliest examples, in The Ridings Centre, occupied a lower level, but the favoured position was an upper or mezzanine floor, with views over the malls. Many early food courts, like that added to the Eldon Square complex, failed either because they were poorly located, or because the American habit of 'grazing' did not initially appeal to British shoppers. Yet another American concept, greedily seized upon by out-of-town malls in the 1980s, was the themed mall. That had less success in an urban context, despite the precocious creation of a perfunctory 'Georgian Arcade' in the Merrion Centre as early as 1973.[47] Superficial local references have, however, crept into designs from time to time: maritime motifs in seaside malls have proved particularly irresistible to designers.

The integration of malls with their environs made great forward strides in the 1980s and 1990s. One of the most acclaimed developments was The Lanes (1984; BDP) in Carlisle, which is often cited as a model urban retail development. Its site (pl. 278c) was criss-crossed by a network of medieval lanes that had been built up with workers' housing, workshops and stables since the eighteenth century, and had stood in a semi-derelict condition for some time. A shopping centre with a tower and podium had been mooted for the site in 1961 but, fortunately for Carlisle, that proposal was shelved. Then, in the late 1970s, BDP was asked to produce a design that would retain the character of the street elevations, behind which would lie a shopping centre, library and multi-storey car park. The alignment of

one lane was retained (Globe Lane), a second was shifted (Grapes Lane) and others were lost, while one completely new lane (New Lane) was created. At first, these lanes were to be open to the sky, but at a relatively late stage it was decided to cover them with glass roofs. Despite this change in design, they were given outdoor finishes and fixtures, such as York stone floors, brick elevations and metal lighting columns. The success of The Lanes may have inspired the glazing of secondary streets in other towns, such as Royal Priors (1987) in Leamington Spa and the Victoria Quarter (1989–90) in Leeds.

The Lanes is lauded for its Scotch Street façade, which involves replicas of the rather ordinary but locally valued buildings that previously occupied the site (pl. 280). One of the first examples of retail façadism was the Castle Shopping Centre in Banbury (1974–7; Frederick Gibberd & Partners), which incorporated the frontage of the Corn Exchange, as well as a number of humbler buildings on the old market place.[48] A slightly different approach was adopted for The Shires on Leicester High Street (1990), where the frontages of numerous Victorian and Edwardian buildings, including the co-op, were retained, while intrusive modern elevations were rebuilt in a matching style. More recently, attempts have been made to incorporate whole buildings into mall developments, such as the Merchant Taylors' Almshouses in Bristol (pl. 281) and the Town Hall in Wimbledon, south London.

280 The Scotch Street elevation of The Lanes Shopping Centre (1984) in Carlisle, which recreated the façades of demolished buildings.

281 (below) Merchant Taylors' Almshouses, built in 1701, now form part of The Galleries Shopping Centre (1991) in Bristol.

279 (facing page) A typical late twentieth-century mall interior: The Shires, which was built behind retained façades on Leicester High Street in 1990.

282   Covent Garden market in London was converted into a bustling speciality shopping centre in 1980. Hardy plants were originally (1830) displayed on the terrace, while fruit and ices were sold from the rooms to its rear.

Conservation-led development has resulted in the conversion of several redundant commercial buildings into malls. In 1980 Covent Garden Market (pl. 282) in central London was converted into an American-style 'festival mall', with street entertainers and crafts stalls as well as a mixture of small shops, designed to attract tourists as much as Londoners.[49] The courtyards of the original wholesale fruit and vegetable market, which had already been glazed over in the Victorian period, were excavated to create basement levels, and the surrounding piazza was pedestrianised. Following this, several department stores, including Bourne & Hollingsworth (1985) on Oxford Street and Whiteley's (1989) in Bayswater, were redeveloped as malls. In Leeds, Cuthbert Brodrick's circular Corn Exchange was adapted as a speciality shopping centre (1989–90), while Bolton Market Hall was given a new lease of life in 1988 by the addition of a new mall.

Since the Government began to limit out-of-town developments in the mid-1990s, large-scale mall construction has resumed in earnest in town and city centres. These malls are on a scale not witnessed within the urban environment since the 1970s, and are frequently linked with existing high street stores and malls to create extremely extensive covered shopping complexes. They are presented by their originators as highly integrated developments which show respect for the local community and its history, and have even been described as new sources of municipal pride.[50] Regardless of this rhetoric, designs still dominate rather than complement their surroundings, and are usually in a Modern rather than a traditional idiom, with large-scale metal and glass elevations. Several of these malls aspire to regional status, and are served by efficient road systems connected to motorway junctions, which mean that shoppers can treat them just like out-of-town complexes.

Large urban malls that have already opened include The Harlequin (1990; 700,000 sq. ft/65,030 sq. m) in Watford, The Oracle (1999; 700,000 sq. ft/65,030 sq. m) in Reading, West Quay (2000; 800,000 sq. ft/74,320 sq. m) in Southampton and Touchwood (2001; 540,000 sq. ft/50,166 sq. m) in Solihull; in addition, a large shopping centre in the form of retail park has opened in the heart of Romford (2002), which now hopes to compete with Bluewater and Lakeside. The Oracle, represented as 'the new heart of Reading', occupies a 22-acre (8.9 ha) site to the south of Broad Street, where several façades have been retained;

283   A riverside view of The Oracle in Reading (which has been dubbed Las Vegas-on-the-Kennet), at night. It opened in 1999.

Manchester's giant Arndale Centre, it will be remembered, occupied a mere 15 acres (6.07 ha). The site of The Oracle is split by the River Kennet, which is lined by a promenade, with cafés and restaurants (pl. 283). Externally the complex is broken into visually separate blocks, with variety in height, materials and elevational treatment: this is a world away from the monolithic, introverted malls of the 1960s and 1970s, but also from the world of traditional shopping represented by nearby Broad Street. Work is currently under way on Castle Quay in Banbury and The

Malls in Basingstoke, both developments that will involve the refurbishment and incorporation of older shopping centres within huge new developments. Other schemes that are proposed or under way at the time of writing include a regional-scale mall at White City in west London (due to open in 2007),[51] and the redevelopment of Elephant & Castle and the Bull Ring (due to open in 2002–3), bringing the story of the English mall full circle.

Big Box Retailing:
Supermarkets and Superstores

SUPERMARKETS REVOLUTIONISED RETAILING and social habits in post-war Britain. Before the war, housewives shopped for food every day; they expected full counter service from their grocer and butcher, and socialised with their fellow customers. The introduction of the self-service system after 1945, and the steady growth in the size of food stores, made shopping a less gregarious experience. Supermarket efficiency, however, met the needs of a new generation with refrigerators and cars, and much less time to shop. Today many people drive out of town to huge superstores to do their weekly shopping, but from the 1950s until the late 1970s most supermarkets occupied town-centre sites, where their size was severely restricted.

The Urban Supermarket, circa 1950–1975

In Britain, the supermarket is generally defined as a food retail outlet with over 2,000 square feet (185.8 sq.m) of selling area.[1] Its main characteristic is self-service, a concept that originated in America in the early years of the twentieth century, and received a boost from labour shortages during the First World War. The opening of the first Piggly Wiggly store by Clarence Saunders in Memphis in 1916 proved a significant breakthrough. Although Piggly Wiggly stores were small and sold only pre-packaged foodstuffs, in most other respects they adopted the full apparatus of supermarket retailing. They were followed by many more self-service food stores during the Depression, such as King Kullen, which opened in New York in 1930. The crucial event, however, was the opening of Big Bear in an empty car manufacturing plant in New Jersey in 1932. Big Bear provided a free parking lot for customers, and dedicated only 30 per cent of its floor area to food, the remainder being let to concessions. It attracted a huge amount of publicity and its cost-cutting approach was widely emulated. One year later, the term 'supermarket' was coined in Cincinnati.[2]

Although English retailers were hesitant about adopting self-service, some notable experiments took place in the 1920s and 1930s. Piggly Wiggly may have been the example in his mind in 1923, when the multiple provision dealer David Greig converted his branch in Turnpike Lane, London, to self-service.[3] Before long the shop reverted to counter service, partly because the system had not been liked by Greig's customers, and partly because too few ready-packaged goods, a prerequisite of self-service, were available. Meanwhile, English shoppers were becoming acquainted with self-selection, a selling technique that was widely adopted by variety stores and the bargain basements of department stores in the 1920s. Self-selection stores had numerous pay-points, rather than a single checkout, and retained an element of counter service.

When self-service was next attempted, during the Second World War, it was referred to as the 'cafeteria' system, revealing widespread familiarity with the concept of self-service restaurants. In 1942, despite limited supplies and rationing, Harold Wicker of the London Co-operative Society was prompted by staff shortages to create a small (176 sq.ft/16.35 sq.m) self-service section on the ground floor of the society's store in Romford.[4] The department made do with existing fittings and had a single counter for payment, rather than a row of tills. Other London Co-operative Society shops followed suit with hybrid conversions during the war,[5] but it was only in the late 1940s that the correct fixtures and fittings for proper self-service conversion could be obtained. That involved specially designed baskets, wall shelves, refrigerated units, island display units (gondolas) and turnstile checkouts. Marks & Spencer, which had introduced self-selection for canned and bottled foods in the 1930s, stole a march on the co-operative societies by opening a newly

284   The aluminium-clad roof of Sainsbury's celebrated store on the Greenwich peninsula in south-east London (1999) incorporates strips of glazing that reduce dependency on artificial lighting. Despite its 'green' credentials, the store is served by 550 car-parking spaces.

285   When the food department in Marks & Spencer's Wood Green branch in north London was converted to self-service in January 1948, it was hailed as the first British example to follow American models. In the first weeks, the average number of purchases per shopper was only two or three.

equipped American-style self-service food department in its Wood Green store in January 1948 (pl. 285).[6] From then on, numerous co-operative societies converted their existing grocery shops to full self-service: the London Society did this in Upton Park in January 1948 and the Portsea Island Society in Southsea in March 1948.[7] By 1951 there were more than 600 self-service co-operative shops.[8]

Before long, self-service shops and supermarkets were being purpose built. Not surprisingly, two of the earliest examples were erected by the co-operative movement: one by CWS architects for the Newton Abbot Society at Kingskerswell, which opened in September 1949, and the other by the architect of the Portsea Island Society, which opened at Bridgemary in October 1949.[9] The latter was a free-standing, single-storey building with a continuous cantilevered canopy above a glazed frontage. Although tilted glazing was recommended for supermarkets, it does not seem to have become as popular as it was for furniture shops, probably because the idea of the supermarket window display was soon abandoned.[10]

The co-op remained in the vanguard of the supermarket movement throughout the 1950s, while many grocery chains struggled to keep up or, to their ultimate detriment, simply shunned this new-fangled method of selling food. Those who moved with the times included Express Dairies, which built supermarkets in London at Earls Court and Streatham Hill (2,500 sq. ft/232.3 sq. m) in 1951, Waitrose, which built a supermarket at Streatham (2,000 sq. ft/185.8 sq. m), in 1955, and Sainsbury's, which converted its Croydon branch (3,300 sq. ft /306.6 sq. m) in 1950, and built a new supermarket in Eastbourne (3,760 sq. ft/349.3 sq. m) in 1952.[11] The Eastbourne supermarket (pl. 286) was in the form of a simple rectangular hall, with a row of columns running down the middle. It was very well lit: a mixture of spotlights and suspended fluorescent lights were attached to the coffered ceiling, while the front wall was completely glazed and fitted with pairs of armour-plated doors.[12] The flank walls were, of course, blind. Such outlets were able to make great economies, especially in the number of staff they needed to employ. Grocery chains that were slow to develop supermarkets, and eventually vanished from the high street, included Maypole Dairy, Home & Colonial and Lipton.[13]

Many of the first supermarkets occupied converted buildings, especially cinemas, a class of building falling redundant at this

286 Sainsbury's Eastbourne supermarket of 1952 was fitted out by Frederick Sage & Co.

time. It was only in the late 1950s, several years after the abolition of rationing, that large self-service shops and supermarkets began to be erected in any numbers.[14] If a supermarket was inserted into an existing streetscape a second floor often had to be added at the insistence of the local authority. That was the case with the Hartlepools Co-operative Society's self-service shop at Owton Manor (1958), which had a mosaic tile fascia that rose the full height of an additional floor.[15] Blind upper floors quickly became the norm, for example at the Premier (i.e. Express Dairies) supermarket in Harrow in west London (1959), which was clad in moulded concrete blocks.[16] Although their proportions and materials looked out of place in the urban environment, such buildings quickly became a component of high streets up and down the country. In design terms, the most successful supermarkets formed part of multi-use complexes, with flats or offices on their upper floors. At street level, their undressed shopfronts gave a view of the cash desks, although the windows were often plastered with crude posters advertising discounts. The frontage was generally sheltered by a cantilevered canopy or a colonnade, creating a recessed space that could be used as a pram park or, in later years, to store trolleys.[17]

Inside early supermarkets, goods were displayed on versatile fixtures, with perimeter shelves and gondolas that were relatively low (average height 3 ft 6 in./1.07 m) by present-day standards.[18] On the ideal circulation route, new lines and 'convenience' foods were placed near the entrance, with 'demand' goods close to the stockroom at the rear and 'impulse' purchases temptingly displayed by the checkout. The co-op experimented with various types of suspended ceilings, fitted with fluorescent lights and tungsten spot lamps, including heated 'Frenger' ceilings (for example, Leicester, 1958), and dark 'Rotterdam' ceilings (as at Carlisle, 1958), which used black paint and careful lighting to camouflage rather than conceal services.[19] Other companies adopted different systems, such as the tidier 'lumenated' ceiling preferred by Sainsbury's (as at Harlow, 1957).[20] Floors were usually covered by colourful linoleum or terrazzo tiles.

The range of goods sold by supermarkets greatly expanded during the 1960s, and companies soon required larger buildings of around 10,000 square feet (929 sq. m) selling area, with aisles that were wide enough to cope with trolley traffic.[21] Soon it became apparent that customer parking encouraged bulk buying, which obviously boosted trade. Few urban sites were large enough to provide a surface car park, so the main chains began to seek units in the new malls that were being erected throughout the country, as these were usually served by large public car parks: Sainsbury's, for example, opened in the Arndale Centre at Poole in 1969. The advantages of these locations were lost, however, when shopping centre managers – often acting for the local authority – banned supermarket trolleys from lifts.[22] It was difficult for supermarket companies to obtain planning permission to build big supermarkets with surface car parks in town centres, and especially difficult to obtain sites wide enough to allow a row of checkout desks along the front. In the late 1960s and early 1970s Sainsbury's erected numerous town-centre supermarkets as part of mixed developments, mostly in a robust style, executed in dark red brick, but all of the major players were now realising that if they wanted to expand they must persuade planners to let them build large superstores with extensive surface parking on cheap off-centre sites.

Hypermarkets and Superstores, circa 1965–1975

As we have seen, large free-standing superstores with ancillary parking facilities first appeared in North America in the 1930s. They proliferated there in the 1950s, often in the form of strip malls: rows of shops in off-centre locations, anchored by a supermarket and provided with communal parking. For twenty years, it was accepted that such developments were not suited to Britain, where fewer shoppers owned the cars and freezers required to support bulk purchasing. The first European country to build off-centre hypermarkets was France, where Carrefour made a dramatic debut at Sainte-Geneviève-des-Bois in June 1963.[23] French hypermarkets sold clothes and household appliances as well as food; they included rows of small shops and services, such as dry cleaners, and had large car parks, cafeterias and cut-price petrol stations. For many years, the size and scope of French *hypermarchés* was greatly admired by British visitors, who had never experienced such Aladdin's caves at home.

In Britain, it is not surprising to find that the initiative was taken by an American company, Gem, which arrived on the scene in 1964 and established two suburban 'supercentres'. The first (West Bridgford, Nottingham, November 1964) occupied a single-storeyed shed clad in ribbed aluminium sheeting, designed by The Austin-Smith/Salmon/Lord Partnership. Essentially a retail warehouse, it was regarded by the trade press as 'a new building type', but its industrial character and windowless walls were deeply distrusted.[24] The second Gem supercentre (Crossgates, Leeds, May 1965) had to be built on two storeys due to the restricted nature of its site, and had less radical aesthetics. In each case the departments were let to concessionaires and the food hall, which was run by Allied Stores, occupied approxi-

mately one-third of the total selling space (60,000 sq. ft/5,574 sq. m). The Gem experiment was not a great commercial success, and both supercentres were sold to the Yorkshire supermarket company ASDA in 1966.[25] Another early hypermarket operator was Woolworth, whose Woolco outlets also sold a mixture of convenience (such as food) and comparison (such as clothing) goods, but were partly, rather than wholly, occupied by concessions.[26] Woolco attempted to learn from Gem's mistakes, and although its first outlets (at Oadby in 1967 and Thornaby-on-Tees in 1968) were simple warehouses on the West Bridgford model, their exteriors were made more attractive by the application of large panels of abstract art works.[27] One of the largest Woolco stores formed the main unit of The Hampshire Centre (1968) near Bournemouth, an early out-of-town shopping centre which adopted the form of a simple strip mall.[28]

By the early 1970s the threatened explosion in off-centre shopping was generating fears for small shopkeepers and car-less consumers. A Government report of 1971, entitled *The Future Pattern of Shopping*, concluded that town centres would not be affected by out-of-town developments as much as local shops.[29] Subsequent guidance for planning authorities on *Out of Town Shops and Shopping Centres* (1972)[30] decreed that all developments over 50,000 square feet (4,645 sq. m; in other words hypermarkets and malls) were to be approved at government level,[31] while local authorities would assess smaller developments (that is, superstores) on their individual merits, giving preference to outlets selling convenience rather than comparison or bulky/durable goods. Some observers held the view that if convenience retailing went off-centre, town centres would be relieved of their traffic congestion and could concentrate on comparison shopping.

The frontiers of out-of-town retailing were pushed forward by supermarket chains in the early 1970s. Now, Britain was ready for this development. Although some maintained that the 'once a week one-stop bulk-buying-car-borne shopper [was] as much a myth as the notion of universal car ownership',[32] lifestyles were swiftly changing. In 1970, 50 per cent of households owned a car and 61 per cent had a refrigerator, if not a freezer.[33] Moreover, the decline of the role of the full-time 'housewife' had the inevitable consequence that household shopping became a concentrated, weekly activity. At the same time, congested urban supermarkets had reached the maximum size permitted by planning authorities.

Around 1970 ASDA and Fine Fare began to open out-of-town superstores, carefully keeping the size below 50,000 square feet to avoid referral to the Secretary of State. Typically, food comprised 75 per cent of the merchandise sold in these early superstores, but it took up only a third of their selling space, which averaged 30,000 square feet (2,787 sq. m). The hypermarkets erected by Carrefour at Caerphilly in Wales, and Telford in

287 The Bretton Centre (1971–2) on the edge of Peterborough, offered large Sainsbury's and Boots stores, and a variety of smaller shops. It was clad in large white metal sheets with a pressed design of alternately raised or sunk hemispheres.

Shropshire, in 1972, were considerably larger, and sold a wider range of non-food products.[34] Hypermarket status could also be claimed by some of the district shopping centres that were being erected on the outskirts of New Towns, such as the Bretton Centre of 1971–2 (pl. 287), which included a large Sainsbury's store, and the Weston Favell Centre of 1975, which offered both Tesco and Supa Centa (see p. 296). The first free-standing off-centre Sainsbury's store was built on Coldham's Lane in Cambridge in 1974, with 376 parking spaces.[35] In the late 1970s several hypermarkets were built in a joint venture between Sainsbury's and BhS, called Savacentre. The first Savacentre, which offered the normal lines of these two retailers, plus white goods and electrical items, opened at Washington (Tyne and Wear) in 1977.[36] By the end of the decade, all of the major chains were competing for viable off-centre sites.

Little can be said about early superstore and hypermarket buildings, which followed the example of the Gem store at West Bridgford, and were denounced by contemporaries for their 'concentration camp' imagery.[37] They were usually glazed along one side, with blind side and rear walls, and their entrances were not always clearly demarcated. Landscaping was kept to a bare minimum, with little thought of creating an attractive external environment for the pedestrian or, indeed, the motorist. Inside, most superstores merely included a sales area – with much taller fixtures than the self-service shops of the 1950s – a stockroom

and staff facilities. Some also offered a delicatessen counter, an in-store bakery, a restaurant and customer toilets. Own-brand petrol was available by the site entrance.

Gilding the Box: Superstore Design, circa 1975–2000

As the novelty of the free-standing off-centre store diminished, the unarticulated 'big box' became less acceptable to planners and to the public. Although most superstores continued to be built as single-storey pavilions with prefabricated steel frames, their external treatment was increasingly adapted to suit local preferences. The 'Essex barn', which dominated superstore design in the 1980s and early 1990s, was first introduced by ASDA at South Woodham Ferrers, a New Town developed by Essex County Council. The store (pl. 288), which was designed by Alcock and opened in 1978, took its inspiration from the medieval tithe barn; it had a skin of handmade bricks, a steeply pitched roof covered in clay tiles and, on the elevation that faced the pedestrianised shopping street, a clock tower. Although described in a contemporary journal as the 'apotheosis of vernacular fakery', it purported to give the New Town shopper a sense of comfort and prosperity.[38]

Around 1980 the restraints that had hitherto limited super-store development went by the board, not due to any single

288 This ASDA store in South Woodham Ferrers, Essex (1978), inspired a rash of superstores that have been described as 'Essex barns'.

legislative change, but as a result of the enterprise culture gen-erated by the Tory government, which encouraged a shift in resources from the public to the private sector.[39] While an average of twenty-five superstores had been built each year in the 1970s, twice as many were erected in the 1980s. Competi-tion for sites was fierce. Numerous redundant industrial sites came up for redevelopment, in both urban (for example, Sains-bury's, Nine Elms, London, 1982) and edge-of-town (for example, Sainsbury's, Canley, near Coventry, 1994) situations, while greenfield development was encouraged as never before.

Some of the earliest attempts to give superstores a ver-nacular appearance were very crude: Tesco's store at Pitsea in Essex (1978), for example, was no more than a big shed with a raked parapet-roof. In the wake of South Woodham Ferrers, however, the 'Essex barn' was reproduced with little variation, its repertoire of brick walls, tiled roofs, hips and gablets being repeated even in areas with no history of these materials and forms. For many years, the clock turret was an almost obligatory feature, proclaiming the presence of the superstore from afar. The culmination of this approach was probably the church-like

Tesco store in Dorchester (1991–2), which was said to have been influenced by the Prince of Wales, who was then constructing Poundbury nearby.[40] In that same year, no less than twenty-three out of twenty-eight new Tesco stores were given clock turrets. Inside, many of these stores had suspended ceilings which con-cealed the girders needed to carry heavy plant on the rooftop. Externally, landscaping attempted to create a humane and inhab-ited setting.

Some superstores of the 1980s rejected the 'Essex barn' in favour of hi-tech, which was applied most extravagantly to canopies and colonnades. One of the first high-profile super-stores in that style was Sainsbury's Canterbury store, designed by Ahrend Burton & Koralek in 1983. Rows of red-painted steel masts rose from the flat roof and supported the canopy. They were said to echo the turrets and spires of the distant cathedral, an analogy that was not entirely convincing. Nevertheless, the store marked a new departure for Sainsbury's.[41] It aspired to raise its architectural image by appointing the architectural critic and historian Colin Amery as adviser to the company's design team, and by opening its major superstores to competition rather than

289 Sainsbury's is well known for commissioning established architects to design its stores. The canopies along the front of the Plymouth superstore of 1994, by Jeremy Dixon & Edward Jones, are made of translucent fibre and are meant to evoke billowing sails.

relying on its in-house team. The most overtly hi-tech design produced by the company was probably the 30,000 square feet (2,787 sq. m) store built on the site of the ABC Bakery in Camden, London (1988; Nicholas Grimshaw Partnership).[42] The column-free sales area was connected to the basement car park by a travelator, and was spanned by an arched roof (clear span: 131 ft/42 m).

Many of Sainsbury's architect-designed stores were essentially big boxes dressed up by well-known architects. One of these was the superstore designed in 1994 by Jeremy Dixon & Edward Jones for a brownfield site at Marsh Mills just outside Plymouth (pl. 289). The architects worked with the engineer Peter Rice, who had been involved in the construction of the Sidney Opera House. The rectangular building was faced with red brick, except for the public elevations, which were of stainless steel. Its most dramatic feature was the canopy that extended along the main frontage like a series of sails, evoking Plymouth's maritime past. Another example of local referencing was the glass-roofed veranda that surrounded Sainsbury's grandiose Harrogate superstore.

Sainsbury's programme of high-profile architectural design culminated, at the end of the century, in its development near the Millennium Dome at Greenwich in south-east London (1999).[43] The building, by Chetwood Associates, was innovative in its use of natural light and energy-saving systems, although Wal-Mart had opened its first eco-store several years previously, in Kansas in 1993.[44] The sales area of the Greenwich store was covered by an aerodynamic aluminium roof with north lights (pl. 284), while solar panels and wind turbines operated the signage, and the toilets were flushed with rainwater filtered through a reed bed on the site. It cost much more than a conventional store to build, but its much publicised 'green features' were seen to set a precedent for future supermarket design.

Since the mid-1990s a sleek neo-modern style has largely superseded the more expensive 'Essex barn'. The chief exponent of this style is ASDA, whose 'Market Hall Concept' stores (pl. 297, top), designed by Aukett Associates in 1995, introduced glass atria. In the late 1990s their stores were characterised by green-tinted glass frontages, streamlined glazing patterns, buff brickwork and shallow arched roofs with north lights. In 1999 the company was taken over by Wal-Mart, the biggest retailer in the world, with 3,000 stores in the USA. The first purpose-built ASDA/Wal-Mart in England, designed by Aukett Europe, opened in November 2001 as part of the first phase of the North Swindon Development. When completed, the development will include 5,500 new homes served by an Orbital Shopping Park with community amenities, reminiscent of the New Town district centres of the early 1970s. Indeed, the modern design of the ASDA store harks back to Milton Keynes Shopping Centre. Instead of being arched, the flat roof slopes upwards towards the

front, where it projects to form a canopy. The vast, spacious interior is lit by a combination of natural and artificial light, its most prominent feature being the exposed ducting which is suspended from the roof in a highly systematic manner. An even bigger ASDA/Wal-Mart, the Eastlands Supercentre (100,000 sq. ft/ 9,290 sq. m), was built in Manchester in 2002.[45]

Over the years, several superstore developments have involved the reuse of historic buildings or, at the very least, the retention of existing façades. In 1977 Tesco's bid to convert the iron and glass railway shed at Green Park Station in Bath into a 65,000 square foot (6,038.5 sq. m) store was turned down, partly because the scheme was too large, but also because the company had a bad reputation at that time with planning authorities. Instead, in 1979, Sainsbury's was permitted to erect a new superstore with a pitched roof to the rear, and use the shed as a car park. Later conversions by Sainsbury's included a disused Victorian church in Wolverhampton (1988): the church itself was used as a coffee shop, while the store was built to one side.

By the year 2000 the big four, Tesco, Sainsbury's, ASDA and Safeway, commanded 70 per cent of the grocery market.[46] Their superstores now offer many services that were unavailable in the 1970s, including dry cleaning, photo-printing, pharmacies, crèches, baby changing facilities, cash-point machines, banks and coffee shops. These services are usually located towards the front of the building. The experience of shopping in superstores has been further revolutionised by computerised cash registers and, since the early 1980s, lasers that scan bar-coded goods. These relay information to stockrooms and provide fully itemised receipts for customers, who now usually pay by credit or debit card rather than cash. For security reasons many supermarkets have one-way pneumatic tubes so that surplus cash in tills towards the front of the store can be sent to a central cash area. The interior itself, although better lit, is still little more than a 'big box'.

These off-centre developments received their first checks in 1996 and 1994, when the Conservative Government introduced Planning Policy Guidance (PPG) Notes 6 and 13. These sought to reduce the amount of car usage generated by new developments, and introduced a sequential test by stipulating that the availability of in-town locations should be investigated before proposals for new off-centre developments receive approval.[47] Although not a blanket ban, this has certainly discouraged out-of-town developments and forced the big supermarket companies to refocus on town centres.

★   ★   ★

The Urban Supermarket, *circa 1975–2000*

In the 1980s and 1990s the supermarket giants all but ceased to build new supermarkets in town centres, and concentrated on off-centre sites. However, many of their older premises remained operational, and town-centre supermarkets were built occasionally, when suitable parking facilities were available. Waitrose continued to retain a foothold in affluent towns, either in the centre or on the edge. Poorer towns, however, came to rely on discount chains like Kwiksave, or such freezer specialists as Bejam and Iceland.

The idea of the blind supermarket superstructure endured into the early 1980s: as late as 1981, for example, the co-op reclad the frontage of its Pricefighter store on Wealdstone High Street in west London, with magnolia-coloured Glassfibre Reinforced Polyester resin (GRP) panels that masked its original windows.[48] Since 1980, however, most town-centre supermarkets have been built in a vernacular style, often with brick gables facing the street.

As a result of PPG6 and PPG13, there has been increased pressure to build supermarkets in towns. Despite this, Tesco met fierce opposition when it proposed to erect a new supermarket on Corve Street in Ludlow, and received permission only after two planning inquiries.[49] The company employed a reputable architect (Richard MacCormac), whom it retained throughout the project, and the completed scheme was commended by the Civic Trust in 2001 'for its worthy contribution to the community'.[50] Other companies have undertaken similar projects: for example, Sainsbury's in Tooting, south London (2000), and Morrison's in Letchworth Garden City (2000). In all cases, planners encourage companies to erect such stores as part of mixed-use schemes. They are required to maintain the line of the street frontage – or to recover it in the case of Ludlow – and to discourage through traffic by establishing good pedestrian routes.

TESCO

In 1995 Tesco overtook Sainsbury's as Britain's leading food retailer.[51] Tesco had come a long way since 1919, when Jack Cohen (1898–1978), the son of an immigrant Jewish tailor, sold a job-lot of salvaged goods in a London street market. In the 1920s Cohen set up market stalls all over London, and he also had a lock-up in Hackney where he relabelled his stock, much of which was of dubious origin. The Tesco name was invented when a tea consignment from T. E. Stockwell was relabelled 'TESCO' tea, combining Stockwell's initials with the first two letters of Cohen's name. In 1931 Cohen began to lease small shops (under 500 sq. ft (46.45 sq. m) in the parades that were being built to serve London's new outer suburbs, beginning at Green Lanes, Becontree, and Burnt Oak, Edmonton.[52] Four years later, he built a distribution warehouse and head office in Edmonton; the premises (41,408 sq. ft/3,846 sq. m) had the potential to service up to 200 shops, but only 100 existed when war broke out in 1939.[53]

Early Tesco shops were identified in a *sans serif* face as 'Tesco The Modern Grocer'; they had open fronts, and the character of market stalls. Inside, two parallel rows of suspended lights illuminated goods stacked from floor to ceiling and 'piled high' on counters, reflecting the founder's mantra, 'pile it high and sell it cheap'. Many of the tightly packed goods were hidden behind extensive price ticketing.

Jack Cohen had seen viable systems of price cutting and self-service in the United States before the Second World War, and returned in 1946 to find that supermarket trading had greatly improved. In 1947 the St Albans branch became the first to convert, albeit on a small scale (660 sq. ft/61.3 sq. m), to self-service.[54] A photograph of an early self-service shop (pl. 290), possibly St Albans, shows goods stacked on the pavement. Behind this, other items are displayed in pigeonhole shelving, open to the street, while signs promoting self-service and cut prices are sited above the central entrance. Although initially successful, the St Albans experiment was brought to a close after twelve months.

Tesco soon resumed its trials with self-service, reconverting St Albans with improved equipment in October 1949. In all, twenty

290 This archive photograph from the 1950s shows a pre-war Tesco shop which has been converted to self-service. The frontage would have been secured by roller shutters at night.

shops were converted by the end of 1950.[55] Conversion usually involved moving existing counters into the middle of the sales floor; not an ideal solution, but none the less successful. Before long, Cohen was persuaded to install windows instead of roller shutters, so that Tesco shops were 'half way to becoming respectable' and shoplifting was reduced.[56] In the mid-1950s, when Tesco had 120 high street shops in London and the Home Counties, it began to acquire other small chains, including 70 Williamson's stores in 1957 and 212 Irwin stores in 1960.[57] Although an unwise purchase in many respects, the latter acquisition gave Tesco its first foothold in the North-West.

Meanwhile, Tesco was experimenting with larger outlets. Its first true supermarket opened in 1956 in a disused cinema in Maldon, Essex, and sold fresh fruit and vegetables as well as groceries and provisions.[58] Around 1960 Cohen decided to sell household goods, along the lines of cut-price department stores. One of the first new-build Tesco stores, which had a Home'n'Wear department as well as a supermarket, opened on the ground floor of a concrete multi-storey car park in Leicester in 1961. It was promoted by the company as 'Super Parking Shopping', and with a sales area of 16,500 square feet (1,532.8 sq.m) was said to be the largest store of its type in Europe.[59] To cater for the car-borne shopper, Tesco subsequently opened a number of supermarkets in malls, but the company's development was

hampered by the fact that most of its outlets occupied small pre-existing units on the high street (pl. 291), often within mixed developments, and with no scope for extension. Indeed, throughout the 1960s, Tesco assembled an extremely diverse property portfolio that showed little uniformity in terms of style or format, ranging from small high street shops to the huge multi-storeyed Crawley store (37,000 sq.ft/3,437.3 sq.m), which opened in October 1968.[60] Regardless of the size of the unit, fascias were usually clad in pale blue mosaic tiles, and bore three-dimensional serifed letters, in red with white outlines, sometimes reading 'Tesco Food Fair', instead of merely 'Tesco'. If there was no fascia – or if the shopfront was recessed – these letters could be applied directly to the façade.

Tesco's expansion in the 1960s owed a great deal to Green Shield Stamps, which were adopted in 1961.[61] Advertisements for stamps, which were redeemed for gifts, now joined the clutter of signs that obscured the glass frontages of Tesco shops. Stamps – despised by Sainsbury's – offered a means of circumventing the restrictions of Resale Price Maintenance (RPM), which enabled manufacturers to control the prices at which their products were retailed. The abolition of RPM, for which Cohen had campaigned long and hard, finally came about in 1964. That allowed the main supermarket chains to develop rapidly, while small independent grocery shops could no longer compete, and fell by the wayside.[62] In 1965–6 Tesco opened a new store on average every ten days. The company's position was further strengthened by the purchase of struggling chains, some of which proved a drain on resources, especially the 217 run-down Victor Value shops bought by Cohen in 1968. By then the company owned a total of 834 outlets, although most were considered inadequate by contemporary standards.

In the course of the 1960s Tesco developed the idea of trading on two levels, with a supermarket on the ground floor and Home'n'Wear above. That idea may have originated at the Cheltenham branch, which was established in an old Woolworth store around 1960.[63] In 1963 the store at Small Heath, Birmingham, opened with 10,000 square feet (929 sq.m) on the ground floor, and 6,000 square feet (557.4 sq.m) above. By the late 1960s new developments with this layout, usually with a travelator or escalator connecting the two floors, were being undertaken by Tesco's own Estates Department, using outside architects. These developments could encompass non-Tesco elements: the Ipswich store (1968; Inskip & Wilczynski; 11,800 sq.ft/1,096.2 sq.m), for example, was built as part of a complex that included a furniture shop (Bowhill, Elliott & White), a flat and an electricity substation.[64] Above the aluminium-frame shopfront, the windowless elevation was clad in a 'Californian "starburst" screen', of moulded concrete blocks. Such facings were very popular with Tesco and with other supermarket chains (pl. 292). At Ipswich, Tesco's stockroom, preparation room and

291 A Tesco supermarket in East Ham, east London, in the mid-1960s, displaying advertisements for Green Shield stamps in the windows.

refrigeration plant were at roof level, where they were concealed from the street by a mansard roof.

Tesco began to expand into the North-East in the early 1970s, opening in Middlesborough in July 1972 and in Gateshead in November 1972.[65] The free-standing Gateshead store (pl. 293) was built on a sloping site next to Luder's Trinity Square complex and measured 30,000 square feet (2,787 sq. m). Only two years later it was extended to include a two-level area for the sale of furniture and other non-food items, and also an in-store bakery.[66]

Tesco was slow to participate in the construction of out-of-town superstores in the early 1970s. Its progress was hampered by its notorious disregard for planning regulations, which made local authorities reluctant to support its schemes.[67] Tesco tried to reform its image by improving its store portfolio: 200 small outlets closed between 1973 and 1979, and in 1975 an American design group, Doody, was called in to modernise the house style. Tesco's profits plummeted in 1974–5, but in 1977 trading stamps were eliminated and prices slashed in an overnight operation called 'Checkout', which was an outstanding success. The exercise bolstered Tesco's market share and strengthened customer and store loyalty.[68] Overheads were cut still further when the company established new central distribution warehouses and expanded its range of own-brand produce.

The first Tesco hypermarket (73,350 sq. ft/6,814.2 sq. m), constructed in Irlam, Greater Manchester, in 1976, was not judged to be a great success, but the company soon began to turn around in the hands of Ian McLaurin, who realised the importance of cultivating a good relationship with planning authorities. The development budget rose, and the company opened its large Pitsea superstore in Essex in July 1978, just before Cohen's death. Increasingly, new stores were designed to appeal to both public and planners, while the Tesco brand was improved through initiatives promoting healthy eating and 'green' issues. Between 1977 and 1983 the store portfolio continued to improve: 371 small supermarkets were closed, and 97 new superstores, with an average size of 30,000 square feet (2,787 sq. m), were erected.

The heritage-style superstore, or 'Essex barn', dominated Tesco's architectural approach during the 1980s and early 1990s (pl. 294). The style was widely adopted in response to the raised expectations of planning officers and community groups who preferred this design, even if it little resembled the true vernacular of their area. Like other supermarket companies, Tesco also restored and redeveloped some historically interesting buildings for supermarket use. In Baldock in Hertfordshire, the façade of a former film studio, later a Kayser Bondor lingerie factory, was retained, and a new superstore was erected to its rear. Ironically, Kayser Bondor had won a High Court action against Tesco, which had cut prices on two of its products, during the

292   Quite a number of new Tesco supermarkets were built in this style in the late 1960s. This example, which was opened by the comedian Jimmy Edwards in 1969, has not been identified.

293   This Tesco store was built in the centre of Gateshead in 1972 and was extended in 1974.

1960s.[69] Tesco's best known conversion to date, undertaken in 1992–3, involved the Hoover Building on Western Avenue (A40) in London (pl. 295).[70] There, the architects Lyons, Sleeman & Hoare created a scheme that restored the main building for office use, while the new superstore to the rear incorporated art

294   In the 1980s and early 1990s Tesco erected many superstores of the 'Essex barn' type. This one is located at Loudwater, just outside High Wycombe, Buckinghamshire.

295 The art deco Hoover Factory on Western Avenue, Perivale, was designed by Wallis, Gilbert & Partners and built in 1931–5. It closed in 1982, and reopened as a Tesco superstore in 1992.

deco details that echoed the original design of 1932 by Wallis Gilbert & Partners.

By the mid-1990s, under the leadership of Terry Leahy, Tesco was opening thirty stores a year, a material expansion that contributed to the company's new lead over its rival, Sainsbury's.[71] Despite some resistance from local planning authorities and the public, Tesco began to move away from the 'Essex barn' towards a modern style, employing glass and steel to produce light spacious buildings that more honestly expressed their function. The company's first neo-modern store, erected in Hemel Hempstead in 1994, was designed by Michael Aukett. Although it had a hipped roof and was faced by a red-brick colonnade, the building was described as 'akin to a giant conservatory' and clearly

marked a break with the past.[72] Around the same time Tesco's chunky lettering was redesigned, with blue 'blips' added below the letters, reflecting the bars on its carrier bags, and a generic interior design was created in 1996 by Future Brand Davies Barron. Another forward step was taken with Aukett's glass and steel superstore for Abbeydale Road in Sheffield (pl. 296), which had a distinctive wave-form roof and won a RIBA award in 1997. By then, the company was persuading local authorities to accept designs that were individually adapted by other consultant architects from Aukett's model. In comparison with past efforts, these stores were low in cost, speedily constructed and energy efficient. Inside, ceilings were left open, exposing ducting and contributing to the more open feel of the building.

296   This modern Tesco superstore is located on Abbeydale Road in Sheffield.

Tesco still builds twenty-five new superstores a year. To cut development costs and maintain design consistency, enabling it to compete with the likes of ASDA, it has reduced the number of architects it works with from forty-two six years ago to ten in 2002 and has moved away from competitive tendering, instead working in close partnership with a limited number of contractors. It has also developed a standardised building shell, or 'flat-pack kit', which was first used at Haverfordwest in Wales in 2000.[73] Tesco's current approach to store design may be economical and modern but it has proved unpalatable for many local authorities, for example in Beverley, where the style of a new store has recently had to be modified.[74]

In the last decade, Tesco has introduced several innovative store concepts. Having identified a neglected market in town centres, largely consisting of professional people who wanted to 'convenience' shop for meals on the way home, or purchase lunchtime snacks, the company launched 'Tesco Metro' in Covent Garden in 1992. Metros (average 12,500 sq. ft/ 1,161.3 sq. m) are usually sited in existing buildings: Leicester Metro is typical, as it represents a downsize of a Tesco supermarket, and is part of an established shopping centre with resi-

dential accommodation on upper floors. Sainsbury's followed in Tesco's footsteps when it opened its first 'Local' store on Fulham Palace Road, south-west London, in 1998.

'Tesco Express' stores (average 2,000–3,000 sq. ft/185.8– 278.7 sq. m) were launched in 1994. These prefabricated flat-roofed modular buildings were located at Tesco filling stations, but difficulties in finding suitable sites for development eventually prompted the company to form an alliance with Esso. Express stores supply basic convenience goods, and include a kiosk where motorists can pay for petrol.

The most recent Tesco concept is 'Tesco Extra', a format that begins with a trading area of 60,000 square feet (5,574 sq. m), but includes two standard models of 80,000 and 100,000 square feet (7,432 and 9,290 sq. m). The first Extra was the extended Pitsea store of 1997, while the first purpose-built examples opened in Peterborough and Newcastle in 2000. In recent years Tesco has expanded greatly overseas, especially in Asia, and its Extra stores reflect this by following an internationally aligned standard format. They devote a high proportion of space to non-food items, and their floor areas are so large that customers' assistants often travel on roller skates to provide a speedy service.

An interesting variation on the Extra format, which evolved from the company's international experiences, is the store-on-stilts. Placing sales at first-floor level over a car park – not unlike the approach at Weston Favell in the 1970s – permits the development of a large store on a restricted site. The first of these in the UK, built in Altrincham, Greater Manchester, was designed by Aukett, and opened in late 2002.

From unconventional and often rocky beginnings, Tesco has evolved to become the leading UK supermarket company and the world's largest Internet retailer. Led by Jack Cohen, it grew haphazardly through the acquisition of existing chains and by disregarding planning requirements. Under the leadership of McLaurin and Leahy, a new relationship was forged with planners, enabling the company to shed its downmarket image and develop a respectable store portfolio.

297   An aerial view showing The Place at the Trafford Centre (1998) near Manchester. The large store to centre-rear is Selfridges.

Shopping Unlimited:
The Move out of Town

ARGUMENTS FOR AND AGAINST off-centre shopping have raged for decades.[1] Planners have tried to protect the livelihoods of town-centre shopkeepers, to minimise traffic congestion and to preserve the countryside, but they have been subjected to enormous pressure from retailers and developers, eager to build massive shopping complexes for car-borne customers on cheap out-of-town land. During the last quarter of the twentieth century, resistance weakened, and off-centre shopping became a reality, a common daily or weekly experience for millions.[2] Superstores, retail parks, outlet villages and malls now encircle our towns and cities, lending some colour to their hitherto non-descript margins, but sapping the economic vibrancy of established urban and suburban centres. Liberated from an urban context, the most efficient forms have evolved for these buildings, offering valuable insights into the more constrained designs of their urban counterparts. They tell us what the retailer and developer would like, given a free hand.

Off-centre retail developments have been discouraged by the planning process since the mid-1990s, and as a result several town centres have acquired large superstores (see p. 283), and a few historic towns are currently being endowed with gigantic new shopping malls, on a scale that has not been seen since the mid-1970s (see p. 272). The extent to which that policy reversal might affect the urban built environment and the economy of smaller towns is only just becoming apparent.

Non-Food Superstores and Retail Parks

It was seen in the last chapter that the first off-centre shopping developments in England were the hypermarkets erected in the mid- to late 1960s by Gem and Woolco, which sold both food and non-food products. While some of these hypermarkets formed single, free-standing units, others – notably Woolco in the

Hampshire Centre, Bournemouth – were accompanied by a row of shops, creating small shopping centres on the precinct model. Gem and Woolco had limited success, and in the early 1970s it was the supermarket chains that took a leading role in the decentralisation of shopping. The first specialised non-food retailers to go down this route were those that sold large items, such as electrical goods, furniture and DIY. These required less parking than food superstores, and occupied smaller units (average 20,000 sq. ft/1,858 sq. m), often located on or close to industrial estates. In many cases existing units were adapted, and the first purpose-built retail warehouses, like those erected in Cambridge Close, Aylesbury, in 1978–81, imitated industrial units by having large delivery doors and small customer entrances on their frontages. Large-scale DIY retailing seems to have originated from diversification by traditional builders merchants, but from the late 1970s more traditional retailers were taking an interest. In 1979, for example, W. H. Smith's purchased eighteen LCP Homecentres and renamed them Do It All. Woolworth acquired B&Q in 1980 and Dodge City stores in 1981, making it the biggest DIY retailer in the country. Garden centres were also jumping on the bandwagon. Drawing on the tradition of nurseries, these took rather more trouble with their appearance. They needed to unite exterior and interior selling areas, and often constructed conservatory or farm style buildings. Sainsbury's Homebase, launched in 1981, was a garden centre as well as a DIY chain. It was only in the 1990s, however, that chains such as Wyevale began to replace independently owned centres in any numbers.

By 1980 retail warehouses were clustering along certain road corridors, such as parts of the North Circular in London, and in 1982 the first planned retail park was built in Aylesbury, possibly representing an enlargement of Cambridge Close, which had initially developed in a piecemeal manner. For once, this was not an American introduction, but a British invention. Few retail

298   A typical out-of-town retail warehouse at Fosse Park, near Leicester, built in the late 1990s.

parks were built before the late 1980s, then their numbers soared, and by the late 1990s no town of any size was without at least one retail park, with anything from five to thirty outlets, which could vary from 10,000 to 100,000 square feet (929 to 9,290 sq. m) with a usual allocation of forty car parking spaces per 1,000 square foot (92.9 sq. m) of retail space. Most retail parks are restricted to outlets selling bulky goods, but some have attracted high street names. One of the first of these was Fosse Park, designed by the Mason Richards Partnership and built outside Leicester in 1989 with units occupied by Marks & Spencer, Mothercare, Burton, Boots and Next.[3] The licence for Fosse Park South (pl. 298), built in 1997–8, was restricted to dealers in bulky

goods, such as Currys, PC World and Maples, to limit further impact on Leicester town centre. Typically, a detached burger restaurant, in this case McDonald's, was marooned in the car park, and a food superstore (ASDA) with a petrol filling station stood nearby. More recently, Fosse Park has opened a food court, a feature more common to malls than retail parks.

In modern retail parks, units are arranged in rows, rather than as detached warehouses. As ever, the buildings are little more than functional, flat-roofed boxes, but delivery entrances are now invariably positioned to the rear. Façades seek to grab the attention of the passing motorist, with brazen displays of names and logos which would be forbidden in an urban area. Entrances are heavily emphasised, and are often contained within a large expanse of glass, topped by an arch or pediment. Some retailers, such as Toys 'R' Us, now concentrate exclusively on retail parks, and have developed a house style appropriate to this new building type. The space requirements of several large non-food retailers such as IKEA exclude them from retail park situations and so, like most large Tesco or Sainsbury's stores, they tend to be free-standing.

★   ★   ★

Outlet Villages

Since 1993 more than thirty outlet villages have opened in the UK. Whether dubbed 'factory', 'designer' or 'discount' villages, they invariably consist of a cluster of up to 130 small shops selling end-of-the-range or last-season brand products at generous discounts, offering the consumer an alternative to the sameness of the mall. American shopping villages, usually offering speciality shopping for sophisticated metropolitan consumers or tourists, originated in the late 1970s and were often themed. One of the first examples, Pier 39 in San Francisco, resembled a rambling fishing village. The concept of the shopping village was prob-

299   Whiteley Village (2000) near Southampton is designed to resemble a genuine English town.

300 Shops, protected by a membrane canopy, ring the central car park at McArthurGlen's Designer Outlet, Ashford, Kent, erected in 2000.

ably allied with that of discounting in America in the 1980s, and the introduction of the outlet village to the UK in the early 1990s was heralded to some extent by free-standing factory shops which sold seconds and spare stock, and by earlier high street discount ventures, such as Next to Nothing.

A few outlet centres, such as the Great Western Designer Outlet Village in Swindon, occupy converted buildings in built-up areas, but most have been erected out of town. While Great Western is a covered mall,[4] most are open-air complexes which follow one of two possible layouts: in the first, the buildings flank pedestrianised streets and are surrounded by surface car parks; in the second, the buildings encircle a central car park. In either case, the complex is inward looking, with well-concealed delivery yards on its periphery. If the car parks are also on the outside, the pedestrian entrance is given particular prominence, often in the form of a monumental archway. Outlet villages

provide similar facilities to malls, such as play areas, food courts and entertainment centres. Many have attracted large superstores, retail parks and pubs to their vicinity, and operators generally make efforts to appeal to tourists as well as those residing within the designated catchment area. Thus, Atlantic Village was sited near Bideford in Devon, not because the area has a high resident population, but because it attracts more than 6 million visitors each year.

The first UK outlet village was built in 1993 by Clark's, the footwear manufacturers, on their redundant factory site in Street, Somerset, following a visit to America by a contingent of company directors. While some former factory buildings were retained as part of the complex, many smaller purpose-built blocks of shops were erected around them. Clark's Village was quickly followed by a brand-new outlet village on a greenfield site near Bicester in Oxfordshire (1995; Lyons, Sleeman &

Hoare). There, a winding street was flanked by weather-boarded buildings in a colonial New England style, with shops on their ground floors. The L-shaped car park enabled shoppers to enter the street at two points, one marked by a monumental arch. On one level, Bicester Village represents the 'ideal' urban shopping street, free from the distraction of traffic and with a distinctly American ambience. Two later developments, Freeport Braintree, Essex (2000), and Whiteley Village, Fareham, Hampshire (2000) (pl. 299), have translated this idea into an English idiom. Their streets are lined with domestic-scale façades in a mixture of pseudo-vernacular styles; Whiteley Village has even adopted a traditional 'crossroads' plan.

Since the mid-1990s the main developer of outlet villages in Europe has been BAA McArthurGlen: a partnership between British Airport Authorities, which runs retailing at UK airports, and an American developer. McArthurGlen's first UK site, at Cheshire Oaks near Ellesmere Port, Cheshire, opened in 1995 and, at 400,000 square feet (37,160 sq. m), is by far the largest outlet village in the country.[5] It is served by a multi-storey car park as well as extensive, zoned surface car parks in the centre of the complex. At McArthurGlen's Designer Outlet Ashford, Kent (pl. 300), the car park in the middle of the tear-drop shaped complex is sunken, creating clear 360 degree vistas from the continuous shopping street. Ashford opened on the site of a former railway works in March 2000 and is perhaps McArthurGlen's best-known development, if only because it was designed by Richard Rogers, architect of the Greenwich Millennium Dome and Chairman of the Urban Task Force. The eighty outlets which ring the car park are spanned by a continuous tented roof which is said to be the longest membrane structure in the world.[6] Outside the complex, an embankment conceals all but the canopy from view: the effect has been likened to a medieval encampment or, by Lord Rogers, to 'a Bedouin tent in an English meadow'.[7] The use of tenting, here and at other outlet villages, produces an ephemeral, fairlike atmosphere.

Consumer Cathedrals: The Off-Centre Mall

The first off-centre shopping complex in the USA is said to have been the Country Club Plaza, which opened in Kansas in 1923.[8] The idea did not take off until the 1950s, when America acquired numerous large out-of-town shopping malls, erected for car-borne shoppers. These developments could assume the size of a major town centre and, typically, included one or two well-positioned 'magnet' or 'anchor' stores which encouraged pedestrian flow past smaller shops. The key components were already present in 1956, when Victor Gruen's covered Southdale Centre at Edina, outside Minneapolis, first opened.[9] That climate-controlled building comprised two shopping levels around a

central court, where events and eating areas were located. Writing about British shopping centres in 1959, Wilfred Burns warned that 'if we do not solve our transport and car parking problems, the American plans may indeed be welcomed; the red warning light is on'.[10]

In fact, as early as 1955, the Glass Age Development Committee, sponsored by Pilkington's, designed an imaginary out-of-town shopping complex called High Market, to serve the West Midlands conurbation (pl. 301).[11] The rectangular building, measuring 2,000 by 400 feet (609.6 × 121.9 sq. m), was strangely prophetic of things to come, although it included some futuristic ideas that would never materialise. It had basement parking and servicing, a market hall covered by parabolic arches, rows of small shops arranged around a mixture of open squares and glazed arcades, two department stores, a cinema, a restaurant and a boating pool. It could be enclosed and air-conditioned in

301 The High Market scheme, put forward by Pilkington's in 1955, was the first British proposal for an out-of-town shopping mall. From *The Architect and Building News*, 8 December 1955, 750.

winter, and shoppers – who might arrive by helicopter or monorail rather than car or bus – could travel round the complex on a two-way moving platform fitted with seats.

The first serious proposal for an out-of-town shopping complex was submitted four years after Wilfred Burns's warning, in 1963. That concerned a regional shopping centre of 1,000,000 square feet (92,900 sq. m) at Haydock Park near Liverpool, but the application was turned down after a lengthy inquiry. The Haydock Report, commissioned from Manchester University, suggested that the proposed development would have a devastating effect on trade in surrounding town centres.[12] For a further twenty years, developers campaigned for the erection of such shopping centres, while planners resisted by pointing out the shortage of available greenfield sites, and stressing the detri-

302 When it was completed in 1975, the Weston Favell Shopping Centre near Northampton was one of the largest off-centre shopping developments in the country.

mental impact that huge malls would have on established interests.

In the event the first non-central shopping malls to open in Britain belonged to the last phase of post-war New Town development. The single-level Bretton Centre (1971–2; Scott, Brownrigg & Turner) near Peterborough was a hybrid development, part-precinct and part-mall, with two large stores (Sainsbury's and Boots) and a number of smaller shops giving a total retail area of 54,000 square feet (5,016.6 sq. m; pl. 287). The much larger Weston Favell Centre (1975; Gordon Redfern) was situated on the A45 to the east of Northampton, which had been designated a New Town in 1968.[13] It stood close to new residential developments, with which it was uncomfortably connected by high-level pedestrian bridges (pl. 302). At this time, many New Town shopping centres, whether district or central in status, were being designed to attract car-owning consumers from a wide area. This approach was adopted because shopping centres in the embryonic New Towns of the 1950s and 1960s had not been sustained, during their early years, by the residential population.

Unlike the Bretton Centre, Weston Favell was a full-fledged mall with a retail area of 210,000 square feet (19,509 sq. m). The windowless, two-level box consisted of shops above a covered car park, with additional open-air parking to north and south (pl. 302). The 600-foot (182.9 m) mall walkway and the North and South Squares were spanned by coffered barrel vaults, while the remainder of the roof was flat. On one side of the mall were two superstores and on the other a row of small shops. Access between the car park and mall was provided by an 'autowalk',[14] as well as escalators, stairs and lifts. By the standards of the time, Weston Favell, with its gallery of growing plants, its white barrel vaults and its marble floor, was considered unusually grand. As one critic put it: 'in this country at present, there isn't another shopping mall quite like it and it is well worth a visit'.[15]

Still in the European vanguard, France enjoyed a boom in the construction of out-of-town shopping centres around 1970, particularly in the Ile-de-France, where Parly 2 (1969), Velizy 2 (1972) and Rosny 2 (1973) were located. In England, the first regional-scale off-centre shopping mall was granted permission in 1972 and opened in 1976.[16] As it was sited at Brent Cross, on the North Circular Road in the north-London suburbs, it cannot accurately be described as an 'out-of-town' development. Nor was it a town centre development, like its contemporary in Milton Keynes. The semi-derelict site was seven miles from Oxford Circus, but within easy reach of several suburban high streets, notably Golders Green. The two-level building (pl. 303), designed by Bernard Engle & Partners for the Hammerson Group, had an American-style dumb-bell plan, with an anchor store at either end. The main feature of the interior, which was brighter than most urban malls of the 1970s, was a solid central dome with stained-glass inserts. Brent Cross was an instant commercial success, despite the 1970s recession, encouraging developers to propose similar complexes elsewhere in England.

In the late 1970s and early 1980s a smattering of smaller off-centre mall developments appeared, including the Hempstead Valley Shopping Centre (1978; Stanley Bragg & Associates) in Kent. This had a hypermarket (Savacentre) and forty-six smaller units arranged along a single-storeyed L-shaped mall.[17] Although merely a district centre, its 'Picnic Parlour' pioneered the communal fast-food area in the UK.[18] Hempstead Valley could not have been more different from the Miesian design of the contemporary mall in Milton Keynes. It was one of the first to have fragmented brick elevations, a varied roofscape featuring both pitched and flat elements, staggered malls that admitted daylight through continuous clerestoreys, and courts lit by pyramidal lanterns. A new era of mall design was dawning.

Over the years, many applications for regional out-of-town shopping centres had been turned down. Attitudes changed in the early 1980s, when the new Conservative Government voiced support for schemes that provided jobs and stimulated investment in areas with social and economic problems, especially

303 This aerial photograph of 2000 shows the Brent Cross Shopping Centre (1976), which is situated in north London. To the front is the John Lewis department store.

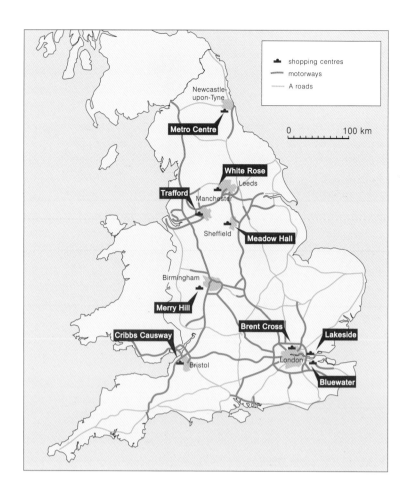

when little or no public subsidy was involved. Thus, between 1984 and 1999, no less than seven malls were built by the private sector, close to motorway junctions, within reach of the country's largest cities (see table, below, and map, pl. 304).[19] Most of the mega-malls created during these years occupy brownfield sites, where some could reap the tax advantages of Enterprise Zone status during their early years.[20] At the most basic level, all of these buildings have extensive malls with glazed roofs and entrance bays, but their architectural treatment and overall layout varies considerably. Most have absorbed American concepts, such as themed areas, the food court and ancillary leisure and entertainment facilities. They usually benefit from the proximity of a retail park, and are served by their own bus and railway stations. In addition, they are enveloped by varying combinations of surface, double-decker and multi-storey car parks, carefully arranged to give entry into different shopping levels, ensuring an even footfall throughout the malls. Their critics denounce these developments as anonymous, American-style blots on the landscape, which suck life from town centres, cause environmental blight and devalue any sense of place, together with the cultural traditions that define it.[21] Others maintain that such

304 (*left*)   This map reveals the close relationship between English motorways and out-of-town mall developments.

Name	Nearest Cities	Road Access	Construction Dates	GLA★	Catchment area★★	No. of shops	Site acreage
Brent Cross	London	A406/A41	1972–6	790,000	1,275,000 20 minutes	82	52
MetroCentre	Gateshead/Newcastle	A1	1984–7	1.5 million	3 million	350	120
Lakeside	London	M25	1990 1998	1.3 million	11 million	230 320	120 200
Merry Hill	Dudley/Birmingham	M5	1985–9	1.5 million	4.7 million	220	125
Meadowhall	Sheffield/Rotherham	M1	1990	1.1 million	4.7 million	223	138
White Rose	Leeds	M62/M621	1998	650,000	9 million	100	not available
Cribbs Causeway	Bristol	M5	1995–8	725,000	1.7 million	131	not available
Trafford	Manchester	M60	1995–8	1.3 million	5.3 million 45 minutes	280	61 acres
Bluewater	London	M25	1999	1.6 million	10 million	320	240

Comparative statistics for out-of-town shopping centres in England, at the time of opening, 1976–99
★ Gross lettable area
★★ People living within one hour's drive unless otherwise stated

305 This aerial view of Bluewater (1999) shows the triangular form of the malls, the central delivery yard, the three main 'break out' areas and peripheral car parking.

attacks are manifestations of British middle-class snobbery and fear of cultural change.[22] Gigantic malls have, certainly, struck a chord with the general public ('guests'), and are especially popular for family days out at weekends.

In the 1980s planners welcomed proposals that promised to regenerate derelict sites within post-industrial landscapes of little aesthetic value. Thus the MetroCentre (1986; Ronald Chipchase & Associates) was built on the coal-ash dump of a power station by the River Tyne, while both Meadowhall (1990; Rodney Carran of Chapman Taylor & Partners) and Merry Hill (1989; Leslie Jones) occupy former steelworks sites. These low sprawl-ing complexes are usually unimpressive when glimpsed from a distance, but Bluewater (1999; Eric Kuhne) (pl. 305) benefits from dramatic surroundings, lifted from the frames of a science fiction movie. As one approaches, it presents a glimmering vision of metal and glass, contained by the sheer sides of the disused

chalk pit it so spectacularly fills. Lakeside (1990; Rodney Carran of Chapman Taylor & Partners) occupies a shallower chalk quarry to lesser effect.

In terms of their external design, malls have become less inward-looking and less monolithic since the heyday of Brent Cross. While the mirror-glass cladding of Merry Hill harks back to Milton Keynes, Meadowhall, Lakeside and Crystal Peaks (1988; BDP), a district centre at Mosbrough, all have brick outer walls, punctuated by fully glazed entrance bays. Cribbs Causeway (1998; BDP) and the White Rose Centre (1997; BDP) opted for a cool and uncluttered Modernist style, while the Trafford Centre (1998; Rodney Carran of Chapman Taylor & Partners) and Bluewater are much more extrovert creations. In each case, the elevations of anchor stores are differentiated from those of smaller shops, giving the impression of a cluster of ele-ments, rather than a single monolithic block. Internally, the main

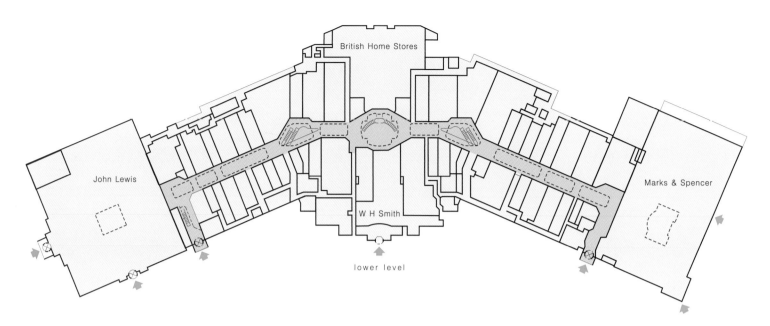

British Home Stores

John Lewis

Marks & Spencer

W H Smith

lower level

306 Cribbs Causeway (1998) near Bristol has a classic angled 'dumb-bell' plan with anchor stores positioned at either end and in the centre.

307 The interior of Cribbs Causeway receives copious daylight and accommodates twenty-eight palm trees, which were imported from Florida.

308   The Trafford Centre is the most grandiose British shopping centre. This shows the central area, under the main dome.

architectural features of all these malls are their expansive glass roofs. To minimise glare and heat, these can be treated in various ways. At Cribb's Causeway (pls 306–7), for example, perforated metal solar shades are suspended from the roof, but elsewhere fritted, or seraphic, glass has been used. One of the first examples of seraphic (ink-printed) glazing, based on a technique observed by architects from BDP during a study trip to America in 1994, was the new dome at Brent Cross, which was extensively refurbished in 1995.[23] Glazed malls are much more fea-

sible nowadays, as natural ventilation can be controlled by sensors that detect rainfall or changes in temperature. Simple heating and chilling has replaced air conditioning, making malls more energy efficient.

The Trafford Centre is described in its own publicity material as 'a powerful shopping machine', visually resembling a walled town. By car, the first glimpse of the building is the green glass cupola, followed by lower glass vaults, rising above the red brick sides of the complex. Close to, one finds that the

310 A water feature in the Mediterranean Village, a themed area in the MetroCentre, Gateshead (1986).

outer walls are treated in a highly eclectic fashion: the main entrance leads through a circular classical courtyard (The Place) (pl. 297), but much of the brickwork to either side incorporates Elizabethan-style diaper work, and the exterior of Selfridges (pl. 190) apes the elevation of its famous Oxford Street store. The interior (pl. 308), as one might expect, is big, bold and brassy, with two-tier barrel-vaulted malls making a pointed reference to Manchester's Barton Arcade, the Trafford Centre of its day.

The notion of incorporating local or regional references to counter accusations of American-style anonymity was taken very much further by Eric Kuhne, the American architect of Bluewater. The space-age exterior has ventilators based on the cowls of local hop-drying oast houses. Inside, Kuhne has tried to tap into Britain's and, more specifically, Kent's cultural roots, and to bring narrative back into architecture. His attempt to create a distinctive English ambience was denounced by one critic as 'about as English as the London of Walt Disney's 101 Dalmatians',[24] but the results are liked by more light-hearted commentators, often despite themselves. Kuhne described the interior as 'Blenheim Palace on speed', and certainly much of the styling is enjoyably whimsical. The three malls composing the triangular plan – the Rose Gallery, Guildhall and Thames Walk (pl. 309) – incorporate literary quotations from Kentish writers (such as Charles Dickens and Vita Sackville-West), mouldings depicting Britain's 106 guilds, and a pavement map of the River Thames, composed of blue and buff limestone inlaid with stainless steel place names. Together with fifty artworks,

309 The design of Bluewater is restrained compared with that of the Trafford Centre. The floor of Thames Walk, one of the three main malls, is inlaid with a map of the River Thames, while the vault has a nautical feel.

311 The Orient Leisure Dome at the Trafford Centre can be separated from the malls to provide access at night.

these details are intended to support Kuhne's claim that Bluewater is 'a city rather than a retail destination'. That this is an *English* city is further intimated by the 'handkerchief' domes borrowed from Sir John Soane, a cross-mall loosely based on London's Burlington Arcade, and a Winter Garden even more loosely inspired by the Palm House at Kew. Throughout, even if one admits that Kuhne's devices are artificial and irrelevant, the finishes and furnishings are of a higher quality than one has come to expect from an English shopping mall. Touchwood in Solihull, West Midlands (2001), demonstrates how the concepts embodied in Bluewater have been adapted, by Kuhne and his team, to a tight urban situation.

Bluewater is the most sophisticated English example of the themed mall, an idea pioneered in America, for example by

Jon Jerde at the theatrical, multi-level Horton Plaza (1985) in San Diego.[25] In the UK, where theming reveals something of an obsession with the Mediterranean, the first mall to incorporate stage-set areas was the MetroCentre, which employed a North American consultancy to design The Forum, Antique Village, Garden Court and Mediterranean Village (pl. 310), all of which are secondary malls.[26] The first main malls to be themed were probably those at Meadowhall and the Trafford Centre, which were designated 'Park Lane', 'High Street' and 'Market Place' and given an appropriate tenant mix. Bluewater followed the idea of designing each mall for a different category of shopper, but – like its clone in Solihull – is too upmarket to incorporate a 'marketplace'. The Rose Gallery is lined by typical high street retailers, while the Guildhall is stocked with fashion labels and designer homeware, and Thames Walk (pl. 309), with its colourful shopfronts, concentrates on toys, sports, games and street fashions. Each has its own 'break-out' area: the child-friendly Winter Garden (pl. 310), the sophisticated Village and the entertaining Water Circus. Essentially, whether shopping or resting, visitors gravitate towards the area where they feel most comfortable. Although less obviously engineered, the same phenomenon of quasi-voluntary social segregation occurs in traditional town centres, which have grown organically. Malls, however, have security systems and police forces that rigidly exclude a social underclass – truants, drunks, beggars and the homeless – whose presence contributes to the discomfort and insecurity felt by many people when shopping on real streets.

Theming often extends to food courts. An American rather than a European idea, these comprise a variety of food stalls arranged around a vast central seating area, enabling customers to refuel and dash back to the shops with the utmost rapidity. In England, the food court was pioneered in the Hempstead Valley Shopping Centre (1978) and, on a larger scale, at the Ridings Centre (1983) in Wakefield. The Oasis in Meadowhall was based on the Plaza de los Naranjas in Marbella and is a circular space surrounded by Spanish 'houses' accommodating various fast food outlets, and a video wall sponsored by Coca-Cola. Even more fantastic is The Orient at the Trafford Centre, a 1,600-seat food court/auditorium with an ocean liner theme, regarded by the management as a 'giant male crèche' (pl. 311).[27] The ship's deck is equipped with a swimming pool and life rafts, and is spanned by a domed ceiling with a painted sky effect and the ability to change from day to night. It is surrounded by two levels of food outlets, with themed areas from around the world, including Morocco, China, Italy, Egypt and America. All malls offer a waiter-service restaurant and several coffee shops, interspersed among the shops, as civilised alternatives to food courts.

Another innovation that originated in North America was retail-with-leisure. Internationally, the best-known examples were the Woodbine Centre (1985) in Toronto and West Edmonton Mall (1981–5) in Alberta, while in Europe, the Forum des Halles (1979) in Paris demonstrated that this combination held great commercial potential. Soon, facilities such as multi-screen cinemas and bowling alleys were being built into or, more usually, close to British malls. These opened at the same time as the shops, but also served to keep centres alive in the evenings. Some of the more interesting developments of recent years include the MetroCentre's Metroland (originally Metro World), a noisy fairground in an enclosed box linked to the main mall by the food court.[28] The MetroCentre also offers Quasar, a laser game, and the Megabowl Entertainment Centre, with twenty lanes of computerised ten-pin bowling. At Meadowhall, leisure pursuits were located in a stand-alone complex, as it was felt that they might compete too much with shopping if they opened off the malls.[29] Lakeside offers a variety of water sports, while Bluewater has a fishing club, a nature trail and a mountain-bike track, set within 50 acres (20.23 ha) of landscaped parkland.

Landscaping, which had a low priority at Brent Cross, has assumed great importance as a means of persuading visitors that they have arrived at an upmarket destination; it also gives them a pleasant environment in which to recharge their batteries in the middle of an exhausting shopping day. The external focus of Cribbs Causeway is a water feature, comprising fountains, cascades and a linear stream set within a grassed and tree-lined avenue which, rather cynically, 'provides the customer with a sanctuary in which to contemplate their next purchase'.[30] Inside, more water features, palm trees and hanging plant galleries are installed on a much more extravagant scale than they were in the 1960s.

For the time being, no new out-of-town malls are planned in England, although several existing malls are being extended. In Britain, or even Europe, we shall perhaps never see anything quite as extravagant or fantastical as the West Edmonton Mall, which is reported to have 'twice as many submarines as the Canadian Navy'.[31] It is the largest mega-mall in the world, covering 3,899,800 square feet (362,291 sq. m), with more than 800 shops interspersed with leisure pursuits remaining open twenty-four hours a day. Visitors can stay in the appropriately named Fantasyland Hotel, and sample the attractions of the Ice Palace, Fantasyland and Deep Sea Adventure, with its life-size model of Columbus's *Santa Maria*. The themed malls include a replica of Bourbon Street in New Orleans, and a European Boulevard with full-height elevations. The West Edmonton Mall makes our own mega-malls seem quite paltry in comparison.

312 Fascia lettering of a disused shop on Botchergate in Carlisle.

14

Conclusion:
The Landscape of Desire

THE ENGLISH RETAIL LANDSCAPE HAS EXPANDED enormously over the last thousand years. Instead of simply purchasing all our needs and wants in the local market, and in a handful of small town-centre or neighbourhood shops, we are offered a huge choice of locations where we can undertake different kinds of shopping. Over the centuries, the high street has been enriched by the introduction of novel forms of retailing, such as the arcade, the department store and the mall. Then, in the course of the twentieth century, towns and cities became ring-fenced by furniture warehouses, car showrooms, retail parks and superstores. We can now drive beyond these to a variety of out-of-town retail destinations, perhaps pausing at a petrol station shop to pick up forgotten items en route. Furthermore, with the arrival of the Internet we can order all sorts of products from our homes. The expansion of retailing has been temporal as well as spatial: many malls now open late into the evening and on Sundays,[1] while some superstores remain open round the clock.

The increase in private car ownership since the Second World War has done more to transform the shopping environment than anything else. It was directly responsible for the unprecedented development of edge-of-town and out-of-town retailing in the last three decades of the twentieth century. By the early 1990s town centres faced a crisis. Rightly or wrongly, blame for blighted high streets, with a surplus of empty shops, was laid at the door of developments such as the MetroCentre, and with a number of mammoth schemes such as Bluewater and the Traf-ford Centre in the pipeline, it seemed that the situation could only get worse. Out-of-town shopping also generated fears about road congestion, the environment, accessibility and social exclu-sion, persuading the government to amend existing planning guidance in an attempt to redress the balance in favour of towns. The emphasis is now on retrieving the vitality and viability of urban centres, something that is inevitably stimulating new developments. These need to be underpinned by a deep under-standing of the history of affected sites, their buildings and their individual contexts, something that was not often achieved in the great redevelopment schemes of the 1960s.

As long as towns have existed, they have been the focus of trading activity. Initially, that was concentrated in the open market place and in shops that occupied ground-floor rooms in houses situated either in the central area or on major approach roads. For centuries, following the pattern established by market traders, shopkeepers tended to group together according to the class of goods they sold. Although that trend is no longer so prevalent, the instinct for retailers to cluster for mutual benefit – whether in rows, arcades or malls – remains a significant feature of today's retail landscape.

Retailers have always been major land users, and the market occupied the largest public space in most medieval towns. Over time, increasing numbers of stalls were protected by shelters, or housed on the ground floors of civic buildings. Similarly, shops often occupied parts of buildings with other primary functions, whether civic, industrial or domestic. For centuries they were restricted to rooms on the street frontage; they had little depth and never spread on to upper floors. The most sought-after loca-tions, known in later years as the 'prime pitch' or '100 per cent position', were corner sites with dual frontages which gave the greatest access to the streets. It was only selds that attempted to exploit the potential of backland sites.

Retailing spread behind rooms on the immediate street frontage once economic and social conditions allowed shop-keepers to sell larger quantities of merchandise to an increasingly affluent public, a development that was particularly evident in late eighteenth-century London. The physical growth of shops exploited technological advances that made it easier to light spaces distant from the façade, and thus to draw customers into the depths of a building. Before disrupting domestic accommo-dation, workshops and stockrooms on upper floors, shopkeepers converted as much of their ground floors as possible into selling space. This often involved building a single-storey extension, lit by a skylight or roof lantern, over the yard or garden to the rear of the premises. The introduction of gas and electric lighting, and the replacement of structural walls by beams and cast-iron columns, made such developments all the more successful. Once the ground floor was operating to full capacity, there was often little option but to open showrooms on the first floor, displacing other activities. The first successful attempts to coax customers upstairs were the exchange 'galleries' of the seventeenth century, and by the late eighteenth century many high-class London shops – usually those without living accommodation – boasted grand first-floor showrooms. Before the introduction of efficient lifts, customers were enticed upwards by sweeping staircases, imposing architectural vistas and – by the third quarter of the nineteenth century – first-floor display windows. Lifts transformed the arrangement of space within stores, enabling Selfridges to open with no less than six trading levels and a rooftop tea garden in 1909. The widespread adoption of escalators in the 1960s, following a handful of highly publicised experiments in the 1930s, did even more to increase the value of upper floors. The most sophisticated methods of encouraging upward movement can be seen in modern malls, with their glass-sided, 'scenic' lifts and tempting top-level food courts.

The architectural form most commonly associated with retail buildings, and especially department stores, is the galleried well which transmits daylight to multiple trading levels through open-fronted galleries. Internationally, the most famous examples are the Bon Marché and Galeries Lafayette in Paris, and although several stunning wells were erected in England in the course of the nineteenth and early twentieth centuries, few survive intact. An early example may have been created by Wedgwood in the 1770s, but the first well-documented gallery formed part of Lackington's bookshop of 1793. The idea was executed on a much larger scale by the bazaars of the 1820s and 1830s, creating the most imposing retail spaces experienced, as yet, by shoppers. These bazaars have been unjustly neglected by historians, perhaps because none survives intact. Architecturally, the impact of bazaars on department stores may have been indirect; there was certainly quite a lull between the opening of the last great bazaar in the early 1860s and the widespread adoption of galleried wells for large drapery stores in the 1890s. In the intervening period French models had come to the fore, but it may be argued that these were themselves deeply rooted in the bazaar tradition.

Developments in cast-iron construction made it easier to construct galleried wells and assisted in the creation of arcades and market halls, some of which operated with limited success on more than one level. As far as furniture dealers and ironmongers were concerned, wells wasted floor space. They preferred to admit daylight through heavily glazed façades, while drapers opted for more substantial and ornamental masonry frontages. Such differences in approach helped to create the variety that is the hallmark of the English streetscape, a variety that is enhanced by the intermingling of shops, stores and arcades with buildings such as banks, libraries and offices. Contrasts in materials, in style, and even in scale, help to generate the sense of place that is unique to any English town.

In debating the appearance of a new building with his architect, the shopkeeper took many factors into account. The nature of the business and the range of functions it encapsulated were clearly of primary importance, but it was also vital for the shopkeeper to consider the lifestyle, the social and economic profile, and even the age and sex, of his target customers. This was as important for the humble corner shop as for the Savile Row tailor. At all levels in the hierarchy, shopkeepers have always relied to some extent on word-of-mouth to develop trade, but they will only 'catch' custom by sending out the right signals. The experienced shopper can make a rapid assessment of any shop from the outside by decoding the subliminal cultural messages contained in the design of the building, the style of the shopfront and the arrangement of the window display. For some the message might be welcoming, for others intimidating, but it is part of the skill of shopkeeping to ensure that the right sort of customer steps over the threshold and the wrong sort passes by. This aspect of the retail landscape was perhaps more evident in the past, when the gap separating social classes was much wider than it is today. Nowadays, although a broad middle market dominates, design is still used on occasion to attract or repel customers as necessary, for example in the premises of niche retailers such as Nike, or the luxury boutiques of Bond Street.

Another major influence on the form and appearance of retail buildings was foreign fashion. The origins of the Stocks and Leadenhall markets have not been satisfactorily pinpointed, but seem to lie on the Continent, either in France or Italy. Gresham's Royal Exchange of 1568 was closely based on the Nieuwe Beurs in Antwerp, and the first glazed shopfronts in London probably emulated examples seen in the Low Countries. By the early nineteenth century, however, Paris was the recognised fashion centre of the western world, and after 1816 French influence poured across the Channel. The arcade was certainly a direct import from Paris, and while the bazaar seems to have originated in England, it was the French who seized upon its architectural form, realising that it was ideal for large retail establishments. The first enclosed market halls were built in England, but again it was the French who erected the most ambitious and modern example of that building type: Les Halles in Paris. As far as large stores are concerned, English retailers were much more conservative than their French counterparts throughout the nineteenth century. Some did, however, take steps to Gallicise their façades. Heals, with its rows of large round-headed windows, harked back to the Galeries du Commerce et de l'Industrie of 1837, while Jeffery's of Liverpool invites comparison with the almost exactly contemporary Magasins Réunis in Paris of 1865–7. The pavilion roofs of Marshall & Snelgrove, in the mid-1870s, were plainly inspired by French models. But it is notable that the windows of English stores remained smaller than their French counterparts, even when they lit showrooms and sales areas rather than staff rooms. English store design may have been restricted by building laws and the practice of living-in, but it was even more inhibited by a strong streak of conservatism.

In the early twentieth century, English retailers shifted their gaze from France to America. Indeed, it is difficult to believe that Michael Marks was not inspired by 'five and dime' stores when he opened his first penny bazaar around 1889. The arrival of Selfridge in 1906 and Woolworth in 1909 created a stir, and stimulated interest in American store design and retail methodology. After a visit to Marshall Field's, Whiteley's manager determined to rebuild his store with a vast central hall, but it was the American 'horizontal' system of unbroken floors, typified by Carson Pirie Scott's, that dominated store design after 1918. Throughout the 1920s and 1930s, influences from France, America and Germany were intermingled. French *deco moderne* was taken up after 1925 and popularised by Joseph Emberton. American skyscraper design was imitated on a reduced scale in stores such as C&A in Newcastle, and the International Modernism of Mendelsohn had a great impact on avant-garde London stores of the mid-1930s. But after 1945 American influence governed all: the artificially lit and air-conditioned department store and shopping mall, the supermarket and the development of off-centre shopping all originated on the other side of the Atlantic.

While high street façades could be grandly impressive, sometimes evoking famous models from other countries, the streets or lanes that ran along the backs of shops and stores were very different in character. In the eighteenth and early nineteenth centuries it was still common for deliveries to be made through carriage arches on the main frontage, which gave access to a yard and stables. Occasionally these entries survive, with metal rails for cartwheels set into a cobbled surface. If there was no carriage arch, a hoist attached to the shopfront could be used to lower goods into a cellar; quite a number of these are shown on Tallis's drawings of around 1840. As businesses grew and towns were 'improved', however, rear service lanes were created if they did not already exist, to avoid the possibility of disturbing pedestrian flow on the pavement. By the late nineteenth century most large businesses had removed their stabling or garaging some distance from their store, merely leaving space on site to admit one or two delivery carts or vans at a time. Not only was that the

cheapest option, but it allowed prime retail sites to be devoted to selling. The introduction of goods and vehicle lifts in the early twentieth century enabled retailers to make even more efficient use of space by positioning delivery bays on different levels within the main building, freeing up space on the all-important ground floor. As the backs of premises were devoted to deliveries, much less trouble was taken with their architectural design, and they were clad in cheaper materials than façades.

As well as affecting the appearance and commercial viability of high streets and back lanes, retail buildings could forge new pedestrian routes within a town centre. The most successful arcades and market halls achieved this, as did some bazaars, department stores and variety stores. It was in the retailer's interests to develop such routes, as they ensured a steady footfall through his premises. Sometimes, however, this redirected pedestrians away from older thoroughfares, causing the focus of an entire shopping centre to shift. That effect could also be brought about by municipal improvement schemes, but in many communities the shopping centre has remained on the very same spot since the Middle Ages.

While town centres have always been in the state of flux, the greatest changes of all were brought about by motor transport. Not only did this affect the atmosphere of the street, but it eventually influenced the design of shops and stores. By the late 1930s some department stores were finding it beneficial to provide customer car parks. New Towns of the 1950s and early 1960s were planned for the motor car, with pedestrianised centres and peripheral or rooftop car parks. Existing towns and cities were remodelled along similar lines, and equipped with precincts, malls and free car parks. Despite these measures, the pressure imposed on urban space by the motor car proved intolerable, and by the late 1960s free-standing hypermarkets were being built in suburban locations. These were followed by superstores, retail parks, outlet villages, megamalls, and even shops in petrol station forecourts. Within a generation the town centre had lost its status as the single focus of shopping activity.

It is undoubtedly true that the character of all too many town centres was spoiled by insensitive development in the 1960s and early 1970s, in particular by the insertion of monolithic blocks with blind façades clad in unsympathetic materials. It is shocking, sometimes, to realise what was sacrificed to make way for these buildings, and for the dual-carriage ring roads that isolated central areas. But just as the rush out of town was gaining momentum, appreciation for the 'traditional', or pre-war, urban shopping environment was growing. Increasingly, redundant department stores and market halls were converted to new uses rather than being demolished. When the demolition of old buildings was inevitable, it became usual, rather than exceptional, to retain their façades. Furthermore, the installation of Victorian-style street furniture and the encouragement of heavily moulded and panelled shopfronts marked a conscious attempt to turn back the clock. That retrospective trend peaked in the 1980s, since which time a sleek modernism has been adopted for new developments in large towns and cities, perhaps indicating that urban centres have regained their confidence and are prepared, once more, to look forward rather than back.

We are left with an urban retail landscape that, despite a Victorian-style veneer, harbours few genuine reminders of what shopping was like before the Second World War. Businesses such as Dyer's in Ilminster, with its old-fashioned counter service and bentwood chairs, are seldom economically viable and rely on local loyalty to sustain trade. When such shops close, museums compete to acquire their fittings: once these have been stripped out, the shell of the shop is of minimal interest or significance, and usually only the shopfront can be preserved *in situ*. Although this situation is far from ideal, it is hard to find a solution. Museums tend to mix and match shop fixtures and fittings to create generic 'traditional' shops, but without imparting information about the provenance or date of individual artefacts, which consequently lose all meaning. Re-creations of specific shops – for example the co-op store at Beamish Museum – are admirable, but once the shop is removed from its urban context its value as a historic document is undermined and becomes suspect. The attempt to retain Dyson's jewellery shop in Leeds is fascinating, since it preserves counters and showcases in the original building, albeit stripped of the patina of age by zealous restoration and enhanced by museum-like displays. The fate of Grout's of Palmers Green is much more typical. Soon after it closed in April 2002, its cash railway was sold to a museum in East Anglia and its counters and shelves were acquired by a second-hand shopfitter.

It is impossible to predict the future of shopping in England, but it will undoubtedly respond to changes in society as a whole. Clearly, the extent of car ownership and the quality of public transport systems will continue to determine where the population shops. Greater numbers of shops, or larger shops, may be needed if the population grows by 4 million by 2020, as expected, and if households continue to fragment at their present rate. The character of shops may alter to reflect the fact that more people will fall into older age brackets, or that customers will be highly aware of environmental issues. In particular, a stronger organic food movement and demand for regional produce may inaugurate a return to smaller food shops.

The relationship between town centres and out-of-town complexes is likely to remain finely tuned. For the time being no major new out-of-town developments are receiving planning approval. Nevertheless, out-of-town shopping complexes are here to stay; they will obtain permission to build substantial extensions, and may even develop as the nuclei of new business communities. Large towns will continue to fight back, either by enhancing existing facilities or by building new malls and superstores on a competitive scale, often linked to a vast catchment area by high-speed access roads. In 2002 Reading and Southampton entered the top ten of the national shopping league published by Experian (Goad), reflecting the fact that both have recently acquired a regional-scale mall which necessitated the redevelopment or closure of existing shops and stores. On a smaller scale, at Romford, an out-of-town-style shopping-and-leisure development with a large surface car park has been grafted on to the edge of the main shopping centre, challenging its urban character. In the future, many more towns may emulate the tactics of the out-of-town centres to enhance their economic viability: that is certainly a much cheaper option than the construction of a carefully integrated mall such as Touchwood in Solihull. Either way, such developments are bound to draw customers away from the smaller centres that fall within their orbits. However, shopping centres of all shapes and sizes are likely to encounter major competition from Internet shopping and digital TV shopping channels, essentially novel forms of old-fashioned home delivery or mail-order services. So far, this has not posed a serious threat to bricks-and-mortar outlets, but if online grocery shopping takes off, today's superstores may become tomorrow's distribution warehouses. Whatever happens, we can be sure of one thing: that the different environments in which we shop will continue to metamorphose in parallel with changes in technology, transport, local and national planning guidance, fashion and a host of other factors, as they always have done in the past.

Notes

CHAPTER 1

1 For general surveys of medieval trade in England, see Salzman 1931, Postan 1972, Britnell 1993 and Miller and Hatcher 1995.

2 Salzman 1931, 352–435.

3 The importance of analysing the topography of medieval towns as a tool to understanding their economies was recognised by Hoskins 1955, and developed by Beresford 1967 and others.

4 Miller and Hatcher 1995, 361ff.

5 Salzman 1931, 14.

6 Davis 1966, 22.

7 Salzman 1931, 43.

8 Cox 2000, 85.

9 Dyer 1991, 25, 45. For problems involved in calculating London's population in the early modern period, see Harding 1990.

10 Salzman 1931, 122; 'Gazetteer of Markets and Fairs in England and Wales to 1516' (*www.history.ac.uk/cmh/gaz/gazweb2.html*).

11 New foundations peaked in 1250–75 (Everitt 1976, 168–9). Britnell has shown that 1,003 markets were founded in twenty-three counties (55 per cent of the area of England) before 1349 (Britnell 1981, 210).

12 Victoria County History, *Wiltshire*, vol. 6, 1962, 17.

13 Everitt 1976, 168.

14 Archer, Barron and Harding 1988, 6.

15 For a discussion of this, see Beresford 1967, 153–60.

16 However, in Winchelsea – the best known example of a planted town in England – the market occupied a wide street.

17 See Taylor 1982.

18 Morley 1994, 324.

19 Harper 1920, 143.

20 Harper 1920, 144.

21 Tittler 1991, 29.

22 Dendrochronological analysis of original timbers, undertaken in 1992 but not published, produced a date range of 1430–60 (information from D. F. Stenning, Essex County Council).

23 Tittler 1991, 134–5.

24 Masters 1974, 13; Archer, Barron and Harding 1988, 5.

25 Archer, Barron and Harding 1988, 4. Le Waleys may have been responsible for constructing the middle row in Newgate Shambles around the same time.

26 Information from Derek Keene. See reconstruction of the Stocks Market by David Crouch in Archer, Barron and Harding 1988, 33.

27 Samuel 1989, 145.

28 Archer, Barron and Harding 1988, 69, 92–3.

29 Archer, Barron and Harding 1988, 75, 95–6.

30 Archer, Barron and Harding 1988, 11, 77, 96–7.

31 Howes 1631, 1024.

32 Smith 1999, 171–9.

33 The chief evidence for the form of these post-Fire markets is a survey carried out by William Leybourn in 1677. See Masters 1974.

34 Leadenhall Market was rebuilt in 1879–80.

35 The Stocks was swept away for the construction of the Mansion House in 1737. It was replaced by the Fleet Market.

36 Masters 1974, 38.

37 Masters 1974, 44 and Plate XIIIa (plan of 1698). Newgate Market was demolished in 1869 for the formation of Paternoster Square, following the establishment of the Metropolitan Meat and Poultry Market at West Smithfield.

38 Smith 2002.

39 *Survey of London, Spitalfields and Mile End New Town*, vol. 27, 1957, 127–32.

40 Latham and Matthews, vol. 7, 1972, 87 (1 April 1666); *Survey of London, The Parish of St James Westminster: Part 1 South of Piccadilly*, vol. 29, 1960, 216–17 and fig. 41; Hobhouse 1975, 17 (fig.). St James's Market was rebuilt in 1817–18 by James Burton.

41 *City Lands Contracts*, vol. 1, 282 (Corporation of London Record Office, Guildhall); Stroud 1971, 147 and plate 48. Honey Lane Market was demolished in 1835 for the erection of the City of London School.

42 See 'Gazetteer of Markets and Fairs in England and Wales to 1516' (*www.history.ac.uk/cmh/gaz/gazweb2.html*).

43 Moore 1985, 23.

44 Moore 1985, 214ff.

45 Victoria County History, *Hampshire*, vol. 5, 1973, 36; Moore 1985, 17–18; Keene 1985, vol. 2, 1091–123.

46 Moore 1985, 146.

47 Defoe 1971, vol. 1, letter 1, 102.

48 Defoe 1971, vol. 1, letter 1, 102–3.

49 Ward 1700, 16.

50 In researching medieval shops, much help was received from D. F. Stenning of Essex County Council.

51 Stone shops are recorded in early thirteenth-century London (Keene 1990, 35).

52 Harris 1994, 47–51.

53 Harris 1994, 30–32; 251.

54 Keene 1990, 34; David Clark 2000, 59.

55 The west wing of 17–21 King Street houses two shops, one of which was probably sublet as a lock-up (Stenning 1985, 37, fig. 9).

56 Pantin 1962–3, 228–9; Brown 1999, 23 and 64.

57 Information from Derek Keene. Faulkner expressed the view that many undercrofts were built on a speculative basis for rent to retailers (Faulkner 1966, 122–3), but that is difficult to substantiate (see discussion in Harris 1994, 228–47).

58 See Coppack 1991.

59 See Schofield 1987.

60 Victoria County History, *Gloucestershire*, vol. 8, 1968, 129.
61 Parker 1971, 66, 127.
62 Pantin 1962–3, 223.
63 Keene 1990, 37; Platt 1976, 66.
64 Pantin 1962–3, 217–18; Brown 1999, 24.
65 Pantin 1962–3, 225–6.
66 Pantin 1962–3, 220, 223.
67 Keene 1990, 38.
68 Keene 1990, 38.
69 Brown 1999, 19.
70 Brown 1999, 20.
71 Keene 1990, 32. Soper Lane is now Queen Street.
72 Keene 1990, 40.
73 Keene 1990, 42.
74 Latham and Matthews, vol. 1, 1970, 277 (29 October 1660).
75 David Clark 2000, 64.
76 For example The Swan in Maldon and The George in Colchester (information from D. F. Stenning, Essex County Council).
77 Harris 1994, 257.
78 Keene 1990, 35–6.
79 David Clark 2000, 64–5.
80 Stenning 1985, 38.
81 For references to early pentices, see Keene 1990, 36.
82 Taylor and Richmond 1989, 268; Parker 1971, 70.
83 Beresford 1967, 33.
84 James and Roberts 2000; Harris 1994, 189–98.
85 It has been suggested that The Rows were inspired by *cornières* (Lawson and Smith 1958, 34).
86 A doorway that may have opened into a shop at 150 High Street, Chipping Ongar, Essex, is dated 1642.
87 Dan and Morgan Wilmott 1907, 3.
88 Dan and Morgan Wilmott 1907, 3. See Whittock 1840, 1, for an illustration of a bulk shop at Temple Bar.
89 Information from Derek Keene.
90 Keene 1990, 34.
91 Keene 1990, 34.
92 Salzman 1952, 478; Pantin 1962–3, 223–5.
93 Keene 1990, 37.
94 Bennell 1989, 201.
95 The present location of this painting is not known. It was illustrated in the *Illustrated London News*, 2 October 1937, 578.
96 See reproductions in Witt Library, Courtauld Institute of Art, and Pevsner 1976, fig 16.5.
97 Hughes 1989, 78–9; Harris 1994, 189–98.

CHAPTER 2

1 The idea of a consumer revolution in the second half of the eighteenth century was proposed by McKendrick, Brewer and Plumb 1982, but has been questioned by other scholars who perceive a strong degree of continuity with the early modern period (see Cox 2000, 2–5).
2 Saunders 1997, 37–9.
3 Saunders 1997, 48, quoting L. Grenade, 'Les Singularitéz de Londres', 1576 (Vatican Library. Reg. Lat. 672).
4 Saunders 1997, 89.
5 Saunders 1997, 93.
6 Saunders 1997, 45.
7 The new building of 1667–71 was designed by Edward Jerman and Thomas Cartwright.
8 See Stone 1957–8.
9 For an account of the entertainment that marked its opening, see Knowles 2002.
10 Quoted by Stone 1957–8, 117.

11 Translated directly from Sorbière 1664, 40.
12 See Latham and Matthews 1970–83.
13 Davis 1966, 142.
14 Keene 1990, 31.
15 Davis 1966, 109.
16 For Aldgate, see Latham and Matthews, vol. 3, 1970, 66 (19 April 1662). For Neville's, see Latham and Matthews, vol. 1, 1970, 277 (29 October 1660).
17 Davis 1966, 111.
18 Latham and Matthews, vol. 4, 1971, 350 (26 October 1663).
19 Sorbière 1664, 39–40.
20 Kirton was ruined by the fire and died in 1667 (Latham and Matthews, vol. 7, 1972, 309 (5 October 1666) and vol. 8, 1974, 526 (11 November 1667). Pepys amassed a library of 3,000 volumes, which is now in Magdalene College, Cambridge.
21 For Fleet Street, see Latham and Matthews, vol. 4, 1971, 80 (20 March 1663). For Pope's Head Alley, see Latham and Matthews, vol. 1, 1970, 298 (21 November 1660) and vol. 3, 1970, 115 (20 June 1662).
22 Latham and Matthews, vol. 2, 1970, 130 (1 July 1661) and vol. 4, 1971, 6 (6 January 1663).
23 Latham and Matthews, vol. 7, 1972, 296 (26 September 1666).
24 Latham and Matthews, vol. 4, 1971, 191 (22 June 1663).
25 Strype 1720, vol. 1, Ch. XXVIII, 234 (quoting Car2.c.3.sect.14 (1667)).
26 Latham and Matthews, vol. 8, 1974, 441 (18 September 1667).
27 Welch 1913, 45. The Royal Exchange was destroyed by fire on 10 January 1838 and rebuilt between 1842 and 1844.
28 Pendrill 1934, 58.
29 *Survey of London, The Strand*, vol. 18, 1937, 123.
30 Fenwick 1955, 165.
31 In 1698 Celia Fiennes noted that the Exchange in Exeter was 'full of shops like our Exchanges are, only its but one walke along as was the Exchange at Salisbury House in the Strand' (Morris 1982, 198).
32 For inventories of opulent London shops in the early eighteenth century, see Cox 2000, 92.
33 Defoe 1727, 262.
34 Defoe 1727, 259.
35 For remarks about this shop, see Schopenhauer 1988, 152–3.
36 Williams 1933, 111.
37 Defoe 1727, 263.
38 This is described by Defoe himself, 1727, 85.
39 The middle classes are thought to have formed 30 per cent of London's population in 1798 (Rule 1992, 78–9).
40 Unlike 'manufactories', 'warehouses' did not usually sell goods that were made on the premises. It has been argued that the term 'warehouse' conveyed the idea that goods were sold at cheap wholesale prices (Mui and Mui 1989, 64). None the less, the term was not disdained by high-class retailers such as Josiah Wedgwood. The term 'magazine' had more stylish overtones.
41 Defoe 1727, 248.
42 Rouquet 1755, 120–21.
43 Des Fontaines 1970, 197; McKendrick, Brewer and Plumb 1982, 118.
44 Des Fontaines 1970, 202–3.
45 *Repository of Arts*, 1st series, vol. 1 (February 1809), 102–7 and plate 7.
46 *Repository of Arts*, 1st series, vol. 2 (August 1809), 122–3 and plate 10.
47 Hughes 1967. Morgan & Sander's business was founded in 1801 and closed in 1822.
48 Rudolph Ackermann opened his combined shop, art library and drawing school at 101 Strand in 1786, and launched his monthly periodical, *The Repository of Arts, Literature, Commerce, Manufactures, Fashions and Politics*, in 1809. John B. Papworth designed a new library for Ackermann in 1812–13 (*Repository of Arts*, 1st series, vol. 9, April 1813, 230 and plate 28) and a new building at 101 Strand in 1827 (*Repository of Arts*, 3rd series, vol. 9, June 1827, 362–3 and plate 31). Boydell's print shop on the Strand had a top-lit room in 1786 (Williams 1933, 238).

49 *Repository of Arts*, 1st series, vol. 9 (April 1813), plate 28, shows Acker-mann's library lit by gas lights and without any top-lighting.

50 The glass illuminators were circular pieces of glass, 5 inches (12.7 cm) in diameter, with convex tops, which were fitted into wooden or metal frames (Patent No. 3058, 1807).

51 McKendrick, Brewer and Plumb 1982, 119.

52 Knight 1877, 240.

53 Lackington 1795, 128. Lackington moved from 46–47 Chiswell Street to Finsbury Square around 1791.

54 *Repository of Arts*, 1st series, vol. 1 (April 1809), 251–2 and plate 17.

55 Watercolour by Henry Cave, dated 1797, published in Murray, Riddick and Green. 1990, 91.

56 Defoe 1727, 340.

57 Fawcett, 1990, 56; Mui and Mui 1989, 231; Des Fontaines 1970, 198–9. According to James Lackington, who had opened his bookshop on Chiswell Street in 1774, 'it was thought, that I might as well attempt to rebuild the tower of Babel, as to establish a large business without giving credit' (Lackington 1795, 211.)

58 McKendrick, Brewer and Plumb 1982, 83. At least one Parisian *marchand de modes*, Le Petit Dunkerque, imposed fixed prices from the 1780s, but the practice seems to have been relatively rare in France (Fairchilds 1993, 238, fn. 73).

59 British Museum Prints and Drawings, Heal Collection, 17.88.

60 'J. Lackington's address to the public on his new elegant and cheap shop', British Museum Prints and Drawings, Heal Collection, 17.84.

61 Hughes 1958; *Repository of Arts*, 1st series, vol. 1 (March 1809), 187 and plate 12.

CHAPTER 3

1 The main existing study of shopfront history is Powers 1989.

2 Southey 1951, Letter XI, 69.

3 See, for example, tinted engraving by T. Loveday, *c.*1750 (Guildhall Library).

4 Davis 1966, 190, quoting Addison in *The Spectator*.

5 Southey 1951, Letter XIII, 77.

6 Williams 1933, 87.

7 Williams 1933, 141.

8 Williams 1933, 142.

9 Kalman 1972, 75–9. See Stroud 1971, 132–3 and plate 41 for the shop and shopfront of Thomas Moore, a carpet warehouseman, designed by Dance around 1777 for one corner of Finsbury Square.

10 Shepherd and Elmes 1827–31 (reprinted 1978), 98.

11 See, for example, photographs of Wisbech in the 1850s in Millward and Coe 1974.

12 See Jackson 1969.

13 Whittock 1840, 4.

14 Pigot & Co. *Commercial Directory and Topography of Hertfordshire*, 1828. The shopfront was very like that of a chemist's shop on Great Russell Street in London (Whittock 1840, 9 and plate 12).

15 Eldridge 1958, 193.

16 For example *The Builder*, 5 August 1848, 381.

17 Colvin 1995, 962. This shopfront was discussed in Knight 1843, 392–3.

18 *Industrial Great Britain*, 1895, 326.

19 Eldridge 1958, 195.

20 Powers illustrated an example at 209 High Holborn, which he dated to around 1820 (Powers 1989, 55).

21 Sandeman and Leighton 1849.

22 Powers 1989, 15 and figure on 64.

23 *Architectural Magazine*, vol. 1 (1834), 114.

24 Eldridge 1958, 194. In 1865 Mayhew reported that the largest plate-glass windows in London measured 15 × 10 ft (4.57 × 3.05 m); they belonged to McLean's looking-glass manufactory on Fleet Street (Mayhew 1865, 208).

25 For information on brass sash bars, see Mayhew 1865, 205–8. The first shops to use them were said to be Everington's shawl emporium on Ludgate Hill, Swan & Edgar's at Piccadilly and E. Moses & Son's on Aldgate.

26 Eldridge 1958, 193. The sheets measured 4 ft 11 in, and 3 ft 2 in. (0.97 m), making a total height of 8 ft 1 in. (2.46 m). Numerous examples of this survive in Ireland.

27 Knight 1843, 392.

28 *The Builder*, 28 December 1861, 902.

29 Information from Mike Seary of Dean's Blinds and Awnings UK Ltd.

30 Such shutter boxes were mentioned in *The Builder*, 7 November 1857, 650.

31 The invention (Whiting's patent) was reported in the *Architectural Magazine*, vol. 4 (1837), 79.

32 *The Builder*, 3 March 1866, 153.

33 Eldridge 1958, 195.

34 Whittock 1840, 7. This was Ablett's outfitting warehouse on Cornhill.

35 Dan and Morgan Wilmott 1907, 26.

36 Eldridge 1958, 193.

37 Robinson [*c.*1869].

38 See Bartram 1978 for a wide variety of illustrations of fascia lettering.

39 See letter in *The Builder*, 19 February 1881, 228.

40 Artley 1975, 9.

41 An early example with several island windows was Allders in Croydon (*The Draper's Record*, 9 October 1909, 99). The actual shopfront was set back 19 ft 6 in. (5.94 m) from the pavement.

42 *Architectural Review*, July 1912, 50.

43 *The Builder*, 10 November 1916, 291–2.

44 The best surviving 1920s shopfront – and, indeed, the best surviving interior – on Regent Street is probably that of Church's shoe shop, which was originally erected for Morny, and was designed by Mewes & Davis around 1922 (see *The Builder*, 19 December 1924, 968).

45 Grundy 1981.

46 Powers 1989, 31.

47 *The Builder*, 11 April 1930, 707.

48 Simpson's windows bear a plaque inscribed 'Patent Invisible Glass pat 354984 & 411046 Pollards London'. The displays at Simpson's were arranged by the Hungarian émigré designer László Moholy-Nagy who had taught alongside Walter Gropius at the Bauhaus in the 1920s.

49 *The Jubilee of C&A: 35 Years of Advertising History*, 91 (seen in C&A archive)

50 *The Architect and Building News* 9 April 1948, 320.

51 Westwood and Westwood 1955, 12.

52 *The Architect and Building News*, 28 November 1962, 41.

53 Powers 1989, 32.

54 Jackson 1998, 34.

55 Somake and Hellberg 1956, 121–5.

56 Marriott 1989, 231.

CHAPTER 4

1 Walsh 1995, 161–3.

2 Mui and Mui 1989, 244; Scarisbrick 1994, 244. John Parker and Edward Wakelin, who took over The King's Arms and Feathers off Haymarket about 1760, had no repair or manufacturing facilities in their shop and used up to seventy-five subcontractors (Clifford 1995, 5–6).

3 Mayhew 1865, 31.

4 Scarisbrick 1985, 55.

5 Scarisbrick 1985, 56.

6 Mayhew 1865, 32.

7 The chandeliers were bought in Paris by Dyson's wife, Lucy Anne, on the proceeds of winnings made in Monte Carlo.

8 This was described by a traveller, Johanna Schopenhauer, in the early nineteenth century (Schopenhauer 1988, 138).

9 For example Matthews 1962, pl. XVI: 'The Apothecary's Shop, opened' by William Faithorne (1616–91).
10 S. Maw & Son was founded in 1807. The firm made surgical instruments and druggists' sundries.
11 Tallis and Arnold-Forster 1991, 47.
12 Pamphlet issued by 'Ye Oldest Chymist Shoppe', Knaresborough.
13 *The Chemist and Druggist*, 24 January 1942, 117.
14 Diamond Jubilee leaflet, seen in shop.
15 A similar arrangement can be seen in Potter's in Buxton.
16 George 1925, 198.
17 George 1925, 199.
18 Jefferys 1954, 373.
19 Birmingham Building Regulation Plan 46769 (Birmingham Record Office).
20 *The Architect and Building News*, 12 February 1932, 222–3. This shop has recently been gutted and redeveloped for HMV and The Disney Store.
21 The National Trust, Wimpole Hall.
22 *Boot and Shoe Trades Journal*, 27 December 1901, 872.
23 *Architectural Design and Construction*, vol. 6, no. 6 (June 1936), 271–3.
24 In 1951 the wood engraver Reynolds Stone was commissioned to design a new Dolcis logo, and throughout the 1950s young artists, such as Lynn Chadwick, were employed by the firm to undertake particular decorative schemes.
25 Rees 1932, vol. 1, 87.
26 Bennell 1989, 201.
27 Mui and Mui 1989, *passim*.
28 Campbell 1747, 188.
29 Rees 1932, vol. 2, 98.
30 Blackman 1967, 110.
31 *Illustrated London*, c.1892, 69.
32 Rees 1932, vol. 2, 251. Home & Colonial Stores became Allied Suppliers Ltd in 1960, and ceased high street trading in 1968.
33 Williams 1994, 27–31. Sainsbury's first dairy on Drury Lane was a much more humble affair.
34 It was recommended that a thick mahogany block be used so that, in years to come, this could be re-planed and varnished rather than being replaced (Tupman 1909, 228). Another well-preserved provision shop is David Greig's branch at 87 High Street, Deptford, dating from around 1928.
35 Williams 1994, 80.
36 Wilkinson 1994.
37 *The Architect and Building News*, 6 January 1955, detail sheets A313 and A314.
38 Knight 1843, 391.
39 Herbert 1928, 14.
40 The use of sawdust in butchers' premises has not been prohibited, as long as it is clean and replaced at least once a day (Meat Products [Hygiene] Regulations 1994, Part II, General Conditions of Hygiene, Part 6).
41 A pulley system survives in the former abattoir at Mr Parker's shop at Abbey Green, Nuneaton, Warwickshire, although it is no longer in use.
42 Herbert 1928, 47.
43 Winstanley 1983, 142.
44 Dewhurst's tiles were manufactured by Carter's.
45 Before the Second World War, there were more than 12,000 licensed slaughterhouses in Great Britain. By March 1999 the total had fallen to 416 (*The Abattoir and Meat Processing Industry in Great Britain*, 1999, 9).

CHAPTER 5

1 The most thorough publications dealing with arcades are MacKeith 1985 and MacKeith 1986. Little attention has been paid to bazaars, which are seldom awarded more than a passing reference. Pevsner dismissed them – unfairly and incorrectly – as 'no more than a fashion in nomenclature' (Pevsner 1976, 261).
2 Southey 1951, 53.
3 Adburgham 1964, 18.
4 *Survey of London, The Parish of St Anne Soho*, vol. 33, 1966, 58–9.
5 Nightingale 1816, 10.
6 Nightingale 1816, 16 and 43–4.
7 The Soho Bazaar displayed artists' works free of charge, but most of its successors charged commission on sales.
8 *A Visit to the Bazaar*, 1818, 11–12; Nightingale 1816, 57–8.
9 View of interior in 1829, Westminster Archives Ashbridge Collection 792.
10 Timbs 1868, 41.
11 The building was depicted in Tallis's *London Street Views*.
12 Geist 1983, 49. For an illustration of the Western Exchange, said to date from about 1820, see Desebrock 1978, 72–3. The Western Exchange was damaged by fire in 1836 (Westminster Archives C138 New Bond Street (20)).
13 This was not the first Parisian bazaar: the Grand Bazar opened in 1825, but had closed by 1830 (Marrey 1979, 18–19).
14 Marrey 1979, 19–20.
15 The Watts family abandoned their trade as retail drapers in 1836 and sold the bazaar to three employees, Kendal, Milne and Faulkner.
16 Adburgham 1964, 49.
17 Adburgham 1964, 49. The bazaar at 26 High Street, Margate, is said to have been extensively refurbished and extended in 1830–31.
18 Ison 1948, 185.
19 The ground floor, which was the original bazaar, is now a bank; the upper floor, used for most of its history as an auction room, is an Indian restaurant.
20 Other documented bazaars include the triangular Victoria Bazaar in Newcastle (1837; Thomas Oliver).
21 Norfolk Record Office SO 18/1–121; White's *Norfolk Directory* 1836, 154; Allthorpe-Guyton 1982, 42–47.
22 Adburgham 1964, 20–21.
23 Colvin 1995, 975.
24 Adburgham 1964, 22.
25 Westminster Archives, ACCM: 495 (deeds and plans). The most famous auction room for the sale of horses and carriages was Tattersall's, which was on Hyde Park Green from 1838 until 1865, when it moved to Knightsbridge.
26 The miscellaneous department was referred to as a 'Ladies' Bazaar' in Smith 1833, 224.
27 *The Builder*, 24 June 1843, 254.
28 Hobhouse 1976, 189.
29 Darby and van Zanten 1974; *The Builder*, 30 October 1858, 719.
30 *Illustrated London News*, 6 November 1858, 440.
31 *The Builder*, 30 October 1858, 720.
32 Adburgham 1979, 141.
33 *Survey of London, The Parish of St James Westminster: Part 2 North of Piccadilly*, vol. 31, 1963, 297–8.
34 There is some uncertainty about this since some writers (e.g. Lancaster 1995, 9) suggest that the bazaar had Parisian origins.
35 For plan, elevation and section of Royal Opera Arcade, see *Survey of London, The Parish of St James Westminster: Part 1 South of Piccadilly*, vol. 30, 1960, pl. 39.
36 MacKeith 1986, 23.
37 Mayhew 1967, 217.
38 Mayhew 1865, 100–01.
39 *The Civil Engineer and Architect's Journal*, vol. 7 (August 1844), 305, with plan.
40 Mayhew 1865, 100.
41 Morrice 2001, 93–100.
42 *The Civil Engineer and Architect's Journal*, vol. 7 (August 1844), 305.
43 *Survey of London, The Theatre Royal, Drury Lane and the Royal Opera*

House Covent Garden, vol. 35, 1970, 81, n. 97; *The Builder*, 15 December 1855, 603–4

44 *Civil Engineer and Architect's Journal*, vol. 18 (1855), 247.
45 Howard 1965, 53–4.
46 MacKeith 1986, 40–44.
47 Later arcades in Manchester included the Old Exchange Arcade (1896) and the Deansgate Arcade (1897).
48 See plans of arcades published in MacKeith 1985.
49 Colchester Record Office, Building Regulation plan D/B6 PB3/4955.

CHAPTER 6

1 Scola 1992, 150ff. Other cities that decentralised markets in this period were Sheffield and Leeds (Markus 1993, 303).
2 Pevsner 1976, 237.
3 Schmiechen and Carls 1999, 28–31, 61–71.
4 Schmiechen and Carls 1999, 51–6.
5 Schmiechen and Carls 1999, 38–41. The Local Government Act of 1858 enabled local authorities to borrow money to build new market halls.
6 Pannier markets had benches, rather than shops or stalls.
7 Schmiechen and Carls 1999, 134.
8 Plans of these French markets were published in Bruyère 1823. They generally had stone piers which carried simple timber roofs with raised lanterns.
9 Stratton 1916, 20.
10 *An Account of St John's Market, Great Charlotte Street, Liverpool*, 1822, 3.
11 *Architectural Magazine*, vol. 2 (1835), 133.
12 Taylor 1964 and Taylor 1968–9.
13 *Architectural Magazine*, vol. 5 (1838), 665–77.
14 Knight 1851, 800.
15 Knight 1851, 802.
16 *Architectural Magazine*, vol. 3 (1836), 14.
17 A similar approach had been adopted for Oxford Covered Market, which was built in the 1770s with four houses along its frontage.
18 This roof was rebuilt in 1901–5.
19 *The Civil Engineer and Architect's Journal*, vol. 8 (1845), 257. Birkenhead Market Hall burned down in 1977.
20 At least two French markets had iron roofs before 1845 (Pevsner 1976, 238, note 24).
21 One exception to this was the gallery of the market hall in Aberdeen (1842).
22 *Stockport Advertiser*, 6 August 1875, cited by Hodson 1998, 36, note 20; *The Builder*, 15 September 1860, 591.
23 Manchester Markets Committee Minutes, 29 October 1854, 348. This structure was for the wholesale and retail meat trade.
24 *The Builder*, 8 January 1853, 24–5.
25 *Illustrated London News*, 2 June 1866, 537. Haywood's Phoenix Foundry had been responsible for the ironwork of the covered markets in Manchester (1853) and Stockport (1860–61).
26 Schmiechen and Carls 1999, 119.
27 Schmiechen and Carls 1999, 119.
28 Schmiechen and Carls 1999, 105–11.
29 Schmiechen and Carls 1999, 107.
30 N. Pevsner, *London II*, The Buildings of England (Harmondsworth, 1952), 72.
31 *Building News*, 17 February 1893, 223–24.
32 London Markets, Special Report of the Public Control Committee, London County Council, 1893.
33 *Lancashire Evening Telegraph*, Souvenir Edition, 31 October 1964, 22.
34 *www.bullring.co.uk* (2). December 2001.

CHAPTER 7

1 Definitions of 'department store' vary enormously. While the simplest description may be 'a large shop selling many different kinds of article' (*Oxford English Dictionary*, second edition, 1989, vol. 4), most historians have accepted Jefferys's rather generous definition, that it 'is a large retail store with four or more separate departments under one roof, each selling different classes of goods of which one is women's and children's wear (Jefferys 1954, 326). A department is generally understood to be separate entity in terms of accounting, buying and staffing, as well as having a distinct physical existence as a sales area devoted to a particular line of merchandise.
2 Owen 1971, 18.
3 Knight 1843, 394.
4 Tallis's prints reveal the presence of swing-loading arms in front of many shops, for lifting goods into cellars.
5 Adburgham 1964, 43 and 137–40; Airey and Airey 1979, 47; Lancaster 1995, 7; Crawford 1990, 29.
6 Airey and Airey 1979, 47.
7 Oliver 1851, 21. Surviving architectural drawings reveal that a very plain rear wing was erected in 1865, and that the main building incorporated at least two top-lit galleries by 1888 (Newcastle Building Plans T186/1775 (1865) and T186/12576 (1888), Tyne and Wear Archives).
8 From directories and prints it is clear that Kendal Milne & Faulkner gradually spread south along Deansgate, from St Ann Street to Police Street, between 1850 and 1870. The firm became cabinetmakers as well as drapers and carpet dealers in the course of the 1850s (Slater's *Directory of Manchester*, 1850; 1861).
9 Whittock 1840, 4 and 12.
10 *Reminiscences of an Old Draper*, 1876, 90.
11 For Hyam's, see Sharpe 1995. By 1852 Hyam's had shops in Colchester, London (Oxford Street), Manchester, Liverpool, Glasgow, Bristol, Birmingham and Leeds.
12 Knight 1843, 392. Moses also had a shop on New Oxford Street in London, which was 'a distinct advance in business architecture, and not without results upon the future' (*The Builder*, 25 November 1876, 1139), and built a branch at the top of Tottenham Court Road in 1860 (*The Builder*, 5 December 1860, 763).
13 Chapman 1993, 16.
14 Knowles and Pitt 1972, 63.
15 Costello and Farmar 1992, 16.
16 *The Builder*, 25 June 1859, 423–5. This shop was located next door to Warwick House (see above) on New Street.
17 Adburgham 1964, 96.
18 For example, Timbs 1868, 40; Knight 1877, 396; and Moss and Turton 1989, 34.
19 For example, Lambert 1938, 18; Chung et al. 2001, 240.
20 *Modern London*, c.1888, 212.
21 Gomme and Walker 1987, 114–16.
22 Goodden 1984, 3.
23 Old photographs show that part of Shoolbred & Cook's nearby store was constructed in a similar manner, but the date of these showrooms is not known (Bedford Lemere photographs, National Monuments Records).
24 This is illustrated in Moss and Turton 1989, 37. The 1855 building superseded a narrow building with a cast-iron façade of 1850, and was itself rebuilt on the same principles, but on a more lavish scale, in 1885; the architect was James Sellars.
25 Moss and Turton 1989, 57. The first hydraulic passenger lift to be installed in England was the 'Ascending Room' of the Colosseum, Regents Park, dating from 1826–9.
26 By another account, the first American store to install a passenger lift was Strawbridge & Clothier in Philadelphia, in 1865 (Pasdermadjian 1954, 25).

27 The Junior Army & Navy Stores had two lifts when it opened in York House in 1879 (Adburgham 1964, 217).

28 Marrey 1979, 22–3; 31.

29 Information supplied by the company.

30 Department of Culture, Media and Sport list description.

31 Knowles and Pitt 1972, 75.

32 It is not clear when shops began to employ shopwalkers. They were mentioned in 1843 (Knight 1843, 399).

33 Rappaport 2000, 153.

34 *Shopping in Cambridge*, W. Eaden Lilley & Co., [*c*.1928], 24 (Cambridgeshire Collection C.27.2, Cambridge Library).

35 *Illustrated London News*, 14 April 1866, 360, 366.

36 *Modern London*, *c*.1888, 152.

37 *The Builder*, 20 July 1878, 752–3. The architect was Octavius Hansard. The site is now occupied by Debenhams (1970; Adrian V. Montague & Partners).

38 Settle 1951, 30.

39 James Smith was the proprietor of the *Sportsman*. He won £48,000 when his horse Rosebery won the Cesarewitch and the Cambridge Stakes in 1876.

40 *The Builder*, 24 March 1877, 289.

41 Many English stores were named Bon Marché, including David Lewis's store on Basnett Street, Liverpool, John Broadbent's in Southport, Ralph Negus's in Cheltenham and Pope's in Gloucester.

42 The only evidence for a glass roof seems to be a statement that the roof 'will consist to a great extent of glass' (*The Builder*, 29 January 1876, 94), and a photograph of around 1910, showing an unlocated ladies' and children's outfitting department (Minet Archive SP16/846/BON.2).

43 A clear understanding of the Bon Marché is hampered by the fact that records do not survive before 1892, the year that James Smith was declared bankrupt with debts of £71,000. Control then passed to a group of five more experienced retailers, including Owen Owen and Edwin Jones.

44 A late nineteenth-century engraving of the store, which was used by Smith in his publicity material during the 1880s, appears to show the rear range as he intended to build it, rather than as it was actually built (Minet Archives SP16/846/BON.6). It may have been erected in phases over a number of years.

45 *The Builder*, 29 January 1876, 94.

46 *The Builder*, 24 March 1877, 289.

47 List of departments (Minet Archive, Bon Marché cuttings file).

48 Around 1888 the basement housed: men's outfitting, with separate departments for boots, hats, shirts and tailoring; cycles; perambulators; tea and coffee, and toys. On the ground floor were: household linen and drapery; furnishing drapery; silk; plain and fancy dress goods; mourning materials; fancy goods; lace; hosiery, gloves and jerseys; Berlin wools &c.; haberdashery; books; foreign fancy goods; patent medicines; stationery; china and glass; ironmongery and hardware; carpets and rugs; auction and estate agency. On the first floor were: millinery; mantles; ladies' and children's outfitting; ladies' and children's boots and shoes. On the second floor was furniture. (*Modern London*, *c*.1888, 140–42.)

49 Adburgham 1979, 139.

50 Similar societies were set up in Dublin and Edinburgh, and the Household Stores Association in Liverpool and Manchester ran along similar lines.

51 Hood and Yamey 1957, 316.

52 Hood and Yamey 1957, 313.

53 *The Builder*, 22 February 1868, 140.

54 Moss and Turton 1989, 277.

55 Ferry 1960, 197.

56 Hood and Yamey 1957, 317.

57 Hood and Yamey 1957, 317, quoting *The Civilian*, 19 February 1870.

58 Adburgham 1964, 156.

59 *The Builder*, 9 July 1881, 44.

60 Whiteley's staff lived in lodgings in the vicinity of the store.

61 *The Builder*, 9 July 1881, 44.

62 *The Draper's Record*, 26 January 1907, 223–4.

63 *Survey of London, Southern Kensington: Kensington Square to Earl's Court*, vol. 42, 1986, 87.

64 Moss and Turton 1989, 282.

65 A two-storey roof-lit extension was built over the back garden in 1873.

66 On the first floor were silver, electric goods, lamps, saddlery and portmanteaux; on the second floor, perfumery, patent medicines and toys; on the third floor, furniture and bedding. The basement was used for storage (Moss and Turton 1989, 322).

67 Basil Street and Hans Crescent were then North Street and New Street respectively.

68 This was 42–60 Kensington High Street (*The Draper's Record*, 18 March 1905, 743).

69 *Survey of London, Southern Kensington: Kensington Square to Earl's Court*, vol. 42, 1986, 88.

70 Another example of this was the Park Mansions Arcade, built between Brompton Road and Knightsbridge in 1910.

71 *Building News*, 23 February 1900, 263.

72 None of these light wells, nor those of the new John Lewis and Peter Robinson stores on Oxford Street, has survived.

73 Moss and Turton 1989, 57–8.

74 Two years later, customers at Macy's in New York were offered shots of whisky as they stepped on to the store's first escalators.

75 Moss and Turton 1989, 58; Adburgham 1975, 43.

76 Corina 1978, 187.

77 Wyman's *Commercial Encyclopaedia*, 1896, 387.

78 *The Draper's Record*, 5 December 1896, 569.

79 Liffen 1999–2000. Cash railways comprised tracks fitted with switches. The cash was inserted into balls of different diameters which ran along the tracks between the sales stations and a central cashier's office. With wireline carriers, a cashbox was propelled along the tracks by a variety of means, usually by pulling a cord. Pneumatic tubes worked by suction.

80 *Modern London*, *c*.1888, 140.

81 The pneumatic tubes in Fairhead's in Ilford were taken out of operation as recently as 1991 and, although they no longer use them for cash transactions, several other stores have kept their pneumatic tubes as a handy method of till clearance. One of the last wire-line carriers could be seen in Grout's in Palmers Green, until it closed in 2002 (Liffen 1999–2000, 97).

82 *The Graphic*, 3 August 1872, 98.

83 *Illustrated London News*, 9 December 1865, 565.

84 Marrey 1979, 40.

85 Briggs 1956, 39–43, 103–4. The store was rebuilt in 1910–23 to a design by the Liverpool architect Gerald de Courcy Fraser, and yet again after the Second World War.

86 Manchester Building Plans, loose drawings.

87 The architect of the Birmingham store was H. R. Yeoville Thomason. The store was on the corner of Corporation and Bull Street and was rebuilt in the years 1917–28.

88 A Sheffield store opened in 1884 but closed in 1888. At a later date, Lewis's stores opened in Glasgow, Leeds, Hanley, Leicester and Bristol. Plans survive for a Leeds store, designed by Thomas Ambler, which was never built (West Yorkshire, Record Office, Building Regulation Plan 12 October 1888, no. 11). Lewis's owned the Leeds site until 1898 (Briggs 1956, 156).

89 Briggs 1956, 87.

90 Adburgham 1964, 46–7.

91 Slater's *Directory*, 1871–2.

92 Cockayne's new premises opened in 1896 (*The Builder*, 2 May 1896, 387).

93 *The Builder*, 22 August 1868, 621.

94 King's Lynn Library, Shops 'J' Cuttings File.

95 King's Lynn Building Control Plans, first series, plan no. 566.

96 Scott 1928, 57; Scott 1929, 12 and 102; Scott 1930, 250.
97 For example: Kent and Kirkland 1958, 106; Hartlepool Museum Service 1984, 28; Stratton 1998, 21; and Stratton 1999, 12.
98 Teeside Archives, Stockton-on-Tees Building Regulation Plans 654 and 883; *The Draper's Record*, 9 May 1896, 299.
99 Teeside Archives, Stockton-on-Tees Building Regulation Plan 1024; *Stockton and Thornaby Herald*, 11 May 1901, 8.

CHAPTER 8

1 *The Guardian*, 9 February 2001, 26.
2 Early co-operative societies tended to have fleeting existences. Between 1844 and 1853, 39 new societies were formed, and between 1854 and 1863, 346 were formed (Fraser 1981, 122). The number in existence briefly reached a peak of 1,770 in 1911, and then declined due to amalgamations (Purvis 1992, 113).
3 Bonner 1970, 9.
4 Fair trading chiefly meant selling unadulterated goods at reasonable prices.
5 The dividend is said to have originated in Lennoxtown in 1812 (Fraser 1981, 121). The 'divi' was abandoned in the late 1960s/early 1970s, and replaced with stamps. These, in turn, have been phased out by several societies and replaced by reward cards.
6 Information from Rochdale Pioneers Museum, Toad Lane, Rochdale.
7 Until 1872 the CWS was called the North of England Wholesale Agency and Depot Society Ltd. From 1870 onwards legal and administrative advice was provided to societies by the Co-operative Union.
8 This cumbersome name was changed to Lincoln Co-operative Society in 1927.
9 These histories are: *Handbook of the 23rd Annual Co-operative Congress, Lincoln*, 1891; McInnes 1911, and Bruckshaw and McNab [*c.*1961]. The quarterly balance sheets are still held by the Society. In addition, building regulation plans for most Lincoln Co-operative Society buildings are held by Lincoln City Council.
10 Lincoln Co-operative Society Quarterly Balance Sheets, 2 April 1872.
11 F. Smith, of 6 Brown Street, Manchester, may have been recommended by the CWS Building Department. In 1894 Smith designed additions to the LCS corn mill, on Waterside North (Lincoln City Council, City Plans, 2404 and 2481).
12 Messrs Wright & Sons (McInnes 1911, 98).
13 The Lincoln Society Building Department, which evolved from a joinery department, was created in 1898 and within a few years had more than 100 employees. Its first manager may have been a Mr Burnett (Lincoln Co-operative Society Quarterly Balance Sheets, 6 April 1898). Its second manager was John G. Hedley (1904–8), who signed a number of architectural plans and drawings (Lincoln County Council, City Plans). A misjudged tender caused the Department to suffer serious losses between 1903 and 1908, resulting in G. Rutherford from the CWS taking over as manager in 1908.
14 The Dispensary was not acquired by the Lincoln Society until 1933.
15 Other societies with rural branches included Ipswich and Banbury (Purvis 1992, 123).
16 Mortimer designed a number of buildings for the LCS between 1883 and 1911 (Lincoln City Council, City Plans).
17 Co-operative societies usually prided themselves on selling home-reared meat.
18 These milk shops were supplied by the Society's own milk depot and dairy farm.
19 New slaughterhouses were built on Brayford in 1916.
20 *Architectural Review*, July 1936, xxv (advertisement).
21 The St Giles branch was built in 1926 with two halls, one with 250 seats and the other with 50. The head of the Building Department at that time was A. Doncaster.

22 Lincoln Co-operative Society Quarterly Balance Sheet, 1 January 1913.
23 Birmingham Central Library, Building Plan no. 25288 (February 1914); Williams 1993, 22 and 28. Other large stores erected at this time included West Hartlepool, a very grand neo-classical building inspired by Selfridges and Whiteley's, which opened in 1915.
24 Souvenir Calendar, Ashton Co-operative Society, 1928, 2 (Co-operative Union Archive).
25 Williams 1993, 46.
26 The Sleaford branch was rebuilt in the form of an emporium in 1937 (Lincoln Co-operative Society Quarterly Balance Sheet, 6 January 1937).
27 Plans for both of these extensions were signed by W. A. Johnson (Lincoln City Council, City Plans, 6696 and 7391).
28 Redfern 1938, 423–4; information supplied by The Co-operative Group, Business Information Unit.
29 *Architectural Design and Construction*, May 1939, 181–2.
30 Obituary from *The Producer*, August 1924, 303 (supplied by The Co-operative Group, Business Information Unit).
31 Johnson had a brief spell in private practice, 1910–14, and was with the Royal Engineers during the First World War (Royal Institute of British Architects Biography file).
32 *Architectural Review*, October 1936, 166. Other stores by Johnson included Sheffield & Eccleshall (1931), Coventry (1932), Southport (1936), Huddersfield (1938) and Stockport (1941).
33 Williams 1993, 84.
34 *The Co-operative Official*, November 1929, 413–14 and *The Producer*, August 1930, 221–3 (supplied by The Co-operative Group, Business Information Unit).
35 *Co-operative Architecture 1945–59*, 1959, frontispiece and caption.
36 Hay became overall Chief Architect of the CWS in 1963, when the London and Newcastle offices lost their autonomy.
37 *Co-operative Architecture 1945–59*, 1959, n.p.
38 Co-ops also suffered from the end of resale price maintenance in 1964, and the introduction of Selective Employment Tax in 1966.
39 Similarly, the North Eastern Co-op incorporates 119 former societies. Nationally, there were 467 societies in 1967, 312 in 1976 and 55 in 1994.
40 These included store concepts named 'Living' and 'Homeworld', respectively town centre and out-of-town outlets.
41 *www.co-op.co.uk* (9 January 2000). The CRS had been formed in 1934 to promote sales in 'co-operative wildernesses' and to help struggling societies. By the 1990s approximately 200 societies had come under its wing.
42 In 2001 the retail societies (excluding The Co-operative Group) had only forty-four superstores between them.

CHAPTER 9

1 *The Draper's Record*, 30 June 1906, 784–5.
2 The majority of later American stores followed the Schlesinger & Mayer approach, although Wanamaker's huge Philadelphia store (1911; D. H. Burnham) had a vast central court, like Marshall Field's.
3 Swales made this claim in the *Architectural Record*, 26 December 1909, 422. He attributed the building to: 'D. H. Burnham & Co., Architects; Messrs. Atkinson & Swales, collaborating'. A different account of his involvement is given by Honeycombe 1984, 31–2.
4 The first store to make use of this technology seems to have been the second Leiter Building in Chicago (Siegel Cooper, by William Le Baron Jenney, 1889–91).
5 Lawrence 1990, 23. These figures can be contrasted with statistics concerning Wanamaker's in Philadelphia, which was the largest store in the world when it opened in 1911. Its twelve storeys rose 247 feet (75.3 m) above the pavement, and its largest compartment contained 1,350,000 cubic feet (125,415 cu. m; Hall 1920, 238–40).
6 *The Draper's Record*, 16 June 1906, 629.
7 Atkinson undoubtedly played a crucial role in persuading the London

County Council to pass the Steel Frame Act of 1909, which permitted thin curtain walls supported on steelwork (London County Council (General Powers) Act, 1909). The 80 foot (24.4 m) height limit and 250,000 cubic foot (7,075 cu. m) limit nevertheless endured for many years, and Swan & Edgar's became embroiled in similar disputes in the 1920s.

8 Lawrence 1990, 26. Bylander had worked in Germany and America and was responsible for the steel frames of the Ritz Hotel and the Royal Automobile Club on Pall Mall.

9 Since most of the internal fire walls were supported by the steel frame, it was possible to remove them at a later date.

10 These wells were floored over in the 1950s (Honeycombe 1984, 144).

11 *The Builder*, 20 March 1909, 332. A more extensive roof garden was designed in 1928–9 by Richard Sudell and Marjory Allen, but it was demolished after the Second World War, when offices were built on the roof (Honeycombe 1984, 161–2).

12 For original departmental layout and photographs, see *The Draper's Record*, 13 March 1909, 798, and 20 March 1909, 942–5. Selfridges sold almost everything except furniture.

13 Selfridge had established a bargain basement in Marshall Field's store in 1885.

14 In Filene's Boston store of 1912 the men's department had to be placed on the first floor, but it was served by an escalator placed just inside the entrance so that men did not have to walk through other departments to reach it (Hall 1920, 242).

15 *The Draper's Record*, 31 July 1909, 285.

16 *The Draper's Record*, 27 February 1909, 503; 13 March 1909, 198–9; 20 March 1909, 942.

17 *Survey of London, Southern Kensington: Brompton*, vol. 41, 1983, 21.

18 *The Draper's Record*, 20 February 1909, 506; 20 March 1909, 925.

19 For Debenham & Freebody, see *Architectural Review*, June 1908, 362–9; *The Builder*, 20 March 1909, 346. For D. H. Evans, see *The Builder*, 18 December 1909, 670–71.

20 *The Builder*, 18 December 1909, 670. Party-wall rules seem to have been waived (*The Draper's Record*, 11 September 1909, 637).

21 *The Draper's Record*, 11 September 1909, 637–8.

22 *Architectural Review*, March 1912, 164–78; *The Builder*, 14 June 1912, 697.

23 *The Builder*, 24 January 1913, 116–19; *Architectural Review*, April 1913, 80–81.

24 *Survey of London, Southern Kensington: Kensington Square to Earl's Court*, vol. 42, 1986, 93.

25 *Architectural Review*, June 1917, 116–21.

26 Goodden 1984, 90.

27 One of the best surviving examples is the Righton Building in Chorlton-on-Medlock, a draper's premises erected in 1905 (see Department of Culture, Media and Sport list description).

28 Moss and Turton 1989, 65.

29 *The Draper's Record*, 7 November 1903, 353.

30 *The Draper's Record*, 30 January 1909, 348.

31 *The Draper's Record*, 3 July 1909, 15.

32 Obituary of Augustus F. Scott, *The Builder*, 10 April 1936, 727. For Bunting's, see: Norfolk Record Office, *N/EN* 12/1/6974, 1911; Salt 1988, 37–8.

33 *Northern Daily Mail*, 20 March 1907. To put this in context, the oldest surviving ferro-concrete building in the country is the CWS warehouse in Newcastle, of 1897–1900.

34 Costello and Farmar 1992, 55.

35 Parkinson-Bailey 2000, 141; Briggs 1956, 106–7.

36 Debenhams took over Marshall & Snelgrove's and Harvey Nichols (1919–20); Barker's took over Derry & Toms (1920); Harrods acquired Kendal Milne's (1919), Swan & Edgar's (1920), D. H. Evans (1928), Shoolbred's (1931) and the Civil Service Co-operative Society (1931). Around the same time Binns purchased several stores in the North. Selfridges had started buying stores in 1918, and by 1926 controlled thirteen stores

in addition to the Oxford Street premises. The Drapery Trust, formed in Scotland by Clarence Hatry in 1925, took over the Bobby Group and Swan & Edgar's. Then, in 1927, Debenhams took over the Drapery Trust and entered the 1930s with Britain's biggest group of stores (seventy in all).

37 Jefferys 1954, 327 and 344.

38 The Quadrant was designed by Sir Reginald Blomfield to harmonise with Norman Shaw's Piccadilly Hotel. Blomfield's design was imposed on Austin Reed's, Aquascutum and Lillywhite's as well as on Swan & Edgar's.

39 *Country Life*, 10 June 1922, 781.

40 Adburgham 1975, 103.

41 *Architectural Review*, May 1924, 180–85. See *Architectural Review*, 6 November 1924, lii, for advertisement for Castle's Shipbreaking Co. Ltd.

42 For plans of the 1924 building, see *The Builder*, 1 August 1924, 164–5.

43 Hall 1920, 242 and 254. This system was advocated in *The Architect and Building News*, 22 March 1929, 396.

44 The Selfridges extension was designed by Albert D. Millar of Graham, Anderson, Probst & White, the successors to Burnham, with Sir John Burnet & Partners as consulting architects. Burnet's firm and Philip Tilden produced numerous designs for the tower (Tilden 1954, figs 34–7).

45 *The Architect and Building News*, 25 August 1939, 213.

46 *The Architect and Building News*, 5 June 1936, 277–82.

47 *The Architect and Building News*, 29 November 1935, 243.

48 *The Architectural Review*, July 1935, 26.

49 Store Guide of *c*.1929, 5 (History of Advertising Trust (HAT) Archive).

50 Hall 1920, 242; *The Architect and Building News*, 1 April 1925, 574.

51 Bentall 1974, 124–8.

52 *The Beehive*, April 1935, 7.

53 Selfridges store guide, HAT Archive.

54 Bentall 1974, 164–6.

55 Lancaster 1995, 96; *The Store*, 1937, 286.

56 Howard Robertson, 'German Architecture of Transition: Two Shop Designs by Erich Mendelsohn', *The Architect and Building News*, 18 October 1929, 479–82; Zevi 1985, 68–9, 74–81, 84–91, 100–07.

57 Others were the Rudolf Petersdorff ladies' dress shop in Breslau (1927–8) and the Cohen-Epstein store in Duisberg (1926–7).

58 Illuminated advertisements were still rare in Europe, and Mendelsohn was undoubtedly inspired by American prototypes, such as the area around Times Square in New York.

59 *The Architect and Building News*, 19 November 1926, 598–9.

60 Howard Robertson and F. R. Yerbury, 'A Modern Dutch Department Store', *The Architect and Building News*, 10 February 1928, 227–30.

61 *The Architect and Building News*, 8 May 1936, 155.

62 Southall 1996, 12.

63 Ferry 1960, 135. William Filene's Sons Co. in Boston also seems to have built an extension for menswear just before the First World War (Ferry 1960, 119).

64 Honeycombe 1984, 149. Barker's opened a men's shop on the first and mezzanine floors of its new building in 1926.

65 *Architecture Illustrated*, April 1941, 52.

66 *Architectural Design and Construction*, May 1938, 191.

67 Calladine 2001.

68 *Architectural Review*, June 1939, 291.

69 *Architectural Review*, June 1939, 294.

70 The architect, Raymond McGrath, published images of the store in his book *Glass in Architecture* (1937).

71 Corina 1978, 140, 145.

72 *Journal of the Royal Institute of British Architects*, vol. 58 (October 1951), 457–61.

73 Banham 1972, 37.

74 *Portsmouth Evening News*, 14 August 1953, supplement.

75 American department stores with multi-storeyed car parks included

Zion's Co-operative Mercantile Institution (ZCMI) in Salt Lake City, built in 1954.

76 Bentall 1974, 84–6.

77 *The Store*, 1937, 289. Busby's of Bradford had a car valeting service for customers (Corina 1978, 187).

78 *Concrete Quarterly*, no. 41 (April–June 1959), 2–4.

79 Klose 1965, 202–3.

80 Klose 1965, 222–3; Banham 1972, 45.

81 Somake and Hellberg 1956, 104.

82 Ketchum 1948, fig. 20.

83 *Building Design*, 7 October 1977, 6.

84 Lancaster 1995, 103.

85 Publicity material, quoted in *www.culture-lab-uk.com* (29 January 2002).

86 *Architectural Record*, February 2001, 32; *www.future-systems.com*

87 D. H. Evans was briefly, and unsuccessfully, renamed House of Fraser in 1987.

CHAPTER 10

1 *Building*, April 1929, 180.

2 Secondary or multiple outlets already existed in the seventeenth and eighteenth centuries (Cox 2000, 227).

3 Adburgham 1964, 46–7.

4 For Tallis, see Jackson 1969, 132 and 140.

5 Jefferys 1954, 401 and 434.

6 Jefferys 1954, 137.

7 Jefferys 1954, 187.

8 Jefferys 1954, 356. Nine of these twenty-one were still trading under their own names in 1950.

9 Jefferys 1954, 296–300.

10 Jefferys 1954, 324.

11 Jefferys 1954, 65.

12 Marriott 1989, 15.

13 Smaller C&A stores in this style were built in Peckham and Lewisham in south-east London, and in Southampton and Portsmouth.

14 The store on Church Street, Blackpool, was designed by John S. Quilter & Son.

15 These were at Kenton, Wembley, Ruislip, Haywards Heath, Amersham (Williams 1994, 78).

16 Scott 1996, 77–9.

17 Marriott 1989, 18.

18 For example in: Neasden, Southgate, Queensbury, Kingsbury, Harrow Weald, Pinner and Rickmansworth (Corina 1971, 82–3).

19 Scott 1996, 48–63.

20 *Building*, September 1929, 399.

21 Benton 1995, 180.

22 Jefferys 1954, 65.

23 *Taywood News*, February 1975 (cutting in Newcastle Central Library).

24 *The Times*, 28 April 2001, 48–9.

25 In one of the most significant and bestselling business books of recent years, Naomi Klein has examined and deconstructed, sometimes with shocking results, the marketing strategies established in the USA by firms like Levi and Nike (Klein 2000).

26 The main published source used in this section was Wilson 1985. Tim Baker-Jones of the W. H. Smith Archive, supplied much additional information.

27 *www.whsmithplc.co.uk* (25 October 2001).

28 Wilson 1985, 17.

29 Wilson 1985, 182.

30 It was not until 1857 that John Menzies opened its first bookstalls north of the border, in Scottish railway stations.

31 *The Civil Engineer and Architect's Journal*, vol. 19 (1856), 142–3; 181.

32 A second Continental branch opened in Brussels in 1920 (Wilson 1985, 430).

33 Wilson 1985, 235.

34 Strand House was erected before 1914 but was requisitioned until 1920. Bridge House, Lambeth, was built in 1933–5 to house an expanded Stationery Department and the Bookbinding Department.

35 *The Builder*, 22 September 1855, 449.

36 *The Builder*, 14 April 1877, 374.

37 *The Newsbasket*, December 1926, 240 (*The Newsbasket* was W. H. Smith's house magazine).

38 *Junior Staff Journal*, April 1933, 299 (W. H. Smith's house magazine).

39 From *Titus Andronicus* IV.i.34.

40 From *Personal Talk*, iii.

41 *The Newsbasket*, February 1922, 26.

42 *Building News*, 19 July 1872, 46–7.

43 In 1905, 200 architects responded to an open competition for a uniform shopfront design. Two entries, by J. & J. B. Ednie of Edinburgh and James W. Morton of London, were awarded prizes but, as the designs have not survived, it is unclear to what extent they were adopted by the company (*Building News*, 3 November 1905, 612).

44 Powers 1989, 26–7, 92–3. Smith's pre-1907 shopfronts were undistinguished, for example that at 566 Rochdale Rd, Manchester, by J. Percival, February 1905 (Manchester Building Plan 6853).

45 This was the basic plan followed by most W. H. Smith's shops, including Southport, Taunton, Newport, York and Dewsbury (*The Newsbasket*, April 1922, 64).

46 In the post-war period, houses in suburban estates were occasionally bought for managers who were remunerated in kind for fiscal reasons (information from Tim Baker-Jones, W. H. Smith Archive).

47 Tea shops existed in Bournemouth, Darlington, Worthing and elsewhere. There does not appear to have been a company policy on catering, leaving it up to branch managers to decide whether it was appropriate. Sometimes tea shops and baking were the responsibility of the manager's wife (information from Tim Baker-Jones, W. H. Smith Archive).

48 By the 1950s the first-floor room, with its fittings and furnishings, was let separately as a restaurant and club.

49 Wilson 1985, 320. At this time the company had approximately 300 shops.

50 Wilson 1985, 326.

51 Chappell registered the name 'Cheap Book Company' for this subsidiary (Wilson 1985, 327).

52 From the late 1950s the Estate Department appears to have been anxious to replace the fittings of as many stores as possible with Vizusell fittings, advertised by W. H. Smith's Newsagents' Services as 'Versatile Fittings (W.H.S.) Ltd.'. Newsagents' Services was set up in order 'to give trade agent customers of the wholesale houses – and any other newsagent – the benefit of vast W.H.S. experience in shopfitting by providing mobile fittings on very reasonable terms' (*Newsbasket*, January 1960, 9).

53 Wilson 1985, 397.

54 *Newsbasket*, January 1960, 20.

55 Smith's sold records from 1958, and had opened twelve record departments by 1960.

56 The second floor was used for offices and staff facilities.

57 *Newsbasket*, November/December 1973, 12–15.

58 Smith's travel agencies subsequently opened as a free-standing chain and could be found in most of their large stores.

59 In 1996 the company disposed of its share in Do-It-All, which had merged with Boots' Payless DIY in 1990; in 1997 Waterstone's was demerged, and in 1998 Smith's share in Our Price was sold to the Virgin Retail Group.

60 In drafting this section, much help was received from Judy Burg, Company Archivist, and Alan Cooper, Design Integration Manager, both Boots Company plc. The main published sources are Chapman 1974 and Weir 1994.

61 Chapman 1974, 35.

62 Nottinghamshire Archives, City Building Plans, 318, 29 August 1878.

63 Nottinghamshire Archives, City Building Plans, 434, 12 October 1881.

64 Nottinghamshire Archives, City Building Plans, 542, 1 March 1882. Boot's lease was extended at the end of 1881, and this may have prompted the decision to rebuild (Chapman 1974, 42).

65 Nottinghamshire Archives, City Building Plans, 944, 22 November 1882; 391, 6 August 1884.

66 Boot seems to have lived here as late as 1887, but had moved to Bon Air, Mapperley, by 1888 (Kelly's *Directory of Nottinghamshire*, 1888).

67 Plans for this shopfront were submitted by Sutton in December 1881, to supersede the plain shopfront planned the previous October (Nottinghamshire Archives, City Building Plans, 470, 21 December 1881). One other Boots shop is known to have had a shopfront with barley-twist columns and pierced spandrels, probably of cast iron: the branch at 1 Oxford Street, Manchester.

68 Nottinghamshire Archives, City Building Plans, 44, 24 April 1885. Part of this outbuilding survives.

69 Chapman 1974, 72.

70 The company was renamed Boots Pure Drug Company Ltd in 1888.

71 Most of these shops were in working-class areas (Alfreton Road, Radford; Arkwright Street; 7 London Road; 253 Mansfield Road; the corner of Mansfield Road and Shakespeare Street). For plans of the central Pelham St. premises, see Nottinghamshire Archives, City Building Plans, 406, 16 March 1892.

72 Brand 1988 and Brand 1989.

73 A few stores, for which Bromley received considerable fees around 1900 (indicating rebuilding or serious alterations), are listed in the Private Ledgers in The Boots Company Archives. These stores include Melton Mowbray, Sheffield (Bridge Street), Cambridge (Petty Cury) and St Albans. Gibbs & Flocton were the architects of 6 High Street, Sheffield.

74 The scroll is thought to have been devised by a sign-writer called Jack Hunt who worked in the Shopfitting Department. It was standardised in 1924. See *Boots News*, 10 April 1974, 15.

75 Bromley's first work for the company appears to have been alterations to the Island Street manufacturing site in 1895.

76 Chapman 1974, 73–4. Unfortunately, Boot's activities on this trip are not recorded.

77 Chapman 1974, 74.

78 Chapman 1974, 74.

79 Documents pertaining to Young's dismissal reveal that he was unwilling to accept M. V. Treleaven as his superior (The Boots Company Archives, A83/15).

80 Nottinghamshire Archives, City Building Plans, 2394, 4 March 1903.

81 Other large stores of this type included: Northampton, Sheffield (West Street), Mansfield, London (Edgware Road and Putney). Smaller stores in a similar style were built in Cambridge (Market Hill), Buxton, Nuneaton, Lewisham, Dover and Newcastle. In addition, a magnificent art nouveau store was erected in Great Yarmouth.

82 Other shops with this type of shopfront included: St Anne's Street, Manchester, Walsall and 18 Moorfields, London.

83 For example, Chapman 1974, 87.

84 King's Lynn Building Control Plans, 1st series, plan no. 945 (possibly never built); Hants Record Office w/CII/2/873 and The Boots Company Archives, Building Plans, Y63.

85 Other 'black and white' stores were: Beeston (1908), Bury St Edmunds (1911), Canterbury (n.d.), Derby (c.1910), Evesham (1919), Exeter (1906–7), Gloucester (1913), Hereford (n.d.), Kingston-upon-Thames (n.d.), Trent Bridge (1906–7), Wellingborough (1906–7) and York (1907–8).

86 Chapman 1974, 86–7; Brand 1988, 8. For illustrations of this building see *The Bee* May 1936, 168.

87 *The Drapers' Record*, 16 November 1907, 420.

88 That building appears to have been erected around 1891 (Kelly's *Directory of Cheshire*, 1891). See illustration in Boots Scribbling Diary 1899 (The Boots Company Archives).

89 For example by Chapman 1974, 87 and Hudson 1983, 28.

90 Binfield 1988, 110.

91 *The Builder*, 15 June 1917, 382 (Bristol) and *The Builder*, 21 December 1917, 362 (Eastbourne).

92 Boots Scribbling Diary 1905 (The Boots Company Archives).

93 Brand 1986.

94 None is known to survive.

95 *The Bee*, February 1927, 139, and March 1927, 187; Lincoln City Council Plans, 5833.

96 There are a number of similarities between the designs of Lloyds Bank in Nottingham (1926, Bromley & Watkins) and the Boots store in Glasgow (1926, Bromley & Watkins).

97 Bromley formed a new partnership with T. N. Cartwright and T. H. Waumsley, but died in 1934. Gregory seems to have entered partnership with a Mr Robinson.

98 *The Architect and Building News*, 22 December 1933, 338.

99 *The Builder*, 26 November 1965, 1187 (emendation to Percy J. Bartlett's obituary).

100 'Some Recent Work for Messrs Boots Pure Drug Co', *Architectural Design and Construction*, vol. 6 (February 1936), 117–21.

101 It is possible that the 'black and white' Hereford store was built in 1928 (date on rainwater heads). The first Canterbury store may date from c.1930.

102 'A Selection of Shops for Boots Pure Drug Company', *Official Architecture and Planning*, vol. 22, no. 2 (February 1959), 73–9.

103 Until the early 1970s a separate Shopfitting Department designed, manufactured and installed the shop fittings and fronts. The Architects, Shopfitting and Estates Departments all belonged to the Property Division of the company, and were supported by a team of retail engineers in the Engineering Division (information from Alan Cooper).

104 The position of Chief Architect was not filled after 1995.

105 Ruston 1999, quoting from *The Guardian*, 30 March 1998.

106 Boots Properties PLC was created in 1989, and has one of the biggest property portfolios in the UK, including 630 out of a total of 1,400 Boots stores. This department controls all property acquisition for Boots, and works with external architects and developers.

107 The main published source used for this section was Sigsworth 1990. Additional information was obtained from the Burton Archive (West Yorkshire Archive Service, Leeds), from Jeremy Burton, grandson of the founder, and from Bob Whiteley, Building Surveyor for Arcadia Group plc.

108 Osinsky first changed his name to Morris (or Maurice) Burton but eventually settled on Montague.

109 Around 1910 the company's letter heading illustrated Progress Mills, but there is no evidence that the building ever existed (Sigsworth 1990, 22–3; 34).

110 The company went public in 1929.

111 Between 1917 and 1920 Burton established four factories in Leeds, which was second only to London's East End as a centre of menswear production.

112 Sigsworth 1990, 42.

113 *The Builder*, 28 December 1923, 994–1009. Other multiples that started to build stores designed by their own architects in the early 1920s included Lennard's (boots and shoes) and David Greig's (provisions).

114 Honeyman, *Well Suited*, 2000, 300–1.

115 *Recollections of Sir Montague Burton by Mr Aubrey Orchard-Lisle* October 1983 (obtained from Jeremy Burton).

116 The nominee was frequently James Walker the jeweller, which was owned by Sydney Saunders, a friend of Montague Burton (Honeyman 1993, 205).

117 Manchester Building Plan 15953 (July 1923); Lincoln City Council Plans 5840 (1923).

118 Architects' Department Box 127 (Burton Archive, West Yorkshire Archive Service, Leeds).

119 A Mr. Wright was noted as head Shopfitting Draughtsman in a letter of

4 October 1939, but Percy Swallow had been responsible for the shopfront at Hull, in 1934.

120 The windows were manufactured by Beacon (advertisement in *The Architect and Building News*, 6 April 1934, n.p.).

121 The original gold leaf has been replaced with gold-coloured spray paint, and the granite cladding secured by bolts, causing some cracking.

122 Another example of this window design survives on the corner of Dale Road and Bristol Road in Birmingham (1937) (fig. 2, no. 9).

123 Another example of this window design survives on High Ousegate, York (1933).

124 Mort 1996, 137.

125 For example: *www.newarkadvertiser.co.uk* (11 December 2000).

126 A letter from Burton to Martin, dated March 1937, reveals that there were six categories of store buildings, ranging from A to F, classified by size and function (letter from Mr Burton to Mr Martin entitled 'Classification of Buildings', dated 15 March 1937, Burton Archive, West Yorkshire Archive Service, Leeds).

127 Plans of store on Victoria Street, Derby (from Arcadia Group plc).

128 Sigsworth 1990, 81.

129 Mort 1996, 139–40.

130 Honeyman 1993, 212.

131 In the 1980s these tiles were sprayed with a textured coating and had small dark red fascias affixed to their surfaces. In some instances, the tiling was not smooth enough for this treatment and so boarding was applied over the tiling and given a textured finish.

132 Ralph Halpern was appointed manager of Peter Robinson in 1961, launched Topshop in 1968, and advanced through the company hierarchy until he became Chairman and Chief Executive in 1981. He revitalised the company during the 1980s and left in 1990.

133 In April 2001 Arcadia disposed of Wade Smith, Warehouse, Principles, Racing Green and Hawkshead to concentrate on their six core brands: Burton, Dorothy Perkins, Topshop/Topman, Evans, Miss Selfridge and Wallis.

134 The main published sources for this section are Rees 1985, Briggs 1984 and Burns and Hyman 1994. Much additional help was received from the staff of the Marks and Spencer Company Archive.

135 Marks is though to have come up with a fixed low price policy without prior knowledge of American 'five and dime' stores, despite these being an earlier phenomenon (Rees 1985, 14).

136 At this time, many of the goods sold by the company came from continental Europe (Rees 1985, 19).

137 Marks & Spencer became a private limited company in 1903, with 30,000 £1 shares. Marks and Spencer were each issued with 14,995 shares, and seven subscribers were each issued with 1. Further issues of shares in 1904 and 1906 increased the number of smaller shareholders, most of whom were associated with the business in one way or another.

138 The head office and warehouse were in Manchester. A new warehouse, built on Derby Street in 1901, was the first building project undertaken by the company.

139 In 1907 the fifteen market stalls had an average turnover of £1,765, with average net profits of £215; the thirty-four shops had an average turnover of £4,180, with average net profits of £375 (Briggs 1984, 113).

140 Rees 1985, 33.

141 Marks & Spencer Minute Books (Marks & Spencer Company Archive).

142 The architect of these buildings is not known, but the building contractors were M. & H. Steel. A dispute concerning their estimate for the Portsmouth store led to the dismissal of the company director, Bernard Steel, who had been responsible for the company's Estates Department since 1908 (Rees 1985, 45).

143 Transcript of an interview with Ernest Edward Shrewsbury, conducted by Mr Eric Estorick on 9 March 1951 (Marks & Spencer Company Archive).

144 Attempts to sell goods for between 4d. and 10d. in some stores between 1908 and 1913 had proved unsuccessful (Rees 1985, 40).

145 Staff comprised a manageress and several female assistants. It was only when stores became larger in the 1920s that male managers were employed.

146 In 1912 two new warehouses were acquired, one in Birmingham and the other in London.

147 Most of the thirty London Penny Bazaars acquired by Marks & Spencer had a distinctive type of shopfront featuring a depressed arch with glazed spandrels set with radial glazing bars.

148 Company headquarters moved to Chiswell Street in London in 1924, and to Baker Street in 1931.

149 Bookbinder 1993, 83.

150 Briggs 1984, 37.

151 The freeholds were valued at £364,650 and the leaseholds at £223,420. In 1955 Marks & Spencer's properties were valued at £35 million, and in 1964 at £100 million. In 2001 the UK property portfolio was worth £2.5 billion (*www.marksandspencer.com*, 9 January 2002).

152 Extracts from the Chairman's Speeches on Store Development, 1927 (Marks & Spencer Company Archive).

153 Extracts from the Chairman's Speeches on Store Development, 1932 (Marks & Spencer Company Archive).

154 The tendering system was replaced by a fee system, first used for the Wood Green store in 1926–7.

155 Burton 1985, 10–11.

156 *The Architect and Building News*, 4 July 1930, 27.

157 According to the architect P. Hickey, these metal windows were of a standard design, made to the specifications of the company. This design was later modified to incorporate security grilles (P. Hickey, *Marks & Spencer Ltd: A Review of 34 Years of Building Development*, March 1960, typescript, Marks & Spencer Company Archive).

158 *The Builder*, 14 September 1928, 346.

159 The Brixton branch of 1931 retains its original ceiling.

160 A handful of stores had cafés and ice cream bars in the 1920s. The cafés were along self-service lines with shiny chrome fittings by Gaby Schreiber and others after the war (information from Isobel Hunter, Marks & Spencer Archive). The Marks & Spencer café was revived in 1997, in Leeds.

161 Burton 1985.

162 Other examples included Lennard's and the HMV shop, both on Oxford Street.

163 'The Pantheon. New Premises for Messrs. Marks & Spencer Ltd.', *The Architect and Building News*, 28 October 1938, 105–8; 'The Pantheon – London's Finest Variety Store', *Chain and Multiple Store*, 22 October 1938, np.

164 Report on a Visit to America, October 1937, by 'WJ' (?W. Jacobson), (Marks & Spencer Company Archive).

165 A Staff Welfare Department was established in 1934.

166 These were: Lowestoft (1950), Leeds (1951), Sheffield (The Moor, 1953) and Southampton (1952).

167 As in the 1930s, other architectural firms occasionally worked for the company. Denis Lasdun & Partners designed the extension of the Brighton store (opened 1960) (*Building with Steel*, vol. 2, no. 2, June 1962, n.p.). At least one 1950s shopfront survives, that of Norwich, which was installed in 1959.

168 *The Store*, February 1948, vol. 12, 17–20. In 1937 it was deemed that self-service 'could hardly be a practicable proposition in our type of stores' (Report on a Visit to America, October 1937, by 'WJ', Marks & Spencer Company Archive).

169 Burns and Hyman 1994, n.p.

170 *Lewis & Hickey Architects*, brochure (Marks & Spencer Company Archive).

171 In 2001 it was announced that half of the building would be handed over to Selfridges, which is building up a department store chain for the second time in its history.

172 The main published source for this section is Winkler 1941. Additional information was supplied by Pat Sullivan, retired Project Manager, Wool-

worths plc, and Ken Trimmer, Architectural Manager, Property Services Department, Woolworths plc.

173 The Kingfisher Group currently owns B&Q, Superdrug and Comet.

174 Winkler 1941, 81.

175 Winkler 1941, 151–2. At that time Woolworth had 230 American stores.

176 'The Woolworth Enterprise', *The Draper's Record*, 14 August 1909, 387.

177 This scheme was illustrated in *The Draper's Record*, 20 September 1902, 729–31.

178 Winkler 1941, 156.

179 Manchester City Architects Building Bye-law Plan No: 740, 1910.

180 *The Builder*, 19 January 1923, 116.

181 This is how Crittall described the Liverpool façade. *Crittall Metal Windows*, catalogue 36, January 1925 (Crittall Archive, Braintree).

182 *Architectural Review*, November 1935, 193.

183 West Yorkshire Record Office, Building Regulation Plan 3 April 1928, no. 95.

184 City of Manchester City Architects Building Bye-law Plan No: 18021, 1929. Woolworth planned this building with three storeys, but the Improvements Committee insisted on five, to preserve the balance of the square (*The Builder*, 21 January 1927, 112). Woolworth responded by adding two floors of offices, which were soon incorporated within the store.

185 The main entrance to the Blackpool store, which opened in 1938, had a pair of revolving doorways separated by a slim display case.

186 Another early example of the 'diamond w' can be seen on the lobby floor of the former St Ives (Cambs) branch (now a DIY shop).

187 The lion and shield logo can still be seen on the consoles of the Strand store (now Boots) and the branch on Piccadilly, Manchester. The lion's head, without the shield, was used occasionally in the 1930s, for example on the parapet of the Peckham store.

188 The price policy was retained until the Second World War. It was then removed from fascias.

189 An 8 foot mahogany counter of *c*.1938 is displayed in the Museum of London, together with price tickets and other Woolworth paraphernalia.

190 This is because Woolworth opened stores in small market towns and suburbs as well as the principle thoroughfares on which Marks & Spencer concentrated.

191 In the mid-1930s the floral design was replaced by smooth tin panels. Plaster panels were introduced in the late 1930s, followed by asbestos, and finally the fissured tiles of today, which slot into a suspended metal grid (information from Pat Sullivan).

192 Simpson 1999, 54–74. An early instance of steel ceilings in an English store was Palmer's in Great Yarmouth (*The Draper's Record*, 3 August 1907, 255). They still survive in part of Arnison's in Penrith.

193 This feature continued into the 1950s. As in Marks & Spencer stores, the pine floors were manufactured by Vigor Floors (information from Pat Sullivan).

194 In Belfast, Woolworth occupied part of a building erected by Burton, in Burton's house style, but clearly intended for Woolworth from the outset. The exact relationship between the two companies is difficult to determine.

195 Another possible mock timber-framed Woolworth is the Shaftesbury branch.

196 Bainbridge's store (233–227 High Street) survives, complete with its original shopfront, while Woolworth has been demolished.

197 Burton Archive, West Yorkshire Archive Service Leeds (Ref: 127). Burton probably meant 'vertical' rather than 'horizontal'.

198 Others included: Hammersmith, Leicester, Newcastle (now Virgin Megastore), Brighton, Durham, Ealing.

199 In the 1920s Woolworth carried out its own shopfitting. From the 1930s to the 1960s it was carried out by two contractors, with a north and south divide: John Curtiss of Leeds, and A. E. Lindsay of Edmonton, London (information from Pat Sullivan).

200 Information from Pat Sullivan.

201 A very rare surviving example of this can be seen at 10 Connaught Road, Frinton-on-Sea, Essex.

202 The original lettering on the façade of the Brixton store still survives (November 2000). Its chrome shopfront probably dates from the 1950s.

203 *Architectural Design and Construction*, May 1938, 189.

204 *Architectural Design and Construction*, May 1938, 188.

205 The total labour force in the 1950s numbered approximately 600 (information from Pat Sullivan).

206 Woolworth Holdings was split into three divisions: High Street, Out-of-Town and Property.

207 *The Times*, 27 July 2002, 50.

208 In 2000 the company purchased six former C&A stores, including Wood Green and Chester.

CHAPTER 11

1 Any discussion of shopping centres is plagued by linguistic ambiguities. The term 'mall' can be applied to both open-air and covered shopping centres, but it also describes individual walkways within a complex. In Britain, open centres tend to be referred to as 'pedestrian precincts', while enclosed centres are simply 'shopping centres'. The central spaces that link mall walkways, creating pedestrian interchanges, are referred to as 'concourses', 'courts' or 'atria'; smaller wells are 'voids'. Upper levels surrounding atria and voids are 'galleries', but the term 'galleria' is reserved for linear shopping centres with spectacular glass roofs, in the arcade tradition. Terms such as 'plaza' or 'pavilion', which have little precise significance, are popular for their respective connotations of a bustling public arena, or a building devoted to pleasurable pursuits.

2 Tripp 1942, 75.

3 New Towns were created primarily to relieve congestion in London, according to principles of decentralisation outlined in the Report of the Barlow Commission (1940), Sir Patrick Abercrombie's Greater London Plan (1944) and the Reith Report of 1946, whose findings were enshrined in the New Towns Act of 1946. Of the twelve English New Towns created by 1950, eight encircled London (Basildon, Bracknell, Crawley, Harlow, Hatfield, Hemel Hempstead, Stevenage and Welwyn Garden City). By 1968 twelve New Towns had been founded in the Midlands and North (Corby, Milton Keynes, Newton Aycliffe, Northampton, Peterborough, Peterlee, Skelmersdale, Runcorn, Redditch, Telford, Warrington, Washington).

4 Somake and Hellberg 1956, 49 and figs 20 and 25.

5 On Sicilian Avenue the shops were strongly differentiated in terms of style and materials from the offices above. The development featured a fountain and flower beds, and was paved with marble.

6 *The Architect and Building News*, 16 December 1927, 923–7.

7 Lewison and Billingham 1969, 34–5.

8 Lance Wright, 'Shopping the Environment', *Architectural Review*, March 1973, 171.

9 Lance Wright, 'Shopping the Environment', *Architectural Review*, March 1973, 179.

10 'Coventry. A Plan for the City Centre', *The Architect and Building News*, 21 March 1941, 188.

11 Somake and Hellberg 1956, 39. In neighbourhood centres, however, it was quite common to build flats or maisonettes over parades of shops.

12 *The Architect*, March 1973, 44.

13 Gibberd et al. 1980, 140.

14 *Survey of London, Poplar, Blackwell and the Isle of Dogs: The Parish of All Saints*, vol. 43, 1994, 229–30.

15 Between 1947 and 1953, private developers had been deterred by a 100 per cent surcharge on the increase in value of land resulting from development, and until 1959 compensation awarded under compulsory purchase was not awarded at market value. Thus, it was only after 1959 that private developers became heavily involved in post-war reconstruction.

16 *The Architects' Journal*, 3 June 1964, 1238.

17 *Traffic in Towns* (Reports of a Steering Group and Working Group Appointed by the Ministry of Transport), 1963.

18 Scott 1989, 8.

19 The 1947 Town and Country Planning Act created Comprehensive Development Areas, which gave planning authorities considerable powers of redevelopment.

20 These were given a futuristic twist in the montage illustrations in Ivor de Wofle (pseud. for Hubert de Cronin Hastings), *Civilia – The End of Suburban Man: A Challenge to Semidetsia*, 1971.

21 The expansion of Basingstoke was a joint scheme by Basingstoke Borough Council, Hampshire County Council and the Greater London Council. The population was planned to rise from 26,000 in 1961 to 80,000 in 1976.

22 This emerged from an agreement between the GLC, Croydon Council and the Government, and the Croydon Corporation Act of 1956.

23 *The Development* (Croydon Local Studies Library, Box: Whitgift Centre f570 (658.8) WHI; Redevelopment Box 1 f570 (711) RED). A smaller precinct had already been built on St George's Walk, between High Street and Park Lane.

24 *Surveyor*, 24 September 1971, 32–4.

25 'Nooks and Corners', *Private Eye*, 28 December 1973, 7. The Vancouver Centre was begun in 1967 and built in two phases.

26 Chequer Street development, files in St Alban's Library; *Building Design*, 21 April 1978, 12–13.

27 *Building*, 20 July 1979, 55–6.

28 Marriott 1989, 215.

29 Mechanical car parks conveyed cars to parking places using lifts and trolleys.

30 The underused upper level of the Elephant & Castle Shopping Centre was converted into a Department of Health and Social Security conference centre in the 1970s.

31 Adamson 1993. The name Arndale combined the names of Sam Chippindale and his partner Arnold Hagenbach.

32 Photographs of Cross Gates in 1968: West Yorkshire Record Office, Leeds City Engineers, Acc. 3733, nos 36355–36356; 37099–37103.

33 *Yorkshire Evening Post*, 20 September 1967, 6.

34 These Arndale Centres were at Bolton (Crompton Place), Bradford (Kirkgate), Dartford, Doncaster (Frenchgate Centre), Eastbourne, Luton, Manchester, Middleton, Morecambe, Nelson (The Admiral), Nottingham (Broadmarsh), Poole (Dolphin Centre), Stretford, Wandsworth and Wellington. The holding company Town & City Properties Ltd became P. & O. Holdings Ltd in 1988, and Arndale Shopping Centres Ltd became P. & O. Shopping Centres Ltd. Cross Gates was subsequently refurbished (*Leeds Weekly News*, 16 November 1989, East Leeds Extra, 6).

35 *Yorkshire Evening Post*, 20 September 1967, 6.

36 Christopher Middleton, 'Centre Shifts', *Guardian Society*, 4 April 2001, 2, quoting a local history society guidebook.

37 Major influences are said to have been Woodfield Mall in Chicago and Parly II in Paris (*Retail and Distribution Management*, vol. 4, no. 60, November–December 1976, 65).

38 Adamson 1993, 23.

39 Adamson 1993, 24.

40 Adamson 1993, 24.

41 Peter Neal, 'Remaking Manchester', *Landscape Design*, no. 273 (September 1998), 29.

42 The first New Town to have a covered shopping centre was Cumbernauld (first phase completed 1967), but it formed part of a building that housed many other central functions, such as a library and offices. Like Milton Keynes, Runcorn also provided an opportunity for the construction of a 'pure' shopping mall.

43 The original area of surface parking soon had to be extended.

44 *Architectural Review*, February 1977, 103–11.

45 Royal Institute of British Architects, *Modern British Architecture since 1945*, London, 1984, 76.

46 One of the first malls to have a glazed entrance bay (with a cast-iron barrel vault) was the Hounds Hill Centre in Blackpool, which was of red brick and had arcading at ground level.

47 *Yorkshire Evening Post*, 27 September 1973, 16.

48 *Building Design*, 27 January 1978, 10. Another example is the development on Leicester Market Place, 1970.

49 A major inspiration for this might have been the Faneuil Centre in Boston of 1976.

50 *The Economist*, 12 May 2001, 36.

51 *The Times*, 13 July 2002, 48.

CHAPTER 12

1 In drafting this section, much assistance was received from Audrey Kirby of The London Institute, London College of Printing, School of Retail Studies. Thanks are also owed to Emily Cole of English Heritage for making her research on self-service shops available.

2 Towsey 1964, 158.

3 *Self-Service Journal*, vol. 1 no. 2 (December 1951), 20.

4 *Co-operative News*, 3 October 1942; *Woman's Outlook*, 10 October 1942, 475. Harold Wicker later founded the Self-Service Development Association.

5 For example at Barkingside in 1944.

6 *The Store*, February 1948, vol. 12, 17–20.

7 The Royal Arsenal Society is said to have had 'the first really comprehensive self-service food shop in Britain' (Corina 1971, 114).

8 *Self-Service Journal*, vol. 1, no. 2 (December 1951), 8–10.

9 Westwood and Westwood 1955, 92–3.

10 Westwood and Westwood 1955, 88.

11 Express Dairies 1964, 7 (Earl's Court); John Lewis Partnership 1985, 187 (Waitrose, Streatham); *Self-Service Journal*, vol. 1, no. 1 (November 1951), 6–8 (Croydon), vol. 1, no. 2 (December 1951), 12–13; 24 (Streatham Hill), and vol. 1, no. 5 (March 1952), 10–11 (Eastbourne).

12 Somake and Hellberg 1956, 108 and plates 58–60.

13 These three firms became part of Allied Suppliers Ltd (see Mathias 1967).

14 Free-standing supermarkets of the 1950s included the co-ops at Darlington (1957) and Hull (1959) (*Co-operative Architecture 1945–1959*, 1959, n.p.). Many other co-op supermarkets formed part of multi-purpose buildings, such as offices or department stores. Overall, there were 175 supermarkets in 1958, 367 in 1960, 2,130 in 1965 and 4,500 in 1970 (*British Supermarkets*, Jordan Dataquest, London 1977, v).

15 *Co-operative Architecture 1945–1959*, 1959, n.p.

16 Express Dairies 1964, 35.

17 Baskets on wheels were first used in 1918 in Houston, Texas (Bowlby 2000, 140).

18 Towsey 1964, 76–94.

19 G. K. Medlock, 'Lighting Installations in Retail Premises', in *This is Progress: A Pictorial Record of Co-operative Store and Shop Development, 1958*, 1959, n.p.

20 Williams 1994, 127.

21 The American group Safeway arrived in Britain in 1962 and acquired eight Gardner and Prideaux supermarkets. The company has claimed that its Wimbledon store, which opened in 1962, was the first of its kind, the first 'proper supermarket' (*Daily Mail*, 10 May 2001, 41). However, the first Safeway designed and built supermarket opened in the Greyfriars Shopping Centre in Bedford in 1963 (*Store Planning and Design*, July–August 1982, 9–10). The branch at Blackfen, of 1964, was described at the time as 'the nearest thing yet to an out of town store' (*Self-service and Supermarket Journal*, vol. 13, May 1964, 46.)

22 Williams 1994, 169.

23 This store had 27,000 square feet (2,508.3 sq. m), while the Carrefour that opened at Creteil in 1968 had 75,500 square feet (7,013.9 sq.m) (Bowlby 2000, 161 and 165). By 1972 France had more than 100 hypermarkets.

24 *The Architects' Journal*, 5 May 1965, 1071–82; *Self-service and Supermarket Journal*, vol. 13 (August 1964), 15.

25 *Self-service and Supermarket Journal*, vol. 15 (December 1966), 15, 21. ASDA's first store opened at South Elmsall near Wakefield in 1965. By 1970 ASDA had more than thirty stores.

26 There were at least eight Woolco stores, including Oadby, Thornaby, Bournemouth, Hatfield and Killingworth.

27 *Self-service and Supermarket Journal*, vol. 14 (April 1965), 36; vol. 15 (November 1966), 21; vol. 16 (October 1967), 14; (15 August 1968), 7–11. The Oadby store was designed by S. Penn-Smith, Son & Partners, and the Thornaby store by Elder, Lester & Partners.

28 The Hampshire Centre (or Castlepoint), originally developed by Second Covent Garden Properties Ltd, is currently being redeveloped by Castlemore.

29 *The Future Pattern of Shopping*, National Economic Development Office, HMSO, 1971.

30 *Out of Town Shopping and Shopping Centres*, Development Control Policy Note 13, Department of the Environment, 1972.

31 This figure rose over time.

32 Mayer Hillman, Irwin Henderson and Anne Whalley, 'In the Market Place: The Hypermarket Debate', *New Society*, September 1972, 543.

33 Statistics from *www.texas.co.uk* (Company History of Sainsbury's), 5 January 1998.

34 The term 'hypermarket' seems to have been imported to this country by Carrefour.

35 Williams 1994, 169–70.

36 Williams 1994, 212–13. Sainsbury's bought out BHS's share in Savacentre in 1989.

37 Wright 1973.

38 *Building Design*, 13 October 1978, 1.

39 *Built Environment*, no. 14 (January 1988), 7.

40 *Building Design*, 26 February 1993, 26.

41 *Architectural Review*, May 1983, 69–73.

42 *Building Design*, 8 August 1986, 10–11.

43 *Building*, 19 November 1999, 48–50.

44 Chung et al. 2001, 312.

45 *The Times*, 6 July 2002, 16.

46 *Building Supermarkets*, June 2000, 32.

47 Department of the Environment PPG 13, 'Transport', March 1994 and PPG6, 'Town Centres and Retail Development', June 1994. PPG6 encouraged mixed-use development, coherent parking strategies, town centre management schemes, good urban design and urban design analysis.

48 *Store Planning and Design*, June 1981, 34.

49 Giles Worsley, 'Architecture's Learning Curve', *Daily Telegraph*, 28 April 2001 (*www.lineone.net/telegraph*; 23 November 2001).

50 Civic Trust Certificate, 2001.

51 This section was co-authored by Audrey Kirby. Much information was provided by Steve Douglas, Head of Development Planning, Tesco plc. The main published sources are Corina 1971 and Powell 1991.

52 Corina 1971, 75–8; 85.

53 Corina 1971, 92.

54 Corina 1971, 119–20; Powell 1991, 66.

55 Hough and Lambert 1951, 11; Powell 1991, 78.

56 Powell 1991, 78.

57 Powell 1991, 83.

58 Corina 1971, 133.

59 'British Empires', Channel 4, 2000; Powell 1991, 96–7.

60 Corina 1971, 167; 180; *Self-service and Supermarket Journal*, 17 October 1968, 8–10.

61 By then, Fine Fare and Pricerite already gave stamps.

62 Numbers of grocery shops fell from 145,000 to 111,000 in the 1960s (Corina 1971, 184).

63 Corina 1971, 165.

64 Ipswich Building Control Plans 31643, 1968.

65 *Newcastle Journal*, 21 November 1972, 4.

66 *Newcastle Journal*, 9 October 1974, 7.

67 Powell 1991, 145.

68 Seth and Randall 1999, 29.

69 Powell 1991, 99.

70 *The Architect's Journal*, 27 January 1993, 37–46.

71 Seth and Randall 1999, 36; Robert East, 'The Anatomy of Conquest: Tesco versus Sainsbury', Occasional Papers Series no. 29, Kingston Business School, July 1997.

72 *Building Design*, 14 October 1994, 3.

73 *Building Supermarkets*, June 2000, 26.

74 *The Architect's Journal*, 18 January 2001, 4.

CHAPTER 13

1 'Off-centre' is an American term. 'Out-of-town' and 'edge-of-town', the usual British terms, are used in various ways and can be ambiguous. 'Out-of-town' can refer to any retail development outside an established shopping area, including those on the fringes of suburbia (i.e. edge-of-town), but it can also be applied exclusively to developments beyond built-up areas. To avoid confusion, or long-winded explanations, the term 'off-centre' is used here as an umbrella term for all shopping developments outside urban areas.

2 The Sunday Trading Act of 1994 deregulated Sunday shopping.

3 Other retail parks with high street traders include Brookfield Park, Cheshunt, and The Fort, Birmingham.

4 Other outlet villages in the form of a mall include Atlantic Village, Bideford and Freeport Talke.

5 It was designed by Benoy.

6 Giles Worsley, 'Lord Rogers Unveils Shopping Centre within Tent', *Daily Telegraph*, 17 March 2000.

7 Giles Worsley, 'Lord Rogers Unveils Shopping Centre within Tent', *Daily Telegraph*, 17 March 2000.

8 Much work for this sub-section was carried out by Dr Ann Robey, former Head of Architectural Projects, Royal Commission on the Historical Monuments of England. An earlier prototype for off-centre shopping was Roland Park Shop Centre, outside Baltimore in Lake Forest (1916). During the 1930s, Frank Lloyd Wright promoted the idea of new spaces created outside traditional centres expressly for the motorist, and put forward a prototype design (Broadacre City).

9 Photographs of the influential Southdale Centre were published in Gruen and Smith 1960.

10 Burns 1959, 10.

11 *The Architect and Building News*, 8 December 1955, 750–53.

12 *Regional Shopping Centres in North West England*, *Haydock Report*, Department of Town and Country Planning, University of Manchester, 1964.

13 At the same time, Northampton town centre was being modernised and provided with its own mall, The Grosvenor Centre, which was developed by a public/private consortium and opened in 1975.

14 Travelators had been installed at an earlier date in some open centres, such as the Merseyway Centre in Southport, the Whitgift Centre in Croydon and the Wulfrun Centre, Wolverhampton.

15 Leath Waide, 'Consumer Cathedrals', *Built Environment*, vol. 4, no. 2 (February 1975), 93.

16 Hammerson put forward their initial proposal for Brent Cross in 1964.

17 Hempstead Valley Shopping Centre has since been extended.

18 Beddington 1991, 166.

19 Very many more were proposed.

20 Enterprise Zones were set up in 1980. They permitted exemption from development land tax and allowed zero rates to be paid for a period of 10 years. Most were designated for vacant sites.

21 Marcus Field, 'Tragedy in the Chalk Pit', *Blueprint*, no. 161 (May 1999), 45–6.
22 Rick Poynor, 'Inside the Blue Whale: A Day at the Bluewater Mall', *Harvard Design Magazine*, Summer 2000 (*www.gsd.harvard.edu*).
23 *Building Design*, 30 June 1995, 18.
24 Hugh Pearman, *Sunday Times*, March 1999.
25 Anderton et al. 1993, 35.
26 The Georgian Arcade erected at the Merrion Centre in 1973 is mentioned in Chapter 12.
27 'The Trafford Centre Information Pack', August 1999, 4. Merry Hill has a 'crèche' for the elderly dependents of workers and shoppers (*The Times Magazine*, 12 May 2001, 85).

28 MetroWorld was conceived by the originators of West Edmonton Mall.
29 *Journal of the Royal Institute of British Architects*, vol. 97 (November 1990), 71.
30 *The Mall Cribbs Causeway: The Way Shopping Ought To Be* (brochure, n.d.).
31 Maitland 1990, 18, quoting the *Washington Post*, 25 November 1985.

CHAPTER 14

1 The Sunday Trading Act of 1994 deregulated Sunday Shopping.

Bibliography

Abel, Deryck, *The House of Sage, 1860–1960: A Century of Achievement*, London, 1960

Ackermann, Rudolph (ed.), *The Microcosm of London*, 3 vols, London, 1808–10

——(ed.), *The Repository of Arts, Literature, Commerce, Manufactures, Fashions and Politics*, London, 1809–28

Adamson, Zia, *Sam Chippendale: Shopping Centre Pioneer*, Bradford, 1993

Adburgham, Alison, *Shops and Shopping, 1800–1914: Where, and in What Manner, the Well-dressed Englishwoman Bought her Clothes*, London, 1964

——, *Liberty's: A Biography of a Shop*, London, 1975

——, *Shopping in Style: London from the Restoration to Edwardian Elegance*, London, 1979

Airey, Angela, and John Airey, *The Bainbridges of Newcastle: A Family History, 1679–1976*, Newcastle upon Tyne, 1979

Alexander, David, *Retailing in England during the Industrial Revolution*, London, 1970

Alexander, Nicholas, and Gary Akehurst (eds), *The Emergence of Modern Retailing, 1750–1950*, London, 1999

Allthorpe-Guyton, Marjorie, with John Stevens, *A Happy Eye: A School of Art in Norwich, 1845–1982*, Norwich, 1982

Amsterdams Historisch Museum / Art Gallery of Ontario, *The Dutch Cityscape in the 17th Century and its Sources*, Toronto, 1977

An Account of St John's Market, Great Charlotte Street, Liverpool, 1822

Anderton, Frances et al., *You Are Here: The Jerde Partnership International*, London, 1993

Archer, Ian, Caroline Barron and Vanessa Harding (eds), *Hugh Alley's Caveat: The Markets of London in 1598*, London Topographical Society no. 137, London, 1988

Artley, Alexandra (ed.), *The Golden Age of Shop Design: European Shop Interiors, 1800–1939*, London, 1975

Aston, Mick, and James Bond, *The Landscape of Towns*, Stroud, 2000 (first published 1976)

Auerbach, Jeffrey, *The Great Exhibition of 1851: A Nation on Display*, New Haven and London, 1999

Augé, Marc, *Non-Places: Introduction to an Anthropology of Supermodernity*, London, 1995

A Visit to the Bazaar, London, 1818

Bailly, Gilles-Henri, and Philippe Laurent, *La France des halles et marchés*, Toulouse, 1998

Baker, J. F., 'Design of Steel Frames for Buildings', *The Structural Engineer*, Jubilee Issue (July 1958), 96–101

Banham, Reyner (intro.), *The Architecture of Yorke Rosenberg Mardall, 1944–1972*, London, 1972

Barnett, David, *London, Hub of the Industrial Revolution: A Revisionist History, 1775–1825*, London and New York, 1998

Bartram, Alan, *Fascia Lettering in the British Isles*, London, 1978, *The English Lettering Tradition from 1700 to the Present Day*, London, 1986

Bath City Council, *Bath Shopfronts*, Bath, 1993

Beddington, Nadine, *Shopping Centres: Retail Development, Design and Management*, London, 1991

Beeching, C. L. T. (ed.), *The Modern Grocer and Provision Dealer*, 5 vols, London, 1919–22

Benjamin, Walter, *The Arcades Project*, trans. Howard Eiland and Kevin McLaughlin, Cambridge, MA, and London, 1999 (German original, 1982)

Bennell, John, 'Shop and Office in Medieval and Tudor London', *Transactions of the London and Middlesex Archaeological Society*, vol. 40 (1989), 189–206

Benson, John, and Gareth Shaw (eds), *The Evolution of Retail Systems, c.1800–1914*, Leicester, 1992

Bentall, Rowan, *My Store of Memories*, London, 1974

Benton, Charlotte, *A Different World: Emigré Architects in Britain, 1928–1958*, London, 1995

Beresford, Maurice, *New Towns of the Middle Ages*, London, 1967

BDP, *BDP Selected and Current Works*, Victoria, Australia, 1998

Binfield, Clyde, 'Holy Murder at Cheshunt College: The Formation of an English Architect: P. R. Morley Horder, 1870–1944', *Journal of the United Reformed Church History Society*, vol. 4, no. 2 (May 1988), 103–34

Blackman, Janet, 'The Development of the Retail Grocery Trade in the Nineteenth Century', *Business History*, vol. 9, no. 2 (1967), 110–17

Bonner, Arnold, *British Co-operation*, Manchester, 1970

Bookbinder, Paul, *Simon Marks: Retail Revolutionary*, London, 1993

Bowlby, Rachel, *Carried Away: The Invention of Modern Shopping*, London, 2000

Brand, Ken, 'Richard Charles Sutton', *Nottingham Civic Society Newsletter*, no. 69 (January 1986), 4–6

——, 'Albert Nelson Bromley', *Nottingham Civic Society Newsletter*, no. 77 (September 1988), 2–9, and no. 78 (January 1989), 14–18

Brewer, John, and Roy Porter (eds), *Consumption and the World of Goods*, London, 1993

Briggs, Asa, *Friends of the People: The Centenary History of Lewis's*, London, 1956

——, *Marks and Spencer, 1884–1984: A Centenary History*, London, 1984

Britnell, R. H., 'The Proliferation of Markets in England, 1200–1349', *Economic History Review*, vol. 34 (1981), 209–21

——, *The Commercialisation of English Society, 1000–1500*, Cambridge, 1993

Brown, Andrew (ed.), *The Rows of Chester: The Chester Rows Research Project*, English Heritage Archaeological Report 16, London, 1999

Brown, Jonathan, *The English Market Town: A Social and Economic History, 1750–1914*, Marlborough, 1986

Bruckshaw, Frank, and Duncan McNab, *A Century of Achievement: The Story of the Lincoln Co-operative Society*, Lincoln, [c.1961]

Bruyère, Louis, *Etudes relatives à l'art des constructions*, vol. 1, Paris, 1823

Burgess, F. W., *The Practical Retail Draper*, 5 vols, London, 1912–14

Burns, Angela, and Barry Hyman, *Marks and Spencer: A 100 Years of Partnership, 1894–1994*, London, 1994

Burns, Wilfred, *British Shopping Centres: New Trends in Layout and Distribution*, London, 1959

Burt, Steven, and Kevin Grady, *Kirkgate Market: An Illustrated History*, Leeds, 1992

Burton, Neil, 'Robert Lutyens and Marks & Spencer', *Thirties Society Journal*, no. 5 (1985), 8–17

Calladine, Tony, ' "A Paragon of Lucidity and Taste": The Peter Jones Department Store', *Transactions of the Ancient Monuments Society*, vol. 45 (2001), 7–28

Callery, Sean, *Harrods Knightsbridge: The Story of Society's Favourite Store*, London, 1991

Cameron, David Kerr, *The English Fair*, Stroud, 1998

Campbell, R., *The London Tradesman*, London, 1747

Chapman, Stanley, *Jesse Boot of Boots the Chemists: A Study in Business History*, London, 1974

——, 'The Innovating Entrepreneurs in the British Ready-made Clothing Industry', *Textile History*, vol. 24, no. 1 (1993), 5–25

Charey, D., 'The Department Store as a Cultural Form', *Theory, Culture and Society*, vol. 1, no. 3 (1983), 22–31

Chartres, J. A., *Markets and Fairs in England and Wales, 1500 to 1860*, Leeds, 1993

Chatterton, Frederick, *Shop Fronts: A Selection of English, American and Continental Examples*, London, 1927

Chung, C. J. et al., *The Harvard Design School Guide to Shopping*, Cologne, 2001

Clark, David, 'The Shop Within? An Analysis of the Architectural Evidence for Medieval Shops', *Architectural History*, vol. 43 (2000), 58–87

Clark, Peter (ed.), *The Cambridge Urban History of Britain*, vol. 2, Cambridge, 2000

——, and Paul Slack, *English Towns in Transition, 1500–1700*, Oxford, 1976

Clarke, Jonathan, 'Early Structural Steel in London Buildings', English Heritage Survey Report, 2000

Clear, Gwen, *The Story of W. H. Smith and Son, 1792–1948*, London, 1949

Clifford, Helen, 'The Myth of The Maker: Manufacturing Networks in the London Goldsmiths' Trade 1750–1790', in Kenneth Quickenden and Neal Adrian Quickenden (eds), *Silver and Jewellery Production and Consumption since 1750*, Birmingham, 1995, 5–12

Cole, G. D. H., *A Century of Co-operation*, Manchester, 1944

Colvin, Howard, *A Biographical Dictionary of British Architects, 1600–1840*, third edition, New Haven and London, 1995

Co-operative Wholesale Society, *Co-operative Architecture, 1945–1959*, Manchester, 1959

——, *This Is Progress: A Pictorial Record of Co-operative Store and Shop Development*, Manchester, 1959

Coppack, Glyn, *Medieval Merchant's House, Southampton*, English Heritage Guide, London, 1991

Corfield, P. J., *The Impact of English Towns, 1700–1800*, Oxford, 1982

Corina, Maurice, *Pile it High, Sell it Cheap: The Authorised Biography of Sir John Cohen, Founder of Tesco*, London, 1971

——, *Fine Silks and Oak Counters: Debenhams, 1778–1978*, London, 1978

Costello, Peter, and Tony Farmar, *The Very Heart of the City: The Story of Dennis Guiney and Clerys*, Dublin, 1992

Cox, Nancy, *The Complete Tradesman: A Study of Retailing, 1550–1820*, Aldershot, 2000

Crawford, David, *British Building Firsts: The First Castle to the First Airport*, Newton Abbot, 1990

Crossick, Geoffrey, and Serge Jaumain (eds), *Cathedrals of Consumption: The European Department Store, 1850–1939*, Aldershot, 1999

Curtis, Philip, *The People's History: Sunderland: A Century of Shopping*, Seaham, Co. Durham, 1999

Curtis, S. O., *Shopfitting and Setting-Out: A Practical Handbook on the Method of Setting out for Modern Shopfronts*, London, 1939

Dale, Tim, *Harrods: The Store and the Legend*, London, 1981

——, *Harrods: A Palace in Knightsbridge*, London, 1995

Dan, Horace, and E. C. Morgan Willmott, *English Shop Fronts Old and New*, London, 1907

Dannatt, Trevor, *Modern Architecture in Britain*, London, 1959

Darby, Michael, and David van Zanten, 'Owen Jones's Iron Buildings of the 1850s', *Architectura*, vol. 1, iv (1974), 53–75

Darlow, Clive (ed.), *Enclosed Shopping Centres*, London, 1972

Davis, Dorothy, *A History of Shopping*, London, 1966

Dean, David, *English Shopfronts from Contemporary Source Books, 1792–1840*, London, 1970

Defoe, Daniel, *The Complete English Tradesman*, London, 1727 (first published 1726)

——, *Tour through the Whole Island of Great Britain*, London, 1971 (first published 1724)

Delassaux, Victor D., and John Elliott, *Street Architecture: A Series of Shop Fronts and Facades*, London, 1855

Delorme, J.-C., and A.-M. Dubois, *Passages couverts Parisiens*, Paris, 1996

Denvir, Bernard, *The Eighteenth Century: Art Design and Society, 1689–1789*, London and New York, 1988

Desebrock, Jean, *The Book of Bond Street Old and New*, London, 1978

Des Fontaines, Una. 'Portland House: Wedgwood's London Showrooms, 1774–94', *Proceedings of the Wedgwood Society*, vol. 2, no. 8 (1970), 193–212

Dyer, Alan, *Decline and Growth in English Towns, 1400–1640*, Basingstoke, 1991

Dyer, Christopher, 'The Hidden Trade of the Middle Ages: Evidence from the West Midlands of England', *Journal of Historical Geography*, vol. 18 (1992), 141–57

Edwards, A. Trystan, *The Architecture of Shops*, London, 1933

Eldridge, Mary, 'The Plate-Glass Shop Front', *Architectural Review*, vol. 123 (March 1958), 192–5

Elliott, C. J., and Stanley Elliott, *The Modern Retailer*, London, 1937

English Heritage, *Shopfronts*, 1990 (Listed Building Guidance Leaflet)

English Historic Towns Forum, *Shopfronts and Advertisements in Historic Towns*, Bath, 1991

——, *Book of Details and Good Practice in Shopfront Design*, Bath, 1993

——, *Retail Guidance*, Bath, 1997

Evans, Bill, and Andrew Lawson, *A Nation of Shopkeepers*, London, 1981

Everitt, Alan, 'The Market Town', in Peter Clark (ed.), *The Early Modern Town: A Reader*, London, 1976, 168–204

Examples of Modern Shopfronts (published by John Weale), London, 1851

Express Dairies, *Express Story, 1864–1964*, London, 1964

Fairchilds, Cissie, 'The Production and Marketing of Populuxe Goods in Eighteenth-century Paris', in John Brewer and Roy Porter (eds), *Consumption and the World of Goods*, London, 1993, 228–48

Faulkner, J., *Designs for Shop Fronts*, London, 1831

Faulkner, P. A., 'Medieval Undercrofts and Town Houses', *Archaeological Journal*, vol. 123 (1966), 120–35

Fawcett, Trevor, 'Eighteenth-Century Shops and the Luxury Trades', *Bath History*, vol. 3 (1990), 49–75

Ferry, John William, *A History of the Department Store*, New York, 1960

Fraser, W. H., *The Coming of the Mass Market, 1850–1914*, London, 1981

Fraser, Sir J. Foster, *Goodwill in Industry*, 1925

Gardiner, Leslie, *The Making of John Menzies*, Edinburgh, 1983

Gardner, Carl, and Julie Sheppard, *Consuming Passion: The Rise of Retail Culture*, London, 1989

Geist, Johann Friedrich, *Arcades: The History of a Building Type*, Cambridge, MA, and London, 1983 (German original, 1969)

George, M. Dorothy, *London Life in the Eighteenth Century*, London, 1925

Gibberd, Frederick et al., *Harlow: The Story of a New Town*, Stevenage, 1980

Gomme, Andor, and David Walker, *Architecture of Glasgow*, London, 1987 (first published 1968)

Goodden, Susanna, *At the Sign of the Fourposter: A History of Heal's*, London, 1984

Gosling, David, and Barry Maitland, *Design and Planning of Retail Systems*, London and New York, 1976

Gruen, Victor, and Larry Smith, *Shopping Towns, USA: The Planning of Shopping Centers*, New York, 1960

Grundy, Joan, 'Inter-war Shop Fronts', *Thirties Society Journal*, vol. 2 (1981), 41–4

Hall, H. Austen, 'The Planning of Some American Department Stores', *Journal of the Royal Institute of British Architects*, vol. 27, no. 11 (10 April 1920), 237–54

Hammond, A. Edward, *Shop Fittings and Display*, London, 1927

——, *Multiple Shop Organisation*, London, 1930

——, *Modern Footwear Display*, London, 1937

Harding, Vanessa, 'The Population of London 1550–1700: A Review of the Published Evidence', *London Journal*, vol. 15, no. 2 (1990), 111–28

Harper, Charles G., 'Market Houses – 1, *The Architect*, 3 September 1920, 143–6

Harris, Roland B., 'The Origins and Development of English Medieval Townhouses Operating Commercially on Two Storeys', D.Phil. thesis, Hertford College, Oxford University, 1994

Hartlepool Museum Service, *Bricks and Mortar: A Celebration of Architecture in Hartlepool, 1834–1984* (prepared by Hartlepool Museum Service to accompany an exhibition to mark the Festival of Architecture, 1984)

Hartnell, A. P., *Shop Planning and Design*, London, [*c.*1944]

Havenhand, G., *A Nation of Shopkeepers*, London, 1970

Heal, Ambrose, *London Tradesmen's Cards of the 18th Century: An Account of their Origin and Use*, London, 1925

——, *The Signboards of Old London Shops*, London, 1947

Hedges, Harry, *This Way to Self-Service*, London, 1957

Herbert, A. F., 'Construction of Retail Premises', *The Retail Meat Trade: A Practical Treatise for Specialists in the Meat Trade*, vol. 2, London, 1928

Herbst, René, *Modern French Shop-Fronts and their Interiors*, London, 1927

Hilton, R. H., 'Medieval Market Towns and Simple Commodity Production', *Past and Present*, no. 109 (November 1985), 3–23

Hines, Thomas S., *Burnham of Chicago: Architect and Planner*, New York, 1974

Historical Publishing Company, *Modern London: The World's Metropolis*, London, 1887–90

Hobhouse, Hermione, *A History of Regent Street*, London, 1975

——, *Lost London: A Century of Demolition and Decay*, London, 1976

Hodson Debbie, 'Civic Identity, Custom and Commerce: Victorian Market Halls in the Manchester Region', *Manchester Region History Review*, no. 12 (1998), 34–43

Holyoake, G. J. *Self-help by the People: History of Co-operation in Rochdale*, London, 1858

Honeycombe, Gordon, *Selfridges: Seventy-Five Years: The Story of the Store, 1909–1984*, London, 1984

Honeyman, Katrina, 'Montague Burton Ltd: The Creators of Well-Dressed Men', in John Chartres and Katrina Honeyman (eds), *Leeds City Businesses, 1893–1993: Essays Marking the Centenary of the Incorporation*, Leeds, 1993, 186–216

——, 'Tailor-Made: Mass Production, High Street Retailing, and the Leeds Menswear Multiples, 1918 to 1939', *Northern History*, vol. 37 (December 2000), 293–305

——, *Well Suited: A History of the Leeds Clothing Industry, 1850–1990*, Oxford, 2000

Hood, Julia, and B. S. Yamey, 'The Middle-Class Co-operative Retailing Societies in London, 1864–1900', *Oxford Economic Papers*, vol. 9 (1957), 309–22

Horwood, Richard, *A Plan of the Cities of London and Westminster: The A to Z of Regency London*, London, 1985

Hosgood, Christopher P., '"Mercantile Monasteries": Shops, Shop Assistants and Shop Life in Late Victorian and Edwardian Britain', *Journal of British Studies*, vol. 38 (1999), 322–52

Hoskins W. G. *The Making of the English Landscape*, London, 1955

Hough, J. A., and Lambert, F., *Self-Service Shops: A Joint Report*, Co-op Union, Manchester, 1951

Howard, Ebenezer, *Garden Cities of Tomorrow*, ed. F. J. Osborn, London, 1965 (first published in 1898 as *Tomorrow: A Peaceful Path to Real Reform*)

Howes, Edmund, *Annales; or, A Generall Chronicle of England* begun by John Stow, continued and augmented to the end of 1631 by Edmund Howes, London, 1631

Hudson, Kenneth, *The Archaeology of the Consumer Society: The Second Industrial Revolution in Britain*, London, 1983

Hughes, Annabelle F., 'On the First Five Hundred Years of Shops and Shopping in Horsham', Horsham, 1989

Hughes, G. Bernard, 'Europe's First Department Store?', *Country Life*, 15 May 1958, 1058–9

——, 'Furniture for the Regency Traveller', *Country Life*, 2 March 1967, 452–3

Iliffe, Richard, and Wilfrid Baguely, *Victorian Nottingham: A Story in Pictures, vol. 9: Streets Shops and Stalls of Nottingham, 1837–1901*, Nottingham, 1972

Illustrated London, [*c.*1892]

Ind, Rosemary, *Emberton*, London, 1983

Industrial Great Britain, London, [*c.*1895]

Ison, Walter, *The Georgian Buildings of Bath, from 1700 to 1830*, London, 1948

Jackson, Lesley, *The Sixties: Decade of Design Revolution*, London, 1998

Jackson, Peter (ed.), *London Street Views, 1838–1840: Together with the Revised and Enlarged Views of 1847*, London, 1969 (first published by John Tallis, 1838–40 and 1847)

——, *George Scharf's London: Sketches and Watercolours of a Changing City, 1820–50*, London, 1987

James, Tom Beaumont, and Edward Roberts, 'Winchester and Late Medieval Urban Development: From Palace to Pentice', *Medieval Archaeology*, vol. 44 (2000), 181–200

Jefferys, James B., *Retail Trading in Britain, 1850–1950*, Cambridge, 1954

Jones, Colin S., *Regional Shopping Centres: Their Location, Planning and Design*, London, 1969

Kalman, H., 'The Architecture of Mercantilism: Commercial Buildings by George Dance the Younger', in P. Fritz and D. Williams (eds), *The Triumph of Culture: Eighteenth Century Perspectives*, Toronto, 1972, 69–96

Kay, William, *Battle for the High Street*, London, 1987

Keene, Derek, *Survey of Medieval Winchester*, 2 vols, Oxford, 1985

——, 'Shops and Shopping in Medieval London', *Medieval Art, Architecture and Archaeology in London: The British Archaeological Association Conference Transactions for the Year 1984*, 1990, 30–46

——, and Vanessa Harding, *Historical Gazetteer of London before the Great Fire*, part 1: *Cheapside*, Cambridge, 1987

Kellett, J. R., 'The Breakdown of Gild and Corporation Control over the Handicraft and Retail Trade in London', *Economic History Review*, vol. 10, no. 3 (April 1958), 381–94

Kent, Lewis E., and G. W. Kirkland, 'Construction of Steel-Framed Buildings', *Structural Engineer*, July 1958, 102–10

Ketchum, Maurice, *Shops and Stores*, New York, 1948

Kilby, I. E., 'The Character of Shopfronts', MA thesis, De Montfort University, Leicester, 1993

King, Thomas, *Shop Fronts and Exterior Doors*, London, 1839

Kirby, David, *Shopping in the Eighties*, London, 1988

Kirkwood, Robert C., *The Woolworth Story at Home and Abroad*, New York, 1960

Klein, Naomi, *No Logo*, London, 2000

Klose, Dietrich, *Multi-storey Car Parks and Garages*, London, 1965

Knight, Charles (ed.), *London*, vol. 5, London, 1843

——(ed.), *Cyclopaedia of London*, London, 1851

——(ed.) *London* (revised by E. Walford), London, 1875–7, vol. 5

Knowles, C. C., and P. H. Pitt, *The History of Building Regulations in London, 1189–1972*, London, 1972

Knowles, James, '"To raise a house of better frame": Jonson's Cecilian Entertainments', in Pauline Croft (ed.), *Patronage, Culture and Power: The Early Cecils, 1558–1612*, Studies in British Art 8, New Haven and London, 2002, 181–95

Lackington, James, *Memoirs of the First Forty-Five Years of the Life of James Lackington*, tenth edition, London, 1795

Lamacraft, Jane, *Retail Design: New Store Experiences*, London, 1998

Lamb, Jim, and Steve Warren, *The People's Store: A Guide to the North-Eastern Co-op's Family Tree*, Gateshead, [*c.*1990]

Lambert, Richard S., *The Universal Provider: A Study of William Whiteley and the Rise of the London Department Store*, London, 1938

Lancashire Illustrated, London, 1832

Lancaster, Bill, *The Department Store: A Social History*, London, 1995

Latham, Robert, and William Matthews (eds), *The Diary of Samuel Pepys*, 11 vols, London, 1970–83

Lawrence, Jeanne Catherine, 'Steel Frame Architecture versus the London Building Regulations: Selfridges, the Ritz, and American Technology', *Construction History*, vol. 6 (1990), 23–46

Lawson, P. H., and J. T. Smith, 'The Rows of Chester: Two Interpretations', *Journal of Chester and North Wales Architectural Archaeological and Historic Society*, vol. 45 (1958), 1–42

Lemoine, Bertrand, *L'Architecture du fer: France: XIXe siècle*, Seyssel, 1986

Lewis, Samuel, *Topographical Dictionary of England*, London, 1831, 1837 and 1842

Lewison, Grant, and Rosalind Billingham, *Coventry New Architecture*, Warwick, 1969

Liffen, John, 'The Development of Cash Handling Systems for Shops and Department Stores', *Transactions of the Newcomen Society*, vol. 71, no. 1 (1999–2000), 79–101

Lincoln Co-operative Society, *Handbook of the 23rd Annual Co-operative Congress, Lincoln*, Lincoln, 1891

Linstrum, Derek, *West Yorkshire Architects and Architecture*, London, 1978

Lloyd, D. W. *The Making of English Towns: A Vista of 2000 Years*, London, 1984

Lobel, Mary D., *The British Atlas of Historic Towns*, vol. 3: *The City of London from Prehistoric Times to c.1520*, Oxford, 1989

Longstreth, Richard, *The Drive-In, the Supermarket, and the Transformation of the Commercial Space in Los Angeles*, Cambridge, MA, and London, 1999

Louw, Hentie, 'Window-Glass Making in Britain *c.*1660–*c.*1860 and its Architectural Impact', *Construction History*, vol. 7 (1991), 47–68

MacHardy, George, *The Office of J. B. Papworth*, RIBA Drawings Collection Catalogue, London, 1977

MacKeith Margaret, *Shopping Arcades: A Gazetteer of Extant British Arcades, 1817–1939*, London and New York, 1985

——, *The History and Conservation of Shopping Arcades*, London and New York, 1986

Macpherson, Hugh (ed.), *John Spedan Lewis, 1885–1963*, Rugby, 1985

Maitland, Barry, *The New Architecture of the Retail Mall*, London, 1990

Malcolm, James Peller, *Anecdotes of the Manner and Customs of London during the Eighteenth Century*, London, 1810

Malton, Thomas, *A Picturesque Tour through the Cities of London and Westminster*, London, 1792

Markus, Thomas A., *Buildings and Power: Freedom and Control in the Origin of Modern Building Types*, London and New York, 1993

Marrey, Bernard, *Les grands magasins des origins à 1939*, Paris, 1979

Marriott, Oliver, *The Property Boom*, London, 1989 (first published 1968)

Marshall, J. D. (ed.), *The Autobiography of William Stout of Lancaster, 1665–1752*, Manchester, 1967

Masters, Betty R., *The Public Markets of the City of London Surveyed by William Leybourn in 1677*, London Topographical Society no. 117, London, 1974

Mathias, Peter, *Retailing Revolution: A History of Multiple Trading in the Food Trades based upon the Allied Suppliers Group of Companies*, London, 1967

Matthews, Leslie G., *History of Pharmacy in Britain*, Edinburgh and London, 1962

Mayhew, Henry (ed.), *The Shops and Companies of London and the Trades and Manufactories of Great Britain*, London, 1865

——, *The Morning Chronicle Survey of Labour and the Poor*, 6 vols, Horsham 1980–82 (first published as a series of articles in the *Morning Chronicle*, 1849–50)

——, *London Labour and the London Poor*, vol. 4, London, 1967 (first published 1851)

McGrath, Raymond, and A. C. Frost, *Glass in Architecture and Decoration*, London, 1937

McInnes, Duncan, *History of Co-operation in Lincoln, 1861–1911*, Manchester, 1911

McKendrick, Neil, John Brewer and J. H. Plumb, *The Birth of a Consumer Society*, London, 1982

Meadows, Cecil A., *The Victorian Ironmonger*, Princes Risborough, 2000 (first edition, 1978)

Miller, Daniel, Peter Jackson, Nigel Thrift, Beverley Holbrook and Michael Rowlands, *Shopping, Place and Identity*, London, 1998

Miller, Edward, and John Hatcher, *Medieval England: Towns, Commerce and Crafts, 1086–1348*, London and New York, 1995

Miller, M. E., *The Bon Marché: Bourgeois Culture and the Department Store, 1869–1920*, New Jersey, 1981

Millward, Michael, and Brian Coe, *Victorian Townscape: The Work of Samuel Smith*, London, 1974

Mitchell, Ian, 'The Development of Urban Retailing, 1700–1815', in Peter Clark (ed.), *The Transformation of English Provincial Towns, 1600–1800*, London, 1984, 259–83

Morley, H. (ed.), *A Survey of London Written in the Year 1598 by John Stow*, Stroud, 1994 (based on edition of 1603; first published in 1912; reprinted with an introduction by Antonia Fraser in 1994)

Moore, Ellen Wedemeyer, *The Fairs of Medieval England: An Introductory Study*, Toronto, 1985

Morrice, Richard, 'Palestrina in Hastings', *Georgian Group Journal*, vol. 11 (2001), 92–100

Morris, Christopher (ed.), *The Illustrated Journeys of Celia Fiennes, 1685–c.1712*, London and Sydney, 1982

Mort, F., *Cultures of Consumption: Masculinities and Social Space in Late Twentieth-Century Britain*, London, 1996

——, and P. Thompson, 'Retailing, Commercial Culture and Mas-

culinity in 1950s Britain: The Case of Montague Burton the Tailor of Taste, *History Workshop Journal*, vol. 38 (1994), 106–27

Moss, Michael, and Alison Turton, *A Legend of Retailing: House of Fraser*, London, 1989

Mui, Hoh-Cheung, and Lorna H. Mui, *Shops and Shopkeeping in Eighteenth-Century England*, London, 1989

Muir, D. Macmillan (ed.), *The Modern Shop*, London and Leicester, 1927

Munby, Julian, 'J. C. Buckler, Tackley's Inn and Three Medieval Houses in Oxford', *Oxoniensia*, vol. 43 (1978), 123–69

Murray, Hugh, Sarah Riddick and Richard Green, *York through the Eyes of the Artist*, York, 1990

Newby, F., 'The Innovative Uses of Concrete by Engineers and Architects', *Proceedings of the Institution of Civil Engineers*, vol. 116 (August–November 1996), 264–82

Nightingale, Joseph, *The Bazaar: Its Origin, Nature and Objects*, London, 1816

Ogden, William Sharp, *Studies in Mercantile Architecture*, London, 1877

Oliver, Thomas, *The Topographical Conductor or Descriptive Guide to Newcastle and Gateshead*, Newcastle upon Tyne, 1851

Owen, Robert, *The Life of Robert Owen Written by Himself*, London, 1971 (first published 1857)

Pantin, W. A., 'Medieval English Town-House Plans', *Medieval Archaeology*, vol. 6–7 (1962–3), 202–39

Parker, Vanessa, *The Making of Kings Lynn*, London, 1971

Parkinson-Bailey, John J., *Manchester: An Architectural History*, Manchester, 2000

Pasdermadjian, Hrant, *The Department Store: Its Origins, Evolution and Economics*, London, 1954

Pendrill, Charles, *The Adelphi*, London, 1934

Perry, Trevor, *Modern Shopfront Construction*, London, 1933

Pevsner, N., *A History of Building Types*, London, 1976

Phillips, Hugh, *Mid-Georgian London: A Topographical and Social Survey of Central and Western London about 1750*, London, 1964

Platt, Colin, *The English Medieval Town*, London, 1976

Postan, M. M., *The Medieval Economy and Society: An Economic History of Britain in the Middle Ages*, London, 1972

Pound, Reginald, *Selfridge: A Biography*, London, 1960

Powell, David, *Counter Revolution: The Tesco Story*, London, 1991

Powers, Alan, *Shop Fronts*, London, 1989

Priestley, Ursula, and Alayne Fenner, *Shops and Shopkeepers in Norwich, 1660–1730*, Norwich, 1985

Purvis, Martin, 'Co-operative retailing in Britain', in J. Benson and G. Shaw (eds), *The Evolution of Retail Systems, 1800–1914*, Leicester, 1992, 107–34

Rappaport, Erika, '"The Halls of Temptation": Gender Politics and the Construction of the Department Store in Late Victorian London', *Journal of British Studies*, vol. 35 (January 1996), 58–83

——, *Shopping for Pleasure: Women in the Making of London's West End*, Princeton, 2000

Reddaway, Thomas Fiddian, *The Rebuilding of London after the Great Fire*, London, 1940

Redfern, Percy, *The Story of the CWS: The Jubilee History of the Co-operative Wholesale Society Limited, 1863–1913*, Manchester, [c.1913]

——, *The New History of the CWS*, London, 1938

Redmayne, R., *Ideals in Industry, Being the Story of Montague Burton Ltd*, Leeds, 1951

Rees, Goronwy, *St Michael: A History of Marks and Spencer*, London, 1985 (first published 1969)

Rees, J. Aubrey, *The Grocery Trade: Its History and Romance*, 2 vols, London, 1932 (first published 1910)

Reilly, C. H., *Scaffolding in the Sky*, London, 1938

Reminiscences of an Old Draper, London, 1876

Richards, Thomas, *The Commodity Culture of Victorian England: Advertising and Spectacle*, Stanford, 1996

Ritchie, Berry, *A Touch of Class: The Story of Austin Reed*, London, 1990

Robinson, John Martin, 'Shop-fronts', in A. Powers (ed.), *Real Architecture: An Exhibition of Classical Buildings by the New Generation of Architects*, London, 1987

Robinson, Joseph Barlow, *A Series of Suggestive Designs for Shop Fronts of a Plain and Elaborate Character Suitable for every Trade or Occupation*, Derby, [c.1869]

Rocque, John, *A Plan of the Cities of London and Westminster: The A to Z of Georgian London*, London, 1982

Rouquet, André, *The Present State of the Arts in England*, London, 1755; facsimile reprint London, 1970 (French original)

Royal Fine Arts Society, *Design in the High Street*, London, 1986

Rule, John, *Albion's People: English Society, 1714–1815*, London and New York, 1992

Ruston, Phil, *Out of Town Shopping: The Future of Retailing*, London, 1999

Sachse, William L. (ed.), *The Diary of Roger Lowe of Ashton-in-Makerfield, Lancashire, 1663–1674*, London, 1938

Sala, George Augustus Henry Fairfield, *Twice round the Clock*, London, 1859

Salt, Rosemary, *Plans for a Fine City*, Norwich, 1988

Salzman, L. F., *English Trade in the Middle Ages*, Oxford, 1931

——, *Building in England down to 1540: A Documentary History*, Oxford, 1952

Samuel, Mark, 'The Fifteenth-Century Garner at Leadenhall, London', *Antiquaries Journal*, vol. 69 (1989), 119–53

Sandeman, R., and G. C. Leighton, *Grand Architectural Panorama of London, Regent Street to Westminster Abbey*, 1849

Sargentson, Carolyn, *Merchants and Luxury Markets: The Marchands Merciers of Eighteenth-Century Paris*, London, 1996

Saunders, Ann (ed.), *The Royal Exchange*, London Topographical Society no. 152, London, 1997

Scarisbrick, Diana, 'A Nineteenth-Century Exeter Goldsmith', *Antique Dealer and Collectors Guide*, July 1985, 55–7

——, *Jewellery in Britain, 1066–1837: A Documentary, Social, Literary and Artistic Survey*, Wilby, Norwich, 1994

Schmeichen, James, and Kenneth Carls, *The British Market Hall: A Social and Architectural History*, New Haven and London, 1999

Schofield, John, *The London Surveys of Ralph Treswell*, London Topographical Society no. 135, London, 1987

——, and Alan Vince, *Medieval Towns*, Leicester, 1994

Schopenhauer, Johanna, *A Lady Travels: Journeys in England and Scotland from the Diaries of Johanna Schopenhauer*, trans. and ed. by Ruth Michaelis-Jena and Willy Merson, London, 1988

Scola, Roger, 'Food Markets and Shops in Manchester, 1770–1870', *Journal of Historical Geography*, vol. 1, no. 2 (1975), 153–68

——, *Feeding the Victorian City: The Food Supply of Manchester, 1770–1870*, Manchester, 1992

Scott, N. Keith, *Shopping Centre Design*, London, 1989

Scott, Peter, 'Learning to Multiply: The Property Market and the Growth of Multiple Retailing in Britain, 1919–1939', *Business History*, vol. 36, no. 3 (1994), 1–28

——, *The Property Masters: A History of the British Commercial Property Sector*, London, 1996

Scott, W. Basil, 'Steelwork. A Short History: ii', *The Architects Journal*, 11 July 1928, 55–7

——, 'Some Historical Notes on the Application of Iron and Steel to Building Construction', *Structural Engineer*, vol. 7, no. 1 (January 1929), 4–12; vol. 7, no. 3 (March 1929), 99–102

——, 'Iron and Steel', in W. R. Gilbert (ed.), *Modern Steelwork*, London, 1930, 238–50

Seth, Andrew, and Geoffrey Randall, *The Grocers: The Rise and Rise of the Supermarket Chains*, London and Dover, NH, 1999

Settle, Alison, *A Family of Shops*, London, 1951

Sharpe, Pamela, '"Cheapness and Economy": Manufacturing and Retailing Ready-made Clothing in London and Essex, 1830–50', *Textile History*, vol. 26, no. 2 (1995), 203–13

Shaw, Gareth, 'The Evolution and Impact of Large-scale Retailing in Britain', in John Benson and Gareth Shaw (eds), *The Evolution of Retail Systems, 1800–1914*, Leicester, 1992, 135–65

Shaw, G., and M. T. Wild, 'Retail Patterns in the Victorian City', *Transactions of the Institute of British Geographers*, n.s. 4 (1979), 278–91

Shepherd, Thomas H., and James Elmes, *Metropolitan Improvements: London in the Nineteenth Century*, London, 1827–31 (reprinted New York, 1978)

Sigsworth, Eric M., *Montague Burton: The Tailor of Taste*, Manchester, 1990

Simmonds, W. H., *The Practical Grocer: A Manual and Guide for the Grocer, the Provision Merchant and the Allied Trades*, 4 vols, London, 1904–5

Simpson, Pamela H., *Cheap, Quick and Easy: Imitative Architectural Materials, 1870–1930*, Knoxville, 1999

Siry, Joseph, *Carson Pirie Scott: Louis Sullivan and the Chicago Department Store*, Chicago, 1988

Smith, Colin, 'The Market Place and the Market's Place in London, circa 1660–1840', Ph.D. thesis, University College London, 1999

——, 'The Wholesale and Retail Markets of London, 1660–1840', *Economic History Review*, vol. 55, no. 1 (February 2002), 31–50

Smith, Thomas, *A Topographical and Historical Account of the Parish of St Marylebone*, London, 1833

Somake, Ellis E., and Rolf Hellberg, *Shops and Stores Today: Their Design, Planning and Organisation*, London, 1956

Sorbière, Samuel, *Relation d'un voyage en Angleterre*, Paris, 1664

Southall, Brian, *The Story of the World's Leading Music Retailer: HMV 75, 1921–1996*, London, 1996

Southey, Robert, *Letters from England*, ed. Jack Simmons, London, 1951 (first published 1807)

Starsmore, I., *English Fairs*, London, 1975

Stenning, D. F., 'Timber-Framed Shops, 1300–1600: Comparative Plans', *Vernacular Architecture*, vol. 16 (1985), 35–9

Stone, Lawrence, 'Inigo Jones and the New Exchange', *Archaeological Journal*, vol. 114–15 (1957–8), 104–21

Stow, John: see entries under Howes 1631, Strype 1720 and Morley 1994

Stratton, Arthur, 'Two Forgotten Buildings by the Dances', *Architectural Review*, vol. 40, no. 237 (August 1916), 20–23

Stratton, Michael, 'Innovation and Conservatism: Steel and Reinforced Concrete in British Architecture, 1860–1905', in: Peter Burman (ed.), *Architecture 1900*, Shaftesbury, Dorset, 1998, 14–28

——, 'New Materials for a New Age: Steel and Concrete Construction in the North of England, 1860–1939', *Industrial Archaeology Review*, vol. 21, no. 1 (June 1999), 5–24

Stroud, Dorothy, *George Dance Architect, 1741–1825*, London, 1971

Strype, John, *A Survey of the Cities of London and Westminster* (by John Stow, corrected, improved and enlarged by John Stype), 6 vols, London, 1720

Tallis, John, *London Street Views*, 1838–40 and 1847; for facsimile, see Jackson 1969

Tallis, Nigel, and Kate Arnold-Forster, *Pharmacy History: A Pictorial Record*, London, 1991

Taylor C. C., 'Medieval Market Grants and Village Morphology', *Landscape History*, vol. 4 (1982), 21–8

Taylor, I., and J. Taylor, *Designs for Shop Fronts and Door Cases*, London, [*c*.1795]

Taylor, Jeremy, 'Charles Fowler: Master of Markets', *Architectural Review*, vol. 135 (March 1964), 174–82

——, 'Charles Fowler (1792–1867): A Centenary Memoir', *Architectural History*, vol. 11–12 (1968–9), 57–73

Taylor, Robert, and Hugh Richmond, '28–32 King Street, King's Lynn', *Norfolk Archaeology*, vol. 40, part 3 (1989), 260–85

Tilden, Philip, *True Remembrances: The Memoires of an Architect*, London, 1954

Timbs, John, *Curiosities of London*, London, 1868

Tittler, Robert, *Architecture and Power: The Town Hall and the English Urban Community, c.1500–1640*, Oxford, 1991

Townley, H., *A Survey of Interiors of Modern Co-operative Stores*, Manchester, 1932

Towsey, Ralph G., *Self-Service Retailing*, London, 1964

Tripp, Alker, *Town Planning and Road Traffic*, London, 1942

Tupman, W. F., *Grocery*, London, 1909

Turner, Michael L., and David Vaisey, *Oxford Shops and Shopping*, Oxford, 1972

Vallance, Aymer, *Old Crosses and Lychgates*, London, 1920

Waide, Leath, 'Consumer Cathedrals', *Built Environment*, vol. 4, no. 2 (February 1975), 91–4

Wainwright, David, *The British Tradition: Simpson – A World of Style*, London, 1996

Walsh, Claire, 'Shop Design and the Display of Goods in Eighteenth-Century London', *Journal of Design History*, vol. 8 (1995), 157–76

——, 'The Newness of the Department Store: A View from the Eighteenth Century', in Geoffrey Crossik and Serge Jaumain (eds), *Cathedrals of Consumption: The European Department Store, 1850–1939*, Aldershot, 1999, 46–71

Ward, Edward. *A Step to Stir-Bitch-Fair*, London, 1700

Ward, Ned, *The London Spy*, ed. Kenneth Fenwick, London 1955 (first published in parts 1698–1700)

Weatherill, Lorna, *Consumer Behaviour and Material Culture in Britain, 1660–1760*, London, 1988

Weir, Christopher, *Jesse Boot of Nottingham*, Nottingham, 1994

Westwood, Bryan, and Norman Westwood, *Smaller Retail Shops*, London, 1937

——, *The Modern Shop*, London, 1955 (first published 1951)

Welch, Charles, *Illustrated Account of the Royal Exchange and the Pictures Therein*, London, 1913

Wheatley, H. B., *Bond Street Old and New, 1686–1911*, London, 1911

Whittaker, Neville, *Shopfront*, Durham, 1980

Whittock, N., *On the Construction and Decoration of the Shop Fronts of London*, London, 1840

W. H. Smith Group plc, *New Technology, New Markets: W. H. Smith through Two Centuries*, London, [*c*.1992]

W. H. Smith, *The Story of W. H. Smith & Son*, London, 1955

Wilkinson, Alan, *From Corner Shop to Corner Shop in Five Generations: A History of William Jackson & Son plc*, Beverley, 1994

Williams, Barrie, *The Underuse of Upper Floors in Historic Town Centres*, York, 1978

Williams, Bridget, *The Best Butter in the World: A History of Sainsbury's*, London, 1994

Williams, Clare (ed. and trans.), *Sophie in London 1786, being the Diary of Sophie v. la Roche*, London, 1933

Williams, Ned, *The Co-op in Birmingham and the Black Country: 150 Years of Co-operation, 1844–1994*, Wolverhampton, 1993

Wilson, Charles, *First with the News*, London, 1985

Winkler, John Kennedy, *Five and Ten: The Fabulous Life of F. W. Woolworth*, London, 1941

Winstanley, Michael J., *The Shopkeeper's World, 1830–1914*, London, 1983

Wofle, Ivor de (ed.) (pseudonym for Hubert de Cronin Hastings), *Civilia: The end of Sub Urban Man a Challenge to Semidetsia*, London, 1971

Yeomans, David, 'The Pre-history of the Curtain Wall', *Construction History*, vol. 14 (1998), 50–82

Young, J., *A Series of Designs for Shop Fronts*, 1828

Zevi, Bruno, *Erich Mendelsohn*, London, 1985 (first published 1982)

Illustration Acknowledgements

All illustrations are © English Heritage or reproduced by permission of English Heritage. NMR other than those listed below. We wish to acknowledge gratefully all those institutions and individuals who have given permission for their material to appear.

Arcadia Group PLC 224, 229, 230, 233; Beamish. The North of England Open Air Museum 78, 87, 143, 150, 195; The Boots Company Archives 213, 214; Birmingham Library Services 126; Private collection, courtesy of Thomas and Brenda Brod, Fine Paintings and Drawings 26; The Cambridgeshire Collection, Cambridge Central Library 16, 67; By permission of The Syndics of Cambridge University Library 33, 34, 36, 48, 57, 96, 97, 116, 124, 142, 161, 176, 261, 301; The Conway Library, Courtauld Institute of Art 27; Corporation of London Records Office 13; © Crown copyright. NMR 55, 59d, 68, 100, 103, 137, 181, 263, 312; EMI Recorded Music 182; D. P. Fitzgerald, Plymouth 223; By permission of The Folger Shakespeare Library 12; Guildhall Library, Corporation of London 9, 25, 29, 38, 46, 86, 91, 92, 95, 110, 127; Company Archive, Harrods Limited 137; House of Fraser 158; T. & W. Ide Ltd, Glasshouse Fields, Stepney, London: frontispiece; King's Lynn Library 141; Leicestershire Museums, Arts and Records Service 170; Lilian Ream Collection 195; Lincoln Co-operative Society 144; Courtesy of Liverpool Record Office, Liverpool Libraries 108; Manchester City Council, City Architects 123; Marks & Spencer Company Archive 234, 235, 236, 237, 240, 241, 243, 246, 285; Maylott Studios, Swindon 221; The National Co-operative Archive at the Co-operative College 153; Newcastle Libraries & Information Service 196; Newham Archives and Local Studies Library 61, 291; Norwich Castle Museum and Art Gallery 4, 93; Norfolk Record Office 92; Ordnance Survey 4 (© Crown copyright, reproduced from the 1883–4, 1863 and 1878 Ordnance Survey Maps), 274 (© Crown copyright, reproduced from the 1919 Ordnance Survey map), 275 (reproduced by permission of Ordnance Survey on behalf of The Controller of Her Majesty's Stationery Office © Crown Copyright. Licence Number GD 03085G/02/01); Pepys Library, Magdalene College, Cambridge 30; Reading Local Studies Library 171; Museum of the Royal Pharmaceutical Society of Great Britain 70; Sainsbury's Archives 286; Selfridges' Archive, at History of Advertising Trust Archive 188; Tesco Stores Ltd 290, 292, 294, 296; City of Westminster Archives Centre 15, 28, 135; W. H. Smith Archive Limited 205, 208, 209; Woolworths plc 193, 251, 254, 256, 257, 258, 259.

While every effort has been made to trace copyright holders, we apologise to any who may have been inadvertently omitted from the above list.

Contemporary photographs for English Heritage are by the following:

Sid Barker: 162; Alun Bull: 7, 5, 23, 45, 53c, f, 55, 56, 59b, 64, 68, 69, 80, 82, 83, 89a, b, d, 122, 146, 147, 149, 151, 154, 156, 157, 172, 198, 204, 210, 218, 228, 252, 253, 260, 265, 277, 279, 288, 298, 302, 309, 211; Tony Calladine: 19; Steve Cole: 17, 18, 70, 139, 239, 287; Nigel Corrie: 295; Damian Grady: 297, 303, 305; Caroline Griggs: 64; Mike Hesketh-Roberts: 22, 43, 51, 88, 120, 202, 207, 219, 267, 299; Derek Kendall: 30, 41, 49, 52, 58, 62, 75, 76, 134, 167, 174, 181, 183, 192, 199, 270, 282, 284; Kathryn Morrison: 39, 59a, 203, 293; James O. Davies: 3, 21, 40, 47, 50, 53g, i, 59c, d, 73, 74, 81, 89e, 90, 99, 106, 185, 201, 217, 222, 263, 264, 281, 307; Patricia Payne: 103; Tony Perry: 24, 53b, 59e, 65, 72, 84, 101, 102, 105, 106, 112, 113, 115, 117, 19, 121, 131, 140, 152, 155, 177, 190, 191, 199, 212, 216, 231, 234, 243, 248, 249, 259, 255, 266, 272, 276, 280, 311, 312; Bob Skingle: 53d, 132, 226, 245, 269; Peter Williams: 1, 2, 53a, e, h, 54, 85, 89c, 186, 189, 227, 283.

Index